Acts of Modernity

In *Acts of Modernity*, David Buchanan reads nineteenth-century historical novels from Scotland, America, France, and Canada as instances of modern discourse reflective of community concerns and methods that were trans-atlantic in scope. Following on revolutionary events at home and abroad, the unique combination of history and romance initiated by Walter Scott's *Waverley* (1814) furthered interest in the transition to and depiction of the nation-state. Established and lesser-known novelists reinterpreted the genre to describe the impact of modernization and to propose coping mechanisms, according to interests and circumstances. Besides analysis of the chrono-topic representation of modernity within and between national contexts, Buchanan considers how remediation enabled diverse communities to encounter popular historical novels in upmarket and downmarket forms over the course of the century. He pays attention to the way communication practices are embedded within and constitutive of the social lives of readers, and more specifically, to how cultural producers adapted the historical novel to dynamic communication situations. In these ways, *Acts of Modernity* investigates how the historical novel was repeatedly reinvented to effectively communicate the consequences of modernity as problem-solutions of relevance to people on both sides of the Atlantic.

David Buchanan is a postdoctoral fellow in the Department of English and Film Studies at the University of Alberta, a tutor in the Centre for Humanities at Athabasca University, and a sessional instructor of English in the Department of Literature and Language at Concordia University of Edmonton.

Ashgate Series in Nineteenth-Century Transatlantic Studies
Series editor: Kevin Hutchings, University of Northern British
Columbia, Canada, and Julia M. Wright,
Dalhousie University, Canada

www.routledge.com/Ashgate-Series-in-Nineteenth-Century-Transatlantic-
Studies/book-series/ASHSER2094

Focusing on the long nineteenth century (ca. 1750–1900), this series offers
a forum for the publication of scholarly work investigating the literary,
historical, artistic, and philosophical foundations of transatlantic culture.
A vital field of interdisciplinary investigation, transatlantic scholarship con-
textualizes its objects of study in relation to exchanges, interactions, and
negotiations that occurred between and among authors and other artists
hailing from both sides of the Atlantic. As a result, transatlantic research
calls into question established disciplinary boundaries that have long func-
tioned to segregate various national or cultural literatures and art forms,
challenging as well the traditional academic emphasis upon periodization
and canonization. By examining representations dealing with such topics as
travel and exploration, migration and diaspora, slavery, aboriginal culture,
revolution, colonialism and anti-colonial resistance, the series offers new
insights into the hybrid or intercultural basis of transatlantic identity, politics, and aesthetics.

Recent titles in this series:

Transatlantic Literary Ecologies
Nature and Culture in the Nineteenth-Century Anglophone Atlantic World
Edited by Kevin Hutchings and John Miller

Performing Authorship in the Nineteenth-Century Transatlantic
Lecture Tour
Amanda Adams

Nineteenth-Century Transatlantic Reprinting and the Embodied Book
Jessica DeSpain

Robert Burns and Transatlantic Culture
Edited by Sharon Alker, Leith Davis, and Holly Faith Nelson

Acts of Modernity
The Historical Novel and Effective Communication, 1814–1901
David Buchanan

Acts of Modernity
The Historical Novel and Effective
Communication, 1814–1901

David Buchanan

LONDON AND NEW YORK

First published 2017
by Routledge
2 Park Square, Milton Park, Abingdon, Oxon OX14 4RN

and by Routledge
711 Third Avenue, New York, NY 10017

Routledge is an imprint of the Taylor & Francis Group, an informa business

© 2017 David Buchanan

The right of David Buchanan to be identified as author of this work has been asserted by him in accordance with sections 77 and 78 of the Copyright, Designs and Patents Act 1988.

All rights reserved. No part of this book may be reprinted or reproduced or utilised in any form or by any electronic, mechanical, or other means, now known or hereafter invented, including photocopying and recording, or in any information storage or retrieval system, without permission in writing from the publishers.

Trademark notice: Product or corporate names may be trademarks or registered trademarks, and are used only for identification and explanation without intent to infringe.

British Library Cataloguing-in-Publication Data
A catalogue record for this book is available from the British Library

Library of Congress Cataloging-in-Publication Data
A catalog record for this book has been requested

ISBN: 978-1-4724-2556-0 (hbk)
ISBN: 978-1-315-55724-3 (ebk)

Typeset in Sabon
by Apex CoVantage, LLC

Cover image: Frontispiece (colored engraving, landscape), 'The Dying Madge Wildfire Pursued by the Mob and Rescued by Staunton' from *The Heart of Mid Lothian; or The Lily of St. Leonard, a Caledonian Tale of Great Interest* (London: Company of Booksellers, 1822), courtesy of University of Aberdeen Special Collections.

Printed and bound in Great Britain by
TJ International Ltd, Padstow, Cornwall

For my parents,
Barbara Kay Buchanan (*née* Sharp)
and
Darryl Desmond Buchanan

All *historiae* are rough.
— Roy Harris, *The Linguistics of History*

Contents

	Acknowledgements	xi
	Introduction	1
1	Meaning-making: a history of reading practices	7
2	Heart of the matter: consequences of modernity in *Clan Albin* and *Tales of My Landlord*	27
3	Nation of readers: chapbook versions of *The Heart of Mid-Lothian*	51
4	How the West was one: historification from *Waverley* to *The Pathfinder*	64
5	Home and away: Leatherstocking reinvented in America and France	88
6	"Spiders in a pot": harnessing juggernaut in *Le père Goriot*	108
7	Industrial productions: from *editions populaires* to a people's history	126
8	Community lessons: Canadian tales of national progress	147

x *Contents*

9 History in action: dramatizations at Montréal, Paris,
New York, and London   171

Conclusion: working the historical novel   190

Bibliography   201
Index   229

Acknowledgements

Many people have played a part in the development of this book but none more so than Gary Kelly, who has provided learning opportunities, professional support, project funding, and regular encouragement; I am grateful for his collegiality and friendship. Irene Sywenky, Albert Braz, James Mulvihill, Len Findlay, Patricia Demers, Mark Simpson, Cecily Devereux, and Andrea Hasenbank offered valuable comments on early research, which I carried out as a doctoral student in the Comparative Literature Program at the University of Alberta. The University of Alberta and the Social Sciences and Humanities Research Council of Canada provided resources and funding for which I am truly thankful. The work would not have been possible without either the excellent resources at University of Alberta Libraries or consistent funding from both provincial and federal sources. I benefitted from access to primary resources at the British Library, Bodleian Library, National Library of Scotland, University of Aberdeen, Bibliothèque Nationale de France, and Maison de Balzac; in relation, I am grateful to the many writers, scholars, editors, publishers, and librarians who have paved the way for my own work on the nineteenth-century historical novel. Financial support also enabled the presentation and publication of work in progress. I profited from the discussion of ongoing research at conferences hosted by the Canadian Comparative Literature Association (Vancouver, 2008); American Comparative Literature Association (Long Beach, 2008; Vancouver, 2011); Society for the History of Authorship, Reading and Publishing (Toronto, 2009); Comparative Literature Program, University of Alberta (Edmonton, 2010); Walter Scott Society (Laramie, 2011); American Society for Eighteenth-Century Studies (Los Angeles, 2015); and North American Society for the Study of Romanticism (Winnipeg, 2015). I appreciate the work of the organizations that made these events possible and the questions or comments offered by those in attendance. Portions of chapter three first appeared in "Scott Squashed: Chapbook Versions of *The Heart of Mid-Lothian,*" *Romanticism and Victorianism on the Net* 56 (November 2009): n. pag.; and part of chapter nine first appeared in "Popular Reception by Dramatic Adaptation: The Case of Walter Scott's *The Heart of Mid-Lothian,*" *European Romantic Review* 22, no. 6 (November 2011): 745–63. I am

xii *Acknowledgements*

thankful to the editor of each journal for permission to adapt previously published material. More recently, Tegan Zimmerman provided useful feedback on the introduction, and Samantha Fitzner offered insightful criticism of the entire manuscript, as did the anonymous peer reviewer arranged by Ashgate. I appreciate the assistance of Routledge editors Liz Levine, Nicole Eno, and Erin Little, the patience of series editors Kevin Hutchings and Julia Wright, and the efforts of the silent contributors (e.g., copy editors, printers, webmasters, distributors) who helped this research into the world. Finally, in more ways than I can count, Zuzana Buchanan (*née* Garayová) has contributed to every page of this book, and although it is truer than true that they prefer to read Dr. Seuss, the same must be said of Matko and Iza.

Introduction

In *Sketches of a History of Literature* (1794), the Scotch poet and prose writer Robert Alves encouraged readers to reject the "whipt syllabub" of romance for the "solid roast beef" of history.[1] Many readers ignored his well-intentioned advice; circulating libraries and shops in Britain were well stocked with novels of romance and adventure. Regardless, the historical novel soon offered both professional critics and common readers something to embrace. Following upon nearly a century of genre experimentation, Walter Scott's *Waverley, or 'Tis Sixty Years Since* (1814) provided a combination of history and romance that gave critics the pound of flesh they demanded and readers the sweet dish they craved. Early critics were effusive with praise, and the supposedly unknown "Author of *Waverley*" quickly became the most popular novelist of the day. However, the historical novel was not and did not become a static form of historical representation. Authors reinvented the genre for their own purposes, given contemporary circumstances and the expectations of readers. In response, critics attempted to shape production and reception by framing interpretative practices. A basic motivator was the understanding of popular reading as a danger to social order. The historical novel was immediately called into question. Questioning the formal resources of the genre meant dictating terms of literary engagement when the novel emerged as a common form of communication. The particularity of critical reading practices remains recognizable today. On the one hand, although Scott is often credited with the invention of the historical novel in its most popular and influential form, no consensus as to the defining characteristics of the genre has emerged over the past 200 years. The historical novel has repeatedly been described as difficult to categorize;[2] critics disagree on historical distance, historicity, and the separation of history and fiction.[3] One of the most influential of critics on the subject, Georg Lukács, questioned whether the historical novel is a genre at all,[4] and a recent introduction comprises so vast an array of sub-genres as to practically defy definition.[5] Many studies of the historical novel specify a national sphere and most survey canonical authors, although the temporal and thematic emphases are wide ranging. On the other hand, the apparent openness to thematic resources and formal variation is misleading; among

2   Introduction

scholars, where to begin and how to proceed are political statements of no small importance. In other words, meaning production is inseparable from the practicalities of reading, yet the reflexivity of literary criticism is rarely considered a contributing factor to such analyses. Given the persistent, often anxious attention to the relationship between historical representation and community formation, much remains to be learned about why the historical novel attracted so much attention in the first place and how it has been used since by authors and critics alike.

The nineteenth-century historical novel was used to answer a deceptively simple question: what does it mean to be modern? Following Anthony Giddens, modernity here "refers to modes of social life or organisation which emerged in Europe from about the seventeenth century onwards and which subsequently became more or less worldwide in influence."[6] Historical novelists considered in this book responded to the emergence of industrial capitalism and the nation-state by describing the consequences of modernization and means to cope with them. The importance of the task is difficult to underestimate. The quality, pace, and scope of changes to the way people lived created risks and opportunities. In response to this new situation, people found new means to understand the world and their place in it. As constituted by and constitutively altering the character of modern social practices, the historical novel was one such act of modernity. As Franco Moretti states, "Well, the nation-state found the novel. And vice versa: the novel found the nation-state. And being the only symbolic form that could represent it, it became an essential component of our modern culture."[7] In relation, the term "effective communication" in the subtitle of this book refers first to the way in which communication practices are embedded within and constitutive of the broader cultural and social lives of readers, and more specifically, to how authors and publishers attempted to communicate effectively with people by adapting the historical novel to interests and circumstances. The historical novel enabled reflection on what was new about the present and how to re-establish a sense of trust in modern practices (and other people). In this way, it was a transatlantic form of communication. The usefulness of the genre, nevertheless, depended on the imaginative combination of history and romance to meet the needs of specific communication situations. As such, I read the historical novel as an instance of modern discourse adapted to community concerns and methods. This enables comparative textual analysis within and between national contexts over the course of the century. More importantly, it points to a process of meaning-making that Roy Harris aptly calls "historification" – a process that is dependent on the "modes of communication practiced by a society at any given place or time, since these determine what kinds of accounts of the past are available."[8] As this book demonstrates, the historical novel was a popular means of contributing to the chronotopic reconstruction of the past – with an eye to the future.

Introduction 3

This view of the historical novel as an essentially practical, popular means of engaging with the past and future of modernization runs counter to much contemporary criticism of the historical novel, but especially to the postmodernist theorization of historical representation that prioritizes the definition of postmodernism.[9] Whether the focus is on a typology of narratives, hybridization, or possible-worlds theory, the seemingly inevitable result is mystification of the concrete processes and material outcomes of history-making. Typically, in such analyses, *Waverley* mirrors historical events and *Gravity's Rainbow* (1973) questions history itself.[10] The juxtaposition of social reflection and self-conscious deconstruction as nineteenth- and twentieth-century forms of historicization depends on an institutionalized reading-in-general of the genre rather than case-by-case consideration of reading-as-subjectivity in particular communication situations. Categorization of the cultural production of history relies upon interpretation – *in theory*; as a result, a formalist text-as-a-text approach to literature makes of historical fiction "a self-theorizing historically referential medium."[11] As a case of meaning-as-use produced by and for postmodernist critics, reduction to abstraction makes perfect sense. Still, it hardly describes the many ways historians, novelists, critics, publishers, translators, editors, and readers historify the representation of modernity – *in practice.*

The premise underlying *Acts of Modernity* is that meaning depends on use;[12] the result is an understanding of the historical novel as an adaptable, reflexive form of expression. The implications of the approach are several. First, although the actions of producers and distributors (e.g., use of thematic resources, marketing, packaging, venues such as theatres) may be taken into consideration, users make meanings. Readerships and audiences are always changing; thus, producers and distributors must reinvent and remediate to adapt to or cultivate a new market. Second, remediators respond to changing markets and new forms of meaning-making by applying available technologies, commercial practices, and new media to refashion cultural artefacts. With these two points in mind, my focus throughout the book is the historical process of meaning-making rather than the imposition of any one meaning on either text or genre. The aim is to better understand how authors worked the historical novel to respond to modern conditions, and how other cultural producers (e.g., publishers, editors, playwrights, directors) made such representations available to people. Accordingly, my initial point of departure is the representation of modernity in the historical novel, but building on recent interest in literary afterlives, I also consider how different modes of communication enabled diverse peoples and communities to encounter historical novels in their own way.

To situate *Acts of Modernity* within a longer history of literary criticism, chapter one begins with a history of reading practices, centered on critical assessments of the early novel and the historical novel, from

4   Introduction

the early-eighteenth century to the present. Chapter two compares two responses to the consequences of modernity in Scotland: Christian Isobel Johnstone's *Clan Albin: A National Tale* (1815) and Walter Scott's *Tales of My Landlord, Second Series* (1818), which is better known as *The Heart of Mid-Lothian*. This contrast highlights the intersection of rights, representation, and modernity; it also shows how early use of the historical novel varied from *Waverley*. In chapter three, after addressing cheap reprints and the reading of Waverley novels, I demonstrate how chapbooks of *The Heart of Mid-Lothian* reinvented this popular but expensive novel for downmarket readers in Britain. Chapter four begins by outlining how Revolutionary War novels of the 1820s and 1830s by James Fenimore Cooper, Lydia Huntley Sigourney, Lydia Maria Child, Catharine Maria Sedgwick, and William Gilmore Simms built upon a *Waverley*esque template to variously shape an emerging discourse on national identity for American readers. This provides the foundation for an in-depth look at Cooper's *The Pathfinder; or, The Inland Sea* (1840), which set forth a less patriotic appraisal of modernity in the American context. In chapter five, I explain how inexpensive editions of Cooper's Leatherstocking novels impacted reading and writing of the historical novel in America and France. The chapter concludes with a look at how Gustave Aimard's adaptation of Cooperesque themes ultimately served both French and American readers. Chapter six considers Honoré de Balzac's *Le père Goriot* (1835) as a chronotopic use of the historical novel to describe the consequences of modernity specific to readers in post-Revolutionary France. In relation, the focus of chapter seven is the industrialization of print and reading in France. I begin with the reproduction of *Le père Goriot* in downmarket editions up to the 1870s and then look more closely at post-1848 novels by George Sand, Eugène Sue, and Émile Zola; this investigation points to the effects of industrialization on the historification of social life in the nineteenth-century novel. Chapter eight analyzes Canadian tales of national progress. The initial focal point is a comparison of historical novels that speak to the politics of nation building in French Canada, especially Philippe Aubert de Gaspé's *Les anciens Canadiens* (1863) and Antoine Gérin-Lajoie's *Jean Rivard* (1862–64). To describe changing use of the genre, the chapter concludes by comparing late-century iterations of the historical novel that spoke, or claimed to speak, to the industrialization of English Canada from the perspective of working-class people. In chapter nine, I examine how several popular historical novels discussed in previous chapters were dramatized for local theatre audiences at Montréal, Paris, New York, and London. The conclusion describes the remediation of *Scott's Ivanhoe: A Romance* (1820) from early operas of the 1820s to contemporary comics, study guides, and films. In these ways, *Acts of Modernity* investigates how the historical novel was, and continues to be, worked to effectively communicate the consequences of modernity as problem-solutions of relevance to all people on both sides of the Atlantic.

Introduction 5

Notes

1 Robert Alves, "A Parallel Between History and Novel Writing," in Nixon, *Novel Definitions*, 182.

2 Alessandro Manzoni, *On the Historical Novel*, trans. Sandra Bermann (Lincoln: University of Nebraska Press, 1984). Manzoni describes the historical novel as a "species of a false genre" (ibid., 81). Alfred Tressider Sheppard, *The Art and Practice of Historical Fiction* (London: Toulmin, 1930). Sheppard writes that historical fiction "presents innumerable, and at first unsuspected, difficulties" (ibid., 12). Joseph Turner, "The Kinds of Historical Fiction: An Essay in Definition and Methodology," *Genre* 12, no. 3 (Fall 1979): 333–57. Turner argues that "all we can say in general about the genre is that it resists generalization" (ibid., 335). Harry E. Shaw, *The Forms of Historical Fiction: Sir Walter Scott and His Successors* (Ithaca, NY: Cornell University Press, 1983). Shaw adds that "historical novels do not constitute a strongly unified, independent genre" (ibid., 30). Richard Maxwell, *The Historical Novel in Europe, 1650–1950* (Cambridge: Cambridge University Press, 2009). Maxwell writes of an "unplaceability" that "can make historical fiction hard to isolate or get into focus" (ibid., 8).

3 The following is a selective description of relevant examples. Leslie Stephen, "Leslie Stephen: Hours in a Library with Scott, *Cornhill Magazine*," in *Walter Scott: The Critical Heritage*, ed. John O. Hayden (London: Routledge, 1995), 439–58. Stephen follows the subtitle of *Waverley, or 'Tis Sixty Years Since*, arguing that a duration of sixty years is definitive (ibid., 455). Sheppard, *Historical Fiction*. Sheppard argues that whether a few minutes or a thousand years ago, it is all history and drawing a line is arbitrary (ibid., 15–17). Harry B. Henderson, *Versions of the Past: The Historical Imagination in American Fiction* (New York: Oxford University Press, 1974). Although his aim is not to set forth a universal definition of the form of the historical novel, Henderson selects novels set in "the world that existed before the author was born" (ibid., xvi). Brander Matthews, *The Historical Novel, and Other Essays* (New York: Charles Scribner's Sons, 1901), https://archive.org/details/cu31924013355916. Matthews argues that "the really trustworthy historical novels are those which were a-writing while the history was a-making" (ibid., 18). David M. Hayne, "The Historical Novel and French Canada" (MA thesis, University of Ottawa, 1945), microfilm. Hayne differentiates between novels "historical in intention" and those that have become historical over time (ibid., 7). Avrom Fleishman, *The English Historical Novel: Walter Scott to Virginia Woolf* (Baltimore, MD: Johns Hopkins Press, 1971). Fleishman argues that "What makes a historical novel historical is the active presence of history as a shaping force" (ibid., 15). George Dekker, *The American Historical Romance* (Cambridge: Cambridge University Press, 1987). Dekker emphasizes the historicity of social and psychological traits: "For fiction to qualify as 'historical,' what more can be required than that the leading or (more to the point) determinative social and psychological traits it represents clearly belong to a period historically distinct from our own" (ibid., 14). Lion Feuchtwanger, *The House of Desdemona; or, The Laurels and Limitations of Historical Fiction*, trans. Harold A. Basilius (Detroit, MI: Wayne State University Press, 1963). Feuchtwanger highlights the importance of a "decisive event" (ibid., 101). Mark C. Carnes, *Novel History: Historians and Novelists Confront America's Past (and Each Other)* (New York: Simon and Schuster, 2001). Carnes describes the historical novel as "inescapably a contradiction in terms: a nonfictional fiction; a factual fantasy; a truthful deception" (ibid., 14).

4 Georg Lukács, *The Historical Novel*, trans. Hannah and Stanley Mitchell (Lincoln: University of Nebraska Press, 1983), 242.

6   *Introduction*

5 Jerome de Groot, *The Historical Novel* (London: Routledge, 2010).

6 Anthony Giddens, *The Consequences of Modernity*, 1st paperback ed. (Cambridge: Polity Press, 1991), 1.

7 Franco Moretti, *Atlas of the European Novel, 1800–1900* (London: Verso, 1998), 17.

8 Roy Harris, *The Linguistics of History* (Edinburgh: Edinburgh University Press, 2004), 226.

9 See Marina Allemano, *Historical Portraits and Visions: From Walter Scott's* Waverley *to Michel Tournier's* Le Roi des Aulnes *and Thomas Pynchon's* Gravity's Rainbow (New York: Garland, 1991); Elisabeth Wesseling, *Writing History as a Prophet: Postmodernist Innovations of the Historical Novel* (Amsterdam: John Benjamins Publishing Company, 1991); Lubomír Doležel, *Possible Worlds of Fiction and History: The Postmodern Stage* (Baltimore, MD: Johns Hopkins University Press, 2010); and Eric L. Berlatsky, *The Real, the True, and the Told: Postmodern Historical Narrative and the Ethics of Representation* (Columbus: The Ohio State University, 2011).

10 Thomas Pynchon, *Gravity's Rainbow* (New York: Viking Press, 1973).

11 Berlatsky, *Postmodern Historical Narrative*, 8.

12 Besides the work of Anthony Giddens on the consequences of modernity and Roy Harris on integrational linguistics, the basis of this approach follows on my reading of Alec McHoul, *Semiotic Investigations: Towards an Effective Semiotics* (Lincoln: University of Nebraska Press, 1996).

1 Meaning-making

A history of reading practices

> Clear thinking about language and society is impeded all too frequently by attempts to project onto the community a linguistic determinacy of the theorist's own invention.
>
> – Roy Harris, *Integrational Linguistics*, 132

Acts of Modernity focuses on uses of the historical novel to communicate chronotopic interpretations of modernity, but it is also about how scholars make histories of literature and reading available to others. Whereas material histories have contributed to the expansion of scholarship on the historical novel in recent years, thematic prioritization and close reading have too often obscured the historical contexts and reading practices that made historical novels meaningful to readers throughout the nineteenth century. For example, in the hands of too many critics, the most popular novelist of the nineteenth century, Walter Scott, is simply ignored, or remains the quintessential man of nineteenth-century letters; his first and best-known novel, *Waverley*, is boiled down to national reconciliation; the Waverley novel represents a masculine genre that obscures feminine (and other) voices, or a means to contrast history and fiction; and the Waverley novels collectively represent entrepreneurial publishing or gesture to the rise of popular reading. Yet, if a point of contention unites critics of the historical novel, then it is, for better and worse, *Waverley* that acts as the first real historical novel for some and the obstacle to better understanding of a wider field of study for others. Either way, it is the elephant in the room. I use it here as the means to enter an introductory discussion of the historical novel that connects historical representation, reading-as-subjectivity, and the historicity of critical reading practices.

The road to *Waverley* involved repeated experimentation with historical representation by authors only lately recognized as significant contributors to the historical novel. In the British context, Diana Wallace recognizes Sophia Lee's *The Recess, or, A Tale of Other Times* (1783), for example, as a critical early intervention.[1] Additionally, Anne Stevens documents historical novels by women in the fifty years prior to *Waverley*, Katie Trumpener

8   Meaning-making

describes national tales in the early-nineteenth century, and most recently, Fiona Price considers how historical novelists turned from ancient constitutionalism to stadial history to describe social transformation.[2] Consequently, *Waverley* may be loosely described as a continuation of an emerging genre. It was, of course, also a unique response to immediate circumstances. The title *Waverley* is itself a reference to characters in recent historical novels: Charlotte Smith's *Desmond: A Novel* (1792) and Jane West's *The Loyalists: An Historical Novel* (1812).[3] The introduction to *Waverley* openly discusses possible titles, noting the well-established conventions attached to sentimental, fashionable, and gothic tales by successful contemporary novelists such as Frances Burney, Charlotte Smith, and Charlotte Dacre. Many other factors contributed to Scott's negotiation of history and romance. Ongoing debates about historical representation and modern progress were a vital aspect of Scott's education at the university in Edinburgh in the 1790s.[4] His literary career began with the preservation of Scottish oral culture and the translation of German romance.[5] In turn, his early narrative poems used the popular ballad form to bring regional and national histories to life.[6] Concurrent with such experiments in the combination of history and fiction, direct criticism of the sentimental novel by Clara Reeve in 1791, Sarah Green in 1810, and many others in the years in between would not have gone unnoticed.[7] Description of the circumstances surrounding or resources available to Scott as he wrote *Waverley* could be extensive. Just as important, Scott built upon a history of critical interpretations that continuously reframed the novel with respect to history and romance.

Much early debate about the novel centered on definitions of the genre, but literary criticism acted as a form of social valuation. For example, the more contentious aspect of the distinction between the novel (as a contemporary reflection on everyday life) and romance (as a fantastic tale derived from the medieval or heroic romance) was the supposed misuse of literature. In the preface to *The Farther Adventures of Robinson Crusoe* (1719), Daniel Defoe was quick to point out the moral and religious usefulness of his work, which he separated from romance.[8] Samuel Croxall was similarly positive in the 1720s, defending the Horatian potential of the novel to inspire the virtues while both entertaining and instructing.[9] As a new form, the novel required a defense; as the genre became popular, authors protected their own interests by attacking or defending it. In the *Gentlemen's Magazine* of December 1787, "R.R.E." argued that novels were a "useless and pernicious commodity" that should be taxed rather than shoes and boots.[10] Ten years later, Thomas Wilson recommended that the number of novels in circulating libraries should be more than double the number of all other books combined.[11] Although assessments of the novel and the impact of novel reading varied throughout the century, critics were overwhelmingly concerned that the novel, like romance, was a threat to morality. Following on comparisons of the instructiveness of Samuel Richardson's *Pamela; or, Virtue Rewarded* (1740) and the dangers of Henry Fielding's *The History of*

Meaning-making 9

Tom Jones, a Foundling (1749), Henry Mackenzie, for example, was most alarmed about the consequences of "mingled virtue and vice."[12] Such fears were pronounced with respect to children and women – those considered vulnerable. Although Vicesimus Knox believed that the novel could help to cultivate a child's imagination,[13] Samuel Pegge's fears of the corrupting influence of romance on young readers were more common.[14] Erasmus Darwin was less than generous when he argued that women should not be "kept in intire ignorance of mankind," as was his patronizing recommendation of specific novel titles to young female readers.[15] Such paternal treatment would later be extended to the working class – another supposedly susceptible section of the population. Overall, William Jones best summarized the ongoing critique of romance (i.e., popular reading) in the late-eighteenth century by suggesting that ignorance was better than the knowledge gained from novels.[16] The impact of such opinions, which were nothing short of self-interested social management, was far-reaching;[17] long before the "Thought Police" of George Orwell's *Nineteen Eighty-Four* (1949), critics taught not only what was worth reading but also how to read it and to what purpose.[18]

In response to the novel, history was deemed the bedrock of a better society. The related prioritization of historical realism over romantic fiction was, like critical reception of the novel, seemingly inseparable from morality. Defoe defended the moral usefulness of *Farther Adventures*, for example, by labeling his most celebrated work as "Fact" rather than "Fiction."[19] In 1721, Penelope Aubin followed by remarking that her virtuous heroine was more realistic than Robinson Crusoe.[20] Using what would become a common means of exploring authenticity, Samuel Richardson created a sense of objective distance by claiming to be editor rather than author of *Pamela*, which was comprised of letters with a "Foundation in *Truth* and *Nature*."[21] Similarly, Eliza Haywood declared that *The Fortunate Foundlings* (1744) was a collection of letters written by "*real Characters*" and attested to by "*Living Witnesses*."[22] More playfully, John Cleland described *Memoirs of a Woman of Pleasure* (1748–49) as "stark naked truth."[23] In one way or another, the novel was repeatedly, consciously positioned as a form of history, which was framed as the only genuine representation of the past.

Authors strove to create legitimacy for the novel as a form of reading and did so on behalf of their own novels. It was not simply a ploy to mask the pleasures of romance or to piggyback upon the more assured standing of history. The novel differed from romance and history in that it represented everyday life in ways that more and more readers could relate to – not because it was a lesser or corrupted form of historical representation. The transformation of romance into fictitious history, or what Hugh Blair called the "Familiar Novel,"[24] was a topic of discussion among critics throughout the eighteenth century.[25] James Beattie categorized types of the "New Romance."[26] Clara Reeve showed how the novel sprung from romance and also how the novel and romance were different by providing detailed analyses of major eighteenth-century novelists.[27] Awareness that the novel had

10   Meaning-making

become something quite distinct from romance emerged again and again in criticism throughout the century. John Moore wrote that Miguel de Cervantes banished the "old romance" and described the development of a "new species of romance" called the novel.[28] One reason for the shift was the changing representation of history. In the eighteenth century, histories of statecraft gave way to histories of everyday life; this was true across genres, including national histories, memoirs, novels, tracts, and chapbooks.[29] As a consequence, Ann Letitia Barbauld, in her history of the novel, defended the novel as a form of "domestic pleasure," while also describing it as a means to further "knowledge of the world."[30] By 1810, the novel, not unlike history, could be understood as a practical resource linking everyday life and the wider world. The turn from both history and romance to the historical novel – a combination of history and romance used to represent changes in everyday life over time – was under way before *Waverley* appeared on the scene.

In 1797, William Godwin, for example, considered the transition from chronology to historical fiction. He opposed romance and invention to history but insisted on their combination to form historical romance, "the noblest and most excellent species of history, . . . which, with a scanty substratum of facts and dates, the writer interweaves a number of happy, ingenious and instructive inventions, blending them into one continuous and indiscernible mass."[31] Not long before Scott's first narrative poem, *The Lay of the Last Minstrel* (1805), and nearly twenty years before the publication of *Waverley*, Godwin viewed historical romance as a means to improve upon historical record: "He that knows only what day the Bastille was taken and on what spot Louis XVI perished, knows nothing. He professes the mere skeleton of history. The muscles, the articulations, every thing in which the life emphatically resides, is absent."[32] Importantly, historical fiction remains an extension of chronology – an improvement rather than something altogether new – a means to get closer to a truthful representation of the past. Godwin's analysis was common in other ways; he described formal rules of construction, for instance, emphasizing the depiction of genius and so-called masculine values – the great men of history were, or remained, front and center. But Godwin also spoke to use of the genre in a way that would enable Scott and others to experiment more freely with historical representation throughout the century: "Modern history indeed we ought to peruse, because all that we wish must be connected with all that we are, and because it is incumbent upon us to explore the means by which the latter may be made, as it were, to slide into the former."[33] Godwin links the use of historical record to future possibilities. In this way, the combination of history and romance was, or at least could be read as, a response to modernization that took up the historical processes and contemporary outcomes of modernity. Novelists of the period, including Clara Reeve, Mary Wollstonecraft, and Maria Edgeworth, as well as Godwin in novels such as *Things as They Are; or, The Adventures of Caleb Williams* (1794) and

St. Leon: A Tale of the Sixteenth Century (1799),[34] experimented with the combination of history and romance for this purpose. Following on anti-Jacobin, gothic, and other instances of the novel in the 1790s, Lady Morgan's (Sydney Owenson) *The Wild Irish Girl: A National Tale* (1806) and Jane Porter's *The Scottish Chiefs: A Romance* (1810), although sometimes more narrowly defined as national tales preceding the emergence of the historical novel proper, also investigated the relationship between historical representation and social progress.[35] In this light, situated at the tail end of a century of genre experimentation, the publication of *Waverley* was a highly self-reflexive treatment of history-making. It was so, in part, because Scott put reading-as-subjectivity – the contribution of reading practices to community methods – at the forefront of his first novel.

In chapter thirteen of *Waverley*, the Baron of Bradwardine and Edward Waverley set out on horseback, conversing as they go. Scott frames the encounter by describing their respective reading practices. The Baron reads a selection of classic, religious, and national poets; more importantly, he "only cumbered his memory with matters of fact; the cold, dry, hard outlines which history delineates."[36] Edward, in contrast, is "wild and romantic in his ideas and in his taste of reading";[37] he "loved to fill up and round the sketch with the colouring of a warm and vivid imagination, which gives light and life to the actors and speakers in the drama of past ages."[38] This contrast between the Baron's "matters of fact" and Edward's "vivid imagination" aligns with Godwin's earlier differentiation of chronology and romance. But the purpose of the novel was not simply to bring history to life – a common refrain among early critics. There was a point to be made about the relationship between reading and subjectivity. The meeting of the Baron and Edward on horseback may be said to point to the potentially productive union of collective history and individualistic romance – that is, forms of reading and acting – but the way in which this happens is important. Despite marked differences in "their characters and habits of thinking," the narrator states that the Baron and Edward "met upon history as on a neutral ground, in which each claimed an interest," and that "they contributed greatly to each other's amusement."[39] To meet "upon history as on a neutral ground" refers to historical facts (a past) held in common. It also suggests the possibility of new beginnings or at least new ways forward – the theoretical basis of reconciliation and progress so often attributed to *Waverley*. But what does this mean in practice? For example, is there a "neutral ground" of history? What would or could this mean? More certainly, though the fact that both parties "claimed an interest" may also indicate overlapping perspectives, the respective interests of the Baron and Edward are not the same, as their reading practices suggest. Although the Baron and Edward both read history and poetry, each does so for his own purposes and in his own way – as a Scot or a Brit, a Jacobite or a Hanoverian, a man of standing or a young man entering the world. In short, reading occurs as part of a real-life communication situation, which necessarily differentiates the two characters, as

12   Meaning-making

it would any two characters. As far as the progress of the novel is concerned, the difference is pointed and yet also the basis of a resolution that is not strictly personal: "cold, dry, hard outlines" sketch both the historical record of nations and the reading practices of the Baron of Bradwardine, whereas Edward's enthusiasm for poetry is framed as the solitary, juvenile wandering of an untutored mind – the divide, like that between Scotland and England, is not left unresolved.

The meeting of history and romance on horseback suggests the pleasant possibility of a fruitful exchange of ideas. Ultimately, though, *Waverley* is a war novel – a story of political conflict and material consequences; the stakes are high: collective, not just individual. Initially, the reading practices of the Baron and Edward point to the individuality of reading as a function of social circumstances, but the novel ultimately outlines an understanding of subjectivity in terms of the actualization of community interests. The end of Edward's Highland wandering is consummated by his marriage to the Baron's daughter – a cross-border union that restores personal fortunes and reconciles national trajectories (for some, at least). With the end of the war, Edward's singular Highland romance also ends. National history begins (again, post-1707), and the Baron's "matters of fact" may be said to prevail, or at least take precedence. The "solid roast beef" of history and the "whipt syllabub" of romance will learn to live together at Tully-Veolan, although not exactly as equals. Ian Duncan touches upon the connection between the historical novel, reading practices, and social outcomes: "In *Waverley*, for the first time, the novel narrates the history of its own formation as a genre – a historicization that touches not just literary form but the function and status of fiction as an institution, a set of material forms and social practices, including our act of reading."[40] Whatever one's interpretation of the politics of reconciliation cemented by the marriage of Edward and Rose, *Waverley* not only put the historical novel in the hands of more readers than ever before, it also tied the act of reading to the act of history-making. As to what readers (and writers) should do with *Waverley*, critics were not slow to offer a guiding hand.

Early reviews of *Waverley* were positive.[41] Francis Jeffrey's description of *Waverley* as "true to nature" in the *Edinburgh Review* was typical.[42] Similarly, the *Monthly Review* found that despite the fictional frame, "the delineation itself is as correct, minute, and spirited a copy of nature as ever came from the hands of an artist."[43] Yet critics rarely missed an opportunity to differentiate literary forms in order to outline social prerogatives. Also in the *Monthly Review*, *Waverley* was distinguished from both historical romance and novels of manners: "It is strictly an historical romance, and yet scarcely belongs to any class of composition usually decorated with that title. Neither is it a picture of existing manners, and therefore not to be placed by the side of *Ennui* or the *Cottagers of Glenburnie*."[44] Not only a new instance of an existing genre, *Waverley* was also separated from popular novels rented out by circulating libraries – ironically, an institution that

Scott would benefit from enormously. The result was a confusing commitment to historical truth somehow separated from the romance genre through which it was communicated. Critics were more successful in driving a wedge between accepted and popular forms of reading. However, Scott represented the former and the novel the latter, thus creating what would seem to be an irreconcilable conflict between critical valuations and reading practices.

The celebration of *Waverley* caused considerable anxiety among critics. The novel was still considered a lower form, equated with common prose rather than "high" (usually lyric) poetry, romance as opposed to history, a form written mostly by women or hacks, or worse, radicals. At the bottom of such interpretations was the transition from a patronage system that served an elite few writers and readers to capitalist modes of production that encouraged entrepreneurial publishing and the making of literature that would sell widely. *Waverley* demanded a response because it was a unique instance of an emerging genre. That the author of this anonymously published novel was Scott (a poorly kept secret) – a professional man of letters and a poet rivaled only by Lord Byron – also played a role in the immediate appreciation of *Waverley*. No less significant, the first edition of 1,000 copies sold out within days. Further editions and novels by the "Author of *Waverley*" followed quickly. Popularity, rather than paving the way for a shift in interpretation, may be said to have hardened the opposition of critics to the novel. Although *Waverley* could be celebrated as a literary achievement leading to comparisons of Scott to Shakespeare, the genre remained under the microscope. *Waverley* appealed to readers; it did not, however, cause an overnight swing in the reading practices of literary critics. The response of reviewers was not merely celebratory but also defensive of accepted norms and familiarly restrictive with respect to the role of reading in everyday life. The *Critical Review*, for example, questioned why "a poet of established fame, should dwindle into a scribbler of novels."[45] This was a question for Scott, who, as a man of letters, should have been more responsible about the representation of national histories, and a shot at women's expression aimed at delegitimizing female authorship and popular reading. The purpose of the review was not just to inform readers of a new work of fiction. For instance, *Waverley*, with its "endless Scotch idioms, Gaelic allusions, scraps of Latin, and a ridiculous French character,"[46] was derided as too national (i.e., too Scottish) for an English audience. The same review also concluded by noting that "the main incidents are merely the rebellion of 1745, treated 'novel wise.'"[47] In other words, *Waverley* was not only vulgar and patriotic (in a disparaging sense), but also concerned a minor episode in the history of Scotland – that desert of the north. Rather than a knee-jerk reaction, this patriarchal, elitist, southern assessment was a typical, calculated response to the seismic shift in communication practices that seemed to threaten appreciation of the past treated "history wise."

Use of the review for reasons of professional self-interest and social management was an extension of longstanding fears of the impact of unfettered

14   Meaning-making

reading practices. Prominent literary critics carried it out in different ways. In the *Quarterly Review*, for example, John Wilson Croker remarked on Scott's historical inaccuracies and on the uncertain mixture of history and romance.[48] Situated alongside the longer history of novel criticism dating back to the early-eighteenth century, his response should not be understood simply as either a personal preference or an expert appraisal. The motivation for this return to verisimilitude was social control, whether intended or unconscious. Following on changes in copyright legislation, the expansion of libraries, and the potential of new printing technologies to manufacture cheaper print, the increasing accessibility of literature added to concerns over the impact of reading on the lower classes. Broadsides and chapbooks already flooded the streets of London and were carried to all corners of the British Isles. Whereas the relative inaccessibility of expensive new novels would not seem to be of significance in this regard, out-of-copyright novels were widely available. The potentially malevolent impact of reading had become all-too-apparent to the self-interested upper classes. Although Thomas Paine's response in *Rights of Man* (1791) to Edmund Burke's attack on the French Revolution is perhaps the best example of the perceived danger,[49] the novel was not exempt; to take one example, Matthew Lewis's *The Monk: A Romance* (1796), for different reasons, highlighted the supposed power of print to mislead citizens and scandalize youth.[50] The upmarket novel did not circulate as widely as a political pamphlet, but the combination of widening appeal, increasing literacy, and cheaper print posed a threat. In this way, the popularity of the historical novel may be said to have hit a nerve that would reverberate throughout the century. The representation of Anglo-Irish relations in *The Wild Irish Girl*, like the description of Scottish resistance to English rule in *The Scottish Chiefs*, had no less consequential social and political dimensions than *Waverley*. But the practical implications of novel reading changed with the publication of a novel that seemed to put the potentially subversive act of history-making in the hands of more readers than ever before.

During the so-called age of revolution,[51] people remained active in their fight for better conditions – protests, riots, petitions, and other forms of agitation were common in the Romantic period. Although often used to reinforce social order, the historical novel aligns with contemporary efforts to both understand the past and reform the present. *Waverley* can be read as a conservative portrayal of national reconciliation in the aftermath of the American and French Revolutions, but the act of making history, as a conceivable challenge to the status quo, struck a chord that put the literary establishment on guard. Critics may have trusted Scott – a lawyer, sheriff, historian, poet, and property owner – who was more conservative in political life than in the imaginary world of his novels. Common readers and popular writers were another matter. As Croker's attack suggests, although already manifest in other forms of fiction, the heightened status of the unwieldy historical novel signaled a twofold menace – the potential of any writer to "fill up and round the sketch" and of any reader to act upon alternative renditions of history. The unique combination of history and romance – and the uncertain outcome of reading itself – made the historical novel a tool to be handled with special care. Put otherwise, what people read and how they did so was critical for two interconnected reasons: first, a persistent belief in the power of literature to send a message to a reader;[52] second, a pervasive lack of trust in the reader's ability to decode a text correctly. History is a contested field of interpretation, but the "mere skeleton of history" is written to dissuade misinterpretation, and official history is something taught, remembered, and regurgitated – an institutionalized form of meaning production. Men of standing such as the Baron of Bradwardine recite the hard truths of historical record for the benefit of young ears. In this way, truth is supposedly protected and passed on. Such notions falsify the communication process, but under these illusions the addition of romance seemed to open the door to the act of remaking the past – of wandering, as with Edward's foray into the Highlands, from the straight and narrow – and thus consciously or inadvertently altering the story of Progress officially known as History, which could then be sent to passive readers from all walks of life. This was also the nature of the conflict between Paine and Burke in the wake of the French Revolution. At stake were the rights of man, but so too were the rights of men and women to rewrite history in ways that reflected their own interests (or, less often, those of others). The issue was empowerment – the power to question established norms, and by doing so, to shape one's place in the world. With the combination of history and romance made visible in a relatively popular form of literature, the process of remaking history was laid bare for readers, or at least potentially so. The historical novel was not the missing ingredient that made literature a radical form of communication; literature of all sorts – novels, pamphlets, tracts, chapbooks, garlands, broadsides, and poems – communicated interpretations of social progress in Britain, and readers were eager to make of them what they could. But by the nature of its constitution (i.e., the combination of history and romance, among many other forms and genres), the potential for revolutionary challenges to social order was imminent in the making and reading of historical novels. Perhaps, then, it is not surprising that in the eyes of Croker and his contemporaries, young men such as Edward, with heads filled to overflowing with romance and yet to establish themselves in the world, were not to be trusted with such tools – the uneducated masses even less so.

As if to affirm the fears of critics, the Waverley novels, and *Waverley* especially, were used throughout the century and across the Western world to both uphold the status quo and reimagine social progress.[53] Although official reactions varied, the overall aim was social management; critics did their part as self-appointed gatekeepers. British critics of the Victorian period, for instance, severely limited reading of the Waverley novels in ways that remain familiar. For John Ruskin, Scott was great because he could

16   Meaning-making

reveal what he saw in a plain way.[54] This seems a backhanded compliment, yet many critics later described Scott in similarly positive terms, as an artist capable of painting society in motion during a period of great transformation. In comparison, Thomas Carlyle claimed that Scott wrote bestsellers to purchase farms.[55] Carlyle's criticism, however, ran much deeper than mere contempt for commercial success, and it proved a more destructive line of attack, as it resonated with (and likely contributed to) modernist approaches to literary studies. In Carlyle's view, Scott was an entertainer with nothing to say about the mystery of existence. Ruskin saw Scott as depicting complex social landscapes, which aligned well with the many nineteenth-century paintings depicting scenes from the Waverley novels;[56] Carlyle, in contrast, offered only slighting references to his health – ironically, a few years after his death, Scott was "one of the *healthiest* of men."[57] In other words, he was merely of the world: "His life was worldly; his ambitions were worldly. There is nothing spiritual in him; all is economical, material, as of the earth earthy."[58] The inner-man of Scott, tellingly compared to working-class reformer William Cobbett, lacked fire; more to the point, in Carlyle's view, Scott had no message, meaning he did not send the right message, which would have consisted of spiritual guidance worthy of the term genius. Although limited interpretations of Scott's novels, Ruskin's positive gloss and Carlyle's stark repudiation are noteworthy as significant precursors to later uses of the historical novel.

According to James Simmons, following "strongly hostile" reactions in the 1850s, "Historical fiction ceased to be considered ancillary to formal history and became accepted on its own as light literature with little pretension to anything weightier."[59] The completion of the Scott monument in Edinburgh in the 1840s would seem to have set in stone the historical novel's position in the literary world (of Scotland, at least), but social ossification was part of the problem. Although Scott cast a long shadow throughout the Western world, novelists combined history and romance in different ways, resulting in Newgate novels, social problem novels, and science fiction novels. Within the context of a late-century appreciation of realism, which only confirmed overt reliance on a sender-receiver model of communication based on verisimilitude, critics could associate the historical novel with "less serious" genres, such as crime fiction, sensation novels, or adventure stories; G. P. R. James, Wilkie Collins, and H. G. Wells were also historical novelists. So, at the end of the nineteenth century, there was nothing new under the sun; disparagement of the historical novel (i.e., popular reading) and the reification of Scott (i.e., a canon of "great" authors) continued. Upholding Scott, nonetheless, often seemed to require some maneuvering, and a strangely Carlylean "appreciation" of his poetry. For example, in his discussion of Scott and the Romantic school, Joseph Devey reads Scott's narrative poems as lacking passion, with nothing to say of the enigmas haunting humanity.[60] Scott's saving grace was that he recorded events; history remained respectable, and so there was something to salvage. Similarly, in the case of Goldwin Smith, the alignment of Scott with Shakespeare and Homer required the caveat that neither mysticism nor politics played a role in his poetry. Smith instead gushes about "A nature so joyous, a life so happy, so full of physical as well as of mental enjoyment, social success so great excluded all questionings about the mystery of being and all sympathy with the desire of change."[61] The appreciation of Scott's seemingly blissful life trumped the analysis of his literary output; unfortunately, the first edition of Scott's journal, which might have deterred the spread of such myths, was a decade away.[62]

Regardless, such handling was always more reflective of the interests of the reviewer, which raises a question. If Scott was no longer of the moment in the second half of the nineteenth century, why did critics keep going back to him? The popularity of the Waverley novels was never greater than after Scott's death in 1832; despite some critical antagonism toward the genre, the reprinting of all Scott's novels as part of a downmarket collected edition from 1829 to 1833,[63] and the many cheaper editions that followed,[64] kept Scott in the public eye and his historical novels in the hands of readers throughout the century. Perhaps more importantly, the combination of Scott's canonical status and narrow assessments by the likes of Carlyle enabled critics to use Scott for their own purposes (e.g., communication with other critics or like-minded readers), which still usually involved vague apprehensions about the impact of reading on public morality. Further, it was not difficult to position Scott as opposed to the literary current. In the wake of the First Reform Act, Scott did not seem to take up a cause, as did, for instance, Harriet Martineau; as opposed to Edward Bulwer-Lytton or Émile Zola, he did not bask in detail; at the turn of the century, he did not sufficiently theorize the form of the novel (e.g., as did Henry James); and with the rise of modernism and close reading, his long novels seemed sprawling tales rather than aesthetic gems. Against this shifting context, Scott could be redeployed, however repetitively, as a useful measuring stick (i.e., in the mud).

The motivation and consequences of such reading practices remained familiar in the twentieth century. In 1901, Brander Matthews followed Carlyle by presenting a humanist interpretation of Scott, praising his "compassionate understanding of his fellow-creatures."[65] Such seemingly benign comments mask a larger purpose – to attack reinterpretations of history in the form of popular reading. History, Matthews contends, was merely added to or subtracted from novels, that is, employed as background or injected into a story. The historical novel as a genre was denigrated in favor of certain types of realist fiction – a division based only roughly upon aesthetic principles and more firmly upon the reification of a narrow understanding of history or acceptable forms of historical representation, as the supposedly truthful depiction of the real world. The "ordinary historical novel," too far from the skeleton of history and not close enough to the ground, was a "drug" that deceived readers into believing they were "improving their minds."[66] It

18   *Meaning-making*

was dishonest because it did not declare itself as pure romance and because it was not realistic enough, for instance, as compared to reportage or naturalism. Following Henry McKenzie and Alessandro Manzoni, among others, the historical novel was, much like melodrama, considered an unwieldy, inconsistent, even unhealthy, mixture. Or, in Matthews's memorable phrase, it was for those who wished to be "ravished out of themselves into an illusion of a world better than the one they, unfortunately, have to live in."[67] No doubt many readers had good reasons to escape their everyday existence, but the question seems to be, how could readers decode the correct message if the genres of history and romance were bundled together in unpredictable or confusing ways? Following John Gibson Lockhart's *Life of Scott* (1837), and Carlyle's review of it, Matthews's framing of Scott as a force for good made the Waverley novels, which he did not consider to be merely ordinary, suitable for fireside family moments. In this way, Scott could be safely displayed upon the mantle, passed from one century to another, marked as a healthy old man with a knack for spinning realistic yarns of yesteryear. In contrast, framing the historical novel as unhealthy was indicative of enduring concerns over the impact of reading on weak minds. The didactic (and ironic) separation of Scott from the historical novel was meant to keep uneducated readers from getting the wrong message. In short, trust in readers, and in forms of communication that wandered from the "cold, dry, hard outlines which history delineates," was limited. Apparently, people needed to be told what to read and how to read it. This perspective was not new, of course, but as part of a seemingly continuous form of social devaluation the implications for the understanding of literature and reading cannot be underestimated, especially as a precedent for and contributing factor to the modernist criticism of popular culture on the one hand and the institutionalization of new criticism on the other.[68]

Chris Baldick describes criticism of the novel in the early-twentieth century as largely restricted to practicing novelists, whereas literary theorists took up poetry; academic interest in the novel followed starting in the 1940s.[69] In turn, "Much discussion of novelistic principles in the early twentieth century resolves itself into a contest between partisans of Art, who tend to invoke the authority of Gustave Flaubert as the novelist's novelist, and champions of Life, who are more likely to invoke Tolstoy or Dickens."[70] This division, as Baldick is aware, oversimplifies criticism of the period, but it is instructive as another instance of meaning-as-use in practice.[71] Echoing an already entrenched Romantic sentiment, Henry James famously focused on creative freedom and execution; fidelity to the external world was secondary to the truth of the artistic impression.[72] The emphasis on formal resources continued with influential works of literary criticism, for example, by I. A. Richards,[73] whose work at Cambridge facilitated the reading of novels as poems, by Q. D. Leavis and others.[74] Methodology and content seemed to dovetail at the right moment; if the (close) reader was so inclined, modernist novels seemed to lend themselves to the study of literariness, which was advertised as a way to unearth the true meaning of a text (as a text).[75] Conversely, just as Scott in his 1830 introduction to *Ivanhoe* (1820) advised taking "a glance on the great picture of life,"[76] H. G. Wells wrote expansively of modern society, taking a sincere interest in the utility of the novel as a means to better understand the new conditions of everyday life at the turn of the century. The division between James and Wells is of course a matter of reading practices, or meaning-making. Formalism, however, was entrenched at the university and integrated into the advance of English as a subject of study. Such developments coincided with catastrophic international conflicts that changed the way people understood life. As Walter Benjamin describes, World War I resulted in a profound rupture in history and culture: "A generation that had gone to school on a horse-drawn streetcar now stood under the open sky in a countryside in which nothing remained unchanged but the clouds, and beneath these clouds, in a field of force of destructive torrents and explosions, was the tiny, fragile human body."[77] For some at least, the revolutionary events of 1848 in Europe furthered a sense that the Waverley novels no longer spoke to contemporary readers of modern circumstances, hence the practicality of social problem, industrial, and proletarian novels in the second half of the nineteenth century. WWI changed everything again. Scott's histories of political reconciliation and social progress might have been read as comfortingly constructive tales, but at a time when nations were destroying each other, who could make sense of the past or claim to have a firm understanding of one's place in the world? From this perspective, formalism was a sort of clean, well-lighted place.[78] Scott seemed of another time; it is no coincidence that already in Virginia Woolf's *To the Lighthouse* (1913) Mr. Ramsey reads one of those books that people do not read anymore, and it is a novel by Scott.[79] Whereas the Waverley novels integrated history and romance to offer problem-solutions of relevance to early-nineteenth-century readers, in the interwar period, critics separated text from context while artists wrote experimental novels to undermine the making of history and question the nature of existence. Histories are made, not given; historical novelists responded to new circumstances, as did their critics.

Criticism of the historical novel during this period was at once strangely familiar and responsive to the historical moment. Herbert Butterfield, to take one example, is best known for two books: *The Whig Interpretation of History* (1931) and *Origins of Modern Science* (1949). But his little-known first book, *The Historical Novel* (1924), set forth a timely description of the historical novel as both "a piece of invention"[80] and as a demonstration of the "impossibility of history."[81] Looking back, he seems to have fused Godwin's combination of chronology and romance with Manzoni's mistrust of the genre. Conversely, the impossibility of history could also be read as reflective of a modernist, post-WWI disillusionment with history itself; in Butterfield's words, "The Memory of the world is not a bright, shining crystal, but a heap of broken fragments, a few fine flashes of light that

20 Meaning-making

break through the darkness."[82] This view of history as an instance of imperfect memory aligns with his later, influential criticism of Whig historicism. Moreover, it makes way for the transition from history "proper" (i.e., linear chronology) to what Butterfield calls the "literature of power."[83] Literature becomes powerful when grounded: "Historical novels are born of romanticism of a kind; but they are a romancing around objects and places; they have a basis in reality, and their roots in the soil."[84] These words might suggest an emerging historical materialism attentive to the situatedness of meaning production. But the formula for making history remained unchanged; romance served history, passing down the timeless truths of social order to passive readers. Butterfield's focus is instructive – how to write a historical novel featuring historic characters (e.g., Napoleon), which is reminiscent of Godwin's emphasis on the individual but otherwise lacking his progressive view of historicization. What begins as a timely post-WWI deconstruction of the historical novel devolves into a rigid, recognizable case for moral instruction. Butterfield's description of the malleable masses as molded by men in high station was not new; considering at least 150 years of opposition and reform, it was politically charged, more so at a moment in history when proletarian movements across Europe and North America were on the rise. Despite the grounded reference to "romancing around objects and places" that would seem to make way for situational interpretations of history, he manufactures an abstract, top-down view of social order. Following a catastrophic war, perhaps this was a comforting means to make sense of the world, though also patriarchal and laced with religious connotations. The great men of history are set above the world of common people and things: "over our heads, as it were, a great history-making is always going on."[85] The historical novelist becomes a mystic who interprets the past, thus raising history and the novel to a "higher power."[86] However attractive the description of "flashes of light that break through the darkness," the "Memory of the World" hinges on a reading-in-general of the historical novel as a genre uniquely placed to set History (and those who make it) apart from everyday life.

Though informed by the history I have just recounted, *Acts of Modernity* begins elsewhere, with an emphasis on communication practices. Mikhail Bakhtin's chronotopic history of the novel,[87] and his related assertion that Scott "achieves the fullness of time necessary for the historical novel,"[88] point to the adaptation of literary form to better communicate the peculiarities of modern progress to contemporary readers. This approach aligns with the most influential of Scott scholars – Georg Lukács. Christopher GoGwilt points to a difference between the two: "Whereas Lukács sees in Scott the crystallization of the modern English nation-state, Bakhtin points toward those centripetal forces (above all, of language) that do away with any insular sense of national-historical time."[89] Yet the instability of language makes possible the literary reinvention of the nation-state. Further, both critics saw the nineteenth-century historical novel as a timely and unique

Meaning-making 21

response to the modernization of social life. Lukács, however, has been the more influential with respect to studies of the historical novel, perhaps in part because Bakhtin's work was not widely known, at least among Western scholars, until after the English translation of *The Dialogic Imagination* in 1982. Lukács's *The Historical Novel* (1937; first English translation 1962) remains the most prominent consideration of the subject – even as it is productively critiqued or sometimes passed over entirely to make room for new approaches or wider scope. Lukács did not adequately address the historical novel prior to Scott, the significant contributions by women and working-class writers, the differences between Waverley novels, or the adaptation of the historical novel by other authors. Further, his denigration of late-nineteenth-century novels as "making private of history" is also insufficient.[90] But *The Historical Novel* was (and remains) useful in its own way. Lukács recognized the way in which "Scott portrays the great transformations of history as transformations of popular life."[91] The Waverley novels were not the first novels to incorporate historical representation or include lower-class characters, but according to Lukács, they were the first and primary example of a kind of novel that historicized the material life of common people.[92] Importantly, Lukács saw the Waverley novels as representative of a "classical period of the historical novel,"[93] a phrase that connects such novels in time as effective expressions of national transformation. In essence, *The Historical Novel* points to a particular use of the historical novel that was timely and has since proven highly influential; in response to Lukács and other persuasive works of social and literary history, such as Ian Watt's *The Rise of the Novel* (1957), critics subsequently shifted the ground of interpretation during the heyday of formalism.[94]

Lion Feuchtwanger, for example, followed Lukács by describing how Scott's "concern for the common man brought him the realization that the masses, the people, are the bearers of history."[95] Scott's primary concerns may be better described with respect to modernization, and in relation, the self-reflexive making of popular histories. Regardless, in the 1970s, the idea of the people as a subject of study was adapted to studies of the novel as it was used (primarily by middle-class novelists) to represent the intersection of historical circumstances and everyday life experienced by the working classes. Building on E. P. Thompson's *The Making of the English Working Class* (1963) and related materialist approaches to social history, representation of the life of common individuals in the industrial world emerged as a point of interest in Victorian scholarship on the novel.[96] More recent studies are interested in the origins, definitions, and scope of the historical novel. As mentioned, others have productively opened an early history of the British historical novel, especially the groundbreaking contributions of women writers. In relation, Richard Maxwell's study of the historical novel in Europe points to the work of women in pre-Revolutionary France, and Brian Hamnett extends the study of Scott and the nineteenth-century historical novel to Germany, Spain, and Russia.[97] More examples of the

22 Meaning-making

increasing breadth of contemporary scholarship on the historical novel in both national and international contexts might be provided, and of course there are many studies of the novel, in all its forms throughout the eighteenth and nineteenth centuries, to provide the basis of formal and thematic comparisons.[98] These and other secondary sources have contributed to this book, which points to early genre development, embraces both canonical and lesser-known novels by women and men, and describes use of the historical novel in national and transatlantic contexts. My focus, however, builds more directly upon the sociological approaches and book history methodologies that have since the 1980s become prominent components of scholarship linking the historical novel and the nation-state,[99] and even more, on recent work connecting Scott to modernity.[100]

Notes

1 Diana Wallace, *The Woman's Historical Novel: British Women Writers, 1900–2000* (Houndmills: Palgrave Macmillan, 2005). Sophia Lee, *The Recess, or, A Tale of Other Times* (London: Cadell, 1785).

2 Anne H. Stevens, *British Historical Fiction Before Scott* (Basingstoke: Palgrave Macmillan, 2010). Katie Trumpener, *Bardic Nationalism: The Romantic Novel and the British Empire* (Princeton, NJ: Princeton University Press, 1997). Fiona Price, *Reinventing Liberty: Nation, Commerce and the Historical Novel from Walpole to Scott* (Edinburgh: Edinburgh University Press, 2016).

3 Charlotte Smith, *Desmond: A Novel* (London: G. G. J. and J. Robinson, 1792). Jane West, *The Loyalists: An Historical Novel* (London: Longman, Hurst, Rees, Orme, and Brown, 1812).

4 Peter D. Garside, "Scott and the 'Philosophical' Historians," *Journal of the History of Ideas* 36, no. 3 (September 1975): 497–512.

5 Walter Scott, *Minstrelsy of the Scottish Border: Consisting of Historical and Romantic Ballads Collected in the Southern Counties of Scotland; With a Few of Modern Date, Founded upon Local Tradition*, 2 vols. (London: T. Cadell Jun. and W. Davies, 1802). Scott translated Gottfried August Bürger's "Lenore" (entitled by Scott "William and Helen") and "Der Wilde Jäger" ("The Chase"); both were first published as part of *An Apology for Tales of Terror* (Kelso: James Ballantyne, 1799), www.walterscott.lib.ed.ac.uk/works/poetry/apology/home.html.

6 First publication details for Scott's most popular poems: *The Lay of the Last Minstrel: A Poem* (London: Longman, Hurst, Rees, and Orme; Edinburgh: Archibald Constable, 1805); *Marmion; A Tale of Flodden Field* (Edinburgh: Archibald Constable; London: William Miller/John Murray, 1808); and *The Lady of the Lake; A Poem* (Edinburgh: John Ballantyne; London: Longman, Hurst, Rees and Orme/William Miller, 1810).

7 Clara Reeve, preface to *The School for Widows*, in Nixon, *Novel Definitions*, 132–33. Sarah Green, preface to *Romance Readers and Romance Writers*, in Nixon, *Novel Definitions*, 96–98.

8 Daniel Defoe, preface to *The Farther Adventures of Robinson Crusoe*, in Nixon, *Novel Definitions*, 65–66.

9 Samuel Croxall, preface to *A Select Collection of Novels*, in Nixon, *Novel Definitions*, 224–25.

10 "R.R.E.," [from *Gentlemen's Magazine*, no. 57, December 1787], in Nixon, *Novel Definitions*, 220.

11 Thomas Wilson, from *The Use of Circulating Libraries Considered*, in Nixon, *Novel Definitions*, 223.
12 Henry Mackenzie, [from *The Lounger*, no. 20, June 18, 1975], in Nixon, *Novel Definitions*, 238.
13 Vicesimus Knox, "On the Efficacy of Moral Instruction," in Nixon, *Novel Definitions*, 234–35.
14 Samuel Pegge (the Elder), [from *Gentlemen's Magazine*, no. 37, December 1767], in Nixon, *Novel Definitions*, 239–40.
15 Erasmus Darwin, "Polite Literature," in Nixon, *Novel Definitions*, 246.
16 William Jones, "On Novels," in Nixon, *Novel Definitions*, 240–41.
17 See, for example, Elizabeth Parker et al., [Students' Prize-winning Essays on "The Love of Novels"], in Nixon, *Novel Definitions*, 251–57.
18 George Orwell, *Nineteen Eighty-Four: A Novel* (London: Secker and Warburg, 1949).
19 Daniel Defoe, preface to *Robinson Crusoe*, in Nixon, *Novel Definitions*, 65.
20 Penelope Aubin, preface to *The Strange Adventures of the Count de Vinevil and His Family*, in Nixon, *Novel Definitions*, 67.
21 Samuel Richardson, preface to *Pamela*, in Nixon, *Novel Definitions*, 68.
22 Eliza Haywood, preface to *The Fortunate Foundlings*, in Nixon, *Novel Definitions*, 71.
23 John Cleland, opening to *Memoirs of a Woman of Pleasure*, in Nixon, *Novel Definitions*, 72.
24 Hugh Blair, "Fictitious History," in Nixon, *Novel Definitions*, 343.
25 See, for example, Pierre-Dabiel Huet, from *The History of Romances*, in Nixon, *Novel Definitions*, 336–42.
26 James Beattie, "On Fable and Romance," in Nixon, *Novel Definitions*, 347–50.
27 Clara Reeve, *The Progress of Romance Through Times, Countries, and Manners: With Remarks on the Good and Bad Effects of It, on Them Respectively in a Course of Evening Conversations*, 2 vols. (Colchester: W. Keymer, 1785).
28 John Moore, "A View of the Commencement and Progress of Romance," in Nixon, *Novel Definitions*, 358–61.
29 See Mark Salber Phillips, *Society and Sentiment: Genres of Historical Writing in Britain, 1740–1820* (Princeton, NJ: Princeton University Press, 2000).
30 Anna Letitia [Aikin] Barbauld, "On the Origin and Progress of Novel-Writing," in Nixon, *Novel Definitions*, 367.
31 William Godwin, "Of History and Romance," in *Caleb Williams*, ed. Gary Handwerk and A. A. Markley (Peterborough, ON: Broadview Press, 2000), 462.
32 Ibid.
33 Ibid., 458–59.
34 William Godwin, *Caleb Williams*, ed. Gary J. Handwerk and A. A. Markley (Peterborough, ON: Broadview Press, 2000); *St. Leon: A Tale of the Sixteenth Century*, ed. William D. Brewer (Peterborough, ON: Broadview Press, 2006).
35 Lady Morgan (Sydney Owenson), *The Wild Irish Girl: A National Tale* (London: R. Phillips, 1806). Jane Porter, *The Scottish Chiefs: A Romance* (London: Longman's, 1810).
36 Walter Scott, *Waverley, or 'Tis Sixty Years Since*, ed. Susan Kubica Howard (Peterborough, ON: Broadview Press, 2010), 124.
37 Ibid., 123.
38 Ibid., 124.
39 Ibid.
40 Ian Duncan, "*Waverley* (Walter Scott, 1814)," in *Forms and Themes*, ed. Franco Moretti, vol. 2 of *The Novel*, ed. Franco Moretti (Princeton, NJ: Princeton University Press, 2006), 178.

24 Meaning-making

41 See Annika Bautz, *The Reception of Jane Austen and Walter Scott: A Comparative Longitudinal Study* (London: Continuum, 2007), 23–31.

42 Francis Jeffrey, review of *Waverley, or 'Tis Sixty Years Since*, by Walter Scott, in *Walter Scott: The Critical Heritage*, ed. John O. Hayden (New York: Routledge, 1995), 79.

43 Review of *Waverley*, from *Monthly Review*, in Howard, *Waverley*, 494.

44 Ibid.

45 Review of *Waverley*, from *Critical Review*, in Howard, *Waverley*, 495.

46 Ibid.

47 Ibid.

48 John Wilson Croker, review of *Waverley, or 'Tis Sixty Years Since*, in Howard, *Waverley*, 481–83.

49 Thomas Paine, *Rights of Man*, ed. Claire Grogan (Peterborough, ON: Broadview Press, 2011).

50 Matthew G. Lewis, *The Monk: A Romance* (London: J. Bell, 1796).

51 See, for example, Eric J. Hobsbawn, *The Age of Revolution: Europe, 1789–1848* (London: Weidenfeld and Nicolson, 1962).

52 On this view of communication, see Roy Harris, *Introduction to Integrational Linguistics*, 1st ed. (Kidlington, Oxford, UK: Pergamon, 1998), 20–22.

53 See Murray Pittock, ed., *The Reception of Sir Walter Scott in Europe* (London: Continuum, 2006).

54 On Ruskin and Scott, see C. Stephen Finley, "Scott, Ruskin, and the Landscape of Autobiography," *Studies in Romanticism* 26 (Winter 1987): 549–72; Elizabeth K. Helsinger, *Ruskin and the Art of the Beholder* (Cambridge, MA: Harvard University Press, 1982), 48–50; and Peter F. Morgan, "Ruskin and Scott's Ethical Greatness," in *Scott and His Influence: The Papers of the Aberdeen Conference, 1982*, ed. J. H. Alexander and David Hewitt (Aberdeen: Association for Scottish Literary Studies, 1983), 403–13.

55 Thomas Carlyle, *Carlyle's Essay on Sir Walter Scott*, ed. Arnold Smith (London: J. M. Dent, 1933), 109.

56 See Catherine Gordon, "The Illustration of Sir Walter Scott: Nineteenth-Century Enthusiasm and Adaptation," *Journal of the Warburg and Courtauld Institutes* 34 (1971): 297–317; and Peter D. Garside et al., *Illustrating Scott* (Edinburgh: University of Edinburgh, 2009), http://illustratingscott.lib.ed.ac.uk/index.html.

57 Carlyle, *Sir Walter Scott*, 47.

58 Ibid., 43.

59 James C. Simmons, *The Novelist as Historian: Essays on the Victorian Historical Novel* (The Hague: Mouton, 1973), 55, 61.

60 Joseph Devey, *A Comparative Estimate of Modern English Poets* (London: E. Moxon, Son, and Co., 1873), 212–25, https://archive.org/details/comparativeestim00deveuoft.

61 Goldwin Smith, "Walter Scott," in *The English Poets: Selections with Critical Introductions and a General Introduction by Mathew Arnold: Volume IV: Wordsworth to Rosetti*, ed. Thomas Humphry Ward, 2nd ed. rev. (London: Palgrave Macmillan, 1892), 188, https://archive.org/details/englishpoetssele04warduoft.

62 Walter Scott, *The Journal of Sir Walter Scott* (Edinburgh: David Douglas, 1890).

63 Following on earlier collections, all of Scott's novels were reprinted with new introductions by Scott in forty-eight volumes under the title *Waverley Novels* from 1829 to 1833. See Jane Millgate, *Scott's Last Edition: A Study in Publishing History* (Edinburgh: Edinburgh University Press, 1987). In contrast, I use the term "Waverley novels" with a lower case "n" to refer to the novels rather than the collected edition.

64 On the publishing history of Scott, see William B. Todd and Ann Bowden, *Sir Walter Scott: A Bibliographical History, 1796–1832* (Delaware, DE: Oak Knoll Press, 1998).

65 Matthews, *Historical Novel*, 11.
66 Ibid., 26.
67 Ibid., 27.
68 See Queenie D. Leavis, *Fiction and the Reading Public* (London: Chatto and Windus, 1932). Leavis describes the corruption of readers by popular fiction (ibid., 244–45). See also Max Horkheimer and Theodor W. Adorno, *Dialectic of Enlightenment*, trans. John Cumming (New York: Continuum, 2000). Frankfurt School philosophers argued that popular culture is an industry that manufactures a passive population. The erroneous assumption critical to all such approaches is that meaning is inherent in texts and therefore transmitted from text to reader.
69 Chris Baldick, "The Novel in Theory, 1900–1965," in Arata et al., *A Companion to the English Novel*, 257.
70 Ibid., 258.
71 The term "meaning-as-use" is from McHoul, *Semiotic Investigations*, vii. McHoul develops the term throughout his book.
72 James Eli Adams, "The Novel in Theory Before 1900," in Arata et al., *A Companion to the English Novel*, 253.
73 See, for example, Ivor A. Richards, *Principles of Literary Criticism*, 4th ed. (New York: Harcourt Brace, 1960).
74 See, for example, Leavis, *Fiction*.
75 Examples are: Percy Lubbock, *The Craft of Fiction* (London: J. Cape, 1926); Edwin Muir, *The Structure of the Novel* (London: Hogarth, 1928); Ford Madox Ford, *The English Novel* (Philadelphia: J. B. Lippincott, 1929); Erich Auerbach, *Mimesis: The Representation of Reality in Western Literature*, trans. Willard R. Trask (Princeton, NJ: Princeton University Press, 1953); R. S. Crane, *Critics and Criticism: Essays in Method*, abridged ed. (Chicago: University of Chicago Press, 1957); Northrop Frye, *Anatomy of Criticism: Four Essays* (Princeton, NJ: Princeton University Press, 1957); and Wayne C. Booth, *The Rhetoric of Fiction* (Chicago: University of Chicago Press, 1961).
76 Walter Scott, *Ivanhoe*, ed. Ian Duncan (Oxford: Oxford University Press, 1996), 12.
77 Walter Benjamin, *Illuminations*, ed. Hannah Arendt, trans. Harry Zohn (New York: Schocken Books, 2007), 84.
78 The phrase "a clean, well-lighted place" is from Ernest Hemingway's short story, "A Clean, Well-Lighted Place," which was first published in *Scribner's Magazine* in 1933.
79 Virginia Woolf, *To the Lighthouse* (London: Dent, 1943), 137.
80 Herbert Butterfield, *The Historical Novel: An Essay* (Cambridge, UK: The University Press, 1924), 4.
81 Ibid., 14.
82 Ibid., 15.
83 Ibid., 24.
84 Ibid., 41.
85 Ibid., 81.
86 Ibid., 87.
87 Mikhail M. Bakhtin, "Forms of Time and of the Chronotope in the Novel," in *The Dialogic Imagination: Four Essays*, ed. Michael Holquist, trans. Caryl Emerson and Michael Holquist (Austin: University of Texas Press, 1981), 84–258.
88 Mikhail M. Bakhtin, "The *Bildungsroman* and Its Significance in the History of Realism (Toward a Historical Typology of the Novel)," in *Speech Genres and Other Late Essays*, ed. Caryl Emerson and Michael Holquist, trans. Vern W. McGee (Austin: University of Texas Press, 1986), 53.
89 Christopher GoGwilt, "The Novel and the Nation," in Arata et al., *A Companion to the English Novel*, 444.

26   Meaning-making

90 Lukács, *Historical Novel*, 199.

91 Ibid., 48–49.

92 Ibid., 282–83.

93 Ibid., 182.

94 Ian Watt, *The Rise of the Novel: Studies in Defoe, Fielding, and Richardson* (Berkeley: University of California Press, 1957). Watt's emphasis on the historical and social context of literature was important at a time when new criticism was dominant. Other books that ran counter to strictly formalist approaches include Richard Hoggart, *The Uses of Literacy: Aspects of Working Class Life, with Special Reference to Publications and Entertainments* (Harmondsworth: Penguin Books, 1957) and Raymond Williams, *Culture and Society, 1780–1850* (New York: Columbia University Press, 1958). Hoggart emphasized active participation of the working classes in the production of their culture. Williams shifted from culture as moral phenomenon to an anthropological conception.

95 Feuchtwanger, *House of Desdemona*, 58.

96 See, for example, Nicholas Rance, *The Historical Novel and Popular Politics in Nineteenth-Century England* (London: Vision Press, 1975); and Andrew Sanders, *The Victorian Historical Novel, 1840–1880* (London: Palgrave Macmillan, 1978).

97 Brian R. Hamnett, *The Historical Novel in Nineteenth-Century Europe: Representations of Reality in History and Fiction* (Oxford: Oxford University Press, 2011).

98 See, for example, Gary Kelly, *The English Jacobin Novel, 1780–1805* (Oxford: Clarendon Press, 1976); Ian Duncan, *Modern Romance and Transformations of the Novel: The Gothic, Scott, Dickens* (Cambridge: Cambridge University Press, 1992); and Michael Gamer, *Romanticism and the Gothic: Genre, Reception, and Canon Formation* (Cambridge: Cambridge University Press, 2000).

99 See, for example, Shaw, *Forms of Historical Fiction*. Before taking a detailed look at several Scott novels, Shaw points to a historicist view of the past with "a sociological sense of both past and present, a recognition that societies are interrelated systems which change through time and that individuals are profoundly affected by their places within those systems" (ibid., 25). For examples of more recent scholarship on the role of Scott's fiction in the development of the nation-state, see Caroline McCracken-Flesher, *Possible Scotlands: Walter Scott and the Story of Tomorrow* (Oxford: Oxford University Press, 2005); Douglas S. Mack, *Scottish Fiction and the British Empire* (Edinburgh: Edinburgh University Press, 2006); Ian Duncan, *Scott's Shadow: The Novel in Romantic Edinburgh* (Princeton, NJ: Princeton University Press, 2007); Kenneth McNeil, *Scotland, Britain, Empire: Writing the Highlands, 1760–1860* (Columbus: Ohio State University Press, 2007); and Price, *Reinventing Liberty*. For research on editions of Scott's works, see, for example, Millgate, *Scott's Last Edition*; Todd and Bowden, *Sir Walter Scott*; introductions to volumes of the *Edinburgh Edition of the Waverley Novels*, ed. David Hewitt (Edinburgh: Edinburgh University Press, 1993–2012); and Pittock, *Scott in Europe*.

100 For example, Andrew Lincoln, *Walter Scott and Modernity* (Edinburgh: Edinburgh University Press, 2007). Lincoln writes, "I see the condition of modernity itself as Scott's deepest concern" (ibid., viii). Also, Duncan, "*Waverley*," 178. Duncan describes the importance of *Waverley* to the rise of the novel as the "national genre of modernity" (ibid.).

2 Heart of the matter

Consequences of modernity in *Clan Albin* and *Tales of My Landlord*

But the nation-state? "Where" is it? What does it look like? How can one *see* it?

— Franco Moretti, *Atlas of the European Novel*, 17

The opening chapter of Christian Isobel Johnstone's *Clan Albin: A National Tale* (1815) has all the makings of folklore.[1] On a dark and stormy night, Ronald Macalbin, a Scottish Highlander known as Hugh the Piper, wandering back from an extended stay at a market fair, crosses the mountains to Glen-Albin, a solitary and remote valley in the Western Highlands. On his way, he comes across a woman fallen at the side of a path, seized with the pains of childbirth. On foot, he takes her to his home at Dunalbin. The unknown woman dies; her baby lives. Unbeknownst to those in attendance, the boy, later named Norman, is the heir of Glen-Albin. This sets the stage for a romance of recovery – the return of the clan chief and the reconstruction of a Highland glen decimated by land enclosures and emigration. In contrast, the opening line of Walter Scott's *Tales of My Landlord, Second Series* (1818) points immediately to social transformation: "The times have changed in nothing more . . . than in the rapid conveyance of intelligence and communication betwixt one part of Scotland and another."[2] The scene is that of a stagecoach racing across the Highlands – partly through enclosures and plantations, and partly through open pastureland – to deliver mail and persons on schedule. The new time-space relations of modernity are brought before the reader's eyes, as are the consequences and opportunities. Just as important as the backdrop of modernized landscapes, the coach crashes. A writer to the signet and an advocate are thrown from the top of the coach; they threaten legal action. The impasse is unresolved, and the coach carries on without them. An elderly, sickly looking person, who had been precipitated into a river – as had the others – is then taken in hand by the two young men to the nearest inn. Although soaked and stranded, the trio's conversation is light, and despite the unexpected mishap, the long-term prospects of all involved are favorable. In line with the extrication of passengers by a sort of "Caesarean process of delivery,"[3] the crash, although

28   *Heart of the matter*

painful in the short term, turns out to be highly productive – Hardie and Halkit come across the case that will establish their careers and Dunover gets a small office that suffices to support his family. Moreover, evening conversation at the Wallace Inn becomes the basis of the novel better known as *The Heart of Mid-Lothian.*

Both *Clan Albin* and *The Heart of Mid-Lothian* were responses to the Agricultural and Industrial Revolutions of the mid-eighteenth century that impacted the life of their nineteenth-century readers. The Clearances starting in Scotland led to the displacement of tenants, transatlantic emigration, changes in land use, and a shift from subsistence farming and widespread land ownership to rent, single-use farms, and market conditions. Transportation networks expanded to access and connect new markets; as such, market influences affected rural areas, which were increasingly linked to the development and exploitation of a transnational capitalist economy. Changes in banking facilitated industry; the landed classes mobilized resources, expanded financial networks, improved efficient mobilization of capital through the bank system, added innovative banking features, carefully reinvested, and increased international trade. Population and urbanization increased at a remarkable rate due to the depopulation of rural areas and because the industrialization of labor centered around manufacturing towns. Such changes led to disastrous life circumstances for many facing poor conditions in unsafe factories and overcrowded cities; agitation for social reform came early and often, although actual change was slow to follow. In relation, communication practices, especially expansion of the print industry, served the interests of an emerging, diverse nation of readers. In this light, the historical novel was one way to answer the deceptively simple question, what does it mean to be modern? As this chapter describes, Johnstone and Scott provided different answers – a contrast that points to the relationship between meaning and use taken up in other ways throughout this book.

Superficially, at least, the heart of the matter in each novel is immediately apparent. Hugh, "the most kind-hearted of men,"[4] acts to preserve the natural rights that all people possess – the rights to preserve life and to be protected from having life foreshortened. The word "heart" is used repeatedly throughout *Clan Albin* to judge actions, label communities, and foster relationships. The heart may be betrayed, noble, desolate, widowed, black, or brave. Black-hearted Protestants figure poorly next to light-hearted Irish. Norman's lover, Monimia, Irish by birth, is "blessed with a warm Highland heart."[5] When Norman hears of her attachment to the Englishman Sir Archibald Gordon, the man who *"put out fifty smokes,"*[6] Norman's heart fails him. The Highland heart – the *warm* heart – is the baseline of sympathy and the center of collective social development. The introductory chapter of *The Heart of Mid-Lothian* instead sets out a game of hearts that is intimately connected to the historicity of rights. In a seeming nod to *Clan Albin*, conversation at the Wallace Inn leads to a series of puns on the word

Heart of the matter 29

"heart"; the heart is sad, close, hard, wicked, poor, strong, and high. Halkit, the writer, concludes, "I have played all my hearts."[7] Such word play is tied to subsequent discussion of the history of the Tolbooth, the prison of Edinburgh, described by Hardie, the advocate, as "a world within itself," with "its own business, griefs, and joys, peculiar to its circle."[8] The Tolbooth is a mine of stories – stories of human hearts encased by historical context. Sympathy has not disappeared: "Poor Dunover, we must not forget him."[9] Hearts remain in play, but here, the consideration of sentiment is tied to social transformation. Referring to the Tolbooth, Hardie asks, "Was it not for many years the place in which the Scottish parliament met?"[10] The question points to the passing of time, the historicity of place, and new forms of social organization – and it is a timely question in two ways: first, the Tolbooth was officially closed in 1817, one year prior to publication of the novel; second, in the opening volume of the novel, the people of Edinburgh burn down the front door of the Tolbooth. Although *The Heart of Mid-Lothian* is a social history of modernization, it does not describe a slow, even, or selective transition. Just as the upturned coach points to the unexpected, dramatic consequences of modern transportation, the violent events depicted in the first volume of the novel point to the historical discontinuity of modernity, and the related, far-reaching negotiation of rights in practice. In this way, the historical novel was used by Scott to frame an interpretation of modernity that was at least in part a response to Johnstone's emphasis on natural rights.

Clan Albin provocatively offers stinging criticism of capitalist modes of production; Johnstone focuses on the transition from arable and mixed farming to more profitable sheep farming, which depended on the clearance of large tenant populations from Highland estates in Scotland. The reader is confronted with the groans and tears of exiled multitudes, with the northern devastation that makes southern splendor possible – in essence, the consequences of modernity. The underlying problem is clear; it is apparent to Norman when he sees the wealth of the Lowlands and, recalling his reading of *The Wealth of Nations* (1776),[11] feels disdain for the division of labor that creates economic disparity. Johnstone links the imposition of industrial capitalism and past violence against the Highlanders. She is, for example, blunt in her condemnation of the events at Glencoe on February 13, 1692; a poem titled "The Massacre of Glencoe" "exhibits but a faint picture of that night of blood which will never be blotted out from the memory of Highlanders."[12] Similarly, she refers to the "butcheries of Culloden,"[13] thus referencing the Battle of Culloden in 1746, which represents the final confrontation and defeat of the Jacobite rising. In this way, industrial capitalism is situated historically as another attack on the Highlands. Johnstone's defense of the traditional Highland glen does not rest with a critique of the early stages of capitalism. Her approach owes much to earlier novelists: Frances Burney's attention to the impact of market fluctuations on workers in *The Wanderer: or, Female Difficulties* (1814),[14] for example, but also

30   *Heart of the matter*

more generally to writers such as Mary Wollstonecraft, William Godwin, and Helena Maria Williams, who stressed the prioritization of sympathy. In relation, Johnstone continues within a broader current in the recent history of literary writing based on natural law. Besides a similar nostalgia for organized community, Oliver Goldsmith's *Deserted Village: A Poem* (1770), to cite one example, offers a complaint against the individualism and greed that fueled land enclosures.[15] As R. S. White notes, "Goldsmith's work contains a natural law subtext and an implicit plea for the violated natural rights of the rural poor."[16] Four chapters in the first volume of *Clan Albin* have epigraphs attributed to Goldsmith, and sentimental poetry similarly frames other chapters. Johnstone's critique of industrial capitalism builds upon knowledge of political economy and the experience of Highland communities. The focus, however, is not on economic production or labor relations. *Clan Albin* is a national tale of social justice. The sense of wrong and the generation of sympathy depend on an affective response to a specific situation by a spectator, which partly explains the numerous monologues directed at the reader. Besides the authors and works already noted, another productive historical connection is to Adam Smith's sense of sentiment in his earlier *Theory of Moral Sentiments* (1759), and to contemporary dialogues between Thomas Paine, Edmund Burke, and others in response to the French Revolution.[17] As with novels by Jean-Jacques Rousseau, as well as Wollstonecraft and Godwin,[18] *Clan Albin* is a form of translated social philosophy – fiction designed to pit natural law against industrial capitalism by provoking the conscience of readers, and especially those who are sensitive to the cultural specificity of the Highlands.

The Heart of Mid-Lothian demonstrates how the actualization of rights depends upon the modernization of community practices. Unlike *Clan Albin*, it is not a national tale focused on the revival of "the kind and generous spirit of the olden time."[19] The marriage of Scottish Norman and Irish Monimia in *Clan Albin* is based on "That love of Scotland, and of the Highlands of Scotland, which glowed unseen in the hearts of both, [which] formed a natural attraction."[20] In contrast, the marriage of lifelong friends Jeanie and Reuben in *The Heart of Mid-Lothian* seems a more mundane contractual arrangement of mutual interests; the novel may tug at the heartstrings, but it likely does so only peripherally. The routinization of social relations in the modern world hinges on the working or legal relationship between the people and the state – in other words, a new, largely unspoken set of social practices. The humorous roadside squabble that opens the novel is only the first of a series of disruptive events that enables description of the new connective tissue that constitutes everyday life in the modern world, hence the related importance of the Porteous riots of 1736 described in the first volume – a visibly violent tear in the social fabric of the day. The tension between the application of positive law (top down, distant) and popular response (bottom up, here and now) is a point of contention throughout the novel: the people of Edinburgh challenge the authority of London by lynching Captain

John Porteous, Captain of the City Guard of Edinburgh, for his part in the death of innocent civilians; Jeanie, the daughter of a cow-feeder, challenges the sentencing of her sister Effie to death for child murder. The story lines dovetail at London. The resolution requires a negotiation between state (Queen) and people (Jeanie), and the journey to London connects old and new social practices; Jeanie's journey to plead her sister's case calls for Laird Dumbiedikes's sacks o' siller (representing inheritance, feudalism), the ringleader Rat's pass (smuggling, alternative economics), lodgings with the tobacco merchant Mrs Glass (capitalism, indentured servitude and slavery by extension), Reuben's letter (family connections, national histories), and the Duke of Argyle's arrangement of affairs (the link of Scottish nation to British state). In these ways, Scott is quite concrete about what constitutes modernity, and especially so in the fourth volume, where the modernization of social practices takes on a specific macro-formation at the Duke of Argyle's estate at Roseneath. The organization of social life at Argyle's estate is centralized, professional, hierarchical, and compartmentalized – in short, modern, and therefore intended to produce commodities, not restore traditions. The novel's final volume sets out (at least) two axes of modernity – capitalism and industrialism – and the consequences of such practices. For example, Argyle is an *absentee* landlord, Duncan's application of justice is *severe*, and Reuben *compromises* in his management of the local community. The actualization of rights – what happens on the ground at an early stage of class-based modern society – is tied to the implementation of state-sanctioned industrial capitalism. Put otherwise, individual and collective rights are historicized with respect to modernity.

Clan Albin makes visible the centrality of natural rights to modern progress. Rights are natural in that they are built upon the graves of ancestors, but responsibilities are learned, hence the twofold importance of preserving the community at Glen-Albin. The focal point of the community is Eleenalin, literally "the beautiful island."[21] Separated from the rest of the glen by water, Eleenalin is the burying place of the chiefs of Clan Albin and the residence of Lady Augusta, the local matriarch. This "sweet retreat of peace and innocence"[22] is the focal point of a tale that sets forth the primacy of sympathy and a related center-margins relationship between community and world. Natural law, upon which Lady Augusta bases her criticism of capitalism, is the center from which Norman interacts with the world. Norman's education begins at Glen-Albin, where he learns Gaelic and is immersed in the Celtic way of life. Still, he also learns English and later continues his studies under the supervision of a zealous Protestant living in a distant village. The traditional community teaches how to be a man of Scotland first – a man of feeling, that is – and a citizen of the world second. The lesson is clear: although useful to know the ways of the world, such knowledge must never impinge upon the warm Highland heart. The successful mediation of one's being in the world, as with Norman's picaresque wanderings through England, Ireland, and Spain, depends on the preservation of sympathy – the

32   *Heart of the matter*

ethical prioritization of human relations – as social epicenter. In relation, positive law is largely absent in the novel and cast only in an extreme light via military discipline, which intrudes upon the sanctity of pure hearts situated by natural law and Highland culture. As if sentimentality and natural law precluded progress, the intervention of a *deus ex machina* (or several) is the primary instrument of change. Just as the heir mysteriously appears in the middle of a dark and stormy night, the fortuitous discovery of a document in a secret repository returns Glen-Albin to the Highlanders. In the first volume, "The days of clanship were gone."[23] In the final volume, the clan chief strolls through a rejuvenated hamlet. The heart persists untouched in this magical world.

The Heart of Mid-Lothian also has its share of fortuitous coincidences, as when Jeanie comes across her children fighting over a cheese wrapping, which just happens to be an old broadside that indicates the possible whereabouts of Effie's lost child. But even this can be explained by events in the novel, and in fact, it may be understood as another indication of the penetration of modern practices, even to far-flung parts of the Western world. More importantly, the logic of narrative progress that interconnects all events is inseparable from the re-embedding of rights within the context of modernity, and more specifically, the advance of industrial capitalism. Rights, in this way, are understood as the means to question how things get done in the modern world. Jeanie's refusal to commit perjury to save her sister in court, for example, sets forth a conflict between ancient and modern codes of law (biblical and legal) that raises serious questions about authority and individual freedom. The existence of a destitute band of Highlanders living at the edge of a commercial farm raises questions about the right to life, liberty, and happiness. The Porteous affair, like the mob at Carlisle that kills Meg Murdockson, raises more specific questions about the right of association, just as Jeanie's journey seems to reaffirm the right of petition – questions that were especially relevant during a period of constant agitation for reform. For Johnstone, sympathy is the basis of an unshakeable ethical priority from which questions of social progress should be answered.[24] Ethics does not disappear in *The Heart of Mid-Lothian*; rather, ethics is situational and the related resolution of rights a historical matter. In *Clan Albin*, the Irishman Bourke is imprisoned by his English superior and publicly lashed. The reader is expected to feel Bourke's pain, just as Norman faints – to feel the moral wrong based upon a universal understanding of natural rights. In this case, condemnation of the hard-hearted English is essential to the plot, but the ethics of the reaction is not tied to nationality or even to the specific events in question. In *The Heart of Mid-Lothian*, wrongs point to the management of rights within the context of the nation-state. Engagement is a matter of reasoned *response* (i.e., a plan, definite steps) rather than affective *reaction* (e.g., outrage, fainting). The crowd in Edinburgh does not weep uncontrollably or run riot in the town when Porteous does not appear at the Grassmarket. Well-organized citizens withdraw, make plans, and then calmly, courteously even, remove Porteous from his prison and hang him. Similarly, the imprisonment of Effie leads to a discussion of the law against child murder, which results in Jeanie's plan to petition the Queen and save her sister. Again, sympathy does not disappear; whether the scene is Effie in the Tolbooth or Madge at the hands of an English mob, sympathy is simultaneously framed by other questions, of the application of state laws or the re-assertion of community interests, to cite two examples. As in *Clan Albin*, rights are collective, but they are negotiated rather than natural, informed by rather than set against modernity. In this respect, the divide between *Clan Albin* and *The Heart of Mid-Lothian* is irreconcilable. For Johnstone, the warm heart remains the inviolable ethical center of progress in the modern world; for Scott, the historical discontinuity of post-feudal life is complete and cannot be undone (or overcome) – all hearts, no matter how warm, are situated upon the plane of modernity.

Johnstone's location of the heart at the center of the modern world depends on a utopian view of Highland culture that may be said to undermine her prioritization of sympathy to dictate social progress. Despite Lady Augusta's long speeches criticizing capitalism and colonialism, Johnstone's romanticization of Highland community seems a fairy tale of Ossianic proportions. For example, at Glen-Albin, there was "no taint of vulgarity, no mean servility; their deference to rank was the homage of sentiment; – no surly selfishness, – none of those coarse features of character which distinguish the peasantry of other countries."[25] Johnstone highlights "that rough, unambitious, unlaborious plenty, which distinguished the days of chieftainship and clannish hospitality."[26] The past is timeless and unreal, populated by black and white caricatures of good Celts and bad Saxons situated by Highland waterfalls to the north and Lowland factories to the south. The last of the clan is "a chosen people, with whom peace and love took refuge."[27] Such an idealistic portrayal may have appealed to readers as an effective means of communicating the necessity of cultural preservation and attention to the heart amid dynamic social transformations with severe consequences for many people. Regardless, there were enough readers to support the publication of two editions in 1815. More to the point here, Johnstone offered a vision of progress that proposed sympathy as a counterweight to the impact of industrial capitalism on Highland communities.

The Heart of Mid-Lothian, on the other hand, is a novel specifically concerned with the fundamental characteristics of modernization. Andrew Lincoln's overarching assessment is correct: "Scott commanded a new audience, and provided a new map for nineteenth-century fiction, because he was able to offer an imaginative space in which his contemporaries could encounter their own anxieties while appearing to escape from them."[28] Or, as Franco Moretti summarizes with respect to the dominant form of social organization in the early-nineteenth century, "Readers needed a symbolic form capable of making sense of the nation-state."[29] The self-reflexivity of modernity was essential to interest in the historical novel and other forms

34   Heart of the matter

of literature that enabled people to understand and cope with social transformation. Unfortunately, *The Heart of Mid-Lothian* is too often read in the shadow of *Waverley* criticism emphasizing a conservative expression of national progress. James Kerr, for example, argues that *Waverley* attempts "to make a violent past palatable to the reader of the present" by reducing historical conflict to "sentimental reminisces."[30] The view is not unwarranted, but it implies that Scott simply paves the way for modernity. Further, the common emphasis on *Waverley*'s depiction of national reconciliation frames the estimate of later novels. For Lincoln, "Scott's progressive vision of history is always in the service of a conservative vision of moderation";[31] similarly, Ian Duncan points to *The Heart of Mid-Lothian* as an instance of "counter-revolutionary containment of radical populist ideologies in the period."[32] In my reading, it is not clear that *The Heart of Mid-Lothian* contains so much as reveals the realities of modern life, which often seem to take directions we did not foresee.

Recent criticism of *Waverley* suggests that Scott separated private life from public history.[33] Duncan argues that the central topic of Scott's historical romance is a version of history "developed from the philosophical historians of the Scottish Enlightenment."[34] More provocatively, he writes that "the Waverley novels discover history in order to discover the horizon at which – as for the individual subject, so for the nation – history comes to a stop."[35] Following Alexander Welsh, he also writes of the private subject as "politically and psychologically grounded upon property," and concludes that, "Correspondingly, it is spiritually grounded upon a domestic space set apart from public life, from politics, and (thus the logical declension) from historical process: 'home', origin and end of the story."[36] Duncan's complex account links the expansive yet fragmented nature of modern time-space connections to individual subjectivity. But the link hinges on a division of public history and private life that is better suited to *Waverley* than to later novels. Edward's Highland romance is a public adventure that takes him away from his private life. As Moretti adds, "He travels backwards through the various stages of social development described by the Scottish Enlightenment."[37] The resolution, in Duncan's view, emphasizes the reclamation of a "primitive patriarchal identity."[38] There is, then, ample justification for his description of the "local, 'objective' restoration of feudal community at Tully-Veolan"[39] as "the recovery of 'archetypal' terms of social relation, crystallized in a revolutionary ferment,"[40] and also for his related observation that "Private life and public history are combined in a dialectic of mutual exclusion."[41] *The Heart of Mid-Lothian*, however, cannot be read in the same way.

"The romance estate," says Duncan, "is a result not of a historical process but of its interruption. Its occupants are not accommodated within a logic of history but delivered from it, by a miraculous grace that translates history into private terms of its own."[42] He views *The Heart of Mid-Lothian* as moving from "historical conflict" to "idyllic repose,"[43] and so he can describe the fourth volume as "an extraordinary movement out of history to grasp a lost cultural formation in the psychically charged space of private life."[44] In this way, Scott's conservative politics drive the construction of a "new domestic patriarchy,"[45] which "keeps history out."[46] The upward mobility of the Deans family is framed as a means to contain radical lines of flight; "a fable of property accumulation and class ascent" is read as "the progress of a family of the elect from tenantry to freehold, under benign ducal patronage."[47] Moreover, Duncan reads the last quarter of the novel as "void of any historical charge."[48] Form and content – romance and history – are combined to contain historical lines of flight. Interestingly, however, Duncan also argues that *The Heart of Mid-Lothian* "invents for nineteenth-century fiction the universal representation of a national society that exceeds and contains any particular local, public or domestic scene."[49] What does this "universal representation of a national society" consist of? In *Waverley*, the construction of national identity may be accounted for in terms of dialectic oppositions, for example, Scots and English, Protestants and Catholics.[50] Such binaries are not so easily established with respect to *The Heart of Mid-Lothian*, however. Duncan remarks, "What kind of a *national* identity might be represented in the last volume of the novel is an interesting question."[51] It is so, I maintain, because there is no binary opposition to contain history by means of a third or middle way, and also because there is no possibility of retreat. Duncan argues that *The Heart of Mid-Lothian* "finds authentic identity not in the national, corporate, public domain, but in private life."[52] I contend that the opposition of private and public life is tenuous at best. Jeanie's journey, to cite one example, connects a personal affair and national issues. Moreover, the Deans family moves forward in time through three distinct domains suggestive of the larger progress of the nation-state. At the beginning of the novel, Deans struggles with poverty as he works the sterile lands owned by Laird Dumbiedikes. He then becomes a dairy farmer or cow-feeder at St Leonard's, renting a cottage and land. Finally, he is headhunted and hired as an agricultural expert at Argyle's fancy farm in the western Highlands. Whereas, in *Waverley*, Edward wanders back through history and the Highlands, a twofold backdrop to the progressive forces of civil war, in *The Heart of Mid-Lothian*, subjectivity is historical as a function of the modernity of time-space, which integrates social trajectories at the level of individuals and families with wider community practices differently. The question of national identity is inseparable from modern identity, and the latter constitutes new instances of the former to a significant degree.

The subtitle "Disembedding identity" used in Lincoln's introduction to *Walter Scott and Modernity* (2007) points to an aspect of Scott's treatment of modernity that is more fundamental than the rejection or containment of either political or economic radicalism. Giddens describes disembedding as "the 'lifting out' of social relations from local contexts of interaction and their restructuring across indefinite spans of time-space."[53] Lincoln writes of

36 *Heart of the matter*

"the historical disembedding of identity from the social, material, and cultural grounds that governed individuals in earlier ages."[54] More specifically, he maintains that the historical novel could be used to respond to "violent disruptions of contemporary history," which resulted in the disembedding of identity, in part by reasserting "traditional moral and religious principles" to "counter the demythologizing heritage of the Enlightenment."[55] Again, the insistence on recovery seems more appropriate to *Waverley*. It cannot be assumed that a sketch of Scott's initial investigation of Scottish history, which was the first of a trilogy including *Guy Mannering* (1815) and *The Antiquary* (1816), can be seamlessly transferred to later novels. Scott's representations of the separation of and transition from past to present required the reinterpretation of identity on several levels; among critics, at least, the *Waverley* phenomenon has put too much emphasis on national reconciliation and obscured the differences between Waverley novels. *The Heart of Mid-Lothian*, which puts especially strong emphasis on the *re-embedding* of past ways considering modern practices, should be read differently.

For Scott, the question of what it meant to be modern was never just a matter of preserving social order or private welfare in the face of political and economic upheaval. Like Duncan, Lincoln describes the fourth volume in terms of an "evasion of the problems introduced at the beginning of the novel – the substitution of a private solution for a public one."[56] But the problem-solutions required were at once private and public, and they were intimately tied to the material realities of modern life. The main action of *The Heart of Mid-Lothian* begins in Edinburgh, the urban center of Scotland prior to the 1760s, which was a critical period in the Agricultural and Industrial Revolutions that continued at an unprecedented pace until the middle of the nineteenth century. According to T. M. Devine, "That decade seems to have been a defining watershed because from then on Scotland began to experience a social and economic transformation unparalleled among European societies of the time in its speed, scale and intensity."[57] Scott's postscript to *Waverley* famously points to this sense of great political and economic change with respect to the kingdom of Scotland in the years 1745–1805.[58] *Waverley* proposed a solution to a problem, namely, the breakdown of traditional forms of social organization in both the Highlands (patriarchal power) and the Lowlands (heritable jurisdictions). As with *Clan Albin*, it made sense to address modernization by setting the *Waverley* trilogy during the heyday of early industrialism in the second half of the eighteenth century. In contrast, through the life span of David Deans (c. 1660–1751), *The Heart of Mid-Lothian* points to a longer history of modernization. Although this would seem to show the gradual change Scott pointed to in the *Waverley* postscript, I contend that *The Heart of Mid-Lothian*, from the initial coach crash in the framing narrative to the final volume, describes modernity as a decisive break from past forms of social life, and more, that the fourth volume maps out the axes of modernity upon which it was constituted.

That Scott is renowned for bringing history to life is largely based on appreciation of his minute descriptions of scenery. In contrast, the final volume of *The Heart of Mid-Lothian* establishes the fundamental characteristics of modernity by emptying place. In *Clan Albin*, the island of Eleenalin is clearly demarcated – an area with distinct boundaries, uses, and meanings essential to the Highlanders of Glen-Albin, which is similarly defined by natural borders. In the fourth volume of *The Heart of Mid-Lothian*, neither Roseneath nor Knocktarlitie are distinctly described; together, they represent a locale – a set of parameters identifiable as modern but not particular to Argyleshire or even Scotland. Giddens contends that "A locale may be understood in time-space in terms of presence-availability."[59] As demonstrated by the movement of the Deans family, time-space relations are inseparable from social relations. At Woodend, families live under one roof and subsistence farming is the primary contact with the land. St Leonard's is located at the outskirts of Edinburgh; the closer relation between country and city facilitates David Deans's enterprising agricultural practices (e.g., he rents out parcels of land) and leads to Effie's eventual placement in Edinburgh as a shop assistant. The visualization of modern social practices culminates in the final volume. In the first volume, the picture of Edinburgh is relatively detailed, whereas Roseneath-Knocktarlitie is schematic: there is a manse at Roseneath; Jeanie and Reuben live in the parish of Knocktarlitie across the water; Deans lives nearby; Highlanders reside in the forest, etc. Although the fourth volume does not lack for action, the setting is strikingly empty; as Giddens says, one consequence of modernity is that "place becomes increasingly *phantasmagoric*."[60] As in *Clan Albin*, there is a village across the water, but the relationship between people and place has changed. The lack of detail may be another reason for the disappointment of critics who view the last volume as commercial fodder, that is, as pastoral melodrama without any substantive literary value (read: realism). But as Avrom Fleishman suggests, "Roseneath is a symbolic landscape of modern Scotland."[61] In my view, it effectively mapped the new, distanciated relations of modernity and their impact on community formation.

The novel begins at the Wallace Inn (the frame-narrative) and the fourth volume returns to Dumbartonshire (the birthplace of William Wallace), thus linking commerce and national identity (through the act of historification). As with the movement of the Deans family from east to west, that is, from the cultural center of Edinburgh to the emerging industrial region of western Scotland, the historicity of Scottish nationalism is inseparable from the axes of modernity. Ina Ferris's comparison of the ending in *The Wild Irish Girl* and the Waverley novels generally is of interest here. In the former, the return is to a remote corner of Ireland to "live in the old way, live in a world outside the linear flow of modern history," whereas, in a Waverley novel, "idylls are always enclosed in and threatened by metropolitan and other worlds that have a different sense of time and value."[62] As in *Clan Albin*, the hero of *The Heart of Mid-Lothian* returns to the place of national

38   *Heart of the matter*

origins. However, in *Clan Albin*, a wandering Highlander sings, "Sad, sad and weary still I roam,/I have wandered mony a mile,/But my heart is in my father's home/Mang the hills of dear Argyle."[63] Whereas Macalbin comes home, Jeanie does not. She will meet her father again, but her arrival in Argyleshire is not a return to (or of) either home or even the same community; her return is a form of displacement – Jeanie is taken to Roseneath just as Dolly is trundled into a boat and carried across the water, against her will. Agency is involved, but more importantly, all actions shape and are shaped by the fact that the community under construction is not merely differentiated from other worlds, as Ferris argues; modernity is fundamentally different from anything that has come before. Rather than an idyll set apart, Roseneath-Knocktarlitie sets forth a dialectical relation between historical community practices (i.e., feudalism, smuggling) and the axes of modernity (i.e., capitalism, industrialism) that resulted in the coordination of a new paradigm of time-space relations. This is a return with a difference.

At Glen-Albin, the high presence-availability of community members is integral to the Highland way of life, which is differentiated from the Lowlands and the emerging factory system; it is a place apart – geographically and socially. Johnstone constructs cultural affinities between the warmhearted people of Scotland, Ireland, and Spain to further characterize (and denigrate) the English model of "improvement." Essentially, tribal social connections are reiterated by a combination of war, wandering, and fate. Moretti's comment about the constitution of space in sentimental fiction might be applied to Norman's picaresque ramblings: "It's still the atmosphere of Greek romances: space as a mythical force."[64] In contrast, in *The Heart of Mid-Lothian*, localization is subordinated to distanciation. Locales "are thoroughly penetrated by and shaped in terms of social influences quite distant from them. What structures the locale is not simply that which is present on the scene; the 'visible form' of the locale conceals the distanciated relations which determine its nature."[65] The point of *Clan Albin* – of the maintenance of Glen-Albin – is to resist the determination of subjectivity by outside forces. At the end of the novel, modernization comes to Glen-Albin, yet the processes remain opaque. Further, Johnstone does not describe the impact on everyday life other than to say that all is as it should be. Norman preserves the Highland community, which is still constituted by "MACS of all clans and kindreds,"[66] in part by selectively administering English improvement. However, there is no fourth volume here; the center-margins structure remains intact. Eleenalin is not breeched; the essence of social life – the heart, sympathy – does not change with the measured use of modern practices by an enlightened community leader.

As "a locally-situated expression of distanciated relations,"[67] Roseneath-Knocktarlitie seems a long way from the beautiful island of Eleenalin. There is no center-margins structuration of traditional and modern forms of living – hierarchies exist, but the connective tissue has changed. Distanciated time-space relations impact all aspects of social life – political, religious, and

Heart of the matter 39

economic. Stages of social development may seem to overlap, temporarily at least, although there is no question of opting out of modernity. Scott's varied use of genre across the four volumes attempts to set forth different aspects of social transformation: volume one, history (national conflict/penetration of borders); volume two, legal records (law/re-establishment of social relations); volume three, fable (journey/imagination of things otherwise); and volume four, melodrama (projection/sketch of how things are). As Moretti suggests, "Each genre possesses its own space, then – *and each space its own genre*: defined by a spatial distribution – by a map – which is unique to it, and which for historical novels suggests: away from the center."[68] Space and genre, like time and space, are not mutually exclusive but inform each other. The four volumes illustrate the historicity of social change, from the breakdown of traditional community structures to the establishment of new forms of organization, leading to the outline of modern practices, which are increasingly determined by things that happen elsewhere. Scott uses the interpenetration of genre and space to describe the actualization of a new chronotope in the fourth volume, or in Mikhail Bakhtin's words: to "see time in space."[69]

In the opening frame-narrative of the novel, the coach emphasizes the "speed, scale and intensity" of modern social transformation. The fact that Jeanie goes on foot to London and returns to Scotland in a coach points again to related changes in time-space relations. But her success in petitioning the Queen on behalf of her sister depends on a variety of factors that underscore the distanciated relations of modernity. She employs money borrowed from Dumbiedikes, a password from Rat, and a letter from Reuben – all of which indicate a situation of low presence-availability. While in London, Jeanie resides with a relative who happens to be a tobacco merchant, thus connecting her to the slave trade; the space of the Virginian plantation is not important in itself – only as it constitutes local space. Jeanie's exchange of letters with Deans and Reuben highlights her separation from her family. Further, she remains in her room, refusing to go sightseeing, thus negating any sense of the local; that her journey takes her to the capital is imperative, even more so is the fact that the spaces of the capital remain unfilled. The face-to-face meeting with Caroline at Richmond Park is constructed as an essential counterpoint, an exception even, to the emptiness of both London and Roseneath-Knocktarlitie. Argyle, who accompanies Jeanie, encourages her to wear her tartan and to speak naturally. This form of authentic – national, localized – communication seems to contrast sharply with the sort of cagey innuendo that passes for dialogue between Argyle and Caroline. Yet both are situated forms of communication determined by the high presence-availability of the intimate meeting at Richmond Park. In fact, the meeting is odd, and not simply because it puts Jeanie before the Queen. The sense of intimacy is at odds with the larger shift in progress to distanciated time-space relations, which facilitate the meeting at Richmond Park and culminate at Roseneath-Knocktarlitie. Situated between the spontaneous journey

40   *Heart of the matter*

to London (mostly) on foot and the arranged return trip in a coach, quaint Jeanie Deans receiving a fifty-pound note from the Queen highlights the fundamental difference in time-space organization as well as a new relationship between private experience and public history.

At Richmond Park, a peasant girl, a Member of Parliament, and the Queen discuss an affair of personal, professional, and public interest. All three are in an awkward position: pleading, mediating, judging – each according to interests and circumstances. The public-private negotiation of problem-solutions in progress points to the complex, case-by-case re-establishment of trust necessary in the modern world. Even more, trust constitutes and is constituted by a new experience of time-space that recreates the public-private world. In the face of the discontinuity of modernity that resulted in drastic changes to social organization, getting on in life required a new basis of stability – of confidence – in leaders (Caroline, Argyle, Reuben), institutions (government, military, church), and everyday life (family, neighbors, co-workers). As such, although a *deus ex machina* of sorts, the inclusion of Argyle is not only highly practical but also logical. As a state representative respected by the people of Scotland, Argyle occupies a medial position of authority. Even more, he is a link between London (state) and the Highlands (nation). Notably, Argyle sends Jeanie to the Highlands, which involves several telling dislocations: first, from her intended destination of Edinburgh to Roseneath, which touches upon the connection between London and Scotland; second, from Argyle's hunting retreat at Roseneath to the adjacent parish of Knocktarlitie, where she will contribute to the modernization of Argyle's farm. Rather than a relic of past days used by Scott to put a hold on the radical discontinuity of modernity, Argyle is situated by (and facilitates) a transition to modern social practices that is illustrated by two interconnected micro-shifts: from Woodend to St Leonard's and from Roseneath to Knocktarlitie. The political relationship between London and Edinburgh highlighted by Jeanie's journey remains central; most importantly, the state facilitates capitalist production on a national (and international) scale. But the smaller movements that constitute the everyday experiences of common people are no less substantial. Put otherwise, the consequences of modernity permeate all aspects of social life.

Community did not disappear with modernity or distanciated relations, but it did – it had to – change dramatically. Even though Jeanie trusts Argyle, a public (nation-state) figure, the implication is that she also places her trust (or must trust) in the axes of modernity that connect Scotland and England, which puts London at the center of a nation-state system underpinned by industrial capitalism and international relations. As in the opening scene of the novel, the modern (not just post-1707) reality of a United (yet uneven) Kingdom is paramount. The purpose of Jeanie's journey to London is to save her sister; the return trip connects the nation-state with the practical experience of modern life depicted at Roseneath-Knocktarlitie. The nation-state thus extends over large spaces and coordinates political and economic activities (in Britain and beyond). As Giddens says, these are the "large areas of secure, coordinated actions and events that make modern social life possible."[70] Security and coordination do not exist without trust, which takes on new forms with respect to the low presence-availability of modernity: "Trust in abstract systems is the condition of time-space distanciation and of the large areas of security in day-to-day life which modern institutions offer as compared to the traditional world. The routines which are integrated with abstract systems are central to ontological security in conditions of modernity."[71] Jeanie's introduction to Argyle is by no means routine, but her arranged residence at Knocktarlitie routinizes this new relationship between individual and state in concrete ways.

Although the Duke of Argyle may be viewed as representative of patriarchal social organization, he is also directly involved in the governance structures that make possible his own participation, and that of others, in the modernization of Scotland. More specifically, Roseneath-Knocktarlitie is an example of the centralized coordination of created spaces particular to social life in the industrial world. Time-space has changed and so too has the relationship between people and the natural world. Nature in the fourth volume of *The Heart of Mid-Lothian* is at once aesthetically pleasing and a threat – this is not Woodend. The surrounding forest is the scene of Effie and David's picturesque tour to the waterfall. More importantly, the differentiation of this undefined space by a seemingly unnecessary foray into the woods points to the role of capitalism in constituting social relations. Land is the source of material power and labor the source of human power in the production of goods, which are the bases of industrialism, and in turn, Argyle's allocative power. The line that divides the farm from the forest is the border of Argyle's property; the border represents a division between those who own land and those who do not. However, both sides – private property and untamed wilderness, middle-class farmers and destitute Highlanders – are constituted by the practices of capitalism.

Capitalism depends upon and reproduces the coordination of a pattern of human activity: as Giddens summarizes, "*Capitalism* is a system of commodity production, centred upon the relation between private ownership of capital and propertyless wage labour, this relation forming the main axis of a class system."[72] The Highlanders living at the edge of Argyle's estate are as much the result of an exploitive capitalist system of commodity production as is the prosperous Deans family at Knocktarlitie. They are not defeated, as in *Waverley*. Instead, the Highlanders persist in the shadow of, and as constituted by, new economic and political relations. Importantly, this anonymous band of outsiders does not represent (not exclusively, at least) the passive sliding away of cultural life – the remnants of a lost civil war (post-1745). If anything, they are the product of a cultural shift dating back to the seventeenth century – modernity – hence the importance of the life span of David Deans. Scott's representation of early modernity necessarily involves the coexistence of different structural types of society:

42   Heart of the matter

tribal (bands, villages), class-divided (symbiosis of city and countryside), and class (created environment) societies.[73] Still, the created environment at Roseneath-Knocktarlitie does not represent a final stage of progress that has already or will overcome all others; the internal border, here separating pre-modern and modern forms of social organization, is of critical importance in this regard. Further, in contrast to the movement of the Deans family from Woodend to Knocktarlitie, the Highlanders embody a mode of living that is integral to class-based industrial societies. On the one hand, the east-to-west movement of the Deans family that differentiates pre-modern and modern ways of life points to the Scottish philosophers who posited a four-stage theory of overlapping, antagonistic social development. On the other hand, the existence of social outcasts on the outskirts of Argyle's estate does not represent an abstract juxtaposition or linear progression of past and present or feudal and modern practices. The outside is constituted by the inside and vice versa. As Giddens points out, "The interlocking of capital and wage-labour in a relation of dependence and interest conflict is the *chief basis of the dialectic of control* in the productive order of the capitalist economy."[74] There are, then, synchronic as well as diachronic representations of historical change at play in the novel. Further, Scott may not seem to focus on modern labor relations; still, the configuration is in place – this is, after all, *Tales of My Landlord*.

On the surface, the inside/outside dynamic constitutes the dangers of modern life: destitute Highlanders are a threat to the estate, and the unruly residents of Knocktarlitie are a community concern. The dangers may be real but the division itself is a façade. Effie's lost son is one of the impoverished Highlanders and Duncan is involved in illicit trade with them; Reuben and Duncan are in fact dependent on the wild parishioners for their livelihood. The interlocking nature of borders is part and parcel of the created space of capitalist urbanism, which Giddens describes as integrating three sets of market relations: "housing, labour and product markets – within both localised and national economic systems."[75] Whether or not the Highlanders and parishioners are yet employees on Argyle's estate, they are already trading partners (i.e., via smuggling) and they will soon, if they do not already, represent a potential labor force used to manufacture goods, likely for foreign markets. In this way, *The Heart of Mid-Lothian* brings together the crucial components of capitalism – private property and wage labor – that transformed the relation of city to countryside and the nature of work. To read the Highlanders as a threat to civilization or in terms of cultural loss is incomplete; they are economic agents situated by modern relations largely, or at least initially, defined by property lines and exchange values. As Giddens notes, "It is of first importance to see that the intersection of the commodification of exchange and of labour-power is what made industrialisation possible, not the reverse."[76] When Jeanie sends cheese to Argyle in London, this seems a form of gratitude reminiscent of village days, but the production of the cheese depends on the labor-power of a largely

Heart of the matter   43

invisible work force. More to the point, to labor on the estate, whether an expert or one of the hands, is to create surplus value for Argyle. The distribution of power is inseparable from the mode of production. There is no surplus without either the expertise to exploit resources or the "free" wage labor utilized by experts and managers; and the surplus is inseparable from Roseneath-Knocktarlitie, which represents the development of an industrial, class-based society that reproduces "the *asymmetrical distribution of power between classes.*"[77]

The emergent sense of community in *The Heart of Mid-Lothian* is dependent on the development of new practices. Usefully, Alec McHoul describes "communities as 'collections of what happens'; that is, as *effective* loci rather than physical groupings of copresent individuals."[78] Kenneth McNeil, in his discussion of *Rob Roy* (1817), makes a related point that applies to *The Heart of Mid-Lothian*: "Circulation – of goods, money, and people – not only links the Highlands with the rest of Scotland, Great Britain, and the empire in the novel, it shapes new transcultural identities."[79] Scott's purpose was not an escape from history, but a demonstration of the historicity of progress in action. As Fleishman argues, the fourth volume especially represents the historical challenges of modern social transformation; in contrast, "To end on the note of a Highland Arcadia would have been to create an apocalyptic realm outside of history."[80] Andrea Henderson suggests that Scott responded to the problem of extreme circulation with the "isolated island of Roseneath," which "aspires to an isolation and self-sufficiency that would ideally and ultimately make any 'peripheries' drop out altogether."[81] Yet Roseneath-Knocktarlitie is neither an island nor a colony, and it is not rendered separate from an urban market economy – just the opposite. As a locale, rather than a place, it is not an isolated community – as at Glen-Albin – apart from geographical location, which is the least significant aspect of the created environment. I read *The Heart of Mid-Lothian* as re-embedding traditional modes of living in a modern locale that looks forward in all respects. In relation, I also read *The Heart of Mid-Lothian* as shifting the focus of modern progress from national reconciliation, which was an essential early step toward the nation-state and the protection of private property, to the irreversible impact of modernity on subjectivity and everyday life. In *Waverley*, the end of Highland culture is romanticized by defeat. A rebellion conducted by the Frenchified MacIvors on behalf of Bonnie Prince Charlie fails. Fergus is put to death and Flora removes herself to a convent on the Continent, whereas English Edward and Scottish Rose take up residence at Tully-Veolan. Cultural conflict at the level of nations and religions is neatly resolved, and the romance of history is, superficially at least, separated from private life. The resolution of *The Heart of Mid-Lothian* employs a similar pattern. Staunton is murdered by his own son, Effie removes herself to a convent on the Continent, and Jeanie and Reuben take up residence at Knocktarlitie. But the focus of the fourth volume is on coping with the new-fangled fabric of modernity rather than the restitution

44 *Heart of the matter*

of older modes of living. Making this transformation visible required not only a demonstration of distanciated time-space relations but also a resolution that linked the historical transition from feudalism to modernity with the lived experience of middle-class readers.

Beyond the more abstract mapping of a modern locale, coping with the consequences of modernity is essential to Scott's representation of community practices. Scott presents a clear division between those who get on in life and those who do not. For the most part, those who stay on the right side of the law prosper and become productive members of the community. David Deans, Jeanie, and Reuben are the primary examples. However, the division is also made visible by the mirroring of social trajectories: Duncan is the estate manager, Donacha is killed; the elder Staunton is a Catholic priest, the younger Staunton (the smuggler Robertson) is killed; Femie (Euphemia) marries a Highland laird, Effie (Euphemia) retires to a convent on the Continent; David Butler becomes a lawyer, his cousin the Whistler is sold and shipped to America, likely as an indentured laborer. Family security and personal progress in the modern nation-state depend on one's relation to the law, military, and marriage (conservative social bonds) as well as social connections, inheritance, and lineage (real and perceived). From a distance, getting on in life does not seem to have changed all that much, but the details are important; upward mobility, for instance, depends upon modern characteristics such as professionalization and specialization. Jeanie becomes Mrs Butler, the well-dressed housewife of a minister. Reuben emerges from poverty through education and social connections to become a minister and representative at the Kirk of Scotland Assembly in Edinburgh. Rat becomes Captain of the Tolbooth, Duncan something like chief of police or estate manager, and Dolly a housekeeper. Mrs Glass is a successful shopkeeper and Archibald is a professional driver. The transition to middle-class distinction and private accumulation continues with Jeanie's sons, David and Reuben, who become a lawyer and an officer, respectively. The generational change mimics what Deans finds upon his return to Edinburgh to settle accounts with Dumbiedikes. The laird's estate is entirely changed: "He found it in a state of unexpected bustle. There were workmen pulling down some of the old hangings, and replacing them with others, altering, repairing, scrubbing, painting, and white-washing. There was no knowing the old house, which had been so long the mansion of sloth and silence."[82] As at Tully-Veolan, the nation-state is taking shape, but a general sense of national reconciliation has shifted to the background. Modernization depends instead, first and foremost, on historically specific characteristics of modern life, including application of the law (Saddletree), commodifiable expertise and recruitment (Deans, Dolly), coordinated law enforcement (Duncan), thrift (Jeanie's jar), investment (Reuben's purchase of land), and social management (Deans, Duncan, Reuben). In all respects, the lived experiences of everyday life constitute and are constituted by modernity – there is no "beautiful island."

Heart of the matter 45

Importantly, for Scott, the lessons of modernity are not all positive. To put it mildly, the coach has an underside – most obviously, the band of Highland smugglers, the bandits on the road to London, and the sale of the Whistler. But the symptoms of a fundamental ethics of exchange that facilitates social interactions at all levels of society are everywhere. After rereading a letter from Effie, Jeanie "could not help observing the staggering and unsatisfactory condition of those who have risen to distinction by undue paths, and the outworks and bulwarks of fiction and falsehood, by which they are under the necessity of surrounding and defending their precarious advantages."[83] This passage aligns so well with the well-trodden image of sweet Jeanie Deans that what follows is easily overlooked. In the same paragraph, Jeanie accepts Effie's gift of money on behalf of her children. The rationale is not left in doubt: "Her sister had enough, was strongly bound to assist Jeanie by any means in her power, and the arrangement was so natural and proper, that it ought not to be declined out of fastidious or romantic delicacy."[84] "Fastidious or romantic delicacy" is simply a cover for the practices – the ethics – of everyday life in the modern world; in other words, moral objection to Staunton's connection to the West Indies (i.e., the sugar trade and slavery) should not hinder social advancement. Jeanie is not alone in making such a compromise. The inheritance of £1,500 after the death of Deans is not enough for Reuben to purchase additional property. Jeanie pulls out a jar from the cupboard stuffed with £50 notes from Effie. Reuben asks about the source. Jeanie says that "If it were ten thousand, it's a' honestly come by."[85] The exchange, including Reuben's acceptance of such a vague answer, is either dishonest or naïve. Rather than an isolated incident, however, it indicates the state of affairs. The management of Argyle's estate, which depends on the clearance of large tracts of land (and people) for producing agricultural exports, points to the capitalist accumulation that underpins the upward mobility and generational stability of the middle-class family. Although perhaps unknowingly, even upstanding moral citizens – the son of "Bible" Butler and the daughter of "Honest" David Deans – exploit the circulation of goods, money, and people fueled by wider social changes. In this way, not only the distanciated relations of modernity tightly link public history and individual practices but also a related ethics of self-interest.

The partnership of Reuben and Duncan, who not only find a way to compromise in their management of the local population but also occasionally play backgammon together, is another example of community practices reshaped by interests that are not local in origin – both work to further the interests of London-based Argyle. But the impact of modernity on the social priorities of everyday life is nowhere more apparent than in the transition of Deans from young religious zealot at Bothwell Bridge to agricultural expert at Roseneath-Knocktarlitie. Deans refers to the decay of religion in the land and "how the love of many is waxing lukewarm and cold,"[86] which is his way of justifying the move west, supposedly to live among like-minded

46   *Heart of the matter*

people. The narrator frames the transition in larger terms: "Honest David had now, like other great men, to go to work to reconcile his speculative principles with existing circumstances; and, like other great men, when they set seriously about the task, he was tolerably successful."[87] This leads to a series of compromises. Deans reconciles himself to the Kirk of Scotland "in its present model."[88] He accepts the lay patronage of the Duke, assuming "the parishioners themselves joined in a general call to Reuben Butler to be their pastor,"[89] but knowing the parishioners will take orders from Duncan. And, apparently, he "altogether forgot to enquire, whether Butler was called upon to subscribe the oaths to government."[90] In short, as with Jeanie and the cash jar, willful forgetting, or what Deans might once have called moral backsliding, plays a role in upward mobility.

As an extension of the ethics of exchange that dominates social relations, new forms of self-knowledge emerge alongside Christian values that are often paraded and selectively practiced. The farm and the church coexist. Ultimately, however, scientific knowledge supplants speculative principles. As Giddens describes, in the modern world, "Religious cosmology is supplanted by reflexively organised knowledge, governed by empirical observation and logical thought, and focused upon material technology and socially applied codes."[91] Deans's new role as agricultural expert, then, is not incidental to the picture of progress taking shape; in fact, it points to the highly self-reflexive, material basis of self-improvement (and accumulation) in the modern world. In this respect, the lifespan of Deans (plus ten years) enables a longer view of the historicity of socialization. On the surface, this points to the moderation of religious custom, from the early days of religious persecution in Deans's youth to his own restraint at Roseneath-Knocktarlitie. But the generational shift in question is of wider import with respect to social practices; not only does Deans become an agricultural expert on an industrial farm, but his grandson, also named David, becomes a lawyer. For much of the novel, Deans stands as a rigid moral authority, but in the end, science and law are the future. Again, rather than a return to "the spirit of the olden times," this is a multi-generational projection of the re-embedding of social relations in new contexts.

In the end, although questions are raised, especially in *Clan Albin*, neither Johnstone nor Scott challenges the capitalist system that underpins the modern experience of rights, but as manuals of modernity, the lessons of each novel are singular. Norman returns to Glen-Albin as clan chief, and after a couple years attending lectures at the university in Edinburgh begins the "improvement of his estate."[92] He builds mills, improves roads, and administers the sort of "English improvement" otherwise disparaged in the novel.[93] The picture of happiness described by Monimia is seemingly without complications, fulfilled: "quiet, contentment, domestic affections, friendly neighbourhood, unostentatious usefulness, with as much of cultivated taste, and polite literature, as may diversify and embellish a life of retirement, without interrupting its business; and as much solid wealth as to scare the gaunt spectre, Poverty, far, far beyond the boundary *crag*."[94] It would appear, then, that the educated use of modern practices can facilitate the preservation of an idyllic version of traditional social life. Andrew Monnickendam argues that, as in Voltaire's *Candide* (1759), the ending of *Clan Albin* is a reflection on the turbulent world rather than the innocent representation of a return to a pastoral idyll.[95] In this light, Johnstone offers a thoughtful consideration of contemporary social concerns; more practically, the preservation of sympathy seems to protect against the harsh realities of modern life. In the final pages, Norman's warm heart guides the patriarchal reconstruction of an idealized Highland glen; Old Moome tells stories, the Piper dances, and Macs of all sorts join in the festivities. It would seem, then, that sympathy can direct the evenhanded application of modernity. As Lady Augusta says, "Society advances with slow, but sure progress."[96] This, however, seems counterintuitive given the rapid modernization of Scotland, and perhaps also misleading given the dire, seemingly irreversible, outcomes upon which the tale is based. Regardless, romance trumps history – the heart of the matter is that *"Macalbin's come home!"*[97] – meaning that there is a home to come back to; Glen-Albin re-emerges as a clan society still intact. The intended lesson for contemporary readers may simply have been that it is not too late to take control of modernization. In this respect, Scott's second series of *Tales of My Landlord* contrasts sharply with Johnstone's *National Tale*; each depends on a fundamentally different view of modernity. In *Clan Albin*, modernity offers new means of improvement to be applied by traditional communities as they (or the clan chief, to be more precise) see fit. In *The Heart of Mid-Lothian*, modernity had already altered the composition of everyday life; to take control of your life was not the same as taking control of modernization. It is, then, likely no coincidence that Scott set *The Heart of Mid-Lothian* much earlier than *Clan Albin*. Johnstone begins her tale in 1783, ten years after the Inclosure Act of 1773, which was symptomatic of the further establishment of legal property rights and the advance of industrialization in Britain. By focusing on the fifty years prior to the 1780s, excluding the longer history of Deans, Scott essentially responded to Johnstone (and others) by arguing that subjectivity and community practices had already been redefined by the discontinuity of modernity. Both types of novel were vital expressions of the way people might understand and cope with social transformation in the early-nineteenth century. But the implications of Scott's reply are radical. Whereas Johnstone's sentimental response to modernity may have pulled the heartstrings (and led to meaningful reforms), the heart of the matter for Scott was that modernization could not be reversed; there were, however, ways to get on in life – for better and worse.

Notes

1 Christian Isobel Johnstone, *Clan Albin: A National Tale*, ed. Andrew Monnickendam (Glasgow: Association for Scottish Literary Studies, 2003), 3–11.
2 Walter Scott, *The Heart of Mid-Lothian*, ed. David Hewitt and Alison Lumsden (Edinburgh: Edinburgh University Press, 2009), 7. The first edition was Walter

48 Heart of the matter

Scott, *Tales of My Landlord, Second Series: Collected and Arranged by Jedediah Cleishbotham, Schoolmaster and Parish-clerk of Gandercleugh. In Four Volumes* (Edinburgh: Archibald Constable and Company, 1818). All citations are to the Hewitt and Lumsden edition.

3 Scott, *Heart of Mid-Lothian*, 9–10.
4 Johnstone, *Clan Albin*, 37.
5 Ibid., 117.
6 Ibid., 135.
7 Scott, *Heart of Mid-Lothian*, 14.
8 Ibid.
9 Ibid., 18.
10 Ibid., 16.
11 Adam Smith, *An Inquiry into the Nature and Causes of the Wealth of Nations* (London: W. Strahan and T. Cadell, 1776).
12 Johnstone, *Clan Albin*, 234.
13 Ibid., 497.
14 Frances Burney, *The Wanderer: or, Female Difficulties* (London: Longman, Hurst, Rees, Orme, and Brown, 1814).
15 Oliver Goldsmith, *Deserted Village: A Poem*, 5th ed. (London: W. Griffin, 1770).
16 R. S. White, *Natural Rights and the Birth of Romanticism in the 1790s* (Basingstoke: Palgrave Macmillan, 2005), 54.
17 Adam Smith, *The Theory of Moral Sentiments*, ed. Knud Haakonssen (Cambridge: Cambridge University Press, 2002).
18 See, for example, Jean-Jacques Rousseau, *Julie ou la nouvelle Héloïse* (1761); Mary Wollstonecraft, *Mary: A Fiction* (1788); and William Godwin, *Things as They Are; or, The Adventures of Caleb Williams* (1794).
19 Johnstone, *Clan Albin*, 123.
20 Ibid., 306.
21 Ibid., 19.
22 Ibid., 81.
23 Ibid., 57.
24 There is an interesting parallel here with Emmanuel Levinas's prioritization of the Other that might be taken up further. See Emmanuel Levinas, "Ethics as First Philosophy," in *The Levinas Reader*, ed. Seán Hand (Malden, MA: Blackwell, 2005), 75–87.
25 Johnstone, *Clan Albin*, 32.
26 Ibid., 277.
27 Ibid., 23.
28 Lincoln, *Scott and Modernity*, 2. See also, James Buzard, *Disorienting Fiction: The Autoethnographic Work of Nineteenth-Century British Novels* (Princeton, NJ: Princeton University Press, 2005). Buzard refers to *Waverley* as providing "an imaginary domain – a space that Raymond Williams labelled a 'court of human appeal' – in which the compromises of modern social life might be redressed" (ibid., 70).
29 Moretti, *European Novel*, 20.
30 James Kerr, "Fiction Against History: Scott's *Redgauntlet* and the Power of Romance," *Texas Studies in Literature and Language* 29, no. 3 (Fall 1987): 238.
31 Lincoln, *Scott and Modernity*, 6.
32 Duncan, *Modern Romance*, 15.
33 The idea may stem from Georg Lukács, who described the historical novel as "making private of history" (*Historical Novel*, 199).
34 Duncan, *Modern Romance*, 9.
35 Ibid., 53.

36 Ibid.
37 Moretti, *European Novel*, 38.
38 Duncan, *Modern Romance*, 100.
39 Ibid.
40 Ibid., 104.
41 Ibid., 111.
42 Ibid., 110.
43 Ibid., 150.
44 Ibid., 166.
45 Ibid., 164.
46 Ibid., 156.
47 Ibid., 167.
48 Ibid., 156.
49 Ibid., 147.
50 See Linda Colley, *Britons: Forging the Nation, 1707–1837* (New Haven, CT: Yale University Press, 1992). With respect to Great Britain, Colley argues that patriotism and war were primary constituents of the construction of national identity (ibid., 5).
51 Duncan, *Modern Romance*, 167.
52 Ibid.
53 Giddens, *Consequences of Modernity*, 21.
54 Lincoln, *Scott and Modernity*, 9.
55 Ibid., 18.
56 Ibid., 177.
57 Tom M. Devine, *The Scottish Nation, 1700–2000*, 1st American ed. (New York: Penguin Books, 2001), 107.
58 Scott, *Waverley*, 450.
59 Anthony Giddens, *A Contemporary Critique of Historical Materialism*, 2nd ed. (Houndmills: Palgrave Macmillan, 1995), 39.
60 Giddens, *Consequences of Modernity*, 19.
61 Fleishman, *English Historical Novel*, 93.
62 Ina Ferris, *The Achievement of Literary Authority: Gender, History, and the Waverley Novels* (Ithaca, NY: Cornell University Press, 1991), 132.
63 Johnstone, *Clan Albin*, 238.
64 Moretti, *European Novel*, 22.
65 Giddens, *Consequences of Modernity*, 19.
66 Johnstone, *Clan Albin*, 557.
67 Giddens, *Consequences of Modernity*, 109.
68 Moretti, *European Novel*, 35.
69 Bakhtin, "*Bildungsroman*," 53.
70 Giddens, *Consequences of Modernity*, 113.
71 Ibid.
72 Ibid., 55.
73 Giddens, *Contemporary Critique*, 159.
74 Ibid., 120.
75 Ibid., 149.
76 Ibid., 123.
77 Ibid., 111.
78 McHoul, *Semiotic Investigations*, ix.
79 McNeil, *Scotland, Britain, Empire*, 56.
80 Fleishman, *English Historical Novel*, 96.
81 Andrea K. Henderson, *Romantic Identities: Varieties of Subjectivity, 1774–1830* (Cambridge: Cambridge University Press, 1996), 161.

50　*Heart of the matter*

82　Scott, *Heart of Mid-Lothian*, 381.
83　Ibid., 422.
84　Ibid.
85　Ibid., 429.
86　Ibid., 355.
87　Ibid., 383.
88　Ibid.
89　Ibid.
90　Ibid., 404.
91　Giddens, *Consequences of Modernity*, 109.
92　Johnstone, *Clan Albin*, 556.
93　Ibid., 119.
94　Ibid., 344.
95　Andrew Monnickendam, introduction to *Clan Albin: A National Tale*, by Christian Isobel Johnstone, ed. Andrew Monnickendam (Glasgow: Association for Scottish Literary Studies, 2003), xv–xvi. Voltaire, *Candide*, ed. Eric Palmer (Peterborough, ON: Broadview Press, 2009).
96　Johnstone, *Clan Albin*, 174.
97　Ibid., 551.

3 Nation of readers
Chapbook versions of
The Heart of Mid-Lothian

> To construct in its historical dimensions this process of the "actualization"
> of texts above all requires us to realize that their meaning depends upon the
> forms through which they are received and appropriated by their readers (or
> listeners).
>
>   – Roger Chartier, "Labourers and Voyagers: From the Text
>   to the Reader," 88

Walter Scott's novels were long and expensive – published in three or four
volumes and sold for up to thirty-two shillings when most new novels sold
for no more than ten shillings. Still, first edition print runs of 6–10,000
were no less unusual, even though few novels of the period reached more
than two editions of 500 or 1,000 copies each.[1] In short, the "Author of
Waverley" was in high demand. Circulating libraries and downmarket editions further extended middle-class reading. In 1819, Archibald Constable
purchased the copyrights of Scott's first seven novels. He published five editions of *Novels and Tales of the Author of Waverley* within seven years;
the format changed, the price dropped, and illustrations were added.[2] Such
innovations preceded the downmarket Magnum edition of 1829–33, which
included all of Scott's novels; the *Waverley Novels* consisted of forty-eight
cloth-bound, decimo-octavo volumes issued monthly for five shillings each.[3]
Sales of Scott's twenty-five Waverley novels reached 500,000 up to 1829
and 3,000,000 up to 1860.[4] Downmarket reprints of Waverley novels were
widely accessible to a reading nation in the Romantic period and beyond.
As such, it is tempting to suggest that the collective reading of Waverley
novels was a powerful means of consolidating national identity. The subject
of Scott's defining role in nation building has been broached many times.
Christopher Harvie points to a critical consensus when he writes, "As a
novelist and folklorist, he was the precursor of those reconstructors of historic identity who propelled European nationalism."[5] Ample evidence, in
Britain and elsewhere, exists to support the assertion.[6] In the nineteenth
century, it was possible to refer to the "Wizard of the North" or the "Great
Unknown," or to characters (e.g., Edward Waverley, Jeanie Deans, Brian

52   *Nation of readers*

de Boisguilbert) and scenes (e.g., Edward and Flora at the waterfall, Jeanie and Queen Caroline at Richmond Park, Brian and Rebecca at Templestowe) from any of the most popular Waverley novels, and be quite sure that such references were known across the Western world. Further, many canonical authors (e.g., Cooper, Balzac, Manzoni, Tolstoy) adapted the Waverley novels in recognizable ways. Still, this should not imply that to read (or adapt) Scott was to automatically or subconsciously take on board a singular worldview. Benedict Anderson's well-known description of the impact of print technologies on reading seems to suggest that a combination of literacy and circulation enabled collective identity formation over wide reaches of time and space.[7] But the actual process of identity construction, and the role of literature in that process, remains a matter of situational reading practices. Although the expansion of print and reading was essential, the underlying assumption is too often that circulation is a direct means of disseminating meaning. This approach to communication depends on two ideas: first, that meaning is inherent in texts,[8] and in relation, that meaning production results from a transfer of information from sender to receiver.[9] Print circulation played a crucial role in identity formation, as it put texts in the hands of readers, but as Ian Duncan reminds, "the novels themselves do not guarantee a particular ideological outcome, as their reception history shows us."[10] As this book further demonstrates, histories of literary production and print reading reveal the many context-specific ways people used literature to manufacture their own sense of modern subjectivity. To facilitate such a turn to material histories and self-reflexive reading practices, this chapter focuses on adaptations of *The Heart of Mid-Lothian* for downmarket readers of chapbooks. In this way, I describe a facet of print culture not often acknowledged in the criticism of canonical historical novels. Further, I demonstrate that communication cannot be reduced to either linear transmission or passive absorption by showing how publishers and authors reinvented one popular historical novel to communicate effectively with working- and middle-class readers before cheap reprints of the Waverley novels were widely available. Finally, following on recent interest in the many afterlives of Scott and his works,[11] this chapter points to a wider media landscape within which the novel was only one means to address the consequences of modernity.

By the early-nineteenth century, history was no longer the reserve of either classical historians or elite readers. As Ina Ferris notes, "The period is filled with signs of an urgent, widespread sense that large numbers of new and diverse readers had appeared on the scene."[12] Readers of all sorts wanted to know more about the past and what was new about the present. Accordingly, history became available to downmarket readers in a variety of accessible forms and popular genres. Although read by others, not excepting Scott, chapbooks were the popular pamphlets of the poor. Like ballad-sheets and garlands, chapbooks began as a sort of printed folklore yet had broader formal and thematic scope. Some retold old romances or fairy tales; others recounted ancient battles, described historical figures, disseminated superstitions and riddles, provided practical advice, and communicated political messages. The chapbook form was altered to meet the individual interests and contemporary circumstances of readers. Early chapbooks were eight to thirty-two pages in length and printed on cheap paper with woodcut images. They sold for as little as a halfpenny and usually for less than sixpence, thus making them widely available to downmarket readers. They were available in the city and the countryside. The potentially wide dissemination among working-class readers made the chapbook attractive to social reformers. Capitalizing on the longstanding popularity of the chapbook, religious activists targeted downmarket readers with conduct literature labeled as cheap tracts and repackaged in chapbook form.[13] Nevertheless, the proliferation and use of chapbooks went well beyond folklore and reform literature. Even at the lowest prices, substantial variation is apparent. When demand for literature was increasing, publishers altered the form and content of traditional chapbooks to maintain, increase, or diversify readership. Popular chapbooks such as *Guy of Warwick* and *Jack the Giant Killer* adapted and sold for as much as one shilling were likely to be longer, printed on better paper, and feature decorative borders and new images. Chapbook versions of out-of-copyright novels such as *Robinson Crusoe* (1719) and *Pilgrim's Progress* (1678) also remained popular.[14] But as Gary Kelly describes, "Around 1800, chapbooks of a new kind began to appear, mainly much shorter versions of books read by the middle classes."[15] Chapbook adaptations of new novels were usually thirty-two to seventy-four pages, cost from sixpence to a shilling, and differed in appearance from the earlier kinds; they were more carefully printed, bound in attractively ornamented blue and yellow paper covers, and accompanied by hand-colored or steel-engraved frontispieces depicting a sensational incident from the story. Authors and publishers, in short, were quick to capitalize on changes to the print market and in reading practices.

The adaptation of new novels by the most popular author of the day played a role in the changing form and use of the chapbook, the success of which was tied to other media forms. Waverley novels were adapted for the stage within weeks of initial publication, and in some cases throughout the nineteenth century. H. Philip Bolton's account of the dramatization of Waverley novels demonstrates the extensive impact of stage adaptations, especially in London but also in Edinburgh and at provincial theatres throughout Britain.[16] In many cases, adaptations for patent and nonpatent theatres were staged simultaneously. Some were printed and sold for two shillings and sixpence. This was not exceptionally cheap, yet staged or printed dramatizations also provided the basis of or otherwise influenced chapbook versions that sold for as little as one penny, which were thus more widely accessible to the working class and more likely to travel to out of the way locations by way of chapmen.

54 Nation of readers

Although early reprints of *The Heart of Mid-Lothian* would not have extended circulation of the novel much beyond a middle-class readership, the print market was varied and publishers responded. A history of the Porteous Riots sold for eight shillings.[17] The print version of Thomas Dibdin's dramatization of *The Heart of Mid-Lothian* sold for two shillings and sixpence.[18] A sixty-three-page pamphlet describing the gruesomeness of Muschat's Cairn, which is the setting of the midnight meeting of Jeanie and Staunton in the first volume, sold for a shilling.[19] According to Coleman Parsons, *Waverley* was not published in chapbook form until 1821, by which time chapbook versions of *The Heart of Mid-Lothian* and other Waverley novels were already available.[20] Chapbook versions sold for as little as twopence. Commercial publishers were keen to cash in on the popularity of Scott, but chapbooks of Waverley novels, like the dramatizations upon which they were sometimes based,[21] were not simply gutted versions of expensive novels. Publishers and authors worked within the formal, thematic, and material resources of the chapbook to communicate with individual and creative readers across a range of reading communities. In other words, if the primary goal of publishers was profit, the means were more complex. Wide socioeconomic accessibility was not indicative of center-margins, linear, or homogenous transmission. As indicated by the price, form, and content of six chapbook versions of *The Heart of Mid-Lothian*, the new chapbook was used to reach existing or cultivate new readerships.[22]

The Heart of Mid-Lothian; or, The Lily of St. Leonard's (ca. 1819) was part of an ongoing effort to reach juvenile or downmarket readers with short versions of popular literature.[23] George Caw and Henry Elder were printers and publishers at the Stamp Office Close in Edinburgh from 1817 to 1821; together, they published *The Edinburgh Juvenile Library* (a series of children's chapbooks), *Ross's Juvenile Library*, and popular abridgements of books with Alexander Peat, a wholesale stationer and bookseller in Edinburgh.[24] Their version of *The Heart of Mid-Lothian* was portable, short, and cheap: ten by six centimeters, twenty-four pages (each part), and only twopence. It fit into a larger catalogue of advertised literary works: *Life and Exploits of Rob Roy*; *Elizabeth, or The Exiles of Siberia*; *Inkle and Yarico, an Affecting and True Tale*; *The Way to Wealth, or Poor Richard Improved* by B. Franklin; *Watts' Divine Songs*; *Songs and Duets in the Play of Rob Roy with Bailie Jarvie's Journey to Aber-foil, and the 'Boys of Kilkenny,' Sung by Mr Weekes*; and *Caledonia's Delight, Choice Songs*. In this list, the importance of popular authorship, topicality, and regional or national distinction is evident; participatory forms of entertainment were also popular. The association of *The Heart of Mid-Lothian* with Sophie Cottin's novel *Elizabeth; or, The Exiles of Siberia* (1806) is of particular interest.[25] As Peter Garside points out, both *Elizabeth* and *The Heart of Mid-Lothian* emphasize lower-class characters and describe an ambitious, successful initiative carried out by a central female character: "In *Elizabeth*, the heroine makes a long trip on foot to plead on behalf of her exiled parents, finally gaining

Nation of readers 55

a pardon through a direct appeal to the Emperor in Moscow. In *The Heart of Mid-Lothian*, Jeanie Deans's journey to London likewise culminates in a similar appeal to the Crown, in the person of Queen Caroline."[26] The positive representation of working-class life, rather than upper-class domestic squabbles over inheritance or the aloof intellectual musings of an educated leisure class, was likely attractive to downmarket readers, as were other features of this version of *The Heart of Mid-Lothian*.

Reference to a "popular resume" in the opening description is indicative of the style and content employed in many chapbooks. The selective listing of events distilled from the novel was common to the form; as Kelly notes, a chapbook typically "lacked the detailed representations of subjectivity, extensive descriptive passages, lengthy social scenes, and literary allusions often found in their sources."[27] Yet a narrative style reminiscent of traditional chapbooks should not be solely attributed to low levels of literacy or a lack of education. Physical considerations such as the availability of space, the quality of shelter, and the quantity of light would have contributed to the popularity of chapbooks and short histories. Moreover, the open-ended structure, formulaic closure, and weak denouement reflect not only the structure of popular melodrama but also a working-class experience of life as repetitive, cyclical, and generally hard.[28] Regardless, the content had to appeal to readers. Although *The Lily of St. Leonard's* is generally faithful to the original – as a resume, of sorts – the inclusion of dramatic or comedic scenes points to a more complex balance of fictional elements required to meet the interests of working-class readers. Even in an educational or moral rendition of the novel, enough of the appeal of the traditional chapbook remains to interest young readers. Other chapbook versions were similarly sensitive to the expectations of readers.

The Heart of Mid-Lothian, or The Affecting History of Jeanie and Effie Deans (1819) by D. Stewart strives to separate itself from the traditional chapbook in several ways.[29] It is fifty-two pages and sold for one shilling, and is thus longer and more expensive than the Caw-Elder version. The frontispiece stresses the relationship between Jeanie and Effie, an emphasis that increased during the Victorian period and continued to the end of the nineteenth century, predominantly on the stage. Moreover, the full-page frontispiece replicates a style and quality found in more expensive books, pointing to a sense of distinction not seen in other versions. Similarly, the title page features neither Shakespeare nor popular ballads; instead, front and center is a quote from Isaac Watts, an eighteenth-century non-conformist theologian and logician best known as a prolific English hymn writer: "To man, in this his trial state,/The privilege is given,/When tost by tides of human fate,/To anchor fast in heaven." The reference to Watts sets a moral tone for a self-respecting, Christian-minded readership. Similarly, the advertisement provides another example of the publisher's attempt to bring this chapbook in line with the expectations of middle-class readers. The work is described as "*Being a true and affecting Display of Filial*

56   Nation of readers

Affection"; it is also accompanied by "an historical Sketch of the celebrated Clan Macgregor By D. Stewart, M.A." and a quote from Wordsworth: "The eagle he was lord above, But *Rob* was lord below." References to *Rob Roy*, *Paul and Virginia*, and *Robin Hood* emphasize the popularity of adventure and romance, national and foreign (French) authors, and traditional and new works. However, each title is framed to highlight truth, history, or improvement: *Rob Roy* comes "With an historical Sketch"; *Paul and Virginia* is written by the author of "Studies of Nature"; and *Robin Hood* is derived "From an original Copy." The intended message is clear: this is serious literature worthy of a proper frontispiece, one shilling, and a selective (i.e., self-conscious) reader.

Stewart's adaptation is, accordingly, also a skillful literary production concerned with modern progress and social position. As Parsons describes, "Stewart's organization of *The Heart of Midlothian* is the most complex as well as the least neglectful of Scott's values."[30] The close rendering of the tale deteriorates quickly when critical events are dropped and the whole ending is quashed: on page fifty, Jeanie meets with Staunton at the rectory on her way to London; it is then only two pages to the end of the story. Perhaps Stewart began writing, planned on two parts, then had to curtail it suddenly, thus resulting in the end of volume three and all of volume four of the original novel squeezed into a few paragraphs. Regardless, this version is not only well written but also "refuses to be sensational,"[31] pointing instead to the accumulation of cultural capital. The chapbook's publisher, Mackenzie and Dent, aimed for a broad, non-sectarian readership with an interest in self-improvement: readers aspiring to become middle class or those that could already afford to pay one shilling and might justify chapbook reading if it was distinguished from the common sort. Stewart's adaptation is downmarket yet neither cheap nor unattractive, and it is a well-written history "from the original" by the popular *and* distinguished "Author of *Waverley*." Higher price, formal innovation, and thematic cultivation attuned to middle-class values contributed to the complex coordination of production and reception in this as in other versions.

In *The Heart of Mid-Lothian, A Romantic Tale, Founded on Facts* (1820), Joseph Claude Mauris reinvented *The Heart of Mid-Lothian* as a form of moral instruction.[32] Like other versions, it is short (24 pp.) and cheap (the price is not listed, twopence seems likely). Like Caw and Elder, the publisher John Duncombe took up many and varied positions within the publishing industry, for example, as a bookseller, printer, music seller, print seller, and newsagent.[33] He was also a prolific publisher of popular literature. For instance, throughout the 1820s and 1830s, Duncombe published chapbooks featuring historical tales, adventure, romance, and comedy.[34] However, published as the third and final part of a collection including *The History of Miss Harriot Fairfax* and *Female Tubrepidity; or, The Dangers of Superstition: A Tale of Modern Times*, Mauris's *Romantic Tale* served a more precise purpose. In fact, the title seems at least somewhat misleading;

this tale may be founded on facts, but it is a strongly moralized version, favoring social norms regarding education and marriage while also stressing the disadvantages of foreign influence. Such didactic use of popular literature was not new, of course. Even Duncombe's pantomimes of Harlequin could be read as lessons. But with respect to the wider adaptation of *The Heart of Mid-Lothian, A Romantic Tale* provides a neat example of meaning-as-use within the context of popular publishing and reading. The first chapter links a history of George Staunton's upbringing in the West Indies to his desultory behavior in England and Scotland, with a description of the disastrous results for Madge and Effie. The initial emphasis on history is self-consciously conservative, as is the suggestive phrase "Founded on Facts," which had long since become a commonplace means of framing the reception of a work of literature. The message is well-defined: because this "romantic tale" is "founded on facts," it may be accepted by readers in search of wholesome literature. Although such subtitles could disguise as well as advertise, here, at least, the use is sincere. The fourth chapter, for instance, contains blunt moral statements that might have belonged to a religious reformer such as Hannah More – in sentiment if not in phrasing. On the way back to Scotland, Jeanie saves Madge from the mob and finds a place for her in an asylum with the assistance of Rector Staunton. Efforts are made to convert her, but she dies a few days later, "a sad example to 'splendid murderers of virtue, who make their vices their boast, and fancy female ruin a feather in their cap of vanity!'"[35] The warning is repeated in no uncertain terms: "What is man!/When the worst heart can wear the brow of virtue,/And false appearance smile us to destruction?/And yet, what is he not, when crowned with truth/And every social virtue?"[36] Continuing the stress on conduct and morality, the conclusion reflects more broadly upon the uncertainties of life:

> Staunton, in the full enjoyment of domestic peace with his adored Effie, had only looked forward to the recovery of his son as the completion of bliss – but alas! happiness and misery are too closely interwoven; we cannot taste the one without drinking the other, and while we inhale the draughts of bliss, the dregs remind us of the uncertainty of its continuance.[37]

The lesson, or sermon, might be summed up thus: do not the ambiguities and dangers of life lead us back to the stability of moral foundations and right actions? The transformation of a complex novel of modernity into a singular statement of moral persuasion parallels what Kelly calls "pseudo-popular print directed at the working classes by middle-class social reformers."[38] The obvious precedent is More's *Cheap Repository of Moral and Religious Tracts* (1795–1817), which "relentlessly attacked the ideology and culture of traditional working-class print and the overt politics of pro-Revolutionary writers."[39] The dissemination of religious literature took

58   *Nation of readers*

various forms; Padmini Ray Murray, for example, writes that "Thomas Nelson's ambition to provide Christian and classical literature for the 'common people' led to his company's publication of the Bible in thirty-two-page installments."[40] That being said, however common (and varied) the practice of spreading the Word, it is no coincidence that the Religious Tract Society sold tracts in bulk and likely depended on middle-class distribution.[41] The aim of wide dissemination at low prices was tempered by the more varied reading interests of working-class readers, who would have read whatever they could get and what interested them, which was not restricted to the Bible or tales intended to propagate Christian ideology.

Religious didacticism was not limited to Mauris's adaptation of *The Heart of Mid-Lothian*, but in line with the wider print market, new chapbook versions also reflected the spectrum of fiction available to readers, as well as the reading practices that made such variation commercially viable. For example, *The Heart of Mid Lothian; or The Lily of St. Leonard, a Caledonian Tale of Great Interest* (1822) manipulates form and content to interest readers in a national tale.[42] The title page makes direct reference to the theatre, and the edition is based on Thomas Dibdin's 1819 melodramatic adaptation for the Surrey Theatre in London.[43] The price of sixpence (i.e., the price of a seat in the gallery) and the moderate length (36 pp.) are typical of downmarket chapbooks for the period. Less typically, this version also incorporates a hand-colored woodcut frontispiece depicting "*The Dying* MADGE WILDFIRE *Pursued by the Mob and Rescued by* STAUNTON."[44] As a "Caledonian Tale," the title plays upon the popularity of Scottish fiction in England. It also references an ongoing debate over national theatre in London,[45] which impacted the adaptation of Waverley novels for the stage. As early as 1820, theatrical adaptations of *The Heart of Mid-Lothian* were frequently subtitled "national drama," "national dramatic tale," "national melo-drama," "Scotch drama," etc.[46] Inserting "The Lily of St. Leonard" in the title points directly to Dibdin's dramatization and also to increasing interest in Effie, as does the incorporation of scraps of old Scottish songs sung by Effie in the novel.[47] The complex negotiation of readership demanded an adept weaving of popularity, distinction, and interest that linked external factors and textual elements: the Surrey was the most distinguished of minor theatres; sixpence was neither cheap nor expensive for chapbooks of the period; although the hand-colored frontispiece was not unique, it was a curiosity; national distinctions were common but topical; and the epigraph employed a traditional ballad that was taken from a new novel. Such negotiations continued as a new sense of historicity usually reserved for the historical novel made its way into a story that is otherwise aligned with the educational concerns of social reformers of the day. A juxtaposition of past and present occurs several times; for example, "Reader the tale I am recording, took place a century ago; but now when our enlightened times spurn the bare idea of superstition";[48] and, "It is to be remembered at the time of which we are writing, travelling was more dangerous, more tardy, and the want of regular conveyances rendered it very expensive."[49] These seem direct references to the original novel's frame-narrative, which points to the impact of modernization on everyday life. But the chapbook continues, and concludes, as a sentimental tale that supports a nation unified by right conduct. The mob pursues Madge to the crags, where Staunton appears to defend her: "Remorse seized Staunton as he held the dying Madge in his arms. She pardoned him, and said, 'She was blest in breathing out her last sigh with him; if poor Effy gets free, be kind to her and reform.' With this liberal sentiment, the unfortunate creature expired."[50] Effy [sic] is being led to her death when Jannie [sic] bursts through the crowd to deliver the pardon. At the news, the "praises of Queen Caroline and Jannie Deans resounded through the town."[51] This conjoining of Caroline and Jeanie references the successful meeting at Richmond Park that resulted in both Effie's pardon and the removal of sanctions against Edinburgh – an event of personal and national significance. The final paragraph brings home a more scrupulous message: "May the snare into which the imprudent Effy drew herself, be a warning to young females; and let parents, while they watch over the actions of their children and train them to virtue, beware of rigid austerity, for it is best to invite confidence, and not repel it between ourselves and our off-spring."[52] Despite the opening appeal to stage popularity and the incorporation of nationalism, the end averts the threat of the chapbook as popular reading; this is still a moral lesson intended for women and children that will appeal to parents (i.e., the likely purchaser). Readers undoubtedly read these and other chapbooks in their own way, but there is little doubt of the intention: to send a message to readers that would reflect and influence social behavior.

The form and price (12 pp., 1d.) of *The Heart of Mid-Lothian* – a chapbook published by William Davison at Alnwick, which is located near the Scottish border – fits a general trend toward length and price reduction that places it after 1820.[53] Although cheaply made with thin paper and woodcut prints, that is, designed for wide dissemination to a downmarket audience, this version strives to distinguish itself from the traditional eighteenth-century chapbook. Davison, like other publishers of popular literature, wore many hats; he was a printer, engraver/etcher, bookseller, stationer, publisher, bookbinder, the owner of a circulating library, and a stereotype founder.[54] As such, formal and thematic innovation in line with contemporary developments might be expected. Not surprisingly, this chapbook is representative of the "new" chapbook. The front and back covers are made of blue paper decorated with borders and a woodcut image. Every page has a border and numerous images accompany the text, all of which are directly relevant to the story. Despite some weak transitions from one scene to the next necessitated by the brevity and paratactic structure of all chapbooks, this is a relatively smooth and even account with little moral judgment tacked on. Notably, as in Daniel Terry's adaptation for the Theatre Royal at Covent Garden in 1819,[55] minor characters are almost non-existent. With no

60   *Nation of readers*

sign of Dumbiedikes, Margery, the bandits Frank and Tom, Archibald, or Mrs Glass, the aim is not to win a crowd through either sympathetic representation or comedic effect. The omissions are not due to an attempt at moral didacticism, however. It is a condensed tale well told without over-emphasizing criminals and violence or virtue and education. Scots language is employed, which may reflect publication location and the interests of an audience near the Scottish border, as well as the localization of the chapbook trade to minimize transportation costs. In this light, it seems a practical version for downmarket readers of local print that wanted the story short, well-written, and without an obvious political or religious slant.

The final chapbook to consider is *Jeanie Deans, and the Lily of St Leonard's*, number eleven of the *Illustrated Historical Library for the Youth of Happy England*.[56] The date is not listed, but the back cover advertises both the *History of Ivanhoe and Rebecca the Jewess* and *Kenilworth Castle; or, The Trials of Amy Robsart*, thus putting publication after 1821 at least. Other parts of the series are *The Albion Primer; or, Guide to Learning*; *Collection of Nursery Rhymes for Children*; *The Royal Menagerie; or, History of Beasts*; *Whittington and his Cat, and Little King Pippin*; *Blue Beard, and Riquet with the Tuft*; *Cinderella, and the Pigeon and Dove*; *The Little Story Teller*; *The Magic Legacy, and Puss in Boots*; *Forty Thieves, Three Wishes, and the Fairy*; and *Daniel O'Rourke, and Rip Van Winkle*. Clearly, the target audience was children, although the readership might have been wider. Each chapbook sold for one penny, or twopence colored. Like the Davison chapbook, this version is a straightforward retelling of the original work, although not without meaningful alterations. Minor characters, for example, play little or no role. The titular focus on Jeanie Deans seems an obvious choice given the target audience, but the reference to the "Lily of St Leonard's" is of greater interest because in this version, Staunton is reconciled with Effie's father: "he became an altered man, and endeavoured to atone for the errors of his past life by a thorough reformation."[57] It would seem that the youth of happy England required tales that featured a role model and ended with moral improvement, which led to a rather drastic adaptation of the original novel. Equally noteworthy, this version takes up the fourth volume of the novel, if only to a minor degree: Argyle arranges for Butler and Deans to take up positions in Argyleshire – upward mobility is coupled with principled instruction.

As this description of six chapbook versions of *The Heart of Mid-Lothian* suggests, the new chapbook was a flexible form used by authors and publishers to communicate with readers situated in varied sociohistorical circumstances. Variations in price, form, and content could be sensitive enough to address community interests and individual preferences in subtle, meaningful ways. Advances in British printing and publishing, such as the steam press and stereotyping, tended to favor wider dissemination at lower prices; still, popular communication was not simply a matter of scattering words. Rather, because of disparities in education, literacy, income, and interests – what

Nation of readers 61

otherwise might be called life circumstances – print markets were as rhizo-matic as the readerships served. Publishing and reading were not inherently chaotic; rather, adapting to modern life, which could be tumultuous, was of concern to everyone, and print reading played an increasingly major role in facilitating the means to cope with all aspects of modernity. Self-education and distinction were not restricted to the upper classes or the readers of Waverley novels. The working classes furnished themselves with the reading material that made the most material and social sense for their own lives, when and how they could get it. The evidence of how people read such mate-rials is incomplete, but the variety of print preserved in archives suggests that chapbooks and other forms of popular print were not just vehicles of transmission. If anything, chapbook versions of *The Heart of Mid-Lothian* describe the socialization of texts pertaining to reading *situations* informed by personal, economic, political, and geographic conditions. As part of a diverse market for popular print, and as valued by the diverse readers of them, chapbooks, too, were acts of modernity as they contributed to the self-reflexive communication practices that helped all readers, in Britain as elsewhere, see and cope with social transformation in the nineteenth century.

Notes

1 William St Clair, *The Reading Nation in the Romantic Period* (Cambridge: Cam-bridge University Press, 2004), 221.

2 See David Hewitt and Alison Lumsden, "Essay on the Text," in *The Heart of Mid-Lothian*, ed. David Hewitt and Alison Lumsden (Edinburgh: Edinburgh University Press, 2009), 500–9. Summary of early collections of the Waverley novels: 1819 (12 vols, 8vo, £7, 4s.); 1821 (16 vols, 12mo, £6. in boards, 1,500 copies ordered); 1822 (16 vols, 8vo, £7, 4s., larger version of the 1821 edition); 1823 (16 vols, 18mo, £4, 4s. in boards); 1825 (16 vols, 12mo, based on the 1821 edition) (ibid.). See also, Peter D. Garside, "*Waverley* and the National Fiction Revolution," in Bell, Finkelstein, and McCleery, *Ambition and Industry 1800–80*.

3 For the publishing history of Scott's Magnum Opus, see Millgate, *Scott's Last Edition*.

4 St Clair, *Reading Nation*, 221.

5 Christopher Harvie, *Scotland and Nationalism, Scottish Society and Politics: 1707–1994*, 2nd ed. (London: Routledge, 1994), 90.

6 See, for example, Carole Gerson, *A Purer Taste: The Writing and Reading of Fic-tion in English in Nineteenth-Century Canada* (Toronto: University of Toronto Press, 1989); Pittock, *Scott in Europe*; and Ann Rigney, *The Afterlives of Walter Scott: Memory on the Move* (Oxford: Oxford University Press, 2012).

7 Benedict Anderson, *Imagined Communities: Reflections on the Origin and Spread of Nationalism*, rev. and exp. ed., 2nd ed. (London: Verso, 1991).

8 On how this is not the case, see McHoul, *Semiotic Investigations*.

9 See Harris, *Integrational Linguistics*, 20–22. Harris describes and critiques what he calls the "talking heads" model of communication.

10 Duncan, "*Waverley*," 179.

11 On the afterlives of Scott, see, for example, Jerome Mitchell, *The Walter Scott Operas: An Analysis of Operas Based on the Works of Sir Walter Scott* (Uni-versity: University of Alabama Press, 1977); Jerome Mitchell, *More Walter*

62   Nation of readers

     Scott Operas: Further Analyses of Operas Based on the Works of Sir Walter Scott (Lanham, MD: University Press of America, 1996); H. Philip Bolton, *Scott Dramatized* (London: Mansell, 1992); Pittock, *Scott in Europe*; Millgate, *Scott's Last Edition*; and Rigney, *Afterlives of Walter Scott*.

12 Ferris, *Literary Authority*, 22.

13 See Susan Pederson, "Hannah More Meets Simple Simon: Tracts, Chapbooks, and Popular Culture in Late Eighteenth-Century England," *The Journal of British Studies* 25, no. 1 (January 1986): 84–113, www.jstor.org/stable/175612.

14 Pat Rogers, *Literature and Popular Culture in Eighteenth Century England* (Sussex: Harvester Press; New Jersey, NJ: Barnes and Noble Books, 1985), 164–65.

15 Gary Kelly, "Fiction and the Working Classes," in *The Cambridge Companion to Fiction in the Romantic Period*, ed. Richard Maxwell and Katie Trumpener (Cambridge: Cambridge University Press, 2008), 209.

16 Bolton, *Scott Dramatized*.

17 *Criminal Trials: Illustrative of the Tale Entitled 'The Heart of Mid-Lothian' Published from the Original Record, With a Prefatory Notice, Including Some Particulars of the Life of Captain John Porteous* (Edinburgh: Constable, 1818). See also, Coleman O. Parsons, "Chapbook Versions of the Waverley Novels," *Studies in Scottish Literature* 3, no. 4 (April 1966): 201.

18 Thomas Dibdin, *The Heart of Mid-Lothian; or, The Lily of St. Leonard's: A Melo-Dramatic Romance, in Three Acts. From 'Tales of My Landlord.' First Performed at the Surrey Theatre, on Wednesday, January 13, 1819. By T. Dibdin, Author of the Metrical History of England, and Many Dramatic Pieces*, 2nd ed. (London: Robert Stodart, 1819).

19 Parsons, "Chapbook Versions," 201.

20 Ibid.

21 See David Buchanan, "Popular Reception by Dramatic Adaptation: The Case of Walter Scott's *The Heart of Mid-Lothian*," *European Romantic Review* 22, no. 6 (November 2011): 745–63.

22 See Parsons, "Chapbook Versions," 197–202; and David Buchanan, "Scott Squashed: Chapbook Versions of *The Heart of Mid-Lothian*," *Romanticism and Victorianism on the Net* 56 (November 2009): n. pag, http://id.erudit.org/iderudit/1001097ar.

23 *The Heart of Mid-Lothian; or, The Lily of St. Leonard's* (Edinburgh: Caw and Elder; Alex. Peat, ca. 1819).

24 *Scottish Book Trade Index*, s.v. "Caw, George," www.nls.uk/catalogues/scottish-book-trade-index.

25 Madame (Sophie) Cottin, *Elizabeth; or, The Exiles of Siberia: A Tale Founded upon Facts: From the French of Madame Cottin*, 3rd ed. (London: S. A. and H. Oddy, 1809).

26 Peter D. Garside, "Walter Scott and the 'Common' Novel, 1808–1819," *Cardiff Corvey: Reading the Romantic Text* 3 (September 1999): n. pag., www.romtext.org.uk/articles/cc03_n02/.

27 Kelly, "Fiction," 219.

28 Ibid., 216.

29 D. Stewart, *The Heart of Mid-Lothian, or The Affecting History of Jeanie and Effie Deans. Abridged from the Original [of Sir Walter Scott]* (Newcastle upon Tyne: Mackenzie and Dent, 1819).

30 Parsons, "Chapbook Versions," 199.

31 Ibid., 200.

32 Joseph Claude Mauris, *The Heart of Mid-Lothian, A Romantic Tale, Founded on Facts* (London: J. Duncombe, 1820).

33 *British Book Trade Index*, s.v. "Duncombe, John," http://bbti.bodleian.ox.ac.uk/details/?traderid=21216.

34 See, for example, *Dramatic Tales and Romances: Pantomimes* (London: J. Duncombe, n.d., ca. 1817–36). One of many volumes of collected tales published as part of a miniature library for children.
35 Mauris, *Romantic Tale*, 23.
36 Ibid.
37 Ibid., 24.
38 Kelly, "Fiction," 209.
39 Ibid., 227.
40 Padmini Ray Murray, "Religion," in Bell, Finkelstein, and McCleery, *Ambition and Industry 1800–80*, 289.
41 Kelly, "Fiction," 227.
42 *The Heart of Mid Lothian; or The Lily of St. Leonard, a Caledonian Tale of Great Interest* (London: Company of Booksellers, 1822).
43 Dibdin, *Heart of Mid-Lothian*.
44 The frontispiece of this chapbook is the cover image for *Acts of Modernity*.
45 See David Worrall, *Theatric Revolution: Drama, Censorship and Romantic Period Subcultures 1773–1832* (Oxford: Oxford University Press, 2006), 41–44.
46 Bolton, *Scott Dramatized*, 266.
47 Scott, *Heart of Mid-Lothian*, 86–87.
48 *Heart of Mid Lothian (Caledonian Tale)*, 17.
49 Ibid., 25.
50 Ibid., 32.
51 Ibid., 33.
52 Ibid., 34.
53 *The Heart of Mid-Lothian* (Alnwick: W. Davison, n.d.).
54 *British Book Trade Index*, s.v. "Davison, William," http://bbti.bodleian.ox.ac.uk/details/?traderid=19096.
55 Daniel Terry, *The Heart of Midlothian, a Musical Drama, in Three Acts; First Produced at the Theatre Royal, Covent Garden, Saturday, 17th April, 1819* (London: William Stockdale, 1819).
56 *Jeanie Deans, and the Lily of St Leonard's* (London: Webb, Millington, n.d.).
57 Ibid., 31.

4   How the West was one

Historification from *Waverley* to *The Pathfinder*

> Signification and contextualization are not two independent elements but facets of the same creative activity.
>
> – Roy Harris, *Signs, Language and Communication*, 164

By the early-nineteenth century, the transatlantic book trade was extensive, and British imports dominated the American market.[1] Walter Scott's *Waverley* novels were especially popular.[2] Just when the nation-state was taking shape and reading was on the rise, American publishers scrambled to get each new novel by the "Author of *Waverley*" to market as quickly as possible. Reading new works of fiction took on an importance hitherto unknown. Besides the novelty of Scott's novels, fiction provided a means to cope with the disorder of a modernizing world.[3] Thus, major publishing houses shifted production from small print runs and old stock works to current works in large runs. David Kaser notes, for example, how Carey and Lea of Philadelphia "began cutting back on its publishing of stock books – of titles that it would take many years to sell off – and began publishing many more popular books, novels and romances, biographies, books of travel, and even some school books."[4] The predominance of law books, the Bible, and atlases of the 1820s gave way to literature that would interest a popular readership adapting to the realities of American life. Along with feedback from traveling salesmen, the popularity of the Waverley novels signaled to publishers what would sell, which led them to actively encourage American writers such as James Fenimore Cooper to follow suit; as William Charvat describes, "Carey & Lea, the ablest of American publishers before 1850, and the shrewdest interpreters of the public, had exercised precisely such influence on Cooper, suggesting again and again that he write this or not write that."[5] At the intersection of transatlantic communication circuits and the realities of modern life, American reading practices changed. As this chapter describes, use of the historical novel by American authors contributed to the Americanization of print reading, in part by offering different views of the past to inform the progress of the American republic.

How the West was one 65

Cooper's transition from *Precaution; A Novel* (1820) to *The Spy: A Tale of the Neutral Ground* (1821), that is, from a novel of manners set in Britain to the first American historical novel, signaled to early critics the connection that would follow "the American Scott" throughout his career.[6] Contemporary critics have been no less preoccupied with the link between Cooper and Scott. Lion Feuchtwanger, for example, writes that "Cooper consciously picks up where Walter Scott left off," and Wayne Franklin argues that "The kind of tale [Cooper] would tell was determined, clearly enough, by his wish to emulate Walter Scott, whose masterful novels of the Scottish borderlands, beginning with *Waverley* (1814), had established a new literary mode."[7] Cooper used this "new literary mode" – the conscious combination of history and romance in the novel form – for his own purposes. Although *The Spy* follows *Waverley* as a national tale set in the midst of a revolutionary war, more important is that Cooper wrote a novel that focused on the political history and cultural identity of American readers.[8] In this respect, John McWilliams's argument, that the unwavering allegiance of Harvey Birch and the questionable practices of George Washington portrayed in *The Spy* turn *Waverley* on its head to communicate the traits (and uncertainties) of American nation building, is all the more powerful.[9] As Winfried Fluck writes, "Scott's lasting achievement was to demonstrate the usefulness of fiction for the purpose of national self-definition."[10] If the immediate popularity of *The Spy* demonstrated anything,[11] it was that the American reading of American fiction was first and foremost a matter of self-interest; as described below, the lesson was not lost on other American writers.

The popularity of *The Spy* impacted the combination of history and fiction in the 1820s. Cooper himself, likely with the fifty-year commemoration of historic events such as the Battle of Bunker Hill in mind,[12] put his Leatherstocking novels aside to write *Lionel Lincoln; or, The Leaguer of Boston* (1825),[13] a Revolutionary War novel based on extensive research into American history. Cooper was not alone. The historical novel became a popular source of information about the Revolution. Yet the combination of history and fiction was about much more than the popularization of history. Historical fiction could be used to set forth a vision of collective progress that galvanized a diverse American republic. Lydia Sigourney's little-known *Sketch of Connecticut, Forty Years Since* (1824) is useful in this context. The title seems derivative of two contemporary works: Washington Irving's *Sketch Book* (1819) and Scott's *Waverley, or 'Tis Sixty Years Since* (1814), which points to the impact of popular publishing and transatlantic networks, as well as the nature and aims of Sigourney's composite construction. Sigourney describes the book as "A tablet of individual, domestick, and social vicissitudes, [that] would serve as a monument to recall the past, and as a way-mark to direct the future."[14] As a collection of historical sketches that informs readers about the assimilation of Native Americans and the defeat of the British, *Sketch of Connecticut* points to potential and

66   *How the West was one*

later uses of the historical novel to project a tidy picture of social transformation for American readers.

Sigourney's account is notable in the first place for the fact that she acknowledges Native ownership of the land and demonstrates the state of the once powerful tribe of Mohegans; she not only attempts to recall Native history and the nobility of their leaders, but also points to Native assistance in the establishment of the colonies. Of more interest here, she parallels Native and Western history in several ways: Uncas is only in need of a Homer to do his story justice; the traits and actions of Native heroes are compared to William the Conqueror; and Oneco is referred to as "lion hearted,"[15] a reference to Richard the Lion-Hearted of England. Such associations attempt to do justice to Native history, yet neither the process nor the outcomes are neutral. To translate Native history into such explicitly Western terms is also to frame a unique cultural past within a singular view of modern progress. As Gary Kelly writes, "She envisioned a republican, agrarian, Christian United States as a new kind of nation."[16] Sigourney is critical of historians "who were more accustomed to stigmatize, than to praise the natives."[17] Her social criticism is rights-based in a truly progressive sense, unhesitatingly welcoming the participation of Native Americans in modern life. But the historical frame is not simply foreign in a general sense; it is specifically Christian and colonial. The sons of Uncas take on biblical names and are eventually institutionalized: the family descends from Oneco to Joshua (eldest son of Oneco), who is succeeded by brother kings Benjamin and Samuel, Mahomet and Isiah Uncas, the last of the line, who received a partial education at the seminary of President Wheelock, in Connecticut. In isolation, this may seem either a sentimental tale of decline or perhaps a more optimistic history of social adaptation. Yet there is an inherent, and inherently dominating, ethics of progress that resituates Native American culture with respect to world history, in line with the noted glory and fall of the kingdoms of Greece, Israel, England, and Persia. The sweep of history necessitates the transition from tribal nations to nation-states that facilitate modernization on a global scale. Although Sigourney, like Scott with the Highlands, does justice to the greatness of a people, the characteristics and priorities of Western progress define their new place in a colonized world.

The broad theme of social transformation plays out in more precise ways in Sigourney's portrayal of Revolutionary America. Conversion stories are prominent: of an ascetic, repentant Native American converted by a Jesuit in Canada; of the Indian Maurice, who served England, was saved by a priest, and lived as a hermit in America; and of Primus, an aged African who memorized the Bible and told stories of his slavery to American children. The right conduct of minorities, institutions, and families is integral to the moral prosperity of the new republic: Beulah and Cuffee are studious, church-going, free blacks; a charitable school helps the poor help themselves; and Farmer Larkin and his family are pious, industrious, respectful, educated, and tolerant of other faiths. Republican education of this sort was not unknown, of course; Susanna Rowson's *Charlotte Temple: A Tale of Truth* (1791) was popular and Catharine Maria Sedgwick's *A New-England Tale; or, Sketches of New-England Character and Manners* (1822) was no less committed to moral instruction.[18] Sigourney's sketches become more interesting as she develops the American mythology of national foundations. She does this in two ways: first, by painting a picture of 200 Mohegans departing for another land, seemingly by choice (some stay behind); second, by retelling patriotic war stories of Benedict Arnold, Bunker Hill, and George Washington. On the one hand, the departure of Native Americans is an unfortunate aspect of world history; on the other hand, tales of American bravery and military exploits bring glory to the republic. This is myth making at its most influential, playing upon archetypal figures – the noble savage and the American soldier – that would occupy a central place in popular culture for years to come. Playing further upon a dominant view of history as linear and progressive, Sigourney makes clear that there was no going back. The final sketch tells the history of Oriana in a letter delivered to a clergyman following her death: she married, traveled to America, and braved the war, which resulted in the death of her husband and her capture by Natives; she was saved by an old "Indian" named Arrowhamet (also known as Zachary), who had been converted to Christianity; and she lived among the Natives as the adopted daughter of Zachary and his wife. In the end, she comes to appreciate their way of life and sees how little is understood of them, before finally becoming ill and dying. In this way, Sigourney ends as she begins, by weaving sketches of Western characteristics and Native decline into world history as it plays out on American soil, that is, within a larger frame that projects a singular path forward – Oriana's increased knowledge of the life of Native Americans, however interesting, does not lead to social integration but instead to a selectively inclusive American project.

In the wake of *The Spy*, the novel became a significant contributor to the many forms of republican education emerging alongside advances in literacy, reading, and education.[19] As Sigourney's *Sketch of Connecticut* indicates, the lessons could be at once didactic and complex. Unfortunately, despite ongoing efforts to recover both popular and obscure texts, critical interpretation of the American historical novel is often limited by analysis of the same few novels through a certain lens. One example is the repeated use of Lydia Maria Child's *Hobomok: A Tale of Early Times* (1824), Cooper's *The Last of the Mohicans: A Narrative of 1757* (1826), and Sedgwick's *Hope Leslie, or, Early Times in the Massachusetts* (1827).[20] Carolyn Karcher is correct when she remarks that American historical novels were "Designed specifically to forge a nationalist consciousness and cultural identity in the newly independent United States."[21] But the repeated evaluation of consciousness and identity through readings of gender and race in this selection of novels cannot speak to the wider scope of novel use in the American republic.

68   *How the West was one*

The aims are laudable: to restore the central place of women in American literary history, partly by tracing a more accurate history of influence with respect to a subject or type of novel. For example, Nina Baym suggests that *The Last of the Mohicans* was a response to *Hobomok* and that *Hope Leslie* was a response to *The Last of the Mohicans*;[22] Karcher adds that Cooper's *The Wept of Wish-ton-Wish: A Tale* (1829) responded to *Hope Leslie*.[23] Johanna McElwee, however, is right to downplay the overemphasis of such connections and also to argue, along with Susanne Opfermann, that each author "employed the theme of Indian-white relations for different reasons."[24] Stephen Arch is more direct in his criticism of anti-historical and over-determined analyses comparing *Hobomok* and *Hope Leslie* to Cooper's novels.[25] Part of the problem is the simplification of a vast oeuvre to a couple of Cooper's novels read narrowly as conservative tales of miscegenation and American progress, although selection is an issue in other ways. For instance, on the one hand, neither *Hobomok* nor *Hope Leslie* is as radical as some critics would have readers believe. In short, both were situated by historical context, as well as authorial interests. More directly, Domhnall Mitchell argues that in both novels, Native Americans are integrated into the plot for conventional poetic reasons; despite the strong characterization of Native Americans, the resolutions, as in Sigourney's *Sketch of Connecticut*, do not project social integration but instead "the disappearance of the Indian as a separate entity. Intercourse leads to the death of the Native American character."[26] On the other hand, although *Hobomok* and *Hope Leslie* do offer groundbreaking portrayals of women and critical representations of race relations in early American society, neither novel represents the diverse work of either Child or Sedgwick. In sum, then, the Child-Sedgwick-Cooper triangle emphasizes a gendered categorization of novel types more reflective of contemporary priorities,[27] thus avoiding the core issue – meaning-as-use – which applied no less to Child and Sedgwick than to Cooper. Authors used the historical novel to communicate their own interpretations of modernity, according to their own experience, circumstances, and interests; the results, even by the same author, were varied.[28]

Patriotic tales of the Revolutionary War were of the moment in the mid-1820s and 1830s. Child's *The Rebels, or, Boston Before the Revolution* (1826) was just such a tale – a melodramatic account of national heroism in turbulent times.[29] The appeal did not fade quickly. Nearly ten years later, John Pendleton Kennedy's bestseller *Horse Shoe Robinson: A Tale of the Tory Ascendency* (1835) took up the Revolution in Carolina and Virginia.[30] Less famously, Sedgwick would also pick up the thread – and like so many others, *Waverley* – in *The Linwoods, or, "Sixty Years Since" in America* (1835). *The Linwoods* is predominantly a romance of republican values set during a moment of national crisis. The Revolution is a historical turning point; alliances separate friends and families – life will not be the same again. Nonetheless, Sedgwick does not trace a historical trajectory so much as set out a patriotic vision of national origins. The action of the novel is situated between broad characterizations of European and American society, especially British colonialism and Yankee republicanism. The glories of the republic depend on heroism in several forms: the down-and-out soldiers of the republic who give up everything for their sons; the sublime figure of Washington; and not least, the strength of character of the American woman. The stage is filled with melodramatic figures. Eliot Lee is the brave, young republican soldier that will lead the fight against oppression. Washington is the God-like genius upon which all depends. American women, the portrayals of which are more convincing, have a powerful impact on both sides of the conflict, which is painted in stark terms. The character of America is forged in the heat of revolutionary struggle. Isabella Linwood – too noble, too independent of mind – cannot marry aristocratic Jasper Meredith, a conniving rake, and remain on the side of the Royalists. Similarly, her brother Herbert Linwood defies his father and sides with the Republicans. The story of the Linwood family is the story of America – of coming-of-age, of generational change, of freedom – a vision of America based on a moral and intellectual ideal of the republic. Notably, national maturity comes as the result of a conflict of values between Americans and Britons; Native Americans are not present. This is not a novel of social criticism in the vein of *Hobomok* or *Hope Leslie*. Similarly, this is not a novel of modernization – political economy, for instance, plays no role in the advancement or definition of American values. As a sentimental novel that pits the feelings and impulses of the popular and generous people (Americans) against the calculations and plans of despised and selfish oppressors (British), *The Linwoods* is a novel of identity construction dependent upon the opposition to British presumption. The victor, American republicanism, comes shining through as the right political organization for a country of unconquerable, noble spirits favored by the will of heaven. As such, *The Linwoods* is another picture of American origins that caters to the populism of patriotic fervor. The complex question is, who are we? The answer is powerful because it is simple: we are Americans. The ending, in fact, is so bright, so neat, that ironies inevitably seep through. Rose, a black woman, watches the British fleet departing New York and declares that "this an't to be the land for them that strut in scarlet broadcloth and gold epaulette, and live upon the sweat of working people's brow."[31]

Famously, William Gilmore Simms fought for just such a land. Just as men and women are often treated as occupying separate spheres of American literary history, Simms – a Southern writer supportive of slavery – almost single-handedly occupies one side of an unbalanced North-South literary divide. The fact that his fiction is remembered as upholding Southern values puts him in an awkward position, to say the least. Cooper may be portrayed as conservative by degrees in relation to Child and Sedgwick, on certain issues at least, but Simms is more easily relegated to the margins of literary criticism due to the controversial politics that define him. Simms, to put it bluntly, wrote for the wrong side – in several ways. And yet for this reason,

70   *How the West was one*

his use of the historical novel is informative. Simms's localization of modern history is of interest here, as is his changing use of the historical novel over the course of a career that stretched from the 1830s to the Civil War.

As with other American novelists, the Waverley novels were a major influence on Simms, who wrote that Scott was "more perfect, more complete and admirable, than any writer of his age."[32] The critical framing of Scott's impact on Simms is important. Mary Ann Wimsatt sees Scott as setting forth a middle way that emerges from the conflict between two extremes, referring specifically to *Waverley* (1814), *Old Mortality* (1816), *Ivanhoe* (1820), and *Woodstock* (1826). This view of Scott derives from Georg Lukács's influential study, *The Historical Novel*, and is perpetuated by a selection of Waverley novels that emphasize civil conflict and national reconciliation. Wimsatt is accurate when she writes of what Cooper and Simms did with Scott: "They employed his basic structures but made changes in them that reflect their perceptions of their country's history, which was different in fundamental ways from that of Britain."[33] Cooper and Simms, like other American novelists, reinterpreted Waverley novels for their own purposes. However, to say that the history of America was fundamentally different masks an important point; modernization fueled international wars as well as domestic conflict. Wimsatt argues that American history was based on expulsion of the enemy rather than the reconciliation highlighted by Scott. But the Clearances were a form of expulsion, and modernity was fundamental in both cases. In turn, capitalism and industrialism facilitated social transformations embodied by emigration, racism, and colonialism on both sides of the Atlantic. Simms's use of the historical novel was first American and later regional, but it was always a response to historical conditions originating from elsewhere. Accordingly, the historical novel was used to address transatlantic continuities as well as situational differences. Unlike Scott, though, the purpose of Simms's localization of the historical novel was to fend off foreign constructions of progress.

Simms's most popular novel, and the one most often cited by critics, is *The Yemassee: A Romance of Carolina* (1835), which is set in the early-eighteenth century.[34] Unfortunately, as Masahiro Nakamura contends, the frequent use of this novel has "often encouraged literary scholars to undervalue him as an epigone of James Fenimore Cooper or to denigrate his Southern-type demythicization of romantic images of the noble savage."[35] Like *Hobomok* and *Hope Leslie*, *The Yemassee* describes early conflict between colonists and Native Americans. Simms's later colonial and Revolutionary War romances are set in the low country from the founding of the Carolina colony in the late-seventeenth century through the Indian Wars and the Revolution. The conflict between Native Americans and colonists does not disappear, but as in *The Linwoods*, the emphasis shifts to conflict between the Americans and the British. Simms was intent on establishing the contributions of South Carolina to the Revolution. *The Partisan: A Tale of the Revolution* (1835), for example, portrays the early stages of the British

How the West was one   71

occupation of the colony, involving patriot losses to the British at Charleston and Camden and the growth of partisan strength in the coastal region under Francis Marion and his militia troops.[36] Again, as in *The Linwoods*, the Revolutionary War romances are strongly biased against the British. As Charles Watson argues, American historical fiction – often patriotic and romantic – was used for didactic purposes, and Simms, like his Northern counterparts, aimed to "supply moral instruction."[37] The purpose, however, was not to align the sensibilities of North and South as a new, modern republic envisioned by the likes of Sigourney or Cooper. The Revolutionary War romances are patriot histories of the South featuring aristocracy from Charleston, the plantations, and the rural middle class on one side, and the indictment of the moneyed aristocracy, or Loyalists, on the other. Though the thematic scope is broader than such an opposition suggests, even in these early novels Simms was interested in protecting Southern civilization from the encroachment of modernity, or progress as defined by the North.[38] To cite one example, in *The Partisan*, Katharine Walton's chastity embodies the rejection of invasion; charming black characters serve their masters well and uphold the system in place; and Robert Singleton, the perfect Southern gentleman and military leader, idealizes aristocratic leadership. Although Simms drew upon themes common to literature of the North and the South, such as American patriotism and anti-British sentiment, over the years, he worked the historical novel for increasingly specific purposes. His response to modernity – and his vision of the South – conformed to a communication situation that required regional differentiation.

In line with Simms's belief in the value of history as a form of moral instruction that could guide the progress of the people,[39] his concern with the fate of the South supplanted the prioritization of nationalism. Wimsatt outlines how his Border romances of 1838–42 present "a clash between the ordered society of the plantation South and the unbridled license of the far frontier."[40] Despite Simms's change in setting, the broad aim of communicating moral instruction remains the same; however, the instructions are more specific to bourgeois readers of romance in the South. In each novel, the lead character returns from the frontier to "the responsible life of the agricultural society that embodies, in Simms's view, the fullest potential of antebellum culture."[41] Simms proposed an antidote to the disorder of Western expansion, and thus to modernity itself, in the form of a chivalric, orderly society epitomized by the Southern plantation. Accordingly, by the late 1840s, the North had become the new enemy. From *Katherine Walton; or, The Rebel of Dorchester* (1851) onward, Simms wrote militant, sectionalist novels.[42] As opposed to colonial origins and national conflict, his novels increasingly responded to contemporary politics, embracing the defense of Carolina, slavery, and the plantation. Famously, in the wake of Harriet Beecher Stowe's *Uncle Tom's Cabin; or, Life Among the Lowly* (1852), Simms responded with *The Sword and the Distaff; or, "Fair, Fat and Forty," A Story of the South, at the Close of Revolution* (1853; later

72 *How the West was one*

renamed *Woodcraft*), which defended slavery as an institution – the Fugitive Slave Act of 1850 in particular – and also called for militancy against the North.[43] Simms's literary and political trajectory was not complete, however; as Watson describes, "In *The Forayers, or, the Raid of the Dog Days* (1855) and *Eutaw: A Sequel* (1856), Simms foresaw the coming of Southern independence in the glorious finale of the American Revolution."[44] From the 1850s, Simms became a regional commentator on issues of national significance and a spokesman for Southern secession in the years leading up to the Civil War; the historical novel was for him a pulpit that had little to do with the early history of America and everything to do with the vindication of Southern values in the face of contemporary threats to social order, which were perhaps signaled most emphatically by the domestic and transatlantic popularity of *Uncle Tom's Cabin*. Identity and prosperity in the South were intimately tied to the use of slave labor – an economic system that was under threat with the growing movement against slavery centered in the North. The changes Simms made for the new and revised edition of his novels published from 1853 to 1860 are indicative of the divide; Simms not only added polemical introductions but also altered the content of individual novels, thus hardening his stance against the North and refining his revisionist history of the South.[45] This, it should be noted, stood in stark contrast to the anti-slavery efforts of, for example, Lydia Maria Child, who was the editor of *National Anti-Slavery Standard* from 1841 to 1843 and the author of *A Romance of the Republic*, a novel designed to counter the popular claims that racial intermarriage was "unnatural" and that slavery was a benevolent institution. Thus, by the 1850s, Simms, despite his early popularity in the North as well as the South, occupied an increasingly isolated position with respect to the main current of American literature. But as Nakamura and other scholars have helped to make clear, Simms's sectional political agenda should not obscure the fact that his novels point productively to varied use of the historical novel to communicate a range of American responses to modernization.[46]

The historical novel was used by American writers to create visions of an American republic that could bring order to a disordered and uncertain new world. Such visions were regional and patriotic in different ways: Sigourney envisioned an agrarian, middle-class, Christian republic; Sedgwick described a revolutionary transformation from British colonialism to American republicanism; and Simms, in his opposition to modernity, set the South against the North. Cooper was no less interested in the future of the American republic, but the basis of his view of America was not specifically moral, patriotic, or regional. Early on, Cooper flirted with the idea of a series of historical narratives closely aligned with the republican histories that underpinned so many popular accounts of the American past. According to John McWilliams, "In 1824–25, Cooper was planning thirteen fully elaborated and historically researched novels, dealing with formative events and personalities of the American Revolution, balancing

How the West was one   73

the claims of the old and new orders, and comprising a collective achievement very like the then-emerging sequence to be titled 'The Waverley Novels.' "[47] Honoré de Balzac would later envision a similar project for France. Notably, neither Cooper nor Balzac took up the historical novel in this way. It was not that the topic had been exhausted; many novels of the sort would follow. But for Cooper as for Balzac, emerging circumstances required an investigation of the origins and development of modernity rather than the projection of national ideals. With *The Pathfinder; or, The Inland Sea* (1840), then, Cooper did not replicate the patriotic Revolutionary War novel popular in the 1820s and 1830s. Like Scott and Balzac, he was interested in how characteristics of modernity shaped larger issues of fundamental importance to his nation-state. Following early novels that placed greater emphasis on the relationship between frontier exploration and settlement, his approach changed after his return from Europe in 1833.

In the 1820s, according to Wayne Franklin, "Cooper had authored something like 10 percent of all the novels published by American authors. He was the dominant creative force in American fiction across that period."[48] In contrast, by most accounts, the 1830s were not kind to Cooper. Stephen Arch, for instance, refers to a "lacuna in the Cooper canon, seven years of work (1832–39) that has been and can be safely ignored by all but the most serious and assiduous of Cooper scholars."[49] Following his stint in Europe from 1826 to 1833, Cooper returned home out of favor, due in part to his blunt criticism of America in *Notions of the Americans: Picked Up By a Travelling Bachelor* (1828).[50] The situation did not change as a result of critical works such as *A Letter to His Countrymen* (1834) and *The American Democrat, or, Hints on the Social and Civic Relations of the United States of America* (1838).[51] Similarly, his travel narratives (all set in Europe) and *History of the Navy of the United States of America* (1839) were not styled to enhance his popularity in America.[52] His satirical novels – social criticism in another form – were no more successful in this regard. So, the story goes that Cooper, at the suggestion of Richard Bentley (his English publisher), returned to the Leatherstocking novels – which began with *The Pioneers*, continued with *The Last of the Mohicans*, and seemed to have ended with the death of the protagonist, Natty Bumppo, in *The Prairie: A Tale* (1827).[53] In this light, *The Pathfinder* seems a calculated return to popular reception after a decade of failures. Steven Harthorn refers to numerous reviews seemingly delighted with Cooper's return to "pure" romance.[54] However, such estimations were shortsighted then and are misleading now. Cooper's return to Natty Bumppo, known also as Pathfinder, and the frontier romance, served a commercial purpose; regardless, the outcome was a consequence of Cooper's travels and writing abroad.

In his European trilogy, Cooper sets each novel in a period of transition, from feudal to modern times. If the emphasis is not specifically on the transformation to capitalist society, the general concern with modern progress

74 *How the West was one*

is clear. *The Bravo: A Tale* (1831) is set during the Renaissance; *The Heidenmauer: A Legend of the Rhine* (1832) is set in the Reformation; and *The Headsman, or, The Abbaye des Vignerons: A Tale* (1833) is set in the Enlightenment.[55] Arch writes that "After witnessing European society, culture, and politics firsthand, Cooper turned in these three novels to a critique of the ways in which all European governments – despotic, aristocratic, republican, or enlightened – warped their citizens by treating them as things, not people."[56] Beyond a critique of government control, I read these novels as a three-part study of how institutions and people constituted and were constituted by social transformation leading to an international system of nation-states. The lessons were especially relevant to an American audience given ongoing experimentation in the new republic. Cooper used various literary forms to communicate such lessons. His travel narratives are similarly acute descriptions of the development of European society that might have been read with an eye to American progress. As fictional extensions of Cooper's observations of European history and culture, his satirical works later in the decade are more directly critical of America. Additionally, with each novel, Cooper travels closer to home. *The Monikins* (1835) is an allegorical sociopolitical novel that critiques American capitalism.[57] *Homeward Bound, or, The Chase: A Tale of the Sea* (1838) depicts a journey from England to New York via adventures in Africa and elsewhere.[58] *Home as Found* (1838) is set in New York.[59] One might argue, however, that Cooper did not really achieve his purpose until 1840, following a decade of work that traces a trajectory from the heart of feudal Europe to the shores of capitalist America. Franklin remarks that Cooper used *The Pathfinder* to reassert a sense of moral authority to counter what he saw as the troubled path of the republic.[60] Arch argues that Cooper returns to "his early profession as a historical romancer, but he would return then as a different kind of artist and a different kind of American."[61] In the first case, it is still a matter of Cooper attempting to instruct Americans; in the second, it was a matter of effective communication. Both points are relevant; I contend that by the end of the 1830s, he could also depict American history in terms of the fundamental axes of modernity, namely capitalism and industrialization, that drove international conflicts and informed America's version of the nation-state. The resurrection of Natty Bumppo was a response to market demand, but the tale itself was a product of Cooper's attunement to the consequences of modernity in the American context.

As noted, in the 1830s, the historical novel often took the form of Indian captivity tales or Revolutionary War romances. Novels such as Montgomery Bird's *Nick of the Woods, or, The Jibbenainosay: A Tale of Kentucky* (1837), which demonized Native Americans, Ann Stephens's *Malaeska; or The Indian Wife of the White Hunter* (1839), which became the first Beadle and Adams Dime Novel in 1860, and *The Linwoods* were written and published, however differently, to interest as many American readers as possible.[62] Wallace argues that with *The Pathfinder*, Cooper wrote a novel "that

How the West was one   75

would find its way into every library, that would have attractions for the feeblest intellects, yet would not be rejected by the strongest – a democratic novel representing the culture of the new nation."[63] Here, too, there is the sense that Cooper returned to commercial fiction in the wake of a decade during which his popularity waned. The conditions were in place; for example, common use of the term "Leather-Stocking" to refer to frontier figures or behaviors was indicative of the furtive ground awaiting Cooper's return to his most popular character, Natty, who had already become an iconic figure of American culture.[64] *The Pathfinder*, like many other novels of the period, may be said to have combined frontier romance and patriotic adventure with the aim of achieving commercial success; and relative to most novels of the period, it was widely read, at least among those who could afford to purchase or borrow a copy. However, it was a "democratic novel representing the culture of the new nation" not because it was an easy read or because it took up commercially viable themes, but because it showed how the transition to industrial capitalism affected national character at an early stage of American history. Franklin notes that "None of the hundred or so novels published before 1820 by Americans had taken up in any serious way the country's decisive post-colonial event – the political and military liberation from Britain."[65] This changed with *The Spy*, but it remained for Cooper, among others, to take up modernization in the American context. *The Pathfinder* was an act of modernity in several ways, not least as it took up the historification of America's past from the perspective of the nation-state, of which the enterprising nature was becoming clearer to American readers by the 1840s.

Early in *The Pathfinder*, Cooper writes, "It will be remembered that this was in the year 175–, or long before even speculation had brought any portion of Western New-York within the bounds of civilization, or the projects of the adventurous."[66] Put otherwise: Western (transatlantic) civilization (modernity) is bounded (defined) by the project (practices) of speculation (capitalism). The setting of *The Pathfinder* is not simply a vast, boundless forest or the unfathomable breadth of Lake Ontario. Nature is something to behold – literally – as in a painting, as is the case for the heroine of the novel, Mabel: "For the first time since she had left her room, Mabel now turned her eyes beneath her, and got a view of what might be called the fore-ground of the remarkable picture she had been studying with so much pleasure."[67] Two interrelated perspectives come into play. First, following this abstracted view of nature from the fort, land is subsequently framed in terms of ownership; Oswego is "one of the extreme frontier posts of the British possessions on this continent."[68] Second, at the intersection of nature and property, American identity and power take shape; although originally occupied by a Scotch battalion, "many Americans had been received, since its arrival in this country, an innovation that had led the way to Mabel's father filling the humble but responsible situation of the oldest serjeant. A few young officers also, who were natives of the Colonies, were to be found in this

76 *How the West was one*

corps."[69] This historical novel does not hinge on a revolutionary break with Britain. For all the violence in the forest, Cooper sets out a rather smooth transition from British colonialism to a new generation of Americans that will carry "projects of the adventurous" forward in the New World. John McWilliams rightly claims that "Rather than leaping to utopian portrayals of agrarian communities, Cooper's novels concern the awkward transition between the State of Nature and the State of Civilization."[70] This, however, is only one of two transitions in progress. In the American historical novels already discussed, sketching this "awkward transition" meant an illustration of political independence and cultural differentiation cloaked in patriotism. Although *The Pathfinder* represents the settlement of the wilderness, the primary transition is in fact a form of continuity – international wars in America are the first step toward the addition of the United States to an interlocking system of nation-states. In this sense, the "awkwardness" of Native dispossession and colonial infighting fade to the background as the transatlantic expression of modernity in the American context comes to the fore with the novel's resolution.

The outcome of the struggle on Lake Ontario says much of Cooper's assessment of modern progress in America. Arrowhead is killed and June is left a widow, isolated from her own tribe; Cap returns to his seafaring way of life and Pathfinder retreats into the forest; Scottish soldiers are massacred, Duncan the Laird returns to Scotland, and of the two villains besides Arrowhead, Lieutenant Muir (Scottish) is killed and Captain Sanglier (French) is released following defeat. Although the Americans remain, the way forward is not at the frontier. Mabel and Jasper marry and move to New York, where Jasper becomes a merchant and Mabel bears several sons. On the way to this highly productive union, Mabel rejects Arrowhead, Muir, and Pathfinder – representative of the "native owners of the soil,"[71] the foreign occupants of the soil, and outsiders who will only look on from the periphery of American progress. The heart of the matter is modernization – how American identity is defined by the context-specific application of modern practices. The novel is often seen as combining two genres, frontier romance and nautical fiction, in part because Cooper excelled at both. The more critical intersection set forth by *The Pathfinder* is that between modern European history and American identity. In this view, to be American is to have the requisite skills to prosper in modern America. Throughout the novel, the skills linked to forest, river, lake, and ocean separate Pathfinder, Native Americans, Jasper, and Cap according to upbringing and education, but this differentiation points more directly to their ability to thrive in modern America. Notably, when Pathfinder is on the Scud, he is least effective; like Cap, he is out of his element on Lake Ontario. The inland sea requires a certain skill set, and only Jasper can save the day. Pathfinder's displacement and Jasper's fit are two sides of the same coin: the space of modernity. As William Kelly notes, "For the first time in the Leatherstocking Tales, we see [Pathfinder] as a confused and troubled figure whose aim is uncertain."[72] He

How the West was one   77

is described by Cap as "being neither brig, nor schooner";[73] he is of "middle age";[74] and for the first time in his life, he attends to a woman rather than the needs of the fort. The implications of his uncertainty are multiple. As George Dekker argues, this

> is the only Leatherstocking tale in which Natty Bumppo at all resembles the wavering hero of a Scott novel. Here for the first and only time we see him waver between the life he has always led – untrammelled by property, responsible only to his own strict code and conscience, free to follow his own bent away from white European society – and the life of a border family man with all that that implies in terms of a wife who must be kept content with her lot, children who must be properly educated, property which must be acquired and protected.[75]

Pathfinder's inability to settle is a recurring theme throughout the Leatherstocking novels, but the context changes over the course of his life. In *The Deerslayer, or, The First War-Path: A Tale* (1841), as a young man experiencing his first adventures, he refuses Judith's proposal – he *will not* settle.[76] Whereas in *The Pathfinder*, about twenty years later, the outcome is out of his hands. At this later date, in this situation, settlement is no longer an option. McWilliams claims that "to acquiesce or to revolt, to remain or to flee,"[77] is the crucial choice before Pathfinder. Ultimately, however, Mabel makes the decision. As Dekker describes, at stake are issues of freedom and responsibility, which are tightly connected to property and thus the emergence of a nation-state. The question is, what does it mean to be American? The answer is, to be modern. For Cooper, this is the fork in the road that points to the larger historical circumstances and social requirements for belonging and advancement in America. Initially, Pathfinder's alienation is framed with respect to spiritual concerns and political loyalty:

> I have attended church-sarvice in the garrisons, and tried hard, as becomes a true soldier, to join in the prayers; for though no enlisted sarvant of the King, I fight his battles and sarve his cause, and so I have endivoured to worship garrison-fashion, but never could raise within me, the solemn feelings and true affection, that I feel when alone with God, in the forest.[78]

Although such terms usefully describe Pathfinder's position and outlook, they also point to the fluidity of the situation. Cap says that he "found scarcely a man in all York" who would think of things as he did, adding that "it is a difficult thing to find a man – I mean a landsman – who views these matters, to-day exactly as he looked at them, forty years ago."[79] Here, perhaps, is a reference to the historicity of *Waverley*'s "sixty years since," but it is better understood as a reference to the sort of social transformation described in a novel such as *The Heart of Mid-Lothian*. As the

78   *How the West was one*

following exchange between Pathfinder and Cap indicates, the practical impact of modernity on social life is incompatible with traditional views of community. Pathfinder says, "And yet God is unchanged – his works are unchanged – his holy word is unchanged – and all that ought to bless and honor his name should be unchanged too!"; Cap responds, "Not ashore. That is the worst of the land, it is all the while in motion, I tell you, though it looks so solid."[80] Speaking from wilderness and sea, respectively, Pathfinder and Cap look upon the dizzying pace of American development from a distance, and seemingly from the past. More to the point, there is no land, only property, which is "all the while in motion"; all is exchange upon the plane of modernity, which creates varying levels of existential anxiety, as well as social divisions. During this conversation between Pathfinder and Cap, Mabel asks, "Do you understand this, Jasper?"[81] The question, whispered no less, suggests a generational difference with material consequences.

The replacement of Pathfinder with Jasper as Mabel's preferred husband further defines Cooper's portrayal of American progress. As McWilliams suggests, "The asocial hero is replaced by a middle-class white frontiersman."[82] But Jasper *Western* ends up a merchant on the East Coast, not a frontiersman. On Lake Ontario, Jasper shows himself a worthy captain in difficult circumstances, and he is proven innocent of the charge of treason. More imperative than such trials, which justify the repositioning of French-speaking Jasper as substantively American, repeated hints of his inclination toward the settlements, despite (or following on) his upbringing on the frontier, describe a coming-of-age that speaks more to urban social development than to personal inclinations; "I would," says Jasper, "go into the settlements and towns."[83] The more essential point is that he can – and does. Even Pathfinder refers to Jasper's education and suitability for marriage with a woman like Mabel: "Then he is quite a scholar – knows the tongue of the Frenchers – reads many books, and some, I know, that you like to read yourself – can understand you at all times, which, perhaps, is more than I can say for myself."[84] Pathfinder confesses to Dunham, "I found myself so much beneath her in idees, that I was afraid to speak of much beyond what belonged to my own gifts,"[85] and Mabel reflects, "To me, Jasper Eau douce appears to know more than most of the young men of his class."[86] The marriage of Jasper and Mabel, in this estimation, is not only a good match in terms of social qualities and personal preferences; it also points to the practicalities of life in New York.[87] The motivating message behind the union of Jasper and Mabel is well-defined – to be modern is to be able to get on in modern life. In this way, *The Pathfinder*, contrary to Cooper's reputation as a writer of frontier romance and in line with many society novels of the period, is a manual of modernity that points east rather than west.

Early on, Pathfinder sees Mabel's choice as one between the forests and the lake, saying, "Here you have both our domains, Jasper's and mine."[88] Once Mabel rejects his suit, he realizes that the choice is between the frontier and the settlements. Dana Nelson writes that Pathfinder is "rejected in

How the West was one 79

favor of a younger man."[89] Mabel's choice, however, is not based on age, although, as noted, there is a generational shift in evidence. The deciding factor is situational possibilities, or more simply, life prospects in modern America. As Mitchell suggests, "this is a novel where directions are just as important as destinations, and which is crucially concerned with a variety of transitions."[90] In contrast, "Pathfinder and Jasper," writes Richard Dilworth Rust, "reflect the major physical dualities of the book, land and water, which are reconciled in the title *The Pathfinder, or, The Inland Sea* and in the closing chapters of the book."[91] But this is not a novel about geography, unless perhaps human geography comes into play. The chief duality is between interconnected stages of development – frontier exploration and commercial civilization – and the related consequences with respect to subjectivity and social practices. Jasper moves to the Eastern Seaboard, where the true heart of capitalist America, despite the popular romance with Western expansion, is taking shape – Pathfinder does not.

One of the more agonizing depictions in Cooper's fiction is that of Pathfinder coming to the realization that he does not belong. He says that if Mabel could fancy a rude hunter and guide, he would quit his wandering ways and try to "humanize" his mind "down to a wife and children."[92] Such sentiments are immediately replaced by doubts: "Do you think the gal will consent to quit all her beloved settlement usages, and her visitin's, and church-goin's to dwell with a plain guide and hunter, up, hereaway, in the woods? Will she not in the ind crave her old ways, and a better man?"[93] Dunham is right when he suggests that a better man would be hard to find, but only because he refers to the frontier rather than the settlements. Pathfinder and Mabel are both white Christians eligible to be united in marriage; with respect to race and religion, there is no issue. But the cultural difference remains; as Pathfinder says, "Mabel and I are so nearly alike, that I feel weighed down with a load that is hard to bear, at finding us so unlike."[94] The more suitable man, in line with America's emerging identity as a middle-class nation-state, is modern Jasper Western.[95]

The novel plays at length with the possibility of a frontier romance; Mabel and Pathfinder appear to reach an understanding when Mabel says, "One feels nearer to God, in such a spot, I think, than when the mind is distracted by the objects of the towns."[96] But for Mabel to settle in the wilderness with Pathfinder would be to remove herself from history – the trajectory of the republic does not rest with a return to nature, but rather, the exploitation of it. As with *The Heart of Mid-Lothian*, this is a tale of tomorrow, designed to reflect on the historical trajectory of a modern nation-state. Tellingly, when Pathfinder answers, "These are our streets and houses; our churches and palaces,"[97] even he effectively puts nature at the service of the state. The divide is complete; there can be no reconciliation. The sublime forests are now mapped, appropriated, even in the mind of Pathfinder, who facilitates exactly such processes through his work as a guide for the British military. Geoffrey Rans describes *The Pathfinder* as suppressing the social and

80   *How the West was one*

political urgency of previous novels; more particularly, he writes that "The replacement of nature unspoiled by settlements is simply not the crucial historical issue it is elsewhere."[98] Instead, he argues that the idealization of Natty is central throughout the novel; as such, "The break with civilization is made by Natty himself – it is *his* recognition, *his* will."[99] I contend that historical circumstances make Natty's alignment with civilization, and thus marriage to Mabel, impossible. Mabel seems to lean toward frontier life:

> I find I'm fast getting to be a frontier girl, and am coming to love all this grand silence of the woods. The towns seem tame to me, and, as my father will probably pass the remainder of his days, here, where he has already lived so long, I begin to feel that I should be happy to continue with him, and not return to the sea-shore.[100]

But as soon as Pathfinder reveals that her father has agreed to their marriage, such fanciful musings are forgotten. Mabel's response is definitive: "While I esteem, respect – nay reverence you, almost as much as I reverence my own dear father, it is impossible that I should ever become your wife – that I –."[101] The word "impossible" here indicates a disconnect between Pathfinder and Mabel but also the discontinuity of two ways of life, as the following exchange confirms: Pathfinder: "I do not – I shall never think in that way, again, Mabel"; Mabel: "A match like that would be unwise – unnatural, perhaps."[102] For the first time, Pathfinder sees that his gifts would not "please the fancy of a town bred gal."[103] Mabel tells Pathfinder that he will forget and think of her as a friend; his response is telling: "This may be the way in the towns, but I doubt if it's nat'ral to the woods."[104] The discord between them is not merely a matter of preferences; as Pathfinder says, "your ways have not been my ways."[105] The matter at hand is one of compatibility, although not so much with each other as with circumstances – the implications are broadly social and historical rather than merely personal. As Pathfinder says, "Like loves like, I tell you, sarjeant, and my gifts are not altogether the gifts of Mabel Dunham."[106] The novel reaches its conclusion, in Mitchell's words, as "The frontier shifts location to the East, and changes period to the historical present. In this uniquely American vision, progress is a programme which merges Christian and commercial elements. Western and Mabel together embody the Jeffersonian ideal, combining Scripture and capitalism simultaneously."[107] Common on both sides of the Atlantic before and after Cooper, the combination of religion and commerce was not a "uniquely American" prescription for progress. More importantly, *The Pathfinder* is not so much a *vision* of American progress as it is descriptive of American *realities*. Accordingly, Cooper rests his case in New York, the heart of urban life in modern America.[108]

Honoré de Balzac reviewed *The Pathfinder* for *Revue Parisienne* on July 25, 1840. He compares Scott to Cooper, stating that "the one initiates you into great human evolutions, the other into the mighty heart of

Nature herself."[109] Although highlighting Cooper's importance to the history of the novel, this generalization hides the more practical aims of *The Pathfinder* as an investigation of modernization. Balzac also emphasizes Pathfinder, describing him as "a statue, a magnificent moral hermaphrodite, born of the savage state and of civilization, who will live as long as literatures last."[110] As perhaps the only truly memorable character in the novel, Pathfinder is the most obvious hero, but Mabel is also referred to as "our hero"[111] and "our heroine."[112] She is the Jeanie Deans of the novel. Her character is rather uninspiring and her trajectory seems common, but that is the point – the lesson is widely applicable; Mabel is every woman, aspiring to the middle-class values and practices that typify the new republic. In the end, "Jasper and Mabel sate, resembling Milton's picture of our first parents, when the consciousness of sin first laid its leaden weight on their souls."[113] But as with the establishment of Jeanie and Reuben at Knocktarlitie in *The Heart of Mid-Lothian*, this new beginning, despite the Christian frame, results from "reason and judgement."[114] The final sight of Pathfinder is iconic: "When last in view, the sinewy frame of this extraordinary man was as motionless, as if it were a statue set up in that solitary place, to commemorate the scenes of which it had so lately been the site and the witness."[115] As Wayne Franklin argues, Cooper may have returned to the Leatherstocking novels in part to resuscitate Natty as a moral counterweight to the direction of the American republic.[116] And as Balzac suggested, people would revisit Natty – a cultural monument to times gone by. But those people, like Mabel and Jasper, would be middle-class Americans who wanted to know more about their past to better gauge the present and make informed decisions about the direction of their own lives. It is possible to read *The Pathfinder* as nothing more than popular melodrama – an addition to the long line of patriotic frontier novels through the 1820s and 1830s – rather than a historical investigation of modern practices that would have been of use to contemporary readers located primarily in urban settings. William Owen, for example, suggests that "The reassertion of the romantic plot at the close of the novel is gratuitous moral reassurance that good triumphs and evil receives its just reward."[117] However, the resolution offers more than generic stereotypes (which could be productive, nonetheless). George Dekker writes that Cooper's "early tales are variants of the historical novel created by Scott," but argues that "*The Pathfinder* does not belong to this genre."[118] Whereas the early tales are concerned with "the fate of rival cultures, rival societies" or "the inexorable movement westward of white civilization,"[119] *The Pathfinder* is a depiction of "community."[120] In my view, this division is unconvincing – early and later novels took up the matter of community development in America – but the emphasis on *The Pathfinder* as a contribution to better understanding of modern practices is accurate. Cooper aimed to do something different in 1840, more than a decade after his last Leatherstocking novel – to make visible the social consequences of modernization in America. In this sense,

82 *How the West was one*

The Heart of Mid-Lothian and *The Pathfinder* have much in common – both described how the West was one, in these respects at least: as constituted by axes of modernity – namely, capitalism and industrialism – that were transatlantic in scope; and in relation, by the historification of the past in ways that made sense to readers coping with their own experiences of the modernization of everyday life.

Notes

1 See Paul Giles, "Transatlantic Currents and the Invention of the American Novel," in *Cambridge History of the American Novel*, ed. Leonard Cassuto, Clare Eby, and Benjamin Reiss (New York: Cambridge University Press, 2011), 22–36. Giles describes how the eighteenth-century American novel "developed across a transatlantic axis and was shaped by European prototypes as much as by US political pressures" (ibid., 34). See also, Robert A. Gross, "Introduction: An Extensive Republic," in Gross and Kelley, *An Extensive Republic*, 28.

2 See, for example, James D. Hart, *The Popular Book: A History of America's Literary Taste* (New York: Oxford University Press, 1950); David Kaser, "*Waverley* in America," *Papers of the Bibliographical Society of America* 51 (1957), 163–67; Eva-Marie Kröller, "Walter Scott in America, English Canada, and Québec: A Comparison," *Canadian Revue of Comparative Literature* 7, no. 1 (Winter 1980), 32–46; St Clair, *Reading Nation*, 388; Fiona A. Black, "North America," in Bell, Finkelstein, and McCleery, *Ambition and Industry 1800–80*, 450; and James N. Green, "The Rise of Book Publishing," in Gross and Kelley, *An Extensive Republic*, 107–8.

3 Ronald J. Zboray, *A Fictive People: Antebellum Economic Development and the American Reading Public* (New York: Oxford University Press, 1993), xvii.

4 David Kaser, *Messrs. Carey & Lea of Philadelphia; A Study in the History of the Booktrade* (Philadelphia: University of Pennsylvania Press, 1957), 50.

5 William Charvat, *Literary Publishing in America, 1790–1850* (Philadelphia: University of Pennsylvania Press, 1959), 56.

6 James Fenimore Cooper, *Precaution; A Novel* (New York: A. T. Goodrich, 1820); *The Spy: A Tale of the Neutral Ground* (New York: Wiley and Halsted, 1821). On Cooper's dislike of being called "the American Scott," see James Franklin Beard, ed., *The Letters and Journals of James Fenimore Cooper*, vol. 2 (Cambridge, MA: The Belknap Press of Harvard University Press, 2004), 84. See also, Gardiner, review of *The Spy*, by James Fenimore Cooper, *North American Review* 15, no. 36 (July 1822): 275–82, www.jstor.org/stable/25109145. Gardiner questions the appropriateness of the term "Scott of America" (ibid.). George Dekker later kept the term alive in the title *James Fenimore Cooper: The American Scott* (New York: Barnes and Noble, 1967).

7 Feuchtwanger, *House of Desdemona*, 87. Wayne Franklin, "James Fenimore Cooper, 1789–1851: A Brief Biography," in *A Historical Guide to James Fenimore Cooper*, ed. Leland S. Person (Oxford: Oxford University Press, 2007), 38. See also, Ursula Brumm, *Geschichte und wildnis in der Amerikanischen literatur* (Berlin: Schmidt, 1980); Alan Leander McGregor, "The Historical Function of Historical Fiction: Walter Scott and James Fenimore Cooper" (PhD diss., University of California, Berkeley, 1984); Dekker, *American Historical Romance*; Barbara Buchenau, "'Wizards of the West'? How Americans Respond to Sir Walter Scott, the 'Wizard of the North,'" in *James Fenimore Cooper Society Website*, ed. Hugh C. Macdougall (webmaster) (Oneonta: State University of New York College, 1999), n. pag., http://external.oneonta.edu/cooper/articles/

How the West was one 83

suny/1997suny-buchenau.html; and Armin Paul Frank, "Writing Literary Independence: The Case of Cooper-the 'American Scott' and the Un-Scottish American," *Comparative Literature Studies* 34, no. 1 (1997): 41–70.

8 See James D. Wallace, *Early Cooper and His Audience* (New York: Columbia University Press, 1986). Wallace notes that "Cooper worked to expand his original audience's horizon of expectations while attracting new readers by adopting the historical romance, transferring his setting from England to America, and adding ethnic and regional characters" (ibid., 64).

9 John McWilliams, "Revolution and the Historical Novel: Cooper's Transforming of European Tradition," in *James Fenimore Cooper Society Website*, ed. Hugh C. Macdougall (webmaster) (Oneonta: State University of New York College, 1991), n. pag., http://external.oneonta.edu/cooper/articles/suny/1991suny-mcwilliams.html.

10 Winfried Fluck, "The Nineteenth-Century Historical Novel," in *Cambridge History of the American Novel*, ed. Leonard Cassuto, Clare Eby, and Benjamin Reiss (New York: Cambridge University Press, 2011), 122.

11 On the popularity of *The Spy*, see Alan Taylor, *William Cooper's Town: Power and Persuasion on the Frontier of the Early American Republic* (New York: Knopf, 1995), 408–9.

12 Donald A. Ringe and Lucy B. Ringe, "Historical Introduction," in *Lionel Lincoln; or, The Leaguer of Boston*, ed. Donald A. Ringe and Lucy B. Ringe (Albany: State University of New York Press, 1984), xv.

13 James Fenimore Cooper, *Lionel Lincoln; or, The Leaguer of Boston*, ed. Donald A. Ringe and Lucy B. Ringe (Albany: State University of New York Press, 1984).

14 L. H. [Lydia Huntley] Sigourney, *Sketch of Connecticut, Forty Years Since* (Hartford: Oliver D. Cooke and Sons, 1824), 164.

15 Ibid., 45.

16 Gary Kelly, introduction to *Lydia Sigourney: Selected Poetry and Prose*, ed. Gary Kelly (Peterborough, ON: Broadview Press, 2008), 33.

17 Sigourney, *Sketch of Connecticut*, 45.

18 Susanna Rowson, *Charlotte Temple: A Tale of Truth*, ed. Clara Marburg Kirk and Rudolf Kirk (New York: Twayne, 1964). Catharine Maria Sedgwick, *A New-England Tale; or, Sketches of New-England Character and Manners* (New York: E. Bliss and E. White, 1822).

19 Cathy N. Davidson, *Revolution and the Word: The Rise of the Novel in America* (New York: Oxford University Press, 1986), 70. Philip Gould, *Covenant and Republic: Historical Romance and the Politics of Puritanism* (Cambridge: Cambridge University Press, 1996), 10.

20 Lydia Maria Child, *Hobomok: A Tale of Early Times* (Boston: Cummings, Hilliard, 1824). James Fenimore Cooper, *The Last of the Mohicans: A Narrative of 1757* (London: R. Bentley, 1826). Catharine Maria Sedgwick, *Hope Leslie, or, Early Times in the Massachusetts* (New York: White, Gallaher and White, 1827).

21 Carolyn Karcher, *The First Woman in the Republic: A Cultural Biography of Lydia Maria Child* (Durham, NC: Duke University Press, 1994), 18.

22 Nina Baym, "How Men and Women Wrote Indian Stories," in *New Essays on The Last of the Mohicans*, ed. H. Daniel Peck (Cambridge: Cambridge University Press, 1992), 68.

23 Karcher, *First Woman*, 36. James Fenimore Cooper, *The Wept of Wish-ton-Wish: A Tale* (Philadelphia: Carey, Lea and Carey, 1829). Other examples of scholarship linking Child, Cooper, and Sedgwick are J. Gerald Kennedy, "National Narrative and the Problem of American Nationhood," in Samuels, *American Fiction*, 12–14; and Robert S. Levine, "Race and Ethnicity," in Samuels, *American Fiction*, 55.

84   *How the West was one*

24 Johanna McElwee, "The Nation Conceived: Learning, Education, and Nationhood in American Historical Novels of the 1820s" (PhD diss., Uppsala University, 2005), 26, www.diva-portal.org/smash/get/diva2:167469/FULLTEXT01.pdf. Susanne Opfermann, "Lydia Maria Child, James Fenimore Cooper, and Catharine Maria Sedgwick: A Dialogue on Race, Culture, and Gender," in *Soft Canons: American Women Writers and Masculine Tradition*, ed. Karen L. Kilcup (Iowa City: University of Iowa Press, 1999), 27–47.

25 Stephen Carl Arch, "Romancing the Puritans: American Historical Fiction in the 1820s," *ESQ* 39, no. 2/3 (1993): 109–11. See also, Gould, *Covenant and Republic*, 91–95.

26 Domhnall Mitchell, "Acts of Intercourse: 'Miscegenation' in Three 19th Century American Novels," *American Studies in Scandinavia* 27, no. 2 (1995): 133, http://rauli.cbs.dk/index.php/assc/article/view/1462/1474.

27 See Karen L. Kilcup, "The Conversation of 'The Whole Family': Gender, Politics, and Aesthetics in Literary Tradition," in *Soft Canons: American Women Writers and Masculine Tradition*, ed. Karen L. Kilcup (Iowa City: University of Iowa Press, 1999), 1–24; and Gould, *Covenant and Republic*, 91–132.

28 Although not discussed here, later novels by Child and Sedgwick were no less attuned to changing circumstances in America than those of Cooper, as recent critical editions suggest. See, for example, Lydia Maria Child, *A Romance of the Republic*, ed. Dana D. Nelson (Lexington: University of Kentucky Press, 2014); and Catharine Maria Sedgwick, *Married or Single?* ed. Deborah Gussman (Lincoln: University of Nebraska Press, 2015).

29 Lydia Maria Child, *The Rebels, or, Boston Before the Revolution* (Boston: Cummings, Hilliard, 1825).

30 John Pendleton Kennedy, *Horse Shoe Robinson: A Tale of the Tory Ascendency*, 3rd ed. (Philadelphia: Carey, Lea and Blanchard, 1835).

31 Catharine Maria Sedgwick, *The Linwoods, or, "Sixty Years Since" in America*, vol. 2 (New York: Harper and Sons, 1835), 278, https://archive.org/details/linwoodsorsixtyy02sedgrich.

32 William Gilmore Simms, "Modern Prose Fiction," *Southern Quarterly Review* 15 (April 1849), 83, quoted in Mary Ann Wimsatt, *The Major Fiction of William Gilmore Simms: Cultural Traditions and Literary Form* (Baton Rouge: Louisiana State University Press, 1989), 36.

33 Wimsatt, *Major Fiction*, 37. See also, C. Hugh Holman, "The Influence of Scott and Cooper on Simms," in *The Roots of Southern Writing: Essays on the Literature of the American South* (Athens: University of Georgia Press, 1972), 50–60.

34 William Gilmore Simms, *The Yemassee: A Romance of Carolina* (New York: Harper and Bros, 1835).

35 Masahiro Nakamura, *Visions of Order in William Gilmore Simms: Southern Conservatism and the Other American Romance* (Columbia: University of South Carolina Press, 2009), 5.

36 William Gilmore Simms, *The Partisan: A Tale of the Revolution* (New York: Harper and Bros, 1835).

37 Charles S. Watson, *From Nationalism to Secessionism: The Changing Fiction of William Gilmore Simms* (Westport, CT: Greenwood Press, 1993), 4, 5.

38 As pointed out by Wimsatt, Simms was seen as representative of Southern attitudes (*Major Fiction*, 11); for examples, see J. Quitman Moore, "William Gilmore Simms," *DeBow's Review* 29, no. 6 (December 1860): 708; and C. Hugh Holman, "The Status of Simms," *American Quarterly* 10 (Summer 1958), 181.

39 Watson, *Nationalism to Secessionism*, 4.

40 Wimsatt, *Major Fiction*, 120.

How the West was one   85

41 Ibid.
42 William Gilmore Simms, *Katherine Walton; or, The Rebel of Dorchester*, new and rev. ed. (Chicago: Belford, Clarke, 1888).
43 Harriet Beecher Stowe, *Uncle Tom's Cabin; or, Life Among the Lowly* (Boston: J. P. Jewett, 1852). William Gilmore Simms, *The Sword and the Distaff; or, "Fair, Fat and Forty," A Story of the South, at the Close of Revolution* (Philadelphia: Lippincott, Grambo, 1853). The Fugitive Slave Act of 1850 required the surrender of runaway slaves, punished those who aided slaves, and denied fugitives the right to a trial by jury.
44 Watson, *Nationalism to Secessionism*, 109. William Gilmore Simms, *The Forayers, or, The Raid of the Dog Days* (New York: Redfield, 1855); *Eutaw: A Sequel* (New York: Redfield, 1856).
45 Watson, *Nationalism to Secessionism*, 80–84.
46 See John Caldwell Guilds, "The 'Untrodden Path': *Richard Hurdis* and Simms's Foray into Literary Realism," in *William Gilmore Simms and the American Frontier*, ed. John Caldwell Guilds and Caroline Collins (Athens: University of Georgia Press, 1997). Guilds argues that any literary assessment of Simms should consider his literary experimentation (ibid., 53). For just such an assessment, see Nakamura, *Visions of Order*.
47 McWilliams, "Revolution," n. pag.
48 Franklin, "James Fenimore Cooper," 43.
49 Stephen Carl Arch, "Cooper's Turn: Satire in the Age of Jackson," in vol. 2 of *Literature in the Early American Republic: Annual Studies on Cooper and His Contemporaries*, ed. Mathew Wynn Sivils and Jeffrey Walker (New York: AMS Press, 2010), 177.
50 James Fenimore Cooper, *Notions of the Americans: Picked Up By a Travelling Bachelor* (Philadelphia: Carey, Lea and Carey, 1828).
51 James Fenimore Cooper, *A Letter to His Countrymen* (New York: J. Wiley, 1834); *The American Democrat, or, Hints on the Social and Civic Relations of the United States of America* (Cooperstown, NY: H. and E. Phinney, 1838).
52 Cooper's travel series included *Gleanings in Europe, Switzerland* (1836); *Gleanings in Europe, The Rhine* (1836); *Gleanings in Europe, France* (1837); *Gleanings in Europe, England* (1837); and *Gleanings in Europe, Italy* (1838). James Fenimore Cooper, *History of the Navy of the United States of America* (Philadelphia: Lea and Blanchard, 1839).
53 See Robert Emmet Long, *James Fenimore Cooper* (New York: Continuum, 1990), 111; and Wayne Franklin, introduction to *The Pathfinder*, by James Fenimore Cooper (Cambridge, MA: Belknap Press of Harvard University Press, 2014), xv–xvi. James Fenimore Cooper, *The Prairie: A Tale* (Philadelphia: Carey, Lea and Carey, 1827).
54 Steven P. Harthorn, "*The Pathfinder* and Cooper's Return to Popular Literature," in *Leather-Stocking Redux, or, Old Tales, New Essays*, ed. Jeffrey Walker (New York: AMS Press, 2011), 211–17.
55 James Fenimore Cooper, *The Bravo: A Tale* (Philadelphia: Carey and Lea, 1831); *The Heidenmauer: A Legend of the Rhine* (Paris: Baudry's Foreign Library, 1832); *The Headsman, or, The Abbaye des Vignerons: A Tale* (London: R. Bentley, 1833).
56 Arch, "Cooper's Turn," 175.
57 James Fenimore Cooper, *The Monikins* (Philadelphia: Carey, Lea and Blanchard, 1835).
58 James Fenimore Cooper, *Homeward Bound, or, The Chase: A Tale of the Sea* (Philadelphia: Carey, Lea and Blanchard, 1838).

86 *How the West was one*

59 James Fenimore Cooper, *Home as Found* (Philadelphia: Lea and Blanchard, 1838).

60 Franklin, introduction to *The Pathfinder*, xxv.

61 Arch, "Cooper's Turn," 189.

62 Montgomery Bird, *Nick of the Woods, or, The Jibbenainosay: A Tale of Kentucky* (Philadelphia: Carey, Lea and Blanchard, 1837). For a discussion of a little-known early version of *Malaeska*, see "From the Periodical Archives: Ann S. Stephens's 'The Jockey Cap' – The First Version of 'Malaeska,'" *American Periodicals* 18, no. 1 (2008): 101–6. The first full version was *Malaeska; or The Indian Wife of the White Hunter*, in *Ladies' Companion* (February, March, and April, 1839). For the better-known dime novel version, see *Malaeska, the Indian Wife of the White Hunter*, in *Beadle's Dime Novels*, no. 1, June 9, 1860, www. ulib.niu.edu/badndp/dn01.html. For a more recent publication in book format, see *Malaeska: The Indian Wife of the White Hunter* (New York: B. Blom, 1971). For a more detailed publishing history, see Colin T. Ramsey and Kathryn Zabelle Derounian-Stodola, "Dime Novels," in Samuels, *American Fiction*, 267–69.

63 Wallace, *Early Cooper*, 108.

64 Franklin, introduction to *The Pathfinder*, xvii.

65 Wayne Franklin, "James Fenimore Cooper and the Invention of the American Novel," in Samuels, *American Fiction*, 413.

66 James Fenimore Cooper, *The Pathfinder, or, The Inland Sea*, ed. Richard Dilworth Rust, approved ed. (Albany: State University of New York Press, 1981), 36. Note: All references are to this edition.

67 Ibid., 112.

68 Ibid., 107.

69 Ibid.

70 John P. McWilliams, *Political Justice in a Republic: James Fenimore Cooper's America* (Berkeley: University of California Press, 1972), 10.

71 Cooper, *Pathfinder*, 8.

72 William P. Kelly, *Plotting America's Past: Fenimore Cooper and the Leatherstocking Tales* (Carbondale: Southern Illinois University Press, 1983), 153.

73 Cooper, *Pathfinder*, 16.

74 Ibid., 18.

75 George Dekker, *James Fenimore Cooper: The Novelist* (London: Routledge and Kegan Paul, 1967), 161.

76 James Fenimore Cooper, *The Deerslayer, or, The First War-Path: A Tale* (Philadelphia: Lea and Blanchard, 1841).

77 McWilliams, *Political Justice*, 14.

78 Cooper, *Pathfinder*, 92.

79 Ibid., 97, 98.

80 Ibid., 98.

81 Ibid., 97.

82 McWilliams, *Political Justice*, 292.

83 Cooper, *Pathfinder*, 55.

84 Ibid., 456.

85 Ibid., 129.

86 Ibid., 174.

87 In this light, it is no coincidence that a later novel such as Sedgwick's *Married or Single?* (1857) depicts social life in New York rather than life beyond the bounds of civilization.

88 Cooper, *Pathfinder*, 110.

89 Dana D. Nelson, "Cooper's Leatherstocking Conversations: Identity, Friendship, and Democracy in the New Nation," in *A Historical Guide to James Fenimore Cooper*, ed. Leland S. Person (Oxford: Oxford University Press, 2007), 139.

How the West was one 87

90 Domhnall Mitchell, "Authority in Fenimore Cooper's 'The Pathfinder,' " *American Studies in Scandinavia* 24, no. 2 (1992): 109, https://ej.lib.cbs.dk/index.php/assc/article/view/2610.
91 Richard Dilworth Rust, "The Art of *The Pathfinder*," in *James Fenimore Cooper: New Historical and Literary Contexts*, ed. W. M. Verhoeven (Amsterdam: Rodopi, 1993), 180.
92 Cooper, *Pathfinder*, 129.
93 Ibid., 131.
94 Ibid., 130–31.
95 A similar novelistic representation of America's commercial future occurs earlier in Charles Brockden Brown, *Arthur Mervyn, or, The Memoirs of the Year 1793* (Philadelphia: H. Maxwell, 1799); the protagonist, Arthur Mervyn, moves from rural America to Philadelphia. See Michael T. Gilmore, introduction to *Early American Literature: A Collection of Essays*, ed. Michael T. Gilmore (Englewood Cliffs, NJ: Prentice Hall, 1980), 8.
96 Cooper, *Pathfinder*, 265.
97 Ibid.
98 Geoffrey Rans, *Cooper's Leather-Stocking Novels: A Secular Reading* (Chapel Hill: University of North Carolina Press, 1991), 180.
99 Ibid., 186.
100 Cooper, *Pathfinder*, 266.
101 Ibid., 270.
102 Ibid., 271.
103 Ibid., 272.
104 Ibid.
105 Ibid., 273.
106 Ibid., 278.
107 Mitchell, "Authority," 109.
108 Long locates the significance of Jasper's departure to become a successful merchant in New York as "part of the conflict in the novel between worldly and ideal values" (*James Fenimore Cooper*, 119), a conflict that seems to indicate the triumph of commercial interests over spiritual potentialities.
109 Honoré de Balzac, review of *The Pathfinder, or The Inland Sea*, by James Fenimore Cooper, *Revue Parisienne*, July 25, 1840, in *Fenimore Cooper: The Critical Heritage*, ed. George Dekker and John P. McWilliams (London: Taylor and Francis e-Library, 2003), 209–10.
110 Ibid., 207.
111 Cooper, *Pathfinder*, 451.
112 Ibid., 459.
113 Ibid., 457.
114 Ibid., 458.
115 Ibid., 461.
116 Franklin, introduction to *The Pathfinder*, xv–xvi.
117 William Owen, "In War as in Love: The Significance of Analogous Plots in Cooper's *The Pathfinder*," *English Studies in Canada* 10, no. 3 (1984): 290.
118 Dekker, *James Fenimore Cooper*, 166.
119 Ibid.
120 Ibid.

5 Home and away
Leatherstocking reinvented in America and France

> That is, all signs are intelligible; some of these act as solutions to socio-logical problems; and some of these solutions become part of "popular memory."
> – Alec McHoul, *Semiotic Investigations*, 136

In nineteenth-century America, print reading facilitated the self-reflexive production of identity. As Ronald Zboray describes, "Between national print culture and local exigencies, readers had to engineer their existence."[1] American authors combined history and romance to enable localized interpretations of modernization. In this respect, the flexibility of the historical novel made it a useful form of communication. But due to a lack of direct evidence, how exactly readers read historical novels "to engineer their existence" is difficult to determine. For example, the popularity of James Fenimore Cooper's Leatherstocking novels and their influence on popular culture is well known. Yet it cannot be assumed that wide readership translated into the production of a singular interpretation of America or American identity. The question of meaning production might be productively addressed otherwise, however. We might instead ask about the circumstances of production and look more closely at the many ways readers encountered Cooper's most popular novels. Histories of production and dissemination indicate that popular American novels were reinvented for a variety of purposes and in forms intended to create, extend, or cater to new and expanding readerships throughout the nineteenth century. The question of identity, then, becomes one of use; put otherwise, what can the reinvention of Leatherstocking novels teach us about the role of print history, reading practices, and the historical novel in the production of modern identity in America? To answer this question, I begin by outlining the publishing context that framed the initial production and downmarket circulation of *The Pathfinder* in America. Taking up the transatlantic nature of print communication circuits, I then consider reproduction of *The Pathfinder* in Europe. Finally, focusing on French novelist Gustave Aimard, I point to the adaptation of Cooperesque themes by popular European authors, and more specifically to how the transatlantic

Home and away 89

exchange of historical novels between America and France contributed to the making and reading of American history.

As Trish Loughran argues, a national discourse in print did not emerge in America until at least the 1830s.[2] That American novelists of the early republic were not successful in reaching a national audience was partly due to the limited state of territorial expansion and because of the use of waterways for transportation, which restricted migration and access to emerging communities. Another impediment to the circulation of American literature was the overwhelming dominance of British literature; Robert Gross writes that "In 1771, on the eve of the Revolution, British North America ranked as the leading export market for London publishers, absorbing more English books than all of Europe did, and as soon as peace returned, businessmen on both sides of the Atlantic rushed to resume that profitable trade."[3] The situation was not static, however; by the 1840s, the number of American works of fiction increased fourfold.[4] The shift from imports to American authorship in this period was not complete, although it was significant: "In 1820 seven out of every ten titles from presses in the United States were originally written and published abroad, but in the 1830s and early 1840s Americans gained a majority share (55–60 percent) of book production."[5] Prior to the 1820s, novels played a relatively small role in American publishing. Increased publication and reading of American novels depended on several factors. From 1840 to 1880, new distribution and communication systems allowed the book trade to distribute print to wider readerships.[6] Copyright and post office legislation, to cite two examples taken up further in this chapter, encouraged the national diffusion of reading material, including popular fiction, especially in downmarket forms such as periodicals. Major publishers with connections and experience were able to capitalize on market opportunities and literary trends. Increasing literacy rates and the related expansion of schools and libraries were also consequential. Kenneth Carpenter, for example, writes that "some 266 social libraries were founded between 1790 and 1840 in New England alone."[7] The institutionalization of reading flourished due to positive economic conditions and because of the reading material offered. Circulating libraries, for instance, succeeded because of "the many current novels, British and American alike, the library ordered annually; in the 1820s and early 1830s, the latest works of historical romance by Scott, Cooper, Irving, Sedgwick, and others accounted for nearly half of all purchases."[8] In sum, despite early obstacles, novel reading in mid-nineteenth-century America emerged as a common, shared activity that impacted the organization of many towns and cities as well as reading practices. It did so as one part of a larger market for popular print, which depended on institutional changes and commercial endeavors.

"Copyright," according to Meredith McGill, "was understood by the founders to be an important tool of nation building."[9] The manipulation of copyright contributed to centralized control over distribution, risk, and

90 Home and away

association. The consequences for the development of American literature and reading were substantial. The 1790 Copyright Act gave American authors copyright in the United States for a period of up to twenty-eight years and allowed American publishers to reprint foreign materials. It was a twofold response to transatlantic trade and the need to protect American literary production; as Gross notes, "Combining nationalism and cosmopolitanism, it simultaneously encouraged the rise of American authorship and bookmaking and the burgeoning of a domestic market for British and European writings."[10] A clear trade-off was involved. On the one hand, the openness to imports increased the circulation of print materials. On the other hand, the lack of international copyright legislation in America until 1890, the popularity of British authors, and the economic advantage of reprinting worked against American authorship. The 1790 Copyright Act was a response to precise conditions that furthered nation building, although more by the stimulation of national reading than by the production of American literature. Under the informal courtesy of the trade agreement (in place of international copyright legislation), the first publisher of a work had publication rights, which stimulated competition to secure the most profitable British authors. The popularity of Scott fueled such practices, leading to booksellers paying for advance sheets from London.[11] Even though the fight over popular British authors brought the price of foreign literature down and increased access to print, in the short term at least, it also provided little incentive to produce American literature and publish American books. In these ways, American copyright legislation, regional trade agreements, and transnational print networks encouraged the circulation of mostly foreign literature.

The expansion of American reading occurred in other ways, however. American forms of downmarket print were stimulated by the Post Office Acts of 1792 and 1794, which "allowed newspapers and magazines to circulate through the mail at cheap rates, subsidized by high charges on personal letters; books were banned from the mail bags."[12] Following on territorial expansion and population growth, the Post Office Acts also contributed to the growth of national communication networks, as evidenced by the dramatic extension of the postal system in the years to follow; as Richard John describes, "In 1800 the network included 903 offices; by 1810, it expanded to 2,300, and by 1820, to 4,500. In 1828, the United States had 74 post offices for every 100,000 inhabitants – far more than the 17 in Great Britain and the 4 in France."[13] The government further aided the circulation of print by eliminating stamp taxes, censorship, and border control. Under these conditions, expansion of the print market took several forms. For example, the downmarket dissemination of religious and periodical literature played a vital role in the expansion of print markets and reading in the early republic. In many ways, religious literature was the first and most influential form of popular literature. With distribution in the millions, the publication of Bibles (often serialized) and tracts was considerable

Home and away 91

throughout the first half of the nineteenth century. But it was the newspaper that was critical to information circulation: "The press grew at an astounding rate, nearly doubling its ranks every decade and a half, faster even than the surging population: 365 newspapers in 1810, 861 in 1828, 1,403 in 1840."[14] On the East Coast, government factions made excellent use of the burgeoning press, with authors and publishers openly promoting political views to garner popular support. Benefitting from the legislative acts already described, newspapers dropped in price and spread in geographical reach, especially through the "penny press," which began to reach a "broad middling audience by the middle of the 1830s."[15] Alongside mainstream publications reaching large readerships, fringe or minority groups used the press as an instrument of influence. The diversification of print accelerated democratic pluralism at least in part dependent on downmarket penetration. John Brooke outlines how "The reading public, once assumed to be confined to the ranks of independent property holders, was transformed into an expansive and unpredictable free market in which editors – still intent on gate keeping, but now faced with lots of competition – had to sell their wares."[16] Publishers, editors, and authors were always keen on instructing readers, but selling was dependent on providing literature that mattered to readers. The popularity of religious literature and the rise of a competitive press speak not only to an increase in the number of readers but also to the fact that readers read what interested them. The prevalence of foreign literature, copyright acts, and the regulation of distribution played roles in the production and reception of literature; ultimately, however, American reading practices made the specificity of American literature possible (or inevitable). The American historical novel, accordingly, depended not only on the earlier prominence of reading in other forms but also on the use of literature to respond to local circumstances.

Nineteenth-century Americans read many forms of literature originating from across the Atlantic, but it is important to remember that they did so as Americans; in other words, they read according to their own interests and circumstances. At the same time, the localization of literary production, whether Bibles, newspapers, or novels, helped make reading meaningful to the increasing number of people who self-identified as American. For example, descriptions of the unknown American countryside as scenic, sublime, and adventurous followed westward expansion. Typical of the travel genre that emerged, "The single most frequently published travel book in the United States before 1810 was a little volume titled *New Travels to the Westward, or Unknown Parts of America*, a report of a journey into the Mississippi Valley interior and of the native people encountered there."[17] That the number of travel and guide books on America increased was no doubt due to curiosity about this unknown land called the frontier. People wanted to know more about the place they called (or might call) home. Whereas atlases aided exploration, travel literature began to fill in the gaps for armchair travelers in urban settings more inclined to read a narrative than a map.

92 Home and away

The localization of content was equally apparent in downmarket forms. For instance, despite continued reliance on imported English chapbooks, some were also produced in America, in line with the expanding print industry and increased attention to local exigencies; as John Simons writes, "Apart from imports or chapbooks directly copied from English originals, American chapbooks often seem to appeal to a different kind of reader. American chapbook producers like Chapman Whitcombe or Andrew Steuart address an audience which already seems to have distinctively American cultural interests."[18] Victor Neuburg summarizes a shift from imitation or reuse of foreign content to authentic adaptation for local readers taking place as early as the seventeenth century: "American chapbooks fell into two broad categories: first there were the traditional titles, printed in America from English versions; then there were those of specifically American interest, the most characteristic of these being the 'Indian Captivity' titles, of which many hundreds appeared in typical chapbook style."[19] The interest, as in later adventure stories in the form of dime novels, was not simply in fiction for the purpose of entertainment, as the reference to "Indian Captivity" titles might suggest. Josiah Priest, for example, was a well-known author of such popular tales, but he was also "an early historian of the American frontier."[20] The two forms of historification no doubt informed each other, and both may be said to have served republican education in different ways. Knowing what came before and thus what was new about the present mattered to all readers in some way. Although the popularity of the ephemeral chapbook is difficult to quantify, the contribution of cheap literature to the life of common people prior to the downmarket availability of novels played a major role in American reading and culture; they were more accessible, and the content was either specific to the interests of local readers or could be read as such. In line with the centralized control of distribution (i.e., copyright legislation, postal services), popular print, whether travel books or chapbooks, contributed to a transition from dependence on foreign works to new American literature situated geographically, socially, politically, and culturally to meet the interests of American readers.

Early on, the production and reception of novels in nineteenth-century America depended on international connections as much as domestic conditions. Trade routes were primarily transatlantic, with most publishers distributing reprints regionally (e.g., by waterway or road) – there was little in the way of national trade. However, international events impacted local production; for example, the union of Ireland with England and Scotland in 1801 ended the reprint trade with Ireland, thus cutting off "one of the main sources of cheap reprints to that point."[21] Also, the War of 1812 caused a financial crisis, contributing to the bankruptcy of many smaller firms.[22] The publisher Mathew Carey of Philadelphia was able to withstand such events, largely due to Bible sales, which ultimately left him in a position to extend his reach beyond the East Coast to the south and west. Besides the deterioration of the courtesy of the trade system, which exacerbated competition by encouraging publishers to get works to press first and thus favored publishers with greater resources, Carey's ability to capitalize on changing circumstances was an excellent reason for Cooper to switch to Carey and Lea for publication of *The Last of the Mohicans* in 1826. As with Scott's publishers in Scotland and England, Carey was an innovator familiar with publishing trends. He recognized the challenges and opportunities of literary production in America, which remained fragmented and poorly connected; he responded by bringing together producers and consumers in other ways: for example, by using traveling salesmen, and by the arrangement of book fairs.[23] Carey was proactive in his efforts to dominate the market for popular works. In one instance, to promote the publication of a new Bible, he "wrote letters to every postmaster in the country in March [1801], asking them to be his agents for the Bible, which entailed gathering subscriptions and forwarding payment."[24] But such efforts, which amounted to the early coordination of a national distribution network, were not restricted to any one work or genre. Carey also began to prepare for future editions of old and new works of fiction; for instance, "Shortly after *Last of the Mohicans* was published, Cooper sold Carey the copyrights of his five previous novels for their remaining terms as well as the right to his next novel, *The Prairie*, for a total of $7,500."[25] Whether Bibles or novels, publishing meant selling products for profit. Entrepreneurial publishing practices, such as the use of stereotyping to reduce the cost of subsequent editions, corresponded with expansion of the print market for fiction as well as developments in print technology and communication networks, for example, "improvements in papermaking, typesetting, and printing machinery, along with new means of distribution in the railroad and steamboat, [which] made books both cheaper for publishers and more accessible for readers."[26] The rise of the large publishing house, which could take advantage of such changes, established an early basis for professional authorship, increased production, and the management of literary output with an eye to sales. As the print history of *The Pathfinder* indicates, the consequences with respect to American reading practices were significant.

To protect British copyright, *The Pathfinder* was first published in London on February 24, 1840 by Richard Bentley, then in Philadelphia on March 14 of the same year by Lea and Blanchard.[27] Although reviews were mixed, Cooper was pleased with reception in Britain and America.[28] Two of the most popular periodicals of the nineteenth century, *Godey's Lady's Book* and *The Knickerbocker*, noted strong sales.[29] It was, by all accounts, a relatively successful return to the character of Natty Bumppo after his many other endeavors of the 1830s. But it was also a return with a difference in so far as *The Pathfinder* was taken up by publishers that had already begun to adapt to and actively push the emergence of popular print culture. Early on, there was no predetermined plan to issue a complete collected edition of Cooper's novels, as with Scott's *Waverley Novels* or Honoré de Balzac's *La comédie humaine*. Nonetheless, following upon the initial success of the first

94 *Home and away*

edition, reprints appeared quickly and frequently, often as part of large sets or collections, on both sides of the Atlantic.

The Pathfinder appeared as number ninety of *Bentley's Standard Novels* in 1843 and again in 1850; in 1854, *The Pathfinder* was the final issue of the ten-volume *Works of James Fenimore Cooper* (1837–54).[30] Reproduction was more intense in America; Richard Rust summarizes the early history of *The Pathfinder* as follows: "The plates of the first American edition were reimpressed by Lea and Blanchard in 1841, 1843, 1845, and 1846, and by Town and Stringer in New York in 1849 and during the 1850s simultaneously with the Author's Revised Edition."[31] High demand depended on the diversity of the print market. American readers, much like working-class and middle-class readers elsewhere, read what they could afford. Publishers acted quickly to capitalize on the expansion of reading. For example, Louise Stevenson describes how "Mid-nineteenth-century readers could choose from inexpensive editions, usually called a 'people's,' or 'household,' edition, of standard authors costing 75¢ or $1.00, or more costly sets in half or full calf, with gilt edges, such as the thirty-four volumes of James Fenimore Cooper's works for $75.00."[32] Following a first series of *Novels and Tales* in 1835–36 by Carey and Lea, *The Pathfinder* was added to a second series in 1841.[33] Robert Spiller and Philip Blackburn describe the first series as "bound in light red cloth with paper labels, and the second in leather, with gold lettering."[34] Distinction could add value and, potentially, profit at the high end of the market. Editions bound in leather with gilt lettering and trumpeting the addition of revisions, corrections, notes, and introductions in "authorized" editions point to the negotiation of niche audiences, and of course the justification of higher prices. But the dominant trend was downmarket. As new works continued to hit the market, Cooper's novels were reprinted in ever-larger editions, many of which would keep the paratextual additions that had become common. Frequent editions and large sets over a short period suggest that the market for American fiction aimed at middle-class readers willing and able to invest in reading was growing and that Cooper was popular enough to warrant repeated reinvention.

The most striking aspect of the print history of Cooper's novels in nineteenth-century America is less the popular reception and more the lengths to which publishers went to connect with readers over the course of several generations. At the end of Cooper's life, American publishers began to reprint his novels in new ways to profit from popular identification with Cooper and specific novels. For example, the 1840 Lea and Blanchard edition of *The Pathfinder* was slightly revised and published in 1851 by George Putnam as the sixth of twelve volumes under the title *The Works of J. Fenimore Cooper* (1849–53); volumes four through eight have the collective title *The Leather-stocking Tales* and are renumbered as volumes I–V, making this the first instance of the Leatherstocking novels arranged in terms of their story sequence; all other titles are ordered by publication date.[35] Rust notes that the most prominent change for this edition was "an increase in dialect forms," which likely played to growing American readership, as well as the popularity of regional novels and the eccentricity of the character Natty Bumppo.[36] *The Pathfinder* was repeatedly reprinted, as part of *The Leatherstocking Tales* and as part of larger sets. Putnam issued a "complete in one volume" edition in 1852 and an author's revised edition in 1853.[37] Stringer and Townsend reissued the author's revised edition numerous times in the 1850s,[38] for instance, as part of *Cooper's Works* in 1852 and 1853 and as volume three of *The Leather-stocking Tales* in 1854.[39] In short, publishers worked Cooper's works. In practice, this meant constantly reworking what was essentially the same content. Another example is *The Pathfinder, or, The Inland Sea* (1856) as volume four of *The Choice Works of Cooper: Revised and Corrected Series: With New Introductions, Notes, Etc.*[40] Similarly presented as a special edition, *Cooper's Novels* (1859–61), described as the first "de luxe" edition, integrated new type on heavy paper, heavy cloth binding with a gold embossed design on the front cover, gold lettering on the spine, and a special steel engraved title page for each volume.[41] The appeal of these editions depended on the popularity of Cooper and the Leatherstocking novels but also on remaking each to capture the attention of new readers, for instance, by the addition of illustrations by Felix Octavius Carr Darley.[42] Wide circulation was also enabled by constant relabeling. Whereas an author's revised edition aims to legitimize, or perhaps facilitates a sense of distinction for the reader, the publication of a "people's edition" of *Cooper's Novels* (1857–60) suggests mass participation at a time when reading was expanding.[43] One publisher followed another, but the pattern remained the same. James Gregory succeeded Townsend; he clearly had no intention of slowing the industrial reproduction of Cooper's novels. Innovations were made; for example, in 1864, Gregory added a "Discourse on the life, genius, and writings of J. Fenimore Cooper" by William Cullen Bryant to *Cooper's Novels*.[44] The publishers Hurd and Houghton, Appleton, Houghton, Mifflin, and Putnam continued to republish Cooper's novels in large editions.[45] Again, in some cases, there were notable adjustments: a household edition by Hurd and Houghton; a five-volumes-in-one edition by Appleton; a household edition with an introduction by Susan Fenimore Cooper and a Riverside edition of the Leatherstocking novels, both published by Houghton, Mifflin; and a Mohawk edition by Putnam.[46] In short, popular editions were repeatedly recast in new guises. Relabeling, however, was not merely cosmetic; the term "household edition," for example, might be interpreted as a way to forge a stronger link between everyday life, Cooper, and reading. If publishers had their say, in the typical American household, a set of Cooper's novels would sit nicely alongside the family Bible. Obviously, forging such a connection between Cooper and the people required some work; the selection and order of specific works were important factors. Ann Rigney contends that cultural remembrance works on a principle of scarcity, tending "to converge on a limited number of figures of memory, which are then continuously re-invested with additional meaning."[47] The

96 Home and away

reworking of Cooper's novels provides an interesting example. Over the course of the century, the Leatherstocking novels were eventually, and then repeatedly, grouped together, first as five separate volumes within a larger collection, then on their own, then as one volume. Further, they were not collected according to publication date but to make the story of Natty's life a coherent progression from his youth in *The Deerslayer* to his death in *The Prairie*. The interests of readers, which meant profit, came first. In relation, in the complete collections, popular novels were placed earlier. The primary question for publishers was not fidelity to the publishing history of Cooper's works but rather the quality of reproduction, meaning the creation of a direct link between Cooper the American author and Natty the popular character and thus between the common reader and the Leatherstocking novels. The contributions of such editorial choices to the production of cultural memory and American identity are many.

Although the localization of thematic content fueled interest in the reading of American novels and the popular dissemination of them, the convergence of industrial publishing and popular reading furthered the expansion of print markets and reading communities. Cooper's career sits at the center of such changes. The repackaging of Cooper's novels depended on entrepreneurial publishing practices, new print technologies, and the growing interest in American literature among men and women who could only afford downmarket print, but like others, wanted reading material, whether guide, chapbook, rag, or novel, that could be read as a meaningful contribution to their own lives. Ronald Zboray writes that "As industrialism spread in antebellum America, the printed word became the primary avenue of national enculturation."[48] With respect to both reputation and sales, Cooper's timing, then, was fortunate in several ways. His writing career and, even more, the subsequent popularization of his works span a key period in the expansion of the literary market and reading in America, thus providing ways for readers to consider the past, present, and future of the nation-state.

Cooper's fiction also got a new lease on life overseas. Just as American reading depended heavily on foreign literature, expansion of the print industry in America was not restricted by American borders. The balance between imports and exports began to change: Michael Winship writes that "Between 1846 and 1876, American book imports grew almost tenfold, exports by a factor of just over thirteen, though imports always exceeded exports by several times."[49] Trade expanded beyond Britain; reprints and collections of Cooper's novels, in English and in translation, were popular across Europe. European interest in American literature put American authors and works in a new position. In 1856, George Sand identified the impact of transatlantic reading practices on the international representation of America: "America owes almost as much to Cooper as to Franklin and Washington: for if these great men created the Union, by skill in legislation and force of arms, it was Cooper, the unassuming storyteller, who broadcast the news of it across the seas by the interest of his tales and the fidelity of his

Home and away 97

patriotic feelings."[50] James Wallace echoes such sentiments: "Quite simply, Cooper created the community of readers whose taste would dominate the market for fiction in America (and for American fiction abroad) throughout the nineteenth century."[51] The community of readers in question was in fact transatlantic in several respects: first, as Cooper's fiction was disseminated throughout Europe; second, as he was reinvented by European authors.

The reprinting of Cooper in Britain started early and progressed quickly. As Willard Thorp writes, "The British reading public adopted Cooper as one of the great novelists of the day."[52] Richard Bentley canonized Cooper by including him in *Bentley's Standard Novels*.[53] Reprints and collections by other publishers continued to the end of the century. Routledge was a major publisher of Cooper, demonstrating various ways of re-presenting Cooper to British readers.[54] *The Novels and Romances of J. Fenimore Cooper* (1864) contained twenty-six titles in thirteen volumes; *The Pathfinder* took a prominent place in volume one along with *The Last of the Mohicans*.[55] *Novels and Romances* was followed by eighteen-volume sets of *Cooper's Novels*.[56] At the same time, the *Leatherstocking Tales* were reprinted separately in one volume or in five volumes.[57] In 1892, *Cooper's Leather-stocking Tales for Boys and Girls: With Illustrations*, which again incorporated all five volumes in one book, demonstrated both the growing market for children's literature and the rebranding of Cooper's novels as suitable for juvenile readers, just as the education system began to expand.[58] In line with Routledge's varied dissemination of Cooper from the 1860s onward, Frederick Warne published an edition of *The Pathfinder* in 1867 as part of a *Notable Novels* series, in 1887 as number eighteen of *Warne's Crown Library* (1886–94), and around 1900 as an illustrated edition.[59] As in America, British editions were differentiated, materially and otherwise, to meet or create the varied and changing expectations of readers.

The reprinting of Cooper's novels in Europe benefitted from the popularity of British literature in established print markets. Cooper added descriptions of the new world of interest to European readers in a form well-known through the works of Scott. Novels in English were also successful in part because they were printed almost immediately, which depended on a culture of reprinting that also made such works cheaper to produce and purchase. By the mid-nineteenth century, many European countries were reading nations that could support the publication of works in English. However, the real and lasting influence of Cooper beyond the borders of English-speaking countries depended on translation, which was quick, extensive, varied, and continued over a relatively long period, coinciding with the increasingly downmarket dissemination of literature.[60] Taking France as an example, Thorp describes how, "Beginning with the translation of *The Spy* in 1822, editions in English and French of Cooper's novels arrived on the Paris stalls as rapidly as the translators and publishers could prepare them, in almost every instance within the year of their publication in English," and adds that "There was some falling off in French enthusiasm for Cooper after 1830 but

98　Home and away

his vogue was renewed late in the decade, especially with the publication in 1840 of *The Pathfinder*, called in French *Le Lac Ontario, ou Le Guide*."[61] In 1840, Gosselin published the first French translation by A. J. B. Defauconpret (also the primary French translator of the Waverley novels).[62] It was reprinted in 1840 as part of *Oeuvres complètes de M. James Fenimore Cooper, Américain* and separately in Brussels, then repeatedly over the next several decades as volume seventeen of *Oeuvres de J.-F. Cooper*.[63] As with Balzac's *Le père Goriot* (1835) and other popular French novels, an illustrated edition of *L'Ontario* (1850) appeared.[64] The *Romans populaires illustrés* series was "reprinted under other titles frequently during the nineteenth century in Paris and elsewhere."[65] Thus, Cooper became part of a down-market publishing industry in France, which made Cooper's novels widely available to French readers and readers of French across Europe throughout the nineteenth century.

The impact of Cooper's fiction was not restricted to reprints or translations. This was true on both sides of the Atlantic. In America, the popularity of Cooper's novels contributed to the development of a new genre – the western – a term that includes a number of sub-genres that shaped the emerging market for popular fiction.[66] Frontier adventure, Indian romance, captivity narratives, and other adaptations of the Leatherstocking novels (or derivatives of them) formed the basis of much popular fiction, so much so that frontier romance was nearly synonymous with early story papers, dime novels, nickel weeklies, and cheap libraries. Cooper, of course, was not the sole source or influence. Others wrote of the frontier in their own way, and lesser-known or anonymous authors contributed to early story papers on related subjects. Yet it is difficult to imagine the many popular novels of later decades without Cooper; the novels of Mayne Reid, such as *The Scalp Hunters: A Romance of the Plains* (1851) and *The Free Lances: A Romance of the Mexican Valley* (1888), and especially later dime novels, following Edward Ellis's *Seth Jones; or, The Captive of the Frontier* (1860) and leading to Edward Wheeler's many *Deadwood Dick* novels (1877–97), would seem to come out of nowhere without the Leatherstocking novels as both direct sources and general reference point, for authors and readers alike.[67] The producers of popular literature made good use of Cooper.[68] *Beadle's Dime Tales, Tradition and Romance of Border and Revolutionary Times* (September 15, 1863 – August 10, 1864), for example, featured stories of border and Indian life, of the American Revolution, of the settlements, and of other American adventures; and *Irwin P. Beadle's American Novels* (also, *Irwin's American Novels* and *American Novels*; October 7, 1865 – December 1868) not only built upon themes popularized by the Leatherstocking novels but also placed a picture of Cooper at the top center of each cover.[69] A longer view of Cooper's impact would take into account everything from dime novels to the westerns of Louis L'Amour to contemporary genre fiction, comics, and film. From the 1820s, American authors (and publishers) made use of the historical novel, especially popular novels like *The Last of the Mohicans*, to connect with readers.

Similarly, in France, descriptions of the American frontier were not left to either reprints or translations of Cooper's novels. Thorp draws connections between Cooper and several prominent French titles – Balzac's *Les chouans* (1829), Eugène Sue's *Les mystères de Paris* (1842–43), and Alexandre Dumas's *Les Mohicans de Paris* (1854).[70] The literary connection between Europe and America was two-way in terms of print dissemination, literary influence, and reading practices. As William Charvat says, "When Cooper became popular in Europe, and was actually imitated in such works as Dumas' *Les Mohicans de Paris*, the cycle was complete – the historical novel, born in the Old World, had been imported by the axis [Philadelphia and New York publishers], acculturated by Cooper, popularized in the interior [of America] by Carey, and returned to the Old World."[71] Given the longer history of transnational literary influence, it is more accurate to say that the cycle continued. Regardless, the point here is that the return to the "Old World" was as much a result of adaptation as it was of dissemination; adaptation depended on formal and thematic repetition to capitalize on the impact of foreign authorship, the rise of popular reading, and a related interest in the "New World" and frontier romance. As in America, the processes involved were transatlantic and local, resulting in narratives of modernization that were at once familiar and new.

French author Gustave Aimard wrote more than twenty such narratives – "Cooperesque novels"[72] that were quickly translated for American readers. *The Frontiersmen*, first published in New York by F. M. Lupton in 1854 (in a book also including a piece of short fiction by Frances Henshaw Baden), is noteworthy as an early instance of Aimard's reinvention of Cooper.[73] The novel is set in Cooper's backyard, the border region of New York in 1783, and the plot is at least reminiscent of *The Deerslayer*, the last of Cooper's Leatherstocking novels, published in 1841. The Senecas capture Singing Bird, the squaw of Eagle's Wing, who immediately takes his revenge by scalping several of the Senecas. To fulfill a debt of gratitude, the settler Barton, his daughter Ruth, and their friend Ralph Weston pledge to protect Eagle's Wing from the Senecas by shielding him in their cabin, which is situated not far from a lake. The essential conflict is between settlers and Native Americans. In terms of characterization, the parallels with Cooper are easy to draw, although not necessarily particular to any one novel. Ralph Weston is a Waverley figure – a young patriot, a man of action, a military Captain, and yet somewhat in limbo with respect to the direction of his life. Ruth Barton, much like Mabel Dunham, finds herself in the wilderness with her father, and adapts admirably; still, she is a product of the settlements. Ralph Weston and Ruth Barton, like Jasper Western and Mabel Dunham, will eventually marry. Ichabod Jenkins is a peculiar adaptation of Natty Bumppo. He is adept at Native ways and understands Native languages; nature is his

100   Home and away

church; he is intensely fond of his rifle, and even though it appears to be of common stature, he is known far and wide as sure of aim. Ichabod, however, is also a proponent of civilization in search of the almighty dollar; his visit to Barton is largely prompted by the idea of setting up a woolen factory in the area. As Ichabod is so evidently in favor of the advance of Western civilization and has no interest in Ruth, he seems only an eccentric counterpoint to the more reserved Ralph; as a result, the romance between Ruth and Ralph does not take on the weight of that between Mabel and Jasper in *The Pathfinder*. The equivalent of Cooper's character Chingachgook is Eagle's Wing, or Moukapec, the great chief of the Coras, of the Del Norte. Well-built, grave, wise, and passionate, a noble warrior with the requisite "gifts" required for life in the wilderness, Eagle's Wing is at once central to the story and yet also only one of a range of stock characters that fill out the novel, including a useful Negro (Sambo, Barton's servant), evil "Injuns" (most notably, Panther, a rival chief), and white scoundrels (i.e., Guthrie, a Loyalist). Although black-and-white characterization allows for the broad representation of political conflict between Native Americans and settlers, frontier politics is defined by familiar clashes between specific tribes (i.e., Oneida and Tuscarora) and between settlers (e.g., Barton the republican and Guthrie the loyalist). As such, the debt to Cooper is great, but the style and content still owe much to the priorities of popular melodrama and a narrow view of colonialism.

As in the Leatherstocking novels, Aimard describes individual gifts to differentiate the nature of races, for instance, by pointing to Ichabod's rejection of the Native practice of scalping. With Cooper, such cultural differences cut deep, bringing into question the survival of nations and the direction of the nation-state. In this early novel, Aimard's representation is more straightforward. The exchange of knowledge between Singing Bird and Ruth concerning the role of women in their respective communities is fairly balanced.[74] Conversely, Ichabod speaks directly of the futility of civilizing Native Americans through Christianity.[75] Instead, he gives the Senecas a lesson in political economy, advising them to buy land cheap, adding that they should clothe themselves for proper society.[76] Given the contemporary popularity of culturally insensitive captivity narratives, it is perhaps less surprising that a lawyer and a bailiff who bring legalese and whisky into a Native camp are tortured and murdered. Further, true to common usage of the sentimental novel for social education, Ruth stops Eagle's Wing from killing his rival by appealing to his sense of forgiveness and redemption.[77] More particular to the blunt application of history in the novel, the conclusion is a history lesson – a reflection seventy years later reveals that villages have sprung up, drunk Natives wander the streets aimlessly, and traditional modes of life have passed away. In short, "progress" is taking shape – for better and worse, obviously.

In the shadow of the Leatherstocking novels, *The Frontiersmen* is at once eerily familiar and yet strikingly empty – *Cooperesque* in a disconcerting

Home and away   101

way. Cooper was influential, but to be successful, adaptations had to be reinventions suited to local reading practices, which were not static. Correspondingly, *The Frontiersmen* is an early example of Aimard's capitalization on the popularity of Cooper and frontier romance in Europe and yet not representative of his entire oeuvre. Although unambiguous oppositions typical of melodramatic novelization remain, a look at later novels reveals sensitivity to social context and the changing interests of readers.

Novels of the American frontier offered a sense of exoticism, much like novels set in the Orient, but they were also read locally, that is, as relevant to contemporary circumstances. In France, since Napoleon's sale of Louisiana in 1803, nostalgia for French colonialism in America was of the moment.[78] French adventures abroad in the second half of the nineteenth century kept the relationship between France and colonial populations before the eyes of readers. As a distant, unknown space, the American frontier empowered authors such as Aimard to investigate colonialism in a way that was less threatening than a novel dealing directly with French colonialism. In this respect, the annexation of Texas in 1845 and the Mexican-American War of 1846–48 caught the imagination of popular writers on both sides of the Atlantic. Mayne Reid's first novel, *The Rifle-Rangers, or, Adventures in Southern Mexico* (1850), and Gabriel Ferry's *Le coureur des bois, ou, les chercheurs d'or* (1850) were both inspired by personal experiences of these events.[79] Aimard also traveled extensively in South America and the Far West of America from the 1830s to the 1850s. Just as Cooper moved on from his early imitation of the British novel of manners by writing a specifically American historical novel, Aimard's later novels were relocated to the Far West, thus moving on from earlier imitations of Cooper. The complexities of Aimard's novels increased with experience of the frontier and as a writer. *Les pirates des prairies* (1858), for example, is full of conventional characters as well as fantastic events, but it can also be read as an illustration of national conflicts, social relations, cultural customs, and racial strife.[80] Although the primary struggle remains that between settlers and Natives, the desert has become a plane upon which questions of subjectivity and community are less certain. In short, the intersection of nations and state, and the related investigation of colonialism, begin to come to the fore differently. Thorp refers to Aimard's novels as "distinctly sub-literary" and notes their popularity among school boys.[81] The latter refrain especially was applied to Scott and Cooper as well. But the hard-boiled characterization and seemingly neat resolutions common to popular genres of the novel are not necessarily indicative of social naivety or a lack of skill; such reinventions roughly maintained the genre expectations of readers of popular fiction while exploring what were sensitive, timely, and practical issues of importance to American as well as French readers.

The history of the frontier romance in America, at least as a popular form of reading, may be said to begin with Cooper's *Pioneers*. However, the American historical novel started earlier, for instance, with the popular

102   *Home and away*

reception of Scott, and continued throughout the century to depend on the exploitation of transatlantic communication circuits. As only one of many possible examples of international reading practices, Aimard's popularity in French was matched only by his popularity in English. His novels were quickly translated and published in London, and then reprinted in America. In the early 1860s, one after another of Aimard's novels appeared in translation. Ward and Lock was the primary publisher of Aimard's novels in Britain; Berger, Clarke, Maxwell, and Vickers, among others, also capitalized on the popularity of Aimard. As usual, Philadelphia and New York were not far behind: Peterson (Philadelphia), Dawley (New York), and Beadle (New York) began reprinting translations in the 1860s. Peterson published complete and unabridged editions as part of his collection of Aimard's novels.[82] Beadle and Adams added Aimard titles to their libraries.[83] In London, Maxwell published twenty-seven volumes of *Aimard's Indian Tales* from 1877 to 1879.[84] Percy Bolingbroke St. John revised and edited shorter adaptations.[85] These popular 125-page abridgements preceded other editions published by well-known publishers of popular literature.[86] In short, just as Cooper adapted Scott and Britons adopted Cooper, Aimard adapted Cooper and readers of English adopted Aimard. Although we do not know exactly how readers read these novels, we do know that they were willing to invest in them. The reasons for doing so were likely many and varied.

Benjamin Spencer writes that Cooper's "fiction both depicted and interested the 'people at large.' "[87] This was no less true of Cooperesque novels that originated elsewhere. In this light, it should be remembered that the literature that has contributed to American reading since the seventeenth century has never been restricted to a place called America or to the writings of Americans. The English adventurer Captain John Smith and the French farmer/diplomat Michel Guillaume Jean de Crèvecœur come to mind, although many other examples might be cited. Regardless, any definition of American literature must consider the making of American identity as dependent on American reading practices, and not simply content. The novels of Scott, popular in America as elsewhere, were not read by Americans as they would have been read by the English or the French. How, then, does the reading of an English translation of a French interpretation of a Cooper novel impact the construction of American identity? The best answer to such a difficult question would be a case study of the actual uses of one or more novels by individual readers. Without such evidence, some tentative answers may be helpful anyway. To start, beyond Aimard's mastery of a popular form of the novel and his first-hand knowledge of his material, his popularization of American history evolved with the times over a long career. Aimard's novels, at first colored by the imitation of Cooper, tended eventually to take up the theme of colonialism in a way that was informed by his own background and interests, those of his readers, and the changing American landscape – social as well as geographical. The shift in focus from New York to the Far West, which coincided with the question of the

Home and away 103

character of new territories, was at once representative of frontier expansion in America and relevant to the colonial adventures of France in the later-nineteenth century. For example, nearly twenty-five years after *Les pirates*, the focus of *Les bandits de l'Arizona* (1882) is the conflict between settlers of the Far West rather than between settlers and Native Americans nearer the East Coast.[88] Although beyond the scope of this chapter, the underlying ethics of Native absence should be questioned. For instance, David Coward notes that, to correct for colonial mistakes of the past, "Aimard called for large-scale emigrations of decent French families to California"[89] – a stance that is ironic at best. The primary point here is chronotopic use of a literary genre with an eye to popular reception, in France and America. With French colonialism and the administration of new American territories in the background, to cite only two possible frames of reference, a relatively minor subplot of *The Frontiersmen* is foregrounded in later novels to address new circumstances that might have been of interest to readers on both sides of the Atlantic in the 1880s. The contention, then, is that the translations of Aimard's novels, much like the novels of both Scott and Cooper, aided the understanding of modernity in America. Aimard's novels offered timely reinterpretations of modernity, thus contributing to the constant self-reflexivity central to modernity itself. In other words, novels were read by individual readers with their own interests in mind. To say that American readers read as Americans to engineer their existence is not to avoid the question of influence. It is, instead, to turn the question on its head by recalling that meaning is not encoded in texts. Authors expressed their own interests and related their own experiences; they aimed to interest and possibly guide readers; and they hoped, along with publishers, to profit from the emergent interest in novel reading. This, however, did not deprive readers of the ability to make their own meanings. In this way, it matters less that Aimard was French and more that American readers identified with or could make use of his novels, as they did with those written by Cooper and others.

Notes

1 Zboray, *Fictive People*, 82.
2 Trish Loughran, *The Republic in Print: Print Culture in the Age of U. S. Nation Building 1770–1870* (New York: Columbia University Press, 2007), 23.
3 Robert A. Gross, "Introduction," in Gross and Kelley, *An Extensive Republic*, 13.
4 Elizabeth Barnes, "Novels," in Gross and Kelley, *An Extensive Republic*, 443.
5 Gross, "Introduction," 44, 46.
6 Michael Winship, "Distribution and the Trade," in Casper et al., *The Industrial Book, 1840–1880*, 129. Jeffrey D. Groves, "Trade Communication," in Casper et al., *The Industrial Book, 1840–1880*, 131.
7 Kenneth Carpenter, "Libraries," in Gross and Kelley, *An Extensive Republic*, 274.
8 Ibid., 281.
9 Meredith L. McGill, "Copyright," in Gross and Kelley, *An Extensive Republic*, 198.
10 Gross, "Introduction," 22.
11 Ibid., 41.

104 Home and away

12 Ibid., 18.

13 Richard R. John, "Expanding the Realm of Communications," in Gross and Kelley, *An Extensive Republic*, 216.

14 Gross, "Introduction," 37.

15 John L. Brooke, "Print and Politics," in Gross and Kelley, *An Extensive Republic*, 185.

16 Ibid., 186.

17 Dana Brown, "Travel Books," in Gross and Kelley, *An Extensive Republic*, 450.

18 John Simons, "Introduction: Why Read Chapbooks?" in *Guy of Warwick and Other Chapbook Romances: Six Tales from the Popular Literature of Pre-Industrial England*, ed. John Simons (Exeter: University of Exeter Press, 1998), 24.

19 Victor E. Neuburg, *The Penny Histories: A Study of Chapbooks for Young Readers over Two Centuries* (London: Oxford University Press, 1968), 48.

20 Ibid., 51.

21 Green, "The Rise of Book Publishing," 90.

22 Ibid., 97.

23 Ibid., 91.

24 Ibid., 92.

25 Ibid., 107.

26 Barnes, "Novels," 443.

27 James Fenimore Cooper, *The Pathfinder; or, The Inland Sea* (London: Richard Bentley, 1840); *The Pathfinder; or, The Inland Sea* (Philadelphia: Lea and Blanchard, 1840).

28 Richard D. Rust, "Historical Introduction," in *The Pathfinder, or, The Inland Sea*, by James Fenimore Cooper, approved ed., ed. Richard D. Rust (Albany: State University of New York Press, 1981), xviii.

29 See Harthorn, "Cooper's Return," 219. Harthorn refers to "Editor's Book Table," *Godey's Lady's Book* 20 (May 1840): 239; and "Editor's Table," *Knickerbocker* 15 (May 1840): 449.

30 James Fenimore Cooper, *The Pathfinder, or, The Inland Sea: By the Author of "The Pioneers" etc.* (London: Richard Bentley, 1843), Standard novels, no. 90; *The Pathfinder, or, The Inland Sea: By the Author of 'The Pioneers,' 'The Last of the Mohicans,' 'The Prairie,' etc.* (London: R. Bentley, 1850), Standard novels, no. 90; *The Pathfinder*, vol. 10 of *The Works of James Fenimore Cooper*, 10 vols. (London: Richard Bentley, 1854).

31 Richard D. Rust, "Textual Commentary," in *The Pathfinder, or, The Inland Sea*, by James Fenimore Cooper, approved ed., ed. Richard D. Rust (Albany: State University of New York Press, 1981), 478.

32 Louise Stevenson, "Homes, Books, and Reading," in Casper et al., *The Industrial Book, 1840–1880*, 319.

33 See Robert E. Spiller and Philip C. Blackburn, *A Descriptive Bibliography of the Writings of James Fenimore Cooper* (New York: R. R. Bowker, 1934), 167. James Fenimore Cooper, *Novels and Tales: By the Author of The Spy*, 26 vols. (Philadelphia: Carey and Lea, 1835–36); *Novels and Tales: By the Author of The Spy*, 2nd ser., 14 vols. (Philadelphia: Carey and Lea, 1841).

34 Spiller and Blackburn, *Bibliography*, 168.

35 James Fenimore Cooper, *The Pathfinder, or, The Inland Sea*, vol. 6 of *The Works of J. Fenimore Cooper*, 12 vols. (New York: George P. Putnam, 1851).

36 Rust, "Textual Commentary," 477.

37 James Fenimore Cooper, *The Pathfinder, or, The Inland Sea: Complete in 1 Vol.* (New York: Putnam, 1852); *The Pathfinder*, author's rev. ed. (New York: G. P. Putnam, 1853).

Home and away 105

38 Rust, "Textual Commentary," 478.
39 James Fenimore Cooper, *The Pathfinder, or, The Inland Sea*, vol. 13 of *Cooper's Works*, 33 vols. (New York: Stringer and Townsend, 1852); *The Pathfinder*, vol. 13 of *Cooper's Works* (New York: Stringer and Townsend, 1853); *The Pathfinder*, vol. 3 of *The Leather-stocking Tales*, 5 vols. (New York: Stringer and Townsend, 1854).
40 James Fenimore Cooper, *The Pathfinder, or, The Inland Sea*, vol. 4 of *The Choice Works of Cooper: Revised and Corrected Series: With New Introductions, Notes, Etc.*, 34 vols (New York: Stringer and Townsend, 1856).
41 Spiller and Blackburn, *Bibliography*, 170–71.
42 See, for example, James Fenimore Cooper, *The Pathfinder, or, The Inland Sea*, illus. Felix Octavius Carr Darley (New York: W. A. Townsend, 1860).
43 James Fenimore Cooper, *Cooper's Novels*, people's ed., 34 vols. (New York: W. A. Townsend and Company [Stringer and Townsend], 1857–60).
44 James Fenimore Cooper, *The Pathfinder, or, The Inland Sea*, vol. 7 of *Cooper's Novels*, 32 vols., illus. Felix Octavius Carr Darley (New York: James G. Gregory [successor to W. A. Townsend], 1864). See also, James Fenimore Cooper, *The Pathfinder, or, The Inland Sea* (New York: James G. Gregory, 1864).
45 Some examples are James Fenimore Cooper, *Cooper's Novels*, 32 vols. (New York: Hurd and Houghton; Boston: E. P. Dutton, 1865); *The Works of James Fenimore Cooper*, 32 vols. (New York: Hurd and Houghton, 1868–72); *James Fenimore Cooper's Novels*, 31 vols. (New York: D. Appleton, 1872–73); and *The "Leather-Stocking" Tales*, 5 vols. (New York: D. Appleton, 1873).
46 James Fenimore Cooper, *The Pathfinder, or, The Inland Sea*, vol. 3 of *Leather Stocking Tales*, 5 vols. (New York: Hurd and Houghton, 1869); *The Pathfinder*, vol. 3 of *'Leather-stocking' Tales*, 5 vols. in 1 (New York: Appleton, 1873); *The Pathfinder, or, The Inland Sea*, introd. Susan Fenimore Cooper, household ed., vol. 3 of *The Leatherstocking Tales*, 5 vols. (Boston: Houghton, Mifflin; Cambridge: Riverside, 1876); *The Pathfinder, or, The Inland Sea, a Tale*, introd. Susan Fenimore Cooper, Riverside ed., vol. 3 of *The Leatherstocking Tales*, 5 vols. (Boston: Houghton, Mifflin, 1898); *The Pathfinder*, vol. 3 of *The Works of James Fenimore Cooper*, Mohawk ed., 33 vols. (New York: G. P. Putnam's Sons, 1895).
47 Rigney, *Afterlives of Walter Scott*, 118.
48 Zboray, *Fictive People*, xvi.
49 Michael Winship, "The International Trade in Books," in Casper et al., *The Industrial Book, 1840–1880*, 148.
50 George Sand, "George Sand on Cooper," in *Fenimore Cooper: The Critical Heritage*, ed. George Dekker and John P. McWilliams (London: Taylor and Francis e-Library, 2003), 274.
51 Wallace, *Early Cooper*, 171.
52 Willard Thorp, "Cooper Beyond America," *New York History* 35, no. 4 (1954): 526, www.jstor.org/stable/24470853.
53 Cooper, [*Pathfinder*], Bentley, 1843; *Pathfinder*, Bentley, 1850; *Pathfinder*, Bentley, 1854.
54 For an early reprint of *The Pathfinder* by Routledge, see James Fenimore Cooper, *The Pathfinder, or, The Inland Sea: By the Author of "The Pioneers" etc.* (London: G. Routledge, 1855).
55 James Fenimore Cooper, *The Novels and Romances of J. Fenimore Cooper: A New Edition in Thirteen Volumes*, 13 vols. (London: Routledge, Warne and Routledge, 1864); *The Pathfinder*, vol. 1 of *The Novels and Romances of J. Fenimore Cooper*, 13 vols. (London: Routledge, Warne, 1864).

106 Home and away

56 James Fenimore Cooper, *Cooper's Novels*, 18 vols. (London: George Routledge and Sons, 1866–67); *The Pathfinder, or, The Inland Sea*, vol. 10 of *Cooper's Novels*, 18 vols. (London: George Routledge and Sons, 1866).

57 James Fenimore Cooper, *The Pioneers; The Last of the Mohicans; The Prairie; The Pathfinder* (London: Routledge, 1867); *Cooper's 'Leather-Stocking' Tales: Comprising, The Deerslayer, The Pathfinder, The Last of the Mohicans, The Pioneers, The Prairie*, 5 vols. (London: G. Routledge and Sons, 1868); *Cooper's "Leather-Stocking" Tales: Comprising, The Deerslayer, The Pathfinder, The Last of the Mohicans, The Pioneers, The Prairie* (London: George Routledge and Sons, 1887).

58 James Fenimore Cooper, *The Pathfinder*, vol. 3 of *Cooper's Leather-stocking Tales for Boys and Girls: With Illustrations*, 5 vols. in 1 (London: G. Routledge and Sons, 1892).

59 James Fenimore Cooper, *The Pathfinder, or, The Inland Sea: By the Author of "The Pioneers" etc.* (London: Frederick Warne, 1867); *The Pathfinder, or, The Inland sea: By the Author of "The Pioneers" etc.* (London: Frederick Warne, 1887), Warne's "Crown" library, no. 18; *The Pathfinder, or, The Inland Sea*, illust. ed. (London: Frederick Warne, ca. 1900).

60 Although my focus in this chapter is on France, German translations were also extensive. See Spiller and Blackburn, *Bibliography*, 188–93; and Preston A. Barba, *Cooper in Germany* (Bloomington: n.p., 1914), 93–104.

61 Thorp, "Cooper Beyond America," 528, 529.

62 James Fenimore Cooper, *Le lac Ontario, ou, le guide*, trans. Auguste-Jean-Baptiste Defauconpret (Paris: C. Gosselin, 1840).

63 James Fenimore Cooper, *Le lac Ontario, ou, le guide*, 2nd ed., 4 vols. (Paris, 1840), *Œuvres complètes de M. James Fenimore Cooper, Américain; Le lac Ontario ou le guide*, trans. Auguste-Jean-Baptiste Defauconpret, 3 vols. (Bruxelles: Meline, Cans, 1840); *Le lac Ontario*, trans. Auguste-Jean-Baptiste Defauconpret, vol. 17 of *Œuvres de J. F. Cooper*, 17 vols. (Paris: Furne, 1839–40); *Le lac Ontario*, trans. Auguste-Jean-Baptiste Defauconpret, vol. 17 of *Œuvres de J.-F. Cooper* (Paris: Furne-Gosselin, 1840); *Le lac Ontario*, trans. Auguste-Jean-Baptiste Defauconpret, vol. 17 of *Œuvres*, 30 vols. (Paris: Furne, 1830–52); *Le lac Ontario*, trans. Auguste-Jean-Baptiste Defauconpret, vol. 17 of *Œuvres*, 30 vols. (Paris: Furne, Pagnerre, Perrotin/Furne, Jouvet, Garnier frères, 1872).

64 James Fenimore Cooper, *L'Ontario*, trans. Emile de la Bédollière (Paris: Barba, 1850), *Romans populaires illustrés*.

65 Spiller and Blackburn, *Bibliography*, 185.

66 For a comprehensive discussion of the popular literary western, see Christine Bold, *Selling the Wild West: Popular Western Fiction 1860–1960* (Bloomington: Indiana University Press, 1987).

67 Mayne Reid, *The Scalp Hunters: A Romance of the Plains* (New York: Beadle and Adams, 1875); *The Free Lances: A Romance of the Mexican Valley* (London: Routledge and Sons, 1905). Edward Ellis, *Seth Jones; or, The Captive of the Frontier* (New York: Beadle, 1860), Beadle's dime novels, no. 8. See, for example, Edward Wheeler, *Deadwood Dick in Leadville: or, A Strange Stroke for Liberty* (New York: Beadle and Adams, 1879), Beadle's half dime library, no. 100.

68 For example, on Cooper's influence on Ellis's *Seth Jones*, see Christine Bold, "Malaeska's Revenge; or, The Dime Novel Tradition in Popular Fiction," in *Wanted Dead or Alive: The American West in Popular Culture*, ed. Richard Aquila (Urbana: University of Illinois Press, 1996), 24.

69 See Albert Johannsen, *The House of Beadle and Adams and Its Dime and Nickel Novels: The Story of a Vanishing Literature*, 1st ed., vol. 1 (Norman: University of Oklahoma Press, 1950).

70 Thorp, "Cooper Beyond America," 531–32.

Home and away 107

71 Charvat, *Literary Publishing*, 24.
72 Thorp, "Cooper Beyond America," 533.
73 First American edition: Gustave Aimard, and Frances Henshaw Baden, *The Frontiersmen: A Novel* (New York: F. M. Lupton, 1854). All references are to Gustave Aimard, *The Frontiersmen: A Novel* (New York: F. M. Lupton, 1892), https://archive.org/details/frontiersmennove00aimarich.
74 Aimard, *Frontiersmen*, 96–98.
75 Ibid., 80.
76 Ibid., 108–9.
77 Ibid., 164.
78 Emmanuel Dubosq, "Aventure, idéologie et représentation du monde indien chez Gustave Aimard" (MA thesis, Université de Caen, 2003), http://docplayer.fr/14464392-Aventure-ideologie-et-representation-du-monde-indien-chez-gustave-aimard.html.
79 Mayne Reid, *The Rifle-Rangers, or, Adventures in Southern Mexico* (London: W. Shoberl, 1850). Gabriel Ferry, *Le coureur des bois, ou, les chercheurs d'or*, new ed. (Paris: Librairie illustrée, 1850). See Thorp, "Cooper Beyond America," 533.
80 Gustave Aimard, *Les pirates des prairies* (Paris: Amyot, 1858).
81 Thorp, "Cooper Beyond America," 533.
82 See, for example, Gustave Aimard, *The Pirates of the Prairies: or, Adventures in the American Desert*, trans. Lascelles Wraxall, complete and unabridged ed. (Philadelphia: T. B. Peterson, 1862), Aimard's novels, v. 2.
83 See, for example, Gustave Aimard, *The Prairie Pirates, or, The Hunter's Revenge* (New York: Beadle and Adams, 1869), Beadle's pocket novels, no. 218; *The Bandit at Bay, or The Pirates of the Prairies* (New York: Beadle and Adams, 1879), Beadle's New York dime library, no. 20.
84 Gustave Aimard, *Aimard's Indian Tales: Author's Copyright Ed.*, ed. Percy Bolingbroke St. John, 27 vols. (London: J. and R. Maxwell, 1877–79).
85 Gustave Aimard, *Works of Gustave Aimard*, ed. and rev. Percy Bolingbroke St. John, 8 vols. (London, 1877–79).
86 See, for example, Gustave Aimard, *The Pirates of the Prairies*, rev. and ed. Percy Bolingbroke St. John (New York: Lovell, 1887), Lovell's library, no. 1011; *The Indian Scout. Being the Conclusion of "The Prairie Flower,"* rev. and ed. Percy Bolingbroke St. John (New York: George Munro's Sons, 1893), Seaside library, no. 1740; *Stronghand*, rev. and ed. Percy Bolingbroke St. John (New York: George Munro, 1895), Boys' dashaway series, no. 46.
87 Benjamin T. Spencer, *The Quest for Nationality: An American Literary Campaign* (Syracuse, NY: Syracuse University Press, 1957), 112.
88 Gustave Aimard, *Les bandits de l'Arizona* (Limoges: E. Ardant, 1882).
89 Coward, "Popular Fiction in the Nineteenth Century," in *The Cambridge Companion to the French Novel: From 1800 to the Present*, ed. Timothy A. Unwin (Cambridge: Cambridge University Press, 1997), 82.

6 "Spiders in a pot"

Harnessing juggernaut in *Le père Goriot*

> The juggernaut crushes those who resist it, and while it sometimes seems to have a steady path, there are times when it veers away erratically in directions we cannot foresee. The ride is by no means wholly unpleasant or unrewarding; it can often be exhilarating and charged with hopeful anticipation. But, so long as the institutions of modernity endure, we shall never be able to control completely either the path or the pace of the journey. In turn, we shall never be able to feel entirely secure, because the terrain across which it runs is fraught with risks of high consequence. Feelings of ontological security and existential anxiety will coexist in ambivalence.
>
> – Anthony Giddens, *The Consequences of Modernity*, 139

The power struggle between the aristocracy and the bourgeoisie during the Restoration period in France was a form of class warfare carried over from 1789. The aristocracy fought to maintain a pre-Revolution level of social authority; the bourgeoisie aimed to take advantage of changes brought about by the Revolution and Napoleon. At the heart of the struggle was wealth. The accumulation of capital enabled upward mobility for the bourgeoisie; for the aristocracy, it was a means to shore up social prestige and other forms of distinction. In other words, financial prosperity meant power – gained or resumed. In this context, marriage continued to be a useful tool; it could provide a profitable link between the new affluence of the bourgeoisie and the nobility of the aristocracy. Nevertheless, what was remarkably different in this period was the means to manufacture the economic resources that reshaped the structure and flow of social power. Economic liberalism "began to make serious progress for the first time during the late 1820s."[1] Assured peace, high tariffs against British products, stable currency, investment in canals, and other factors enhanced the ability to plan investment and broaden markets.[2] The impact was felt at all levels of society, though unevenly. The rewards could be pronounced for those able to cultivate connections and opportunities; at the other end of the social spectrum, life remained a battle. Widespread social transformations resulting from capitalist modes of production made the question of modernization the focal point of both public discourse and collective resistance.

"*Spiders in a pot*"   109

Reformers set out intellectual arguments against capitalist individualism;[3] industrial workers acted upon their own experiences of modern life and fought for better conditions.[4] Radical opposition highlighted the extreme consequences of unfettered capitalism. The stakes were high. Everyday life seemed to pit each against all in a fight for dominance, upward mobility, or survival – depending on one's position in society.

In this context, Honoré de Balzac began his career as a writer. In the early-nineteenth century, the canonical authors of French literature were dramatists of the eighteenth century. Not surprisingly, then, Balzac's first literary work was a tragedy in blank verse; *Cromwell* (1819), however, went unproduced and was not published during his lifetime.[5] His next step, a turn to novel writing, was both of the moment and practical.[6] The publication of novels was on the rise.[7] Romance, adventure, and crime novels sold well enough to support writers such as Paul de Kock, whose "pictures of Paris life amused France for half a century with tales of concierges, artisans, and amiable *rentiers* who pursue accommodating *grisettes*."[8] The growing market for prose fiction did not rely solely upon an appetite for entertainment; much new fiction carried on a tradition of social criticism more commonly associated with dramatists such as Jean Racine and Molière. In the early-nineteenth century, the *roman d'intrique sentimentale*, the *roman noir*, and the *roman gai* were popular forms of the novel: the sentimental mystery novels of Sophie Cottin and Sophie Gay criticized contemporary marriage and other forms of social constraint; François Guillaume Ducray-Duminil wrote dark adventure novels that tapped into deep-seated social fears; and Charles-Antoine-Guillaume Pigault-Lebrun added his own mixture of realism and social observation, usually of the lower classes or underground crime, with stories that "pitted beleaguered lower-class heroes against foreign agents, convicts, money-men and conspirators who oppress the vulnerable."[9] Balzac experimented with all three forms, and their corresponding themes, in his early works as well as later in novels collected under the title *La comédie humaine*.[10] For example, in *Physiologie du mariage* (1829), he wrote of women and married life; in *Le père Goriot* (1835), he entered into the mysteries of the underground world of Paris; and strong descriptions of social setting inclusive of a range of classes are common to early and later novels. In short, Balzac wrote novels of social transformation, but he also integrated formal and thematic resources usual to popular fiction. In this chapter, I show how he used the historical novel to dramatize history in a way that was relevant to the everyday life of readers in modern France.

Balzac's development of the popular novel in France and the historical novel more specifically depended on continued attention to the demands of readers.[11] Many of the most popular authors and works of the period incorporated or dealt directly with historical representation.[12] Pamela Pilbeam notes "a fivefold increase in historical works between 1812 and 1825,"[13] and Françoise Parent-Lardeur describes a vogue in historical romance from 1815 to 1832 inspired largely by the success of Walter Scott.[14] Balzac's first

110 *"Spiders in a pot"*

historical novel, and the first of his novels not published under a pseudonym, *Les chouans* (1829), is based on the defeat of a royalist insurrection, following in the footsteps of Scott's *Waverley*. As Richard Maxwell explains, early French historical novels such as Madame de La Fayette's *La princesse de Clèves* (1678) and Abbé Prévost's *Le philosophe Anglois ou histoire de Monsieur Cleveland* (1731–39) were influential precursors to the combination of history and romance in nineteenth-century historical novels – in France and Britain.[15] However, in the first half of the nineteenth century, the impact of the Waverley novels on writing, publishing, and reading was overwhelming.

With no international copyright agreements in place, the Waverley novels were quickly reproduced throughout Europe.[16] French publishers were hungry for English novels. As William St Clair describes, "By the late 1820s, every new British novel was on sale in Paris within three days of its publication in London, in a beautiful, well printed, convenient, cloth bound, single-volume edition, at a quarter of the British price."[17] English works were popular enough among expatriates and French readers of English to be repeatedly reprinted as single volumes and as part of collections.[18] The circulation of Waverley novels in translation was even more extensive, involving reprints, collections, and illustrated and downmarket editions. As indicated by reading room catalogues, Scott was one of the most read novelists in France.[19] Maxwell's remarks concerning the impact of the Waverley novels on French literature are accurate although perhaps understated: "Over the course of a century, they were, for all practical purposes, assimilated into the literary and even the political history of France."[20] New editions were not only corrected or revised but also, for example, redesigned for children to take advantage of the popularity of illustrated editions, and thus to make Scott more accessible to a new generation of readers. Entrepreneurial publishers responded to, and actively cultivated, the modernization of print and reading in France by repeatedly reprinting Waverley novels such as *The Heart of Mid-Lothian*.[21] In this way, the reproduction of Scott in France facilitated the reading and writing of historical and other types of novels – in France and throughout the world; as Ian Duncan states, "Scott, in short, belonged to French literature, and thence to the world republic of letters, quite as much as he did to Scottish and British traditions."[22]

The practical outcomes of Scott's popularity on the writing of historical novels in France were many and varied. Perhaps due to the popularity of *Ivanhoe* (1820) and *Quentin Durward* (1823), several prominent French historical novels of the 1820s were set in the Middle Ages and emphasized military conflict between nations.[23] The historical novel was also used to chronicle the manners of distant historical periods, as in Prosper Mérimée's *Chronique du règne de Charles IX* (1829), or to investigate philosophical themes, as in Alfred Victor de Vigny's *Cinq-Mars* (1826), the third edition of which was published by Balzac.[24] Nevertheless, the shift in popular taste noted by James Smith Allen, "from a traditional folk to a more modern

"Spiders in a pot" 111

popular culture,"[25] led to practical uses of a different sort. As evidenced by the explosion of print reading in the aftermath of the Revolution, readers in France wanted to know more about the world around them, especially as journalism began to make knowledge of contemporary events more accessible, and as historical novels described what was new about the present. The adventures of Napoleon and the impact of the 1830 Revolution intrigued readers, who were interested in current events as well as the literary works that described them, which enabled reinterpretations of their own experiences of the modern world. Entrepreneurial publishers and historical novelists responded to the self-reflexivity that readers brought to their lives, and in turn, to their reading. As such, Balzac's response to the Waverley novels, and more, the implications of modernity in France, spurred his own development of historical fiction.

Balzac's path toward *La comédie humaine* echoed a shift to "modern popular culture," understood as the representation of modernization in popular forms of communication. Early in his career, "Balzac made notes for two historical novels, one, *Le Capitaine des Boute-Feu*, with a fifteenth-century setting, and the other, *Le Gars* [later to become *Les Chouans*], set in the very recent period of the royalist insurrection known as the Chouannerie."[26] Stéphane Vachon puts the change in focus in the following terms: "It is not a discovery made only by Balzac, but rather a resolution which comes out of the confrontation with Walter Scott, read as historian of his nation, observer of its people and its costumes, rebuilding the past from the present."[27] Either setting could have been used to address issues of interest to contemporary readers, but the terms of Balzac's engagement with the past were as particular to national context as Scott's. Balzac used the recent past to further popular understanding of the post-Revolution social transformation in France, and more, to describe the impact of economic liberalism on everyday life. However interesting the reign of Charles IX, as either a subject of study or a point of comparison, the lived experience of modernity – in urban Paris, principally – would have interested many readers attempting to understand and adapt to modern life. Similarly, in 1825, Balzac outlined a series of novels to be titled *Histoire de France pittoresque*, noting that "each century of French history has its emblematic figure and must be the subject of a study and of a novel."[28] As with James Fenimore Cooper's early plan to emulate the Waverley novels, the idea to bring a long view of national history to French readers was likely inspired by the success of the Waverley novels, the settings for which stretch from the eleventh century (in *Count Robert of Paris* [1832]) to the near present (in *Saint Ronan's Well* [1824]), as well as the popularity of historiography with French readers.[29] By the end of the 1820s, Balzac's historical project had come to focus on the more recent, radical points of departure that captured the popular imagination and more openly influenced everyday life in contemporary France. The 1789 Revolution was without question the defining historical moment of the period, but in the shadow of 1789 and the Napoleonic Wars, the expansion of capitalist

112   *"Spiders in a pot"*

economics from the Restoration to the 1830s could not be ignored. Following the 1830 Revolution, the fundamental nature and consequences of modernity took center stage, as signified by Balzac's timely shift from the *Waverley*esque representation of national conflict in *Les chouans* to the investigation of modernization in *Le père Goriot*.

Just as the Waverley novels are often glossed by general reference to *Waverley* or as representative of society in motion, Scott's shadow may mask the chronotopic specificity of Balzac's use of the historical novel to respond to modernity. The events of *Le père Goriot* take place from November 1819 to February 1820. Rather than a *Waverley*esque "sixty years since," the difference between setting and publication is only fifteen years. Vachon locates this temporal shift with respect to the press, arguing that as "journalism takes Balzac towards the history of the present and not only the past, he becomes the secretary of 'the history of manners in action.' Journalistic activity is indeed primarily responsible, in 1830, for the 'turn' or swing from *Histoire de France pittoresque* to *Études de mœurs*."[30] Of significance here is Balzac's attention to the localization of historical representation. Andre Maurois's comment is apt: "For a period to become matter for an historical novel it needs to have lapsed a little into the past; but 'a nation sometimes grows more in a decade than in a century.' "[31] Both *The Heart of Mid-Lothian* and *Le père Goriot* speak to early development of the nation-state, but each sets forth a chronotopic history of modernization. First, both locate a key moment in the transition to modernity. Initially, *The Heart of Mid-Lothian* is concerned with the Porteous riots of 1736–37, but the plot of the novel plays out over the following two decades, leading to the 1760s, a critical temporal juncture in the Industrial and Agricultural Revolutions that fueled modernization in Britain. Similarly, Rastignac's lifespan covers the transformation of France to a modern nation-state – predominantly capitalist, more democratic, increasingly industrial – from 1789 to the middle of the nineteenth century; the time between setting and publication further emphasizes the dramatic changes from Restoration to July Monarchy. Second, for both Scott and Balzac, responding to contemporary circumstances took precedence over nostalgia for traditional sociopolitical structures.[32] In each case, this meant that historification, initially at least, had to conform to local priorities. As such, for Balzac, effective description of the conditions, mechanisms, and consequences of modernization in France required a depiction of historical transformation fitted to the here and now of everyday life as experienced by most French readers, hence Balzac's rather cryptic statement in the opening pages of *Le père Goriot*: "Will it be understood outside Paris? One may doubt it."[33]

Paris was the center of change in modern France. As France remained largely agricultural, change occurred first in the cities, specifically Paris, where the "population doubled in the first half of the century, reaching a level of over a million."[34] The government was decided in Paris throughout the century, and a large, literate, and sometimes radical working-class

"*Spiders in a pot*" 113

population made the capital a hotbed of political conflict.[35] *Le père Goriot*, however, is even more precisely located. The focal point of the narrative is a middle-class boarding house, Maison Vauquer, at the lower end of Rue Neuve-Sainte-Geneviève, which was inaccessible by carriage, immersed in the shadows and silence of the Latin Quarter. David Coward writes that "most novels [of the 1830s] were *romans de mœurs* set in elegant drawing rooms (balls, gambling, conversation) where dramas of finance and adultery were played out."[36] *Le père Goriot* also introduces the reader to elegant drawing rooms – those of the Faubourg Saint-Germain – but they are, pivotally, in contrast to Maison Vauquer, which provides an uncomfortable space of struggle inhabited by a range of social types. More decisively, this out-of-the-way boarding house is the focal point of a novel that responds to modernization by describing the integration of people, place, and practices that constitute and are constituted by the practices of modernity. The fifty-year-old Madame Vauquer, for example, as the proprietor of Maison Vauquer, is inseparable from the post-Revolution social transformations her establishment embodies: "When she is there the picture is complete."[37] The assimilation of person and place may be understood in terms of the impact of historical circumstances on human behavior. But instrumental formulation neglects the complexities of historical agency. Madame Vauquer is "a product of the life she lives here,"[38] and not simply of broad historical currents. She is what she does – she copes with her own experience of modern life. The result seems morally despicable; nevertheless, the real question is one of community methods. Maison Vauquer, the existence of which spans the Revolution to the Restoration (1779–1820), is a microcosm of the inseparable interconnections of social context and individual action. The results are dramatic; the incessant pursuit of financial gain turns Madame Vauquer's good heart cold – a theme that returns with a vengeance as the novel concludes. Of first importance, however, is that the pursuit itself is historical. Maison Vauquer functions as a snapshot of the people's struggle against the seemingly unstoppable force of modernity: "The chariot of civilization, like the chariot of Juggernaut, is scarcely halted by a heart less easily crushed than the others in its path. It soon breaks this hindrance to its wheel and continues its triumphant course."[39] As such, the lowly boarding house takes on a contextual duality, representing the localization of modern forces that do not originate in and are not contained by Paris. Regardless, the real issue is how to cope with the juggernaut that is modernity. The answer defines the practices of everyday life and community formation in modern France.

The cracked and frayed wallpaper of the Maison Vauquer depicts scenes from Fénelon's *Les aventures de Télémaque* (1699). In other words, despite *Télémaque*'s continuing popularity,[40] readers required new lessons suited to modern times – hence the story of Eugène de Rastignac, a twenty-one-year-old law student come to Paris from the neighborhood of Angoulême to support a noble family in humble circumstances. The focal point of Balzac's

114 *"Spiders in a pot"*

investigation of modernity, Rastignac's "observant curiosity,"[41] makes the novel something of a journalistic unraveling of modern circumstances. As a *Waverley*esque figure, Rastignac reveals the social trajectory of the provincial nobleman aiming to find a foothold between the Parisian nobility and the *haute bourgeoisie* (the 90,000 males who could vote). However, the lessons are more widely applicable to the modernization of France. *Le père Goriot* is a novel of "progress" with national implications, though less so because of the symptomatic bridging of class divides and more so because it portrays the consequences of modernity at the heart of daily life for all people. Rastignac's coming-of-age depends upon his engagement with three mentors, each representing a different layer of society: Madame la Vicomtesse de Beauséant, a family relative and leading light of the Faubourg Saint-Germain; Jacques Collin, alias Vautrin, agent and banker of the underworld; and Goriot, a retired industrialist.

According to Madame de Beauséant, to stand on higher ground requires the execution of rational, self-interested steps toward concrete goals: "The more cold-bloodedly you calculate the farther you will go. Strike ruthlessly and you will be feared. Regard men and women only as you do post-horses that you will leave worn out at every stage, and so you shall arrive at the goal of your desires."[42] A view of the world from above, where men and women, like horses and servants, are mere objects for personal pleasure or gain, makes visible a modernized world of lenders and debtors. The pursuit of power is not itself a direct result of modernity, but the understanding of people as well as things in terms of exchange value aligns with a capitalist ethics that persists throughout the novel; in *Le père Goriot*, everything has a price, whether a pair of gloves or a smile. Madame de Beauséant provides Rastignac with his first, broad lesson in social economics and political outcomes. The pronounced difference between the Hôtel de Beauséant and the Maison Vauquer, the luxurious center of the Faubourg Saint-Germain and a miserable boarding house filled with guests who feed "like animals at a trough,"[43] provides an initial frame of reference for the more concrete choices that await Rastignac.

Vautrin puts Madame de Beauséant's advice into starker terms and, ultimately, into action. Following *Télémaque*, Vautrin revels in the role of teacher: "Like Mentor, Vautrin is a site of truth."[44] His aims appear malevolent: "The wisdom of virtue is here replaced by the wisdom of crime."[45] Yet the superficial opposition between virtue and crime unravels quickly and otherwise disguises Vautrin's purpose – to reveal means and ends. The ethics of advancement is clear enough; in Vautrin's own words, "There are no such things as principles, there are only events; there are no laws, there are only circumstances: the man who is wiser than his fellows accepts events and circumstances in order to turn them to his own ends."[46] This moral disrobing leads to a bleak assessment of the life trajectories available to Rastignac, at least as he is situated at Maison Vauquer: subsistence, a career, perhaps marriage – servitude or compromise in every direction – the desperation of

"*Spiders in a pot*"   115

struggle and the dangers of uncertainty, not the freedom and prosperity that young men dream of upon entering the world. Crucially, Vautrin brings his lesson to life by drawing a vivid picture of the masses groveling and fighting for scraps, and concludes: "You must devour each other like spiders in a pot."[47] As Madame de Beauséant says, "the world is vile."[48] Vautrin's response to the modern world, in contrast to that of Madame de Beauséant, is not set against a world of salons and carriages but amid poverty and hopelessness. Yet his advice for Rastignac is familiarly cruel: "You must cut a pass through this mass of men like a cannon-ball, or creep among them like a pestilence. Honesty is of no avail."[49] In short, a Hobbesian world of each against all dominates, and in Vautrin's eyes, "the honest man is the common enemy."[50] Vautrin's own plan is both rational and unethical – to live like a monarch off the backs of slaves in the deep south of America. To advance this plan, he makes Rastignac an offer: Victorine Taillefer, a resident of Maison Vauquer, has been cut out of her family inheritance, but the "untimely" death of her brother in an arranged duel would leave Victorine an inheritance of one million francs; as she has already shown an interest in Rastignac, this sum would fall to him after their marriage. In return for arranging matters, Vautrin would receive twenty percent to fund his foreign exploits. With this practical lesson, Rastignac's illusions begin to fade away.

What exactly is revealed? In a section of *Capitalism in the Twenty-First Century* (2014) titled "Vautrin's Lesson," Thomas Piketty argues that the choice at hand is between work and inheritance.[51] Piketty notes that in a Balzac novel, a character had to have about thirty times the average income of the day to rise above mediocrity or live with a minimum of elegance. Obviously, no profession could provide this sort of separation from the majority, hence Vautrin's lesson – work does not pay – and his plan to take a cut of Victorine's inheritance, leaving Rastignac with a large, secure income. At a rate of return of five percent, Victorine's dowry of 800,000 francs (after Vautrin's cut) would have yielded 40,000 francs a year – about forty times the average annual income. Even more, Vautrin offers to leave his projected American fortune to Rastignac. Why doesn't Rastignac take this path? Rastignac's aversion to Vautrin's immoral plan or his preference for Delphine are obvious but unsatisfying responses. Based on the choices available to Rastignac, I argue that the answer depends on the re-embedding of social practices with respect to the broader circumstances of modernity.

"Virtue, my dear student, is indivisible: it either is, or it is not."[52] Theoretically, Vautrin may be correct; however, in practical terms, actions are inseparable from context. Each of Rastignac's three mentors capitalizes on circumstances by using the most effective weapon at their disposal: Madame de Beauséant relies on social status, Vautrin on connections in the underworld, and Goriot on industry. Although occupying different social strata, with respect to ends, they are essentially mirrors of each other – only the means change with context. Associated with the underground world of crime, Vautrin seems to be painted with a different brush, but the difference

116   *"Spiders in a pot"*

is cosmetic. Whereas Madame de Beauséant's view of the world depends on strict adherence to social order, Vautrin's view from below necessitates thought and action that borders on anarchy. Set against the tyranny of institutions upon which the aristocracy depends, he is labeled part of a " 'dangerous class' resulting from the 'working classes.' "[53] But this is merely part and parcel of the view from above. Vautrin is situated opposite to the Madame de Beauséants of the world; his views, like his path forward, cannot be the same. A closer look reveals that he has much in common with the banker Nucingen; Vautrin sets up as an agent and banker in the underworld. Further, he becomes agent and advisor to the Society of the Ten Thousand – sharks who will not touch anything for a profit of less than ten thousand. Nucingen above and Vautrin below – both are predators nonetheless, positioned to make money off the despair, trust, and ignorance of others. The detective that arrests Vautrin says, "his hoard of money and his brains are always at the service of vice, supply the funds for crime, and maintain a standing army of scamps who wage incessant war against society."[54] No doubt, but at base, the characterization is misleading. Vautrin, like Nucingen, is not so much against society as he is against anyone who will restrict his advancement; Vautrin makes use of what is available to him. Just as no one is exempt from the consequences of modernity, the logic (advantage), means (exploitation), and ends (prosperity/struggle) are consistent – above ground and below.

Noble Goriot, crushing silverware with his bare hands in a boarding house to serve his daughters, would seem to be another exception. Does he not love his daughters completely, unselfishly? Is he not the opposite of Vautrin? In fact, he laid the foundation of his fortune after the Revolution by selling flour for ten times as much as it cost him and sharing profits with the Committee for Public Welfare; his rise depended on exploitation and corruption. To put it bluntly, when the people were hungry, Goriot raked in the profits. Moreover, his attempts to find a foothold in his daughters' lives are fostered by his business acumen, a euphemistic term for the dishonesty that greases the wheels of accumulation in capitalist society. Actions speak louder than words: Goriot is unmatched in his undying, fatherly passion for his daughters, so much so that he threatens to kill, kidnap, and blackmail to establish them in life. His blindness to all that affects others is evident: when Rastignac tells him of the duel and the likely death of Victorine's brother, Goriot answers, "What is that to you?"[55] When Vautrin is arrested and Taillefer is dead, Goriot says, "Well, what matter? That's nothing to do with us."[56] His scheme to make millions by cheating import laws may be for the love of his daughters, but ethically, there is little to separate him from either Vautrin or Nucingen. All are spiders in a pot; harnessing juggernaut is everything.

The situation is this: "Obedience was boring, Revolt impossible and Struggle hazardous."[57] The only response available to Rastignac is exactly what Vautrin teaches: "It's a matter here of playing for high stakes; if you

"*Spiders in a pot*" 117

don't you're trifling, you cut no ice, and goodbye to you!"[58] In private, Rastignac soon begins to repeat this mantra to others: "There are circumstances in life, you see, when you have to play for big stakes and it's no use wasting your luck picking up pennies."[59] He first plays roulette with Delphine's money;[60] later, with money borrowed from his mother and sisters, "He played for high stakes, won or lost large sums of money and ended by taking the extravagant life of a young man about town as a matter of course."[61] The relevance of Rastignac's speculations goes well beyond the irresponsible behavior of a young man in Paris. While a property-owning middle class began to emerge in the nineteenth century, a strong divide remained between elites and the rest of society. Rastignac does not wish to settle for middle ground. To remove himself from the scene of struggle and uncertainty, he needs capital. Each mentor gives him, as Vautrin says, "a glimpse of the mechanism of the social machine."[62] The question is where exactly to attach himself. Rastignac has two choices.

On the one hand, as Piketty shows, "inheritance occupied a structurally central place in nineteenth-century society – central as both economic flow and social force."[63] Vautrin's proposal thus provides one option: by marrying Victorine, Rastignac would inherit the large fortune necessary to avoid labor. Further, in line with Balzac's own conservative views, it was a means to maintain social stability. As Ronnie Butler describes, after 1830, "Intermarriage was now clearly in the interests of both bourgeoisie and aristocracy and could make a valuable contribution to the social reconciliation which, for Balzac, was the prerequisite of national unity and revival."[64] In *Le père Goriot*, bourgeois women marry aristocrats (e.g., Anastasie marries the Comte de Restaud) and financiers (e.g., Delphine marries Nucingen). The transfer of capital is from women to men – not vice versa. In this way, marriage between classes did not change the patriarchal relationship between husband and wife. It was not uncommon for men to take control of their wives' property – through management if not ownership. For example, Anastasie is forced to cede control of her property to her husband; everything will go to the first-born son and nothing to the children resulting from an affair. Marriage and patriarchy seem to be clear, and evidently interconnected, responses to the dissolution of aristocratic family structures and the related threat of extreme capitalist circulation, encouraging the combination of noble men and wealthy women to continue a longstanding system of social differentiation based on class and gender.

While the importance of inheritance did not diminish over the course of the nineteenth century,[65] marriage was only one route to the actualization of social continuity and economic prosperity in the modern world. Marriage, in fact, was re-embedded as a function of modernity. Rastignac ends up with Madame de Nucingen in a newly furnished apartment in the Rue d'Artois, located between the Latin Quarter and the Faubourg Saint-Germain. Notably, he is not married; of greater significance, "he cast his provincial slough and slipped easily and effortlessly into a position which

118   *"Spiders in a pot"*

opened a fair prospect before him."[66] What constitutes this "fair prospect"? The new space occupied by an unmarried couple speaks more specifically to the centrality of speculation to the new social order. As Anthony Giddens states, "we shall never be able to control completely either the path or the pace of the journey."[67] Still, Rastignac's apartment is prepared by the industrialist Goriot and funded by the banker Nucingen. This is playing the game well. Lucienne Frappier-Mazur suggests that "The rule of the game is revolt. . . . it is the revolt of the new order against that of the former."[68] I argue instead that the socioeconomic context recommends a different point of emphasis; in fact, all are playing the same game, although not with the same advantages or for the same stakes. Rastignac is seeking out his point of greatest leverage – the point at which he can maximize his use of the machine, of juggernaut; this is the essence of the drift from Victorine to Delphine – a calculated gamble.

That the novels of *La comédie humaine* return repeatedly to the question of capitalism is no coincidence – it mattered to readers of all classes. *Le père Goriot* is more specific, however. Speculation played a relatively minor role during the Restoration, the setting of the novel, but the shift from 1830 to 1848, when the novel was published, is clear:

> The number of firms whose shares were quoted on the 'Bourse' rose from eight in 1816 to 42 in 1826 and to 88 in 1836, after which they increased dramatically to reach 260 by 1841. Sixty-eight coal companies were formed between 1835 and 1838, with a capital of 142 million. The 1840s saw a corresponding proliferation in railway companies, accompanied by a similar wave of speculation.[69]

Though the stock market was only beginning to play a significant economic role in 1820, the Restoration "appears above all as a period of intense speculation in which fortunes fluctuate rapidly, when personal triumphs are completed and disasters suffered."[70] Put otherwise, social transformation in modern France increasingly depended on new capital flows, which caused uncertainty and required new practices. Balzac brings this shift to bear upon the progress and outcomes of the novel. Delphine thus provides a second relevant path forward – a connection with her husband, Nucingen, who plays for high stakes with other people's money, as Rastignac himself learns to do.

The available means of accumulating capital represented in the novel are historical in different ways – yet only one looks forward. Vautrin's plan, as it begins with murder and ends with slavery, seems an unlikely option for Rastignac, who clings, unsuccessfully, to a provincial sense of ethics throughout most of the novel. In other ways, however, the proposed venture was a shrewd financial move suited to contemporary conditions; as Piketty writes, for the period 1770–1810, "All told, southern slave owners in the New World controlled more wealth than the landlords of old

Europe."[71] Following the rise of labor-intensive cash crops such as tobacco and rice, and the invention of the cotton gin in 1793, the subsequent expansion and entrenchment of slavery in the American South made Vautrin's plan to profit from slavery a lucrative option. Conversely, in retrospect, it seems a backward plan given the international movement to abolish slavery and considering the emergent modes of industrial manufacturing and capitalist economics on both sides of the Atlantic. Slavery was not abolished in the United States until ratification of the Thirteenth Amendment in December 1865; more importantly, although inequality remained largely stable throughout the nineteenth century, the nature of capital in France had already changed from landed capital to industrial and financial capital and real estate.[72] Although marriage as a means of transferring or accumulating property remained central to social life, the impact of modernization on capital flows is evident throughout the novel: Goriot, for example, made his fortune through industry and invested his profits in safer government bonds, which funded his daughter's marriages; Nucingen plunges Delphine's dowry, founded by Goriot's exploitation of the people during a moment of national crisis, into "shady dealings" – land developments used for "swindling poor people out of their money."[73] In this light, Rastignac's second option, Delphine, has everything to do with making the right bet – with an eye to the future. The real issue is how to maximize the longer-term acquisition of capital given the conditions of modernity. As reiterated in the novel, he "must attach himself to part of the machinery if he wanted to rise to the top of the machine."[74] As Pierre Berbéris emphasizes, the part he chooses "Is at *the home of Madame de Nucingen*, the banker's wife who can refuse him nothing and whose husband will help him to make his fortune as a partner."[75] With a view of Paris and Vautrin's lessons in mind, Rastignac makes a self-conscious transition from past ways to new circumstances by placing himself at Nucingen's feet. As later Balzac novels demonstrate, this enables him to take advantage of the economic opportunities afforded by "high" finance without losing out on the more traditional assurances of a large inheritance.

La maison Nucingen (1838) takes the form of a conversation among friends in 1836. The dialogue, however, recalls events in 1826–27, several years after the final scenes of *Le père Goriot*. The first part shows how Nucingen came to make his vast fortune; the second part shows how his association with Nucingen enabled Rastignac to establish an income of 40,000 a year. The accumulation of capital, and thus also economic freedom and social distinction, is all; Nucingen's guiding idea is that "capital is a power only when you are very much richer than other people."[76] He is a swindler, plain and simple, yet he is grand rather than petty. Rastignac helps Nucingen along in a minor way at an opportune moment; thus, he comes into his relatively paltry wealth. In this sense, Rastignac is peripheral to Nucingen, who lays bare the scale of exploitation and the cutthroat conditions underlying advancement. The lesson is clearly stated: "Our age is no better than

120 *"Spiders in a pot"*

we are; we live in an era of greed; no one troubles himself about the intrinsic value of a thing if he can only make a profit on it by selling it to somebody else; so he passes it on to his neighbor."[77] The incentive is not hidden either: "everybody longs to have money without working for it."[78] "Vautrin's lesson" resurfaces, and so too do the social consequences of modernity.

With *La maison Nucingen*, Balzac modernized Plato's *Symposium* (ca. 385–70 BC). Men at a drinking party in Paris discuss financial accumulation rather than love; the difference is the point – love, like marriage, is re-embedded by modernity. At the beginning of *Le père Goriot*, in front of the Maison Vauquer no less, a statue of the god of love is abandoned and deteriorating. A sketch of the state of human relationships develops as the novel progresses: Rastignac is separated from his home and will not return; Anastasie and Delphine reject their father and despise each other; Delphine's marriage is a "horrible mockery";[79] the Comte de Restaud disinherits Anastasie and her illegitimate children; Victorine is disowned by her father and brother; Madame de Beauséant is left by her lover; and Nucingen prefers an adulterous wife, as does the Vicomte de Beauséant. The situation appears dire. *Le père Goriot*, after all, is a story in which the protagonist pens a letter to his mother threatening to blow his brains out if he does not get the money to, as he says, "dig out my path."[80] The inevitable solution appears to be the separation, or removal, of sympathy from everyday life: Delphine exclaims, "To mix money with love! Isn't it horrible?";[81] Goriot concludes, "Let there be no more marriages!"[82] Such reactions are misleading, however; love and marriage continue, as reconstituted by modern usage – in the end, Rastignac will marry Nucingen's daughter. There was, then, no need to marry Victorine.

Would *Le père Goriot* be understood outside of Paris? As an act of modernity, undoubtedly, yes. Balzac makes direct reference to both Scott's *The Heart of Mid-Lothian* and Cooper's novels of the American frontier.[83] The comparisons are apt, pointing to a wider context through which to understand the novel. In the first case, Balzac gestures to Scott's tale of Jeanie Deans to situate his own illustration of individual progress in the modern world; in the second, Vautrin compares Paris to a "forest in the New World." A sense of transatlantic continuity is palpable, even as each author attempts to represent the conditions and consequences of modernity that interested local readers. In *Le père Goriot*, as in *The Heart of Mid-Lothian*, the heart is neither haven nor center, but rather in circulation. Rastignac's family life in the country provides a subtle, constant point of comparison throughout the novel, between a world in which the heart (supposedly) remains free to love, as in the Highlands of Christian Isobel Johnstone's *Clan Albin*, and a world in which the heart, like property, is something to "make a profit on by selling it to someone else." Relationships, like stocks, are either profitable or not – both are a gamble. The connection between sympathy and modernity is simplified; yet, it was perhaps an effective form of instruction for

"Spiders in a pot" 121

this reason. As in both *Clan Albin* and *The Heart of Mid-Lothian*, *Le père Goriot* includes many references to the heart, which, in the final third of the novel, is trampled, traded, silenced, sold, and crushed beneath the weight of juggernaut. The novel begins with this telling statement: "*All is true*, so true that everyone can recognize the elements of the tragedy in his own household, in his own heart perhaps."[84] Overall, then, the novel travels to a point where all can recognize the consequences of modernity, not merely in the selfishness that fuels social climbers like Rastignac and Nucingen, but also in the common relationships and everyday practices that are impacted in Paris as elsewhere. Despite his boundless love, Goriot is, in the end, victim of an "elegant parricide."[85] Experience teaches a hard lesson: "the two daughters had struck blow after blow, without remission or respite, at their father's heart."[86] Rastignac does not emerge unscathed: "He already loved selfishly."[87] In the final pages of the novel, Goriot provides Rastignac's final, heart-wrenching lesson: "Money buys everything, even daughters."[88] Over and over, the heart is questioned. Goriot wants to save it, at all costs: "Cut off my head, leave me only my heart."[89] But the diagnosis is otherwise, as the medical student, Bixiou, says, "The mechanism still works; but in his case it's a pity; it would be far better if he died."[90] The fate of Goriot is also the fate of Rastignac: "A strange pang shot through his heart when he saw that it was impossible for him to reach Delphine."[91] Still, Rastignac descends from Père Lachaise to dine with his lover; the Faustian bargain is made – he will exchange heart for fortune. Can it be any wonder that the novel ends with a declaration of war? In Paris, where all are "spiders in a pot," harnessing juggernaut is not only a matter of work or pleasure, but also of life and death. This, no doubt, was a lesson that readers from all walks of life could take to heart. With the repeated, varied reproduction of *Le père Goriot*, the opportunities to do so were omnipresent throughout the nineteenth century.

Notes

1 Gordon Wright, *France in Modern Times: From the Enlightenment to the Present*, 4th ed. (New York: Norton, 1987), 153.
2 Jeremy D. Popkin, *A History of Modern France*, 3rd ed. (Upper Saddle River, NJ: Pearson/Prentice Hall, 2006), 88.
3 Prominent socialist thinkers of the period included Henri de Saint Simon, who argued for a return to communitarian society, and Charles Fourier, a critic of individualism and bourgeois society.
4 See Pamela M. Pilbeam, *Republicanism in Nineteenth-Century France, 1814–1871* (New York: St. Martin's Press, 1995), esp. chapter 5, "Revolution and Popular Unrest: Republicans 1830–35," 95–128. Pilbeam, for example, notes that "Since the onset of the depression there had been constant marches and demonstrations in central Paris by artisans complaining about shortage of work and food and the soaring price of basic foods" (ibid., 96). She also highlights the association of workers among other responses to modernization (ibid., 115).

122 *"Spiders in a pot"*

5 On the production details for Balzac's early works, see André Maurois, *Prometheus: The Life of Balzac*, trans. Norman Denny (London: Bodley Head, 1965), 65–69.

6 On the history of Balzac's early novels, prior to those included in *La comédie humaine*, see Maurois, *Prometheus*, 565. In 1822, Balzac published two collaborative efforts, *L'héritage de Birague* and *Jean Louis, ou la fille trouvée*, under the pseudonym Lord R'hoone, and *Clotilde de Lusignan*, *Le centenaire* and *Le vicaire des Ardennes*, written under the pseudonym Horace de Saint-Aubin; in 1823, *La dernière fée* under the pseudonym Horace de Saint-Aubin; in 1824, *Annette et le criminel (Argon le pirate)*, again under the pseudonym Horace de Saint-Aubin, and *Du droit d'ainesse* and *Histoire impartiale des jésuites*, both of which were published anonymously; and in 1826, *Wann-Chlore*, also by Horace de Saint-Aubin, and *Code des gens honnêtes*, again anonymously (ibid.).

7 See, for example, James Smith Allen, *Popular French Romanticism: Authors, Readers, and Books in the 19th Century* (Syracuse, NY: Syracuse University Press, 1981). Allen records an increase in the production of novels "from only 210 titles in 1820, to more than 400 in 1838, its highest point in the romantic book trade" (ibid., 131).

8 David Coward, *A History of French Literature: From* Chanson de geste *to Cinema* (Oxford: Blackwell, 2002), 267.

9 Ibid., 265–66.

10 *La comédie humaine* is Balzac's multi-volume collection of more than ninety interlinked novels and stories (as well as stand-alone essays) depicting French society from 1815 to 1848. Honoré de Balzac, *La comédie humaine, Œuvres complètes de M. de Balzac* (Paris: Furne, Dubochet, Hetzel and Paulin, 1842–48).

11 For a different view, see Marion Ayton Crawford, introduction to *Old Goriot*, by Honoré de Balzac, trans. Marion Ayton Crawford (Harmondsworth: Penguin Books, 1983). Crawford argues that Balzac's early writing of popular novels corrupted his later work (ibid., 15–16).

12 See Martyn Lyons, *Reading Culture and Writing Practices in Nineteenth-Century France* (Toronto: University of Toronto Press, 2008), 23, 33.

13 Pilbeam, *Republicanism*, 73.

14 Françoise Parent-Lardeur, *Les cabinets de lecture: la lecture publique à Paris sous la restauration* (Paris: Payot, 1982), 155. Note: All translations of Parent-Lardeur are my own.

15 See Maxwell, *Historical Novel*, 11–58.

16 See Paul Barnaby, "Timeline of the European Reception of Sir Walter Scott, 1802–2005," in *The Reception of Sir Walter Scott in Europe*, ed. Murray Pittock (London: Continuum, 2006), xxvi–xli. For example, reprinting of *The Heart of Mid-Lothian* in Europe occurred early and often: in France and Switzerland (1818, extracts), Germany (1821), Denmark (1822), Italy (1823), Sweden (1824), the Netherlands (1825), Russia (1825), Poland (1826), Belgium (1827), Spain (1831), Denmark (1832–56, Collected Works), Hungary (1832; Pest), and Portugal (1839) (ibid.).

17 St Clair, *Reading Nation*, 296.

18 Scott was a mainstay for French publishers of popular literature in English. See Giles Barber, "Galignani's and the Publication of English Books in France from 1800 to 1852," *The Library*, 5th ser., 16 (1961): 267–86, http://library.oxford journals.org/content/s5-XVI/4/267.full.pdf.

19 Parent-Lardeur, *Cabinets de lecture*, 28.

20 Maxwell, *Historical Novel*, 101.

21 A select chronological list of French adaptations of Scott's *The Heart of Mid-Lothian* includes *La prison d'Edimbourg: nouveaux contes de mon*

"Spiders in a pot" 123

hôte, recueillis et mis au jour par Jedediah Cleishbotham (Paris: H. Nicolle, 1819); *La prison d'Édimbourg: nouveaux contes de mon hôte, recueillis et mis au jour par Jedediah Cleishbotham, maître d'école et sacristain de la paroisse de Gandercleugh* (Paris: Henri Nicolle, Ladvocat, 1821); *Oeuvres completes*, trans. Auguste-Jean-Baptiste Defauconpret (Paris: C. Grosselin and A. Sautelet, 1826–33); *La prison d'Édimbourg: conte de mon hôte, par Sir Walter Scott, traduction nouvelle*, trans. A. and P. Chaillot (Paris: F. Denn, 1829); *La prison du Mid-Lothian ou la jeune Caméronienne*, trans. Albert Montémont (Paris: Didot, 1835); *Le coeur de Mid-Lothian ou la prison d'Edimbourg*, trans. Louis Vivien (Paris: P. M. Pourrtat, 1837); *Oeuvres de Walter Scott*, trans. Albert Montémont (Paris: Firmin-Didot frères, 1840); *La prison d'Édimbourg*, trans. Auguste-Jean-Baptiste Defauconpret (Paris: G. Barba, 1844); *La prison du comté d'Edimbourg*, vol. 7, pt. 1 of *Les veillées littéraires illustrées*, trans. Louis Barré (Paris: J. Bry aîné, 1852); and *La prison du comté d'Edimbourg*, vol. 4 of *Oeuvres complètes de Walter Scott*, trans. Louis Barré (Paris: Librairie Centrale des Publications illustrées à 20 centimes, 1857).

22 Ian Duncan, "The Trouble with Man: Scott, Romance, and World History in the Age of Lamarck," in *Romantic Circles Praxis Series: Romantic Frictions*, ed. Theresa M. Kelley (September 2011): n. pag. (section 11), www.rc.umd.edu/praxis/frictions/HTML/praxis.2011.duncan.html.

23 Allen makes note of, for example, Augustin Thierry's *Histoire de la conquête de l'Angleterre* (1825) and Louis Édouard Gauttier du Lys d'Arc's *Histoire des conquêtes des Normands, en Italie, en Sicile, et en Grèce* (1830) (*Popular French Romanticism*, 41).

24 Maurois, *Prometheus*, 133.

25 Allen, *Popular French Romanticism*, 33.

26 Maurois, *Prometheus*, 133.

27 Stéphane Vachon, *Les travaux et les tours d'Honoré de Balzac: chronologie de la création balzacienne* (Paris: Presses Universitaires de Vincennes, Université de Paris VIII; Montréal: Les Presses de l'Université de Montréal, 1992), 17. Note: All translations of Vachon are my own.

28 Ibid., 16–17.

29 Walter Scott, [*Count Robert of Paris*] *Tales of My Landlord, Fourth and Last Series: Collected and Arranged by Jedediah Cleishbotham, Schoolmaster and Parish-Clerk of Gandercleuch. In Four Volumes* (Edinburgh: Robert Cadell; London: Whittaker, 1832). *Saint Ronan's Well: By The Author of "Waverley," "Quentin Durward," etc. In Three Volumes* (Edinburgh: Archibald Constable; London: Hurst, Robinson, 1824).

30 Vachon, *Travaux*, 19.

31 Maurois, *Prometheus*, 134.

32 With respect to Balzac, see Ronnie Butler, *Balzac and the French Revolution* (London: Croom Helm, 1983), 256.

33 Honoré de Balzac, *Old Goriot*, trans. Marion Ayton Crawford (Harmondsworth: Penguin Books, 1983), 27. Note: All translations of *Le père Goriot* (as *Old Goriot*) are by Crawford.

34 Popkin, *Modern France*, 109.

35 Robert Tombs, *France 1814–1914* (London: Longman, 1996), see esp. chapter 9, "Paris: Seat of Power," 185–92.

36 Coward, *French Literature*, 269.

37 Balzac, *Old Goriot*, 33.

38 Ibid.

39 Ibid., 28.

40 See Lyons, *Reading Culture*, 20–27.

124 *"Spiders in a pot"*

41 Balzac, *Old Goriot*, 35.
42 Ibid., 103.
43 Ibid., 106.
44 Jean-Jacques Hamm, "De Télémaque à Rastignac (suite)," in Gengembre, *Le père Goriot*, 319. Note: All translations from Gengembre are my own.
45 Ibid.
46 Balzac, *Old Goriot*, 134.
47 Ibid., 129.
48 Ibid., 102.
49 Ibid., 129.
50 Ibid., 130.
51 Thomas Piketty, *Capital in the Twenty-First Century*, trans. Arthur Goldhammer (Cambridge, MA: The Belknap Press of Harvard University Press, 2014), 238–40.
52 Balzac, *Old Goriot*, 135.
53 Gérard Gengembre, "Upstairs, Downstairs," in Gengembre, *Le père Goriot*, 133.
54 Balzac, *Old Goriot*, 188.
55 Ibid., 198.
56 Ibid., 228.
57 Ibid., 271.
58 Ibid., 130.
59 Ibid., 157.
60 Ibid., 164.
61 Ibid., 174.
62 Ibid., 182.
63 Piketty, *Capital*, 379.
64 Butler, *Balzac*, 216.
65 Piketty, *Capital*, 379.
66 Balzac, *Old Goriot*, 242.
67 Giddens, *Consequences of Modernity*, 139.
68 Lucienne Frappier-Mazur, "Les échecs: Jeu et société," in Gengembre, *Le père Goriot*, 323.
69 Butler, *Balzac*, 228.
70 Ibid., 142.
71 Piketty, *Capital*, 160.
72 Ibid., 342.
73 Balzac, *Old Goriot*, 249.
74 Ibid., 150.
75 Pierre Barbéris, "L'amour: Ambiguïtés et contradictions," in Gengembre, *Le père Goriot*, 441.
76 Honoré de Balzac, *La maison Nucingen*, trans. James Waring, *The Firm of Nucingen* (Champaign, IL: Project Gutenberg, 2013), www.gutenberg.org/ ebooks/1294. Note: All translations of *La maison Nucingen* are by Waring.
77 Balzac, *Firm of Nucingen*, n. pag.
78 Ibid.
79 Balzac, *Old Goriot*, 166.
80 Ibid., 108.
81 Ibid., 167.
82 Ibid., 290.
83 For the reference to Scott's *The Heart of Mid-Lothian* in *Le père Goriot*, see Balzac, *Old Goriot*, 150; for the comparison of Paris to the New World, see Balzac, *Old Goriot*, 133.
84 Balzac, *Old Goriot*, 28.

85 Ibid., 270.
86 Ibid., 262–63.
87 Ibid., 271.
88 Ibid., 284.
89 Ibid., 289.
90 Ibid., 291.
91 Ibid., 302.

7 Industrial productions

From *editions populaires* to a people's history

> The claim then is no longer for their truth as one might seek to define that by an authorial intention, but for their testimony, as defined by their historical use.
> – D. F. McKenzie, "The Book as an Expressive Form," 45

Honoré de Balzac's *Le père Goriot* addressed a timely subject of relevance to all French readers – how to cope with modernity. It was also published at a critical juncture with respect to the expansion of print and reading in France, which helped to keep it in the hands of French readers throughout the century. The print industry in post-Revolutionary France changed considerably from 1789 to 1835. As Martyn Lyons puts it, the 1789 Revolution "swept away the corporate system which had governed the book trade and the printing industry for centuries."[1] In its place emerged what Christine Haynes has described as a "freewheeling business."[2] Changes in legislation, distribution, and publishing were critical for writers, publishers, and readers; for example, "The Law of 1793 made the written text the legal property of its author for his or her lifetime and for ten years after the author's death," which, as Lyons notes, put the works of authors such as Voltaire and Rousseau in the public domain.[3] At the same time, thousands of newspapers, journals, and pamphlets flooded urban and rural markets in the period 1789–99.[4] Publishing supported by patronage gave way to more democratic forms of production dependent on the capitalist market system and popular reading. The publisher emerges as a specialized profession for the first time in this period. Moreover, the publisher became "A speculator in literary capital."[5] The transition from *éditeur* to *libraire*, from the man of letters who published literary works for select readers to the modern entrepreneur who sells cultural commodities to as many as possible, was meaningful in at least three respects. First, the number of publishers increased drastically: from about 160 in the 1770s to more than 500 in the 1830s.[6] Second, book production increased "from only 2,547 titles in 1814, to 8,273 in 1826, the peak for the entire first half of the century."[7] Third, such changes reflected and drove the diversification of print materials and reading practices. Thus, the book trade became a commercial endeavor, with publishers and authors eager to exploit popular new genres such as the historical novel, which changed with the times to meet or cultivate the interests of a broad spectrum of readers. Just as important, not only did the lower classes have access to more print material than ever before, they also became a focal point of the fiction they read. As I explore in this chapter, the industrial production of literature then takes on a new meaning: the lower classes are produced by the work they do in more ways than one. They become the product of the conditions that are reflected in working-class narratives, but through the self-reflection made possible by these representations, they are also produced as conscious citizens, all through increased access to the industrialized book trade.

The early print history of Balzac's fiction shines some light on the impact of changes to the production and dissemination of literature in nineteenth-century France. *Le père Goriot* started out as a short story but became a serialized novel, appearing in four installments of *Revue de Paris* beginning December 14, 1834 and ending February 11, 1835.[8] Authors of the period often published in serial publications, which could serve as advertising and as a testing ground prior to publication in book form.[9] Martin Kanes records that *Le père Goriot* was well received: "As soon as it was published, *Le Père Goriot* caused an upheaval in the press. It was reviewed in the major Parisian papers and magazines, . . . This in itself is an indication of the novel's great popular success and explains Balzac's boast about having at last 'arrived.'"[10] However, Rose Fortassier notes that Balzac's enthusiasm was likely overstated,[11] and Kanes elaborates that the reviews ranged from celebration to criticism.[12] Further, it was not uncommon for writers or publishers to place puffs to support friends or vilify competitors; the literary landscape was political and contentious. For example, regarding an earlier novel, *La peau de chagrin* (1831), Balzac wrote to the publisher Gosselin, saying that he "can undertake to get something out of" the press (he lists ten periodicals), adding, "I will see to it that the reviews are good and promptly forthcoming, which will greatly facilitate your task as a publisher."[13] In short, publishers and authors worked the market as well as literary form to sell print. In turn, the long-term popularity of *Le père Goriot* depended on the repeated exploitation of market possibilities.

The preface to *Le père Goriot* published on March 8, 1835 in *Revue de Paris* references near simultaneous publication of the book edition. The first *édition librairie* (bookshop edition), *Le père Goriot, histoire parisienne*, was published in two volumes by Werdet and Spachmann on March 2, 1835.[14] At a price of fifteen francs, it was upmarket and thus unavailable to most readers. But two advertisements at the end of volume one point to the extended literary market for popular historical novels emerging in France. The first is for *Librairie de Werdet* (Werdet's Bookshop), which contains an extract from a current historical memoir on Louis XVIII; the second advertises two cheaper forms of Balzac's works – a collected edition and single-volume novels. Capitalization on the popularity of historiography is noteworthy, but so

128   *Industrial productions*

too is the act of repackaging aimed at downmarket readers. Well before publication of the better-known collection *La comédie humaine* (1842–48), Balzac's novels were not only situated alongside other popular selections but also compiled with considerable economic variation; small, multi-volume collections of older works were cheaper than larger, more recent editions of newer works. The difference in price between a thirty-volume, duodecimo collection for fifteen francs and a two-volume, octavo edition for the same amount points to the market diversity that increased access to print across socioeconomic categories.

The varied reproduction of *Le père Goriot* after 1835 depended on the emergence of a modern publishing industry driven by the speculation of entrepreneurial publishers. Literacy in France increased dramatically over the course of the century; a growing interest in education was consequential, although as in Britain, the institutionalization of education for children came late, for example, with Jules Ferry's education laws of 1881–83; and the centralization of literary production in Paris contributed to the decline of patois. Literacy, education, and language standardization facilitated the expansion of reading, which depended on increased production of and access to print materials. But the key factor underlying the emergence of modern publishing practices was liberalization, meaning the ability of publishers to profit from the making and selling of print. The new-made men of the post-Revolution era entered the literary trade as entrepreneurs and dominated the scene by treating books as merchandise to be shifted. Literature was no longer a family affair. The new publishers were speculators and did not hesitate to innovate for profit, which fueled interest in new forms of production and distribution stimulated by cutthroat competition. The government controlled the book trade by legislating intellectual property rights, trade restrictions, and censorship control;[15] as a result, publishers were encouraged to take responsibility for the production of new material. For example, the 1819 Serre Laws, which governed press laws in France, made the publisher the legally responsible property owner and thus the primary figure in the production of a work.[16] Responsibility led to innovation. Publishers adapted to and furthered developments in printing, distribution, and format designed to reach more readers. Industrial printing was not effective in France until the 1860s, when papermaking from wood chips was perfected and rotary presses were adopted.[17] Important changes were underway earlier in the century, however. Mechanical presses slowly replaced early hand presses, leading to major increases in output.[18] Further, decreases in the price of machinery enabled publishers to take advantage of these new technologies.[19] Other aspects of printing were similarly improved: paper manufacture was industrialized as rags were replaced by straw and then wood pulp, and paper cutting, folding, and binding were industrialized.[20] The effectiveness and availability of the mechanical press, along with improvements in literacy and education, facilitated the circulation of larger print runs and cheaper editions. New modes of distribution

Industrial productions 129

also extended circulation. In the early-nineteenth century, distribution took three primary forms: *colporteurs* (peddlers), *étalages* (street shelves), and *cabinets de lecture* (commercial lending libraries). Although Paris continued as the center of the book trade, publishers began to access and cultivate readerships across France in new ways, for example, using booksellers and wholesalers to extend distribution. Adding to the new modes of production and distribution aimed at achieving the national consumption of print, the new presses enabled expansion of the periodical press.[21] The number of volume-format books increased in the period,[22] but "Expensive, multi-volume historical novels produced for the rental libraries could not compete with serialized adventure stories in the press."[23] The modernization of publishing was inseparable from changes in reading practices.

People wanted to know what was going on around them, and to enjoy their reading material, just as publishers wanted to profit from the sale of it. Format and content were adjusted accordingly in the form of new journals and newspapers that began to offer the latest works of fiction. Claude Witkowski records the first instance: "In October 1836, *La Presse*, the daily newspaper created on 1 July, set the precedent – for the first time in the history of journalism a new novel, *La vieille fille de Balzac*, appeared."[24] The reinvention of *Le Figaro* at the end of 1836 further defines the changes in format, content, and readership underway; the new paper was octavo in format, sixteen pages in length, and most notably, the final eight pages were taken from or formed a work of fiction. In short, what and how people read was changing. The outcome became clearer in the following decades. Martyn Lyons notes, for example, that "By the end of the nineteenth century, readers all over France were buying or borrowing novels like Hugo's *Notre-Dame de Paris*, or Dumas's *Les Trois Mousquetaires*."[25] This was a substantial shift in reading practices from earlier in the century, when eighteenth-century classics and religious reading were dominant. Lyons summarizes the result of the expansion of reading as follows: "A homogeneous reading public had been created, and the distinctive audiences of learned literature on one hand, and the popular texts of the Bibliothèque bleue [in English, "blue library," a form of downmarket literature] on the other had become merged in the formation of a new mass audience."[26] The reading public may be said to have become homogeneous in that most people had access to print in some form by the end of the nineteenth century. Additionally, upmarket and downmarket readers had access to at least some of the same materials. For example, longer fiction could be printed as a book, as part of a downmarket collection, or serialized in a periodical. Homogeneity, then, may be understood as dependent on a diverse print market that made it possible for more people than ever before to participate in and benefit from the act of reading. Emerging at just the right time, Balzac's novels were central to these changes.

The renegotiation of existing and the creation of new publishing networks made Balzac's novels available to wider audiences. For example, problems

130   *Industrial productions*

with Werdet led to a new contract with Delloye, Lecou, and Bohain in November 1836.[27] One early result was the downmarket serialization in twenty-five parts of *La peau de chagrin* from December 1837 to July 1838 in *Balzac illustré*, which was followed by a one-volume octavo edition for fifteen francs.[28] A subsequent contract with Charpentier, signed by Balzac on November 12, 1838, led to a new edition of *Le père Goriot*, revised and corrected, published in Paris on March 16, 1839 for three-and-a-half francs as part of a "Collection of the Best Works, French and Foreign, Old and Modern" in the *format anglais* (18mo, compact typography).[29] As elsewhere, low prices broadened access to fiction. Isabelle Olivero describes the significance as follows: "By point of comparison, the average wage of a Parisian worker for one working day in the 1840s was between 1.50 and 2 francs – the price had been reduced from approximately ten working days to slightly over two working days for those earning the most meagre salaries."[30] Charpentier thus increased the availability of Balzac's novels in France. Output also increased: "Between October 1838 and January 1840 Charpentier published 15 volumes of Balzac's works, including 34 titles."[31] These changes were a response to international as well as domestic factors. Several editions of *Le père Goriot* were published in Brussels in 1835,[32] and Belgian publishers were not alone in trying to profit from the reprinting of Balzac novels; other foreign editions in the same year included *Vater Goriot* in Germany and *Papa Goriot* in Italy.[33] French publishers would find new ways to compete.

Broadly, profiting from the sale of literature meant getting print into the hands of more readers; the means to do so developed into a predictable pattern. A novel was serialized, possibly dramatized (which would involve print copies of the play), printed as a multi-volume book primarily for reading rooms, and then reprinted in duodecimo or decimo-octavo format as a single-volume book at a reduced price. *Le père Goriot* is one example among many: four installments in *Revue de Paris*; adapted as a *drame-vaudeville* for the theatre;[34] published in two volumes by Werdet and Spachmann; followed by a cheaper, single-volume edition by Charpentier. The next development was a collected edition to reproduce previously published works for an even lower price, allowing publisher and author to once again profit from reproduction. The twelve-volume *Études de mœurs au XIXe siècle* (1834–37) was the first of such endeavors but not the most influential.[35] On October 2, 1841, Balzac signed a contract for the publication of his complete works, the aim of which he described in a letter: "I have made progress with the complete edition of my works, which will be exploited by a large bookshop and will be published with great luxury and a low price."[36] Notably, the capitalist terminology (e.g., *exploiter*) and details of production and circulation (i.e., luxury and low price) are continuous with the subsequent print history of *Le père Goriot*. The first book of *La comédie humaine* was published on April 12, 1842 for half a franc;[37] *Le père Goriot* appeared on November 7, 1843.[38] Vachon notes that publication of the complete works was irregular and circulation was relatively low: "At 3,000 copies printed, *La Comédie humaine* was not a sales success."[39] However, Furne published two downmarket reprints, the second of which decreased the cost of each volume by half: 160 parts at half a franc per volume (16 vols.) in October 1846 and 340 parts at a quarter of a franc per volume (17 vols.) in February 1849.[40] As such, however lavish the initial product, the cost of reading *Le père Goriot* dropped considerably in a relatively short period of time – a development indicative of the wider impact of industrialization and the related democratization of print on the lives of French readers.

The transformation of print and reading in the second half of the nineteenth century that furthered access to *Le père Goriot* could not have occurred without the social and economic modernization of France. The *pays legal* (those who could vote) doubled between 1830 and 1848 and the first free election involving universal male suffrage was in 1848. Education for boys improved in the first half of the nineteenth century; similar expansion of the education of girls followed in the period 1850–80.[41] Such changes in political representation and access to education contributed to urbanization and industrialization in the same period: "Industrial production doubled between 1852 and 1870; foreign trade tripled, outstripping the growth of any other European nation; the use of steam power rose fivefold; railway mileage was increased sixfold."[42] In relation, increased public spending, private speculation, and the first investment banks – indicators of the advance of economic liberalism – added to the "vigorous stimulation afforded the economy."[43] Although the working classes were not the first or primary beneficiaries of such transformations, the related liberalization and industrialization of the publishing industry meant that new investments in reading were increasingly possible, and perhaps necessary, as the nature of labor and wider social circumstances changed. In this moment of economic expansion and social diversification, print was not only more accessible – reading itself took on new meaning. In what ways this occurred is of some importance as regards the later, downmarket print history of *Le père Goriot*. The serialization of Eugène Sue's *Les mystères de Paris* (1842) in *Le Journal des débats* was important: "Although *Débats* counted only twelve to thirteen thousand subscribers, everyone was speaking about the novel, the *fouriéristes* carried it to the newborn, everyone wanted to read the serial of the day, reading rooms and cafés were taken by storm."[44] Other publishers were quick to exploit the situation. For example, Gosselin published a three-volume edition of *Les mystères de Paris* from 1843 to 1844 and Maresq followed later with a six-volume illustrated edition from 1850 to 1855.[45] Because of these and other downmarket publishing successes, competition for authors that could shift product increased. Sue's *Juif errant* was published in *Le Constitutionnel*, which guaranteed Sue 100,000 francs a year for fifteen years in return for ten volumes per year; the result for the publisher was a print run of more than 20,000 for January 1, 1845.[46] In comparison, the circulation of most periodicals through the 1830s was not

132 *Industrial productions*

often more than 5,000.[47] Following on the incremental steps toward down-market accessibility in the 1830s, the industrialization of literature was well under way by the late 1840s.

Further pointing to the expansion of print and reading as an integral part of the industrialization of France, Isabelle Olivero describes the period 1850–70 as "The first golden age of the series."[48] She relates how publishers responded to economic circumstances and the high price of books by creating *bibliothèques* aimed at working-class readers, including cheap reprints of popular fiction sold daily, weekly, or monthly and collections forming a library of critical works in small format for a low price.[49] *Romans-feuilletons* (serialized novels) of the 1830s led to the further expansion of downmarket periodicals in the 1840s and into the Second Empire.[50] After 1848, downmarket periodicals, some publishing only fiction, were a major outlet for novelists.[51] In January 1848, the first of the *Romans à 4 sous* appeared: "booklets of 16 pages with 2 columns, in the format 21 x 30 cm, illustrated with four wood engravings and sold for 20 centimes."[52] In terms of circulation, the results were remarkable: from 1851 to 1855, the number of volumes of these large, cheap, illustrated publications reached a maximum of 10,000,000 each year and more after 1853 due to reprints.[53] Popular editions with few or no illustrations, including *Les Complements* (with 114 installments of Balzac), were also common in the 1850s and 1860s, as were collections for one franc per volume (16 pp., 11 x 17 cm or 12 x 18.5 cm, 1 vol. of 5 parts at 20 centimes each).[54] Popular editions of this sort reached more than 14,000,000 volumes from 1855 to 1862 and *journaux-romans* (serial publication of novels illustrated with woodcuts; 8 pp., 21 x 30 cm, 5 centimes) surpassed 20,000,000 from 1861 to 1866, reaching a maximum of 23,000,000 in 1864.[55] Published on April 7, 1855, *Le Journal pour tous* lasted for twenty years and spawned more than fifty imitators, many of which only lasted a few months.[56] Arguably, the culmination of such changes occurred with "The advent of the daily newspaper for 5 centimes in 1863: *Le Petit journal*; with 250,000 published copies by the end of 1865 it would continue at this level until 1870 and would be imitated."[57] In summary, from the late 1840s to the early 1860s, the price of fiction dropped, resulting in a yearly subscription rate of eighteen francs, or one sou per day, for *Le Petit journal*. Following the price reductions made by the daily presses and Charpentier in the late 1830s, downmarket publishers continued to reprint well-known authors and works, producing new formats suited to the wider dissemination of popular fiction – acts of modernity inseparable from the interrelated expansion of reading markets and industrial capitalism.

Despite developments in the print industry that would seem to lead readers away from longer works of fiction in book form and toward mixed-format periodicals, the historical novel remained popular, accounting for about half the *feuilletons* published during the Second Empire.[58] Correspondingly, the literary impact of *Le père Goriot* continued after 1848 due to new editions: for example, "On 20 December 1850 a contract was concluded with the bookshop of Marescq and Co. for the publication of a large in-4 edition of the *Illustrated Works of Balzac* (8 volumes published in 160 parts of 16 pages each from 1851–1852) for 20,000 F."[59] *Œuvres illustrées de Balzac* followed, including *Le père Goriot*.[60] Other publishers offered their own popular editions. Bureaux de "Siècle," for instance, published a sixty-nine-page edition of *Le père Goriot* in 1856.[61] The publication of *Le père Goriot* in collected editions by popular publishers such as Lévy, Bourdilliat, and Houssiaux was more common. In sum, modernization facilitated varied downmarket print production, enabled the integration of reading and eveyday life, and thus helped make the novel a common form of reading and Balzac a popular choice among new generations of readers.

As described, working-class readers had better access to fiction beginning in the late 1830s, culminating in a period of downmarket expansion starting in the 1850s. At the same time, the fictional representation of those readers and the circumstances that brought their stories to life changed as well. As indicated by the continued popularity of *Le père Goriot*, Rastignac and Vautrin retained their appeal; yet, whether a petty nobleman rising among the elites of Paris or an underground scoundrel keen on owning a plantation in the American South, such depictions were not reflective of the everyday experiences or expectations of common readers. What, then, was the appeal of Balzac's novel? In contrast to François-René de Chateaubriand's popular novella *René* (1802), which takes a philosophical approach to the exploration of uncertainty and ugliness in the modern world, in the novels of *La comédie humaine*, Balzac repeatedly focuses on the real-world impact of capitalism.[62] As chronotopic interpretations of social transformation, both had their uses. But Balzac engaged more directly with the concrete consequences of modernity, which changed not only with the modernization of France but also with the related expansion of reading. Similarly, following on social criticism by the likes of Saint-Simon and Fourier, other novelists began to question the progress of modernity from a perspective more in line with the realities faced by most readers. The answers changed with the times. For example, in early novels before and after *Le père Goriot*, George Sand addressed social equality,[63] but discourse on modernity also developed as a more fundamental challenge to industrial capitalism. As Donna Dickenson writes, "Sand's view is in contradistinction to the dominant position in the political economy of her day, namely that increased production and demand within a capitalist system of private ownership could ultimately benefit both workers and capitalists."[64] Modernization changed the way people lived and worked; efforts to document (and shape) such changes followed. To cite one example of non-fiction, as early as 1841, Durand described the state of workers in Paris in the fifty years following the 1789 Revolution.[65] Alongside theoretical critiques of capitalist society, such studies were important as they could inform more popular works of fiction. With a steady supply of new information about contemporary circumstances, the focus of fictional representation shifted from the social climbers of the *petite*

134 *Industrial productions*

bourgeoisie represented by Rastignac to the everyday life of the anonymous working classes. Alongside social reformers and historians, novelists like Sand offered problem-solutions to address the conditions of modernity in a literary form that was popular among and increasingly accessible to all fiction readers.

With respect to the potential uses of the novel to respond to modernity, the difference between Sand's *Le meunier d'Angibault* (1845) and *Le père Goriot* is instructive. *Le meunier d'Angibault* explores the construction of cooperative communities based on socialist principles.[66] More specifically, Sand illustrates a transfer of power from the selfish farmer Bricolin, who is ultimately ruined, to the miller Grand-Louis, who takes on a central role in the village of Angibault as provider. The characterization of ethics in the modern world delineates two contrasting responses to modernity: on the one hand, Bricolin exploits people to accumulate personal wealth; on the other hand, Grand-Louis ensures the collective prosperity of the community. As in *Le père Goriot*, there is a lesson to be learned, but the difference is noteworthy; rather than a description of how the upper classes exploit modern conditions for personal gain, Sand sets forth a social alternative centered on an ethically aware collective of workers. In *Le meunier d'Angibault*, modernity demands a radical reformation of community practices. In contrast, Balzac's novels of the 1840s demonstrate the interpenetration of capitalist practices and everyday life. In his novels, the working class is no better than the bourgeoisie – all are rascals, whether in the city or the country, before and after the Revolution of 1830. The struggle for power over others continues in new ways; the means change with circumstances – the motivations remain familiar. Like Christian Isobel Johnstone in *Clan Albin*, Sand focuses instead on the cultivation of community in spite of (or, in opposition to) "improvement." Whereas agency in *Le père Goriot* is a matter of Rastignac's getting ahead, in *Le meunier d'Angibault*, agency is achieved through collective responsibility for social welfare. Broadly, the historical novel continued to inform responses to modernity; more specifically, it offered contrasting views of possible ways forward.

Coping with modernity meant something different before and after 1848. For example, *Les mystères du Paris* features a working-class character, but Sue's *Les mystères du peuple* (1849–56) focuses more squarely on the life of the proletariat.[67] Lion Feuchtwanger remarks that *Les mystères du peuple* is not exactly a historical novel as "The tiny bits of historical meat are drowned in a sea of spiced sauce," but more important than the balance between history and fiction is the proletarian sympathy in evidence, also noted by Feuchtwanger: "Inasmuch as he was sympathetic to socialist ideas he frequently mixed Saint-Simonianistic and Marxist ideas into his ambiguous creations and contributed a large part of his gigantic royalties to the cause of the proletariat."[68] *Les mystères du peuple* offered working-class readers a form of fiction that reflected, to some degree at least, their own situation after 1848. Sue was not alone in responding to the changing

Industrial productions 135

interpretations (e.g., Marxist) and circumstances (i.e., industrial capitalism) of modernity. Georg Lukács argues that in the wake of 1848, "the proletariat enters upon the world-historical stage as an armed mass."[69] Revolutionary fervor took fictional form, but in the hands of mostly middle-class writers, responses tended to be progressive rather than radical. In Sand's *La ville noire* (1859), for instance, working-class Lower Town is the base upon which Upper Town thrives – labor produces wealth.[70] But neither the trajectory nor the resolution follow through on what initially appears to be a radical socialist interpretation of social change. The young metalworker Sept-Epées struggles to overcome his ambition while his lover Tonine and others build relationships in the community. When Sept-Epées returns from his wanderings a more mature man ready to embrace family and community, he finds his factory crushed by a powerful storm – nature overcomes individual greed and a new harmony is possible. Tonine, a respected resident of Lower Town, inherits a small fortune, including a local factory, resulting in changes in technology, education, the administration of medicine, labor organization, local transportation, resident safety, and housing. In short, because of Tonine's benevolence and industry, the people of Lower Town respond to industrial capitalism by building a new community that overcomes divisions: the old miser and the philanthropist are accepted, Upper Town and Lower Town unite to celebrate the wedding of Tonine and Sept-Epées, and the doctor marries a working-class woman and moves to Lower Town. And yet, despite the many practical advances toward collective prosperity, coping with modernity depends not only on a stroke of luck (e.g., Tonine's inheritance), but also, more importantly, upon social cohesion in a capitalist world; while questioning the status quo, there is no question of revolution.[71]

In post-1848 France, fictional representation of the working class and capitalist critique emerged more fully with Émile Zola's *Les Rougon-Macquart: histoire naturelle et sociale d'une famille sous le Second Empire* (1871–93).[72] Set between the start of the Second Republic (1848) and the Paris Commune (1871), the novels of *Les Rougon-Macquart* address the situation faced by those left behind. Following on more conservative representations of social life, the voice is startling: "Respectable people . . . What bastards!"[73] So ends *Le ventre de Paris* (1873). Like his other novels, it was an industrial production in two ways. First, it was initially serialized in sixty-one installments in the journal *L'État* from January 12 to March 17, 1873; it was then published in April of the same year in book format and sold for three-and-a-half francs by Charpentier.[74] Second, it describes the opposition between the bourgeoisie and social reformers, thus not only shifting the ground from Balzac's earlier depiction of conflict between the aristocracy and the bourgeoisie but also questioning the underlying values and practical characteristics of modern progress in France. At the center of *Le ventre de Paris* is Florent, who, having been falsely accused of involvement in a *coup d'état* and deported to Devil's Island, escapes and returns to Paris. He is taken in

136 *Industrial productions*

by his brother Quenu and his wife, Lisa Macquart, who own a deli near Les Halles, the new food markets built at the beginning of the Second Empire. The oppressed, starved, and bedraggled Florent represents the "thin" as opposed to the "fat" – symbolic terms with wider implications. Even before the December 1851 *coup d'état* that brought Napoleon III to power, Florent was an idealist: "he would dream of the great moral and humanitarian reforms which would change the city from a place of suffering to a place of bliss."[75] In other words, he is a revolutionary, someone who seeks dynamic, some might say utopian, social change. Conversely, the "fat" of the world, represented by Lisa, work toward solid bourgeois comfort: "Prosperity and security were her great goals."[76] From her vantage point, the thin are suspicious: "A man capable of living without food for three days struck her as a highly dangerous character. Respectable people never put themselves in that position."[77] Lisa encourages Florent to settle down: "You'll come back to be with your own class, a class of decent, respectable people, and live like everyone else."[78] The underlying question is, on which side of the barricades were you in June 1848? Temporarily, Florent succumbs to Lisa's demands; as a result, "He felt, as it were, the titillation of fat forming all over his body. His whole being was slowly being invaded by the languid contentment of a shopkeeper."[79] As inspector of the fish market, he becomes accustomed to constant food and attention, to routine and ease; he begins to feel soft, eventually reaching a state of complete boredom, overcome by a vague feeling of anxiety. The "foul atmosphere of Les Halles" leads him back to revolutionary action.[80] In this way, the novel does not depict a slow slide into bourgeois acceptance but rather reignites a fundamental difference that questions the nature of modern progress itself. Florent attends secret meetings comprised of anarchists, socialists, and communists; eventually, he leads a failed plan to overthrow the government. Rather than a dead end, the failure highlights alternative paths. To Florent, the belly of Paris – the crowded, fat, smelly, greasy Les Halles – is representative of the brutal victory of capitalism over all that might have been. In contrast, according to Lisa, "Only fools go tilting at windmills."[81] Whereas Florent is greatly afflicted by the abundance and meanness of the Parisian markets, Lisa sees his thinness – essentially, the unwillingness to take advantage of present circumstances – as perversity. The outcome of this conflict reflects the dominance of modern practices, as well as the impact of modernity on identity and belonging; Florent is arrested and convicted, discharged from the great belly of market society. And yet, as in other novels of *Les Rougon-Macquart*, the end is the basis of a new beginning. The historical significance and social outcomes of Les Halles require further attention; in the words of Claude the painter, "Since the beginning of this century, only one original building has been built that has not been copied from somewhere else and has sprung naturally from the spirit of the times, and that is Les Halles. . . . It's a brilliant creation, although it only gives us a vague understanding of what we'll see in the twentieth century!"[82] The brilliance of Les Halles lies

Industrial productions 137

in the organic manifestation of modernity; the markets, then, act as the new center of modern France, a point from which Zola continued to investigate the impact of the capitalist mode of production in Paris and across the country.

L'assommoir (1877), for example, is a novel about the working-class districts of Paris in the 1850s and the devastating effects of urban poverty on families and communities.[83] As a brutally honest portrayal of people living at the margins of Paris in the nineteenth century, it was unique. Zola's tragic heroine is not trim and proper like Jeanie Deans of *The Heart of Mid-Lothian*; rather, the truth here is arrived at through down-and-out Gervaise. Aware of the shift, Zola writes in the preface to the novel that "It is a work of truth, the first novel about the common people which does not tell lies but has the authentic smell of the people."[84] The depiction of everyday life is gritty, even chilling – violence, debt, alcohol, work, sex, and poverty are front and center. The outcome, however, is not simply a journalistic report on urban poverty. In *Les Rougon-Macquart*, Zola is concerned, as the full title suggests, with the intersection of natural and social history rather than reportage for the sake of moral judgment: "And it must not be concluded that the masses as a whole are bad, for my characters are not bad, but only ignorant and spoilt by the environment of grinding toil and poverty in which they live."[85] However, as at the Maison Vauquer in *Le père Goriot*, people are never simply at the mercy of mysterious historical forces; agency constitutes and is constituted by social conditions. In this light, the story of Gervaise (the sister of Lisa in *Le ventre de Paris*), a laundress with two children trying to lead a respectable life in a working-class district of Paris, is a story of coping, and a formidable lesson.

As in *Le ventre de Paris*, the characters of *L'assommoir* hope to make a better life. The building manager, for example, "had had a hard pull himself, but work would take you anywhere."[86] Although the belief in upward mobility is familiar, the practice is particular to circumstances. "Anywhere" is not 40,000 a year and freedom from labor but instead a stable life in which work leads to security. Gervaise "dreamed of setting up in a little shop and employing workgirls herself. She had it all worked out. If the business went well they could buy an annuity after twenty years or so and retire on it into the country."[87] In short, those left behind after the uprising of June 1848 in Paris want bourgeois respectability – the heart of the matter is how to attain it. In this respect, self-employment is of some importance: Lantier once owned a hat factory, Gervaise runs her own laundry until it goes under, Virginie eventually sets up a confectionary shop in the same space. The lessons of *Le père Goriot* remain applicable, but in this case, rather than removing oneself entirely from the world of work, the humbler aim is to simply stand on one's toes, and if possible, to command the work of others. For most, day-to-day survival remains the primary objective; all else is either longing or mere fantasy, although these too can be important means of coping with a sense of everyday life as hard and unforgiving. Regardless,

138 *Industrial productions*

the failure of Gervaise, among others, to advance in life highlights the plight of those without social advantages – those fighting for scraps at the lowest level of a social and political system that depends upon the exploitation of their labor. In relation, even Goujet, the clean-living, hard-working factory worker, seems destined to fail: "The day would come, of course, when the machine would kill the manual worker; already their day's earnings had dropped from twelve francs to nine, and there was talk of still more cuts to come."[88] The outlook is bleak; the sense of fatalism is striking in part because it seems to be systemic and irreversible. *L'assommoir* ends accordingly, with misery, madness, and death: as the narrator concludes, "Yes, yes, it was a pretty picture in this corner of Paris, with men and women herded on top of each other through poverty!"[89] Vautrin's reference to spiders in a pot comes back with renewed force. With each novel of *Les Rougon-Macquart*, the social consequences of modernity were clearer, as was the need for solutions other than hard work, from which there seemed to be no escape, and clean living, of which most could only dream.

L'assommoir provides no concrete solutions; the vicious circle of despair continues for Gervaise and those around her. But the transition from one generation to another that extends across *Les Rougon-Macquart* allows for the possibility of change in other ways. In *L'assommoir*, Lantier spouts radical sentiments: "I demand the suppression of militarism and the brotherhood of nations. . . . I demand the abolition of privilege, titles and monopolies. I demand equal wages and shares in profits, the glorification of the proletariat . . . All the freedoms, do you understand? All the freedoms! *And divorce!*"[90] At first glance, one might think that the Revolution of 1789 never happened, but Lantier's socialist demands may be understood as a renewal of the Revolution considering modernization, at the center of which was the proletariat. Importantly, Lantier gives Étienne, who is about to leave for Lille to continue his apprenticeship, advice of some consequence: "Remember that the producer is not a slave, but whoever produces nothing is a drone."[91] Étienne later becomes the working-class hero of *Germinal* (1885),[92] a story of industrial strife pitting working-class miners against wealthy capitalists in France during the 1860s. From one novel to the next, Zola re-historicized the implications of and responses to modernization, making *Les Rougon-Macquart* a series of historical sketches documenting the life of the working class in the age of modernity.

The suppression of unions under Napoleon III and industrial strife in the 1870s and early 1880s, for example at Anzin in 1878, Denain in 1880, and Montceau-les-Mines in 1882, made *Germinal* a timely publication.[93] The Montsou Mining Company featured in the novel came into existence during a great coal boom in eighteenth-century France. Over the course of several generations, the company prospers by the exploitation of resources and workers. The conditions down in the pits are abominable and the poverty of the families living in company housing is appalling. Zola does not mince his words: "A whole race of people dying down in the pits, sons after

Industrial productions 139

their fathers, so that bribes could be given to Ministers and generations of noble lords and bourgeois could give grand parties or sit and grow fat by their own firesides!"[94] More than an abstract indictment of monopoly and corruption, he portrays grueling labor in horrific conditions. Diseases result from extended periods in the pits; injuries or death result from overwork, malnutrition, and poor safety standards. The picture of industrial life is unambiguous. So, too, is the conflict between oppressed and oppressor: "They, poor devils, were just machine-fodder, they were penned like cattle in housing estates, the big Companies were gradually dominating their whole lives, regulating slavery, threatening to enlist all the nation's workers, millions of hands to increase the wealth of a thousand idlers."[95] Unlike a Balzac novel, there is an enemy here; further, the conditions for revolt – slavery – are expected to culminate in a workers' revolution: "But now the miner was waking up under the ground, germinating in the earth like good seed, and one fine morning you would see him springing up like corn in the fields; yes, men would spring up, an army of men to bring justice back into the world."[96] Here, then, is the promise of a step from individual maturity to collective action that seems to leave the moderate coping mechanisms of Balzac and Sand far behind.

Étienne, a mechanic on the verge of starvation, works in the pits and lives amongst the miners. A Waverley figure finding his way in the world, he encounters two potential mentors: the anarchist Souvarine and Pluchart, the Workers' International representative. His progress toward leadership of the striking miners is tied directly to his education, which causes Étienne to experience abstraction: "Now he spent hours lying on the hay turning over vague ideas which he did not recognize as his own, a sensation, for instance, of superiority which set him apart from his mates, as though his intellectual progress had raised his whole being to greater spiritual heights."[97] The tension between solidarity and individualism becomes untenable. Étienne leads the strikers in revolt while also attempting to hold the desperate group back from committing acts of violence. The divide threatens to separate Étienne from the collective enterprise he has spearheaded: "Gradually his vanity at being their leader and the constant necessity of doing their thinking for them was setting him apart and creating within him the soul of one of the bourgeois he hated so much."[98] *Germinal*, however, is not an inward-looking novel; Étienne's struggle is a response to an industrial crisis in need of a concrete solution. In the end, the resolution is as neat as it is expected: Deneulin loses his mine to Montsou and the workers are forced back to work under the conditions they fought against in the first place – capitalists win, workers lose. As in earlier novels, the sense that the juggernaut of modernity cannot be stopped is strong. In contrast, the symbolic emergence of Étienne from the collapsed mine suggests that the experience has not been entirely in vain. Étienne rises from the depths and is encouraged by the workers, who seem to recognize that the fight must go on, although they descend to the pits once again. The terms of his engagement with the future are

140   *Industrial productions*

eerily familiar; Étienne "thought about himself, and knew that he was now strong, matured by his hard experience down in the pit. His apprenticeship was over, and he was going forth fully armed as a fighting missionary of the revolution, having declared war on society, for he had seen it and condemned it."[99] Although the primary actors of the conflict have changed, the declaration of war reminds one of Rastignac at Père Lachaise. Similarly, Étienne's preparation – a theme common to proletarian novels on both sides of the Atlantic – progresses through a series of mentors, although in this case representing three branches of left-wing thought: anarchism, possibilism (representing legislative reform in collaboration with the capitalists), and communism. Thus, he is prepared to go forth and fight, with working-class experience and bourgeois refinement, for the people; the internal tension between individual and group is seemingly resolved by a socialist education. A collective way forward remains open, as the final lines of the novel indicate: "Men were springing up, a black avenging host was slowly germinating in the furrows, thrusting upwards for the harvests of future ages. And very soon their germination would crack the earth asunder."[100] This representation of working-class radicalism is not the same as the middle-class coping mechanisms emphasized in social problem novels, yet both are means of managing modernity; in this way at least, Sand and Zola have much in common. Though a far cry from the cooperation between capitalist and labor interests in a novel such as *La ville noire*, *Germinal*, too, is a manual of modernity, in its own way. Fifty years after *Le père Goriot*, working-class readers had their Rastignac. Yet, one might still wonder if the specifics of the coming revolution, like the details of Rastignac's rise, would be addressed.

With *Le ventre de Paris* and *L'assommoir*, Zola described the social consequences of industrial capitalism in Paris; with *Germinal*, he brought his portrayal down to the ground, literally; with *La terre* (1887), he comes full circle in two ways: by addressing the farming communities of rural France that supply the food markets of Les Halles, and by highlighting the conflict between farmers and industrialists.[101] Perhaps more than other Zola novels, *La terre* is a damning account of the intersection of human nature and modern conditions. A pessimistic description of rural life in nineteenth-century France, beyond vulgar language and low comedy, *La terre* is uncompromisingly violent, involving rape, incest, starvation, mutilation, and murder. In *Le père Goriot*, the heart is questioned; in *La terre*, one wonders whether there is anything to question at all. Like other Zola novels, however, the power of *La terre* does not rest with description alone but rather with historical representation of the proletariat. The Fouan family's struggle to expand their holdings occurs over several generations. Further, family history is linked to larger patterns of social transformation dating back to the Civil Code of 1804 and, more decisively, the 1789 Revolution; for example, "when the Revolution of 1789 finally established his rights, Joseph-Casimir, the Fouan of the day, owned twenty-one acres wrested from the former manor lands over the space of four centuries."[102] The Revolution did not

Industrial productions   141

bring equality; in 1793, confiscated land was declared to be the property of the nation, opening up the possibility of acquisition, but in reality such opportunities were available to the professional class: "lawyers and financiers were the only people to profit from this decision of the Revolution."[103] The Fouan family's fight for property in the 1860s is the continuation of a revolutionary struggle that had taken on a different character in post-1848 France: "These rich townsfolk nowadays were even worse than the old aristocrats: when the share-out took place, they kept the lot, they made the laws to suit themselves and their wealth came at the expense of the wretched plight of the poor!"[104] As such, *La terre* is positioned as a recent episode in a longer history of class struggle, in this case, between middle-class farmers and urban industrialists. Hourdequin says: "That's the dreadful thing. On the one hand we farmers need to sell our corn at an economic price, and on the other the industrialists want to push prices down so that they can pay lower wages. It's open warfare and how's it going to end, tell me that?"[105] Again, a declaration of war – the scene shifts, the sides change, but the underlying conditions remain.

In some ways, the resolution of the novel is reminiscent of that in *Germinal* – both end with destruction, a sense of continuity, and the prospect of new directions. In *La terre*, the industrialist Rochefontaine wins the local election; in contrast, Hourdequin's modern farm goes bankrupt, he is killed by a jealous lover, and the farm is set ablaze. Moreover, the education trumpeted by Hourdequin only speeds up emigration to the towns, where the younger generation take up new occupations with hopes of material comfort. In this case, education is not preparation to fight against modernity – just the opposite, modernity proceeds apace. What of the people, then? As in *Germinal*, workers will continue to work because they must, although the potential for revolution remains, and radical coping mechanisms are proposed; the drifter Canon, for example, shouts revolutionary ideas picked up in the poorer suburbs of Paris: "Listen to me, you lot, you land-workers, what would you say if you saw a notice stuck up on the door of the town-hall opposite, printed in large capital letters: THE REVOLUTIONARY COMMUNE OF PARIS: First, all taxes are abolished; secondly, military service is abolished. Well, what would you say, you clodhoppers?"[106] Mentors abound, and the student appears to be the working class as a whole. However, without any description of concrete steps or likely outcomes, the path forward seems still to remain at the level of an emotional appeal. Has anything changed? Is change even possible?

La terre describes the impact of modernity in rural France and sets forth several possible responses. However, the greater lesson of *La terre*, and of *Les Rougon-Macquart*, is perhaps the understated proposition that history can (or must) be rewritten. About one-third of the way through *La terre*, the young carpenter-cum-farmer Jean reads "a dramatized history of the peasantry before and after the Revolution, under the doleful title *The Misfortunes and Triumph of Jacques Bonhomme*."[107] This people's history of

142 *Industrial productions*

France from the Gauls to the Revolution emphasizes the continuous oppression of a peasantry at the mercy of "the threefold justice of king, bishop and lord, crucifying the poor peasant as he sweated over the soil."[108] In this tale, suffering over the centuries leads to the 1789 Revolution – a social trajectory from monarchy to republic, from tyranny to social justice. This version of history seems to put the present in a new light, to empower the people. Yet, in the end, the peasant is applauded for maintaining traditional ways, that is, for clinging to the land rather than accumulating monetary wealth. More importantly, the lesson takes a spiritual turn: "Make no mistake, Jacques Bonhomme, money is an empty delusion. The only real wealth is peace of mind!"[109] Not surprisingly, the peasants listening to Jean are incredulous: "Was the book pulling their leg? Money was the only good thing there was and they were poverty-stricken."[110] Workers – the silent majority in factories and on farms – are disenfranchised, and asked to be content with religious dreams rather than worldly riches. A generational difference is apparent in the two responses that follow: the young man, Jean, suggests that what is needed is more education; in contrast, old Fouan concludes, "a peasant's a peasant!"[111] Optimism on the one hand, pessimism on the other – no immediate solutions either way. But Jean's emphasis on education points to the awareness needed to remake social history from the perspective of the people – a stance that refers to the historical novel itself. With the tale of *Jacques Bonhomme, La terre* embeds one history within another, thus gesturing to the act of modernity that made *Les Rougon-Macquart* possible, and powerful – the self-reflexive act of history-making that could redefine the progress of national and other communities.

Notes

1 Martyn Lyons, *A History of Reading and Writing: In the Western World* (Houndmills: Palgrave Macmillan, 2010), 120.
2 Christine Haynes, *Lost Illusions: The Politics of Publishing in Nineteenth-Century France* (Cambridge, MA: Harvard University Press, 2010), 1.
3 Lyons, *Reading and Writing*, 121.
4 Ibid., 122–23.
5 Haynes, *Lost Illusions*, 1.
6 Ibid., 23.
7 Allen, *Popular French Romanticism*, 128.
8 Honoré de Balzac, *Le père Goriot*, in *Revue de Paris*, December 1834–February 1835. Balzac published frequently in *Revue de Paris*, including *L'elixir de longue vie* (October 24, 1830), *L'auberge rouge* (August 21/28, 1831), *La femme de trente ans* (April 29, 1832), and *Histoire des treize I. Ferragus, chef des dévorants* (March 10/17/31 and after April 10, 1833). See Honoré de Balzac, *Le père Goriot*, in vol. 7 of *Collection of Stories by Honoré de Balzac Extracted from the Revue de Paris, 1830–1835* (Paris: Au Bureau de la revue de Paris, 1830[–35]). See also, David Bellos, *Honoré de Balzac, Old Goriot* (Cambridge: Cambridge University Press, 1987). On the readership of the serialization of *Le père Goriot*, Bellos writes that "It is almost certain that the success of the *Revue*

Industrial productions   143

de Paris rested not on the aristocratic readership it claimed to serve, but on a much broader, more diverse public" (ibid., 7).

9   See Claude Witkowski, *Les editions populaires 1848–1870* (Paris: Les Amours des Livres, GIPPE, 1977), 76. Witkowski writes that "It was not uncommon for a daily to buy the publication rights to an unfinished work and for a book publisher to purchase the publication rights a little before the series was complete, so that if the series was successful the publicity would further book sales" (ibid.). Note: All translations of Witkowski are my own.

10   Martin Kanes, *Père Goriot: Anatomy of a Troubled World* (New York: Twayne, 1993), 13.

11   Rose Fortassier, introduction to *Le père Goriot*, by Honoré de Balzac, in vol. 3 of *La comédie humaine*, ed. Pierre-George Castex (Paris: Gallimard, 1976), 33.

12   Kanes, *Père Goriot*, 14–15.

13   Maurois, *Prometheus*, 180.

14   Honoré de Balzac, *Le père Goriot, histoire parisienne*, 2 vols. (Paris: Werdet and Spachmann, 1835).

15   Haynes, *Lost Illusions*, 26.

16   Ibid., 30–31.

17   Ibid., 26.

18   König's steam-driven cylindrical press, invented in 1811, could produce 1,000 impressions an hour; by 1834, Philippe Taylor had refined the König machine to print on both sides of the page, enabling up to 3,600 impressions an hour, which made larger and cheaper editions possible (Allen, *Popular French Romanticism*, 112).

19   For example, "The initial price declined from 36,000 francs in 1815 for a clumsy Nicolson press, to 12,000 francs in 1848 for a more efficient Keonig model" (Allen, *Popular French Romanticism*, 113).

20   Lyons, *Reading and Writing*, 139.

21   See Coward, "Popular Fiction," 74.

22   "In 1820 editions in the *belles lettres* and history averaged 1,130 copies; in 1841, a comparable economic year, they averaged 2,253" (Allen, *Popular French Romanticism*, 115).

23   Ibid., 125.

24   Witkowski, *Editions populaires*, 69.

25   Lyons, *Reading Culture*, 43.

26   Ibid.

27   Vachon, *Travaux*, 31.

28   Ibid., 168.

29   Ibid., 32. Honoré de Balzac, *Le père Goriot, nouvelle édition revue et corrigée* (Paris: Charpentier, 1839).

30   Isabelle Olivero, "The Paperback Revolution in France, 1850–1950," in *Authors, Publishers and the Shaping of Taste*, ed. John Spiers, vol 1. of *The Culture of the Publisher's Series*, ed. John Spiers (New York: Palgrave Macmillan, 2011), 76.

31   Vachon, *Travaux*, 32.

32   See, for example, Honoré de Balzac, *Le père Goriot: histoire parisienne* (Bruxelles: J. P. Meline, 1835); *Le père Goriot: par M. de Balzac* (Bruxelles: A. Wahlen, 1835); *Le père Goriot*, in vol. 3 of *Oeuvres de H. de Balzac* (Bruxelles: Meline, Cans, 1837).

33   Honoré de Balzac, *Vater Goriot* (Stuttgart: Hallberger, 1835); *Papà Goriot: storia parigina* (Milano: Pirotta, 1836).

34   Emmanuel Théaulon, Alexis Decomberousse, and Ernest Jaime, *Le père Goriot: drame-vaudeville en 3 actes* (Paris: Marchant, 1835), http://gallica.bnf.fr/ark:/12148/bpt6k104328x.

144 Industrial productions

35 Honoré de Balzac, *Études de moeurs au XIXe siècle* (Paris: Béchet, 1834–37).
36 Vachon, *Travaux*, 37.
37 Ibid., 210.
38 Ibid., 227.
39 Ibid., 40.
40 Ibid., 210.
41 John Lough and Muriel Lough, *An Introduction to Nineteenth Century France* (London: Longman, 1978), 220–21.
42 Wright, *Modern Times*, 158.
43 René Rémond, *The Right Wing in France: From 1815 to de Gaulle*, trans. James M. Laux (Philadelphia: University of Pennsylvania Press, 1969), 147.
44 Witkowski, *Editions populaires*, 72.
45 Eugène Sue, *Les mystères de Paris* (Paris: Charles Gosselin, 1842); *Oeuvres illustrées d'Eugène Sue* (Paris: Maresq, 1850–55).
46 Witkowski, *Editions populaires*, 37.
47 Lough and Lough, *Nineteenth Century France*, 241.
48 Olivero, "Paperback Revolution," 78.
49 Ibid., 79.
50 For example, *L'Echo des feuilletons* (1840–64) and *Le Magasin littéraire* (1841–48).
51 Coward, "Popular Fiction," 74.
52 Witkowski, *Editions populaires*, 21.
53 Ibid.
54 Ibid., 21–22.
55 Ibid., 23.
56 Ibid., 89.
57 Ibid., 93.
58 Coward, "Popular Fiction," 82.
59 Roger Pierrot, *Honoré de Balzac* (Paris: Fayard, 1994), 515–16. Note: All translations of Pierrot are my own.
60 Honoré de Balzac, *Œuvres illustrées de Balzac* (Paris: Marescq, 1851–53).
61 Honoré de Balzac, *Scènes de la vie parisienne: Le père Goriot* (Paris: Bureaux du "Siècle," 1856), http://gallica.bnf.fr/ark:/12148/bpt6k58487109.
62 François-René Chateaubriand, *Atala; René*, trans. Irving Putter (Berkeley: University of California Press, 1980).
63 See, for example, George Sand, *Indiana*, trans. Sylvia Raphael (Oxford: Oxford University Press, 2000); and *Mauprat*, ed. and trans. Sylvia Raphael (Oxford: Oxford University Press, 1997).
64 Donna Dickenson, introduction to *The Miller of Angibault*, by George Sand, trans. Donna Dickenson (Oxford: Oxford University Press, 1995), xii.
65 Durand, *De la condition des ouvriers de Paris, de 1789 jusqu'en 1841, avec quelques idées sur la possibilité de l'améliorer* (Paris: J. B. Gros, 1841), http://gallica.bnf.fr/ark:/12148/bpt6k6465840n/f1.image.r=histoire%20des%20ouvriers.
66 George Sand, *Le meunier d'Angibault*, trans. Donna Dickenson, *The Miller of Angibault* (Oxford: Oxford University Press, 1995). Note: All translations of *Le meunier d'Angibault* are by Dickenson.
67 Sue, *Mystères de Paris*; *Les mystères du peuple, ou, histoire d'une famille de prolétaires à travers les âges* (Paris: R. Deforges, 1977).
68 Feuchtwanger, *House of Desdemona*, 30.
69 Lukács, *Historical Novel*, 171.
70 George Sand, *La ville noire*, trans. Tina A. Kover, *The Black City* (New York: Carroll and Graf, 2004). Note: All translations of *La ville noire* are by Kover.

Industrial productions 145

71 For a more in depth discussion of George Sand and *La ville noire*, see Robert Godwin-Jones, *Romantic Vision: The Novels of George Sand* (Birmingham, AB: Summa Publications, 1995), see esp. chp. 9, "Helping Sweet Providence: Sacrifice and Reward in *La Ville noire* and *Le Marquis de Villeme*." See also, David A. Powell, ed., *Le siecle de George Sand* (Amsterdam: Rodopi, 1998), see esp. in pt. 3, Mary Rice-Defosse, "The Woman Writer and the Worker: Social Mobility and Solidarity in *la Ville noire*," 95–102.

72 My translation of the subtitle: *Natural and Social History of a Family Under the Second Empire*.

73 Émile Zola, *Le ventre de Paris*, trans. Brian Nelson, *The Belly of Paris* = *Le Ventre de Paris* (Oxford: Oxford University Press, 2007), 274. Note: All translations of *Le ventre de Paris* are by Nelson.

74 Armand Lanoux and Henri Mitterand, "Notes et variantes: Le ventre de Paris," in vol. 1 of *Les Rougon-Macquart: histoire naturelle et sociale d'une famille sous le Second Empire*, ed. Armand Lanoux and Henri Mitterand (Paris: Bibliothèque de la Pléiade, 1960), 1607–8.

75 Zola, *Belly of Paris*, 42.

76 Ibid., 45.

77 Ibid., 85.

78 Ibid., 88.

79 Ibid., 89.

80 Ibid., 123.

81 Ibid., 148.

82 Ibid., 186.

83 *L'assommoir* was originally published in several formats: in two parts, the first part (chapters 1–6) in the daily *le Bien public* from April 13 to June 7, 1876, and the second part (chapters 7–13) in the weekly *la République des Lettres* from July 9, 1876 to January 7, 1877; by Charpentier in 1877, sold for three-and-a-half francs; and as an illustrated edition in 1878 by Marpon and Flammarion, sold for six francs. See Henri Mitterand, "L'assommoir: Notice," in vol. 2 of *Les Rougon-Macquart: histoire naturelle et sociale d'une famille sous le Second Empire*, ed. Armand Lanoux (Paris: Bibliothèque de la Pléiade, 1961), 1533–34.

84 Émile Zola, *L'assommoir*, trans. Leonard Tancock, *L'Assommoir* (New York: Penguin Books, 1970), 21. Note: All translations of *L'assommoir* are by Tancock.

85 Ibid.

86 Ibid., 137.

87 Ibid., 120.

88 Ibid., 177.

89 Ibid., 273.

90 Ibid., 243.

91 Ibid., 244.

92 *Germinal* was originally published in the daily *Gil Blas* from November 26, 1884 to February 25, 1885; by Charpentier in 1885, sold for three-and-a-half francs; and as an illustrated edition by Férat in 1885–86. See Henri Mitterand, "Germinal: Étude," in vol. 3 of *Les Rougon-Macquart: histoire naturelle et sociale d'une famille sous le Second Empire*, ed. Armand Lanoux (Paris: Bibliothèque de la Pléiade, 1964), 1808–9.

93 On the situation of workers as represented in the novel, see David Baguley, "*Germinal*: The Gathering Storm," in *The Cambridge Companion to Émile Zola*, ed. Brian Nelson (Cambridge: Cambridge University Press, 2007), 140–41. Baguley writes, for example, "In France, since 1852, only mutual aid societies under state surveillance were authorised and, even after the fall of the Empire, the workers' movement fared little better under the conservative dominance of the early years of the Third Republic. The Commune had been brutally repressed and

146 *Industrial productions*

the International was widely held responsible for the upheaval. Labour unions, though tolerated earlier, were not authorised until 1884 and only after October 1886, when the first French workers' congresses took place, did the movement gain impetus" (ibid., 141).

94 Émile Zola, *Germinal*, trans. L. W. Tancock (New York: Penguin Books, 1963), 279. Note: All translations of *Germinal* are by Tancock.

95 Ibid.

96 Ibid., 167.

97 Ibid., 358–59.

98 Ibid., 359.

99 Ibid., 495.

100 Ibid., 499.

101 *La terre* was originally published in the daily *Gil Blas* from May 29 to September 16, 1887; by Charpentier in 1887, sold for three-and-a-half francs; and in an illustrated edition by Duez et al. and Marpon and Flammarion in 1889, sold for six francs (59 parts at 10 centimes). See Henri Mitterand, "La terre: Étude," in vol. 4 of *Les Rougon-Macquart: histoire naturelle et sociale d'une famille sous le Second Empire*, ed. Armand Lanoux (Paris: Bibliothèque de la Pléiade, 1966), 1491–92.

102 Émile Zola, *La terre*, trans. Douglas Parmée, *The Earth* (Harmondsworth: Penguin, 1980), 48. Note: All translations of *La terre* are by Parmée.

103 Ibid., 100.

104 Ibid., 73.

105 Ibid., 152.

106 Ibid., 363.

107 Ibid., 87.

108 Ibid., 88.

109 Ibid., 95.

110 Ibid.

111 Ibid.

8 Community lessons
Canadian tales of national progress

> The reflexivity of modern social life consists in the fact that social practices
> are constantly examined and reformed in the light of incoming information
> about those very practices, thus constitutively altering their character.
> – Anthony Giddens, *The Consequences of Modernity*, 38

The speed and scope of modernization in Canada was especially apparent in the second half of the nineteenth century. In this context, cultural
producers provided community lessons at critical moments of the transition from British North America to Canadian Confederation, and then with
respect to the modernization of the Dominion of Canada. With this rough
division of early national and later socioeconomic questions in mind, this
chapter first considers how French-Canadian novelists addressed community formation in the 1860s, and then how English-Canadian novelists of
the later-nineteenth century responded to the consequences of industrialization. In both French and English Canada, the question of national progress
depended on a context-specific understanding of modernization. Authorial
interests, social context, and the particularity of the communication circuits
involved in disseminating new information determined the various answers
provided. The historical novel, alongside newspapers, periodicals, dramas,
and other forms of popular communication, played a central role in the
reflexivity of modern life, which consisted of the constant examination of
social practices with the aim of altering behaviors and adapting to changing circumstances. As one of many acts of modernity, the historical novel
gave writers and readers the opportunity to participate in the formation of a
localized understanding of subjectivity and community. Such interventions
could be highly contentious; questions of community are complex and were
especially political at a time when the practicality of a bi-cultural nation-
state was uncertain. The political divide between the French and the English
was real, yet all people experienced the consequences of modernity. So, the
two cultural spheres were connected by longstanding historical conflict on
the one hand and the inescapable realities of modernity on the other. This
chapter continues the work of better understanding the chronotopic use of

148   *Community lessons*

the historical novel; more specifically, through the juxtaposition of French and English Canada, as well as earlier and later periods within the Canadian context, I further explore the impact of cultural specificity on the integration of modern practices, as well as the ethical limits of the historical novel as it was used to investigate the social consequences of modernization.

Canadian tales of national progress were local endeavors for several reasons, not least the historical circumstances leading up to the production of politically charged historical novels in the 1860s. From the Conquest, the acquisition of Canada by Great Britain in the Seven Years' War (1756–63), to Confederation in 1867, the relationship between the British government and local communities was contentious, and always in a state of transition. Early attempts to govern the Province of Québec were hardly successful, resulting in the 1774 Québec Act, which lifted restrictions on French Catholics, authorized French civil law, and enabled the continuation of the seigneurial system.[1] Although the 1791 Constitutional Act, which created Upper and Lower Canada, is generally understood as a step toward Confederation, the general purpose of the Act was to assimilate each colony's constitution to that of Britain.[2] The Rebellions of 1837–38 in both Upper and Lower Canada symbolized discontent with colonial governance. The Earl of Durham's *Report of the Affairs of British North America* (1838) put the especially precarious position of Lower Canada into stark terms by making it clear that submission to British rule was expected.[3] Following a recommendation from Durham's *Report*, the 1840 Act of Union united the colonies of Upper and Lower Canada as the Province of Canada. Although initially unfair to Lower Canada, many of the one-sided provisions were repealed and the union eventually proved economically prosperous for both Upper and Lower Canada.[4] In 1854, the seigneurial system of land distribution dating back to the establishment of New France in 1627 was abolished. Representing more than economic distribution, the change pointed at once to the consolidation of British influence on French-speaking Canada and the need of French Canadians to continue cultivating their own social practices. In broader terms, the negotiation of power in Canada was continuous and contentious, more so as urbanization, western exploration, and population growth altered the shape and consistency of the emerging nation-state. In this setting, historical novels in English and French looked back at moments of national crisis with the inherently political intent of projecting progress; the perpetual re-examination of the past invariably occurred with new circumstances and community interests in mind.

Rosanna Leprohon's *The Manor House of De Villerai: A Tale of Canada Under the French Dominion* (1859–60) was not the first historical novel in Canada and it was not written either in French or by a French Canadian.[5] Andrea Cabajsky, however, argues that it "is the first historical novel, in either English or French, to portray the fall of New France from the French-Canadian point-of-view."[6] Leprohon first wrote novels of manners set in England. Like James Fenimore Cooper's early transition from *Precaution*, a novel of manners set in England, to *The Spy*, a Revolutionary War novel set in America, she later adapted to the situation and interests of local readers with *The Manor House*, which considers the culture and history of French Canada. *The Manor House* was first published in installments in the weekly *Family Herald* from November 16, 1859 to February 8, 1860.[7] It was also popular in French translation: serialization in the French-Canadian newspaper *L'Ordre*, book publication in Montreal by Lovell and Desbarats in 1861 under the title *Le manoir de Villerai*,[8] followed by five editions of the translation by Joseph-Edouard Lefebvre de Bellefeuille, also titled *Le manoir de Villerai*, between 1884 and 1925.[9] In *The Manor House*, Leprohon unites a peasant girl with a military captain, French protagonists marry and return to France, and the heroine Blanche remains unmarried and stays behind to do charitable work. In this way, Leprohon historicizes a range of responses to the fall of New France, which helped pave the way for further political use of the historical novel leading up to Confederation. The use of marriage to project political paths, long a staple of romance in its many forms, was not new to British North America; for example, Carole Gerson describes Catharine Parr Traill's *Canadian Crusoes: A Tale of the Rice Lake Plains* (1852) in the following terms: "After the children are found, the narrative stage expands to national dimensions as the tale is eventually rounded off with a double marriage blending the country's British, French, and Indian heritages, the latter two being subsumed into the dominant white, English-speaking order."[10] Depictions of racial "blending," or more likely, separation, were common in American historical novels from the 1820s onward, many of which made their way north. What is new is that, as a tale of Canada under French Dominion, *The Manor House* offers a path forward that speaks to the experiences and interests of French Canadians. In this sense, Cabajsky rightly points to the novel's "rejection of historiography written from the perspective of history's victors."[11] Put otherwise, Leprohon adapted the historical novel to a communication situation informed by political difference – a situation soon to be exploited further by others working in French and English.

The sympathetic view of French-Canadian history put forward by *The Manor House* followed earlier histories of French Canada by Michel Bibaud and especially François-Xavier Garneau,[12] which led to more explicitly patriotic uses of the historical novel. The most famous is Philippe Aubert de Gaspé's *Les anciens Canadiens* (1863).[13] Paul Perron writes, "Although not the first historical novel written in Québec, Philippe Aubert de Gaspé's *Les Anciens Canadiens* . . . constituted a radical break from previous novels and was by far the most popular and widely read novel in nineteenth-century French Canada."[14] Not surprisingly, Aubert de Gaspé's radical break builds not only upon historical accounts of French Canada but also upon the Waverley novels, as David Hayne notes: "If *Les Anciens Canadiens* is truly the first genuine historical novel in French Canada, it is also further indication of the importance of Scott's influence for the young genre."[15] Questions

150   *Community lessons*

of authenticity and genre aside, Scott set forth a combination of history and romance that was useful to Aubert de Gaspé and others as a means to address social transformation within the new social and political realities of French Canada. As a member of *Club des Anciens*, an elite group of writers, artists, and historians dedicated to preserving the cultural identity of French Canada, Aubert de Gaspé was part of "An intellectual and literary renaissance [that] was beginning for French-Canadians."[16] Accordingly, the stated ambition of *Les anciens Canadiens* is "To set down a few episodes of bygone days, a few memories of youth, alas! long past."[17] For most of the twentieth century, the novel was thus seen as a nostalgic remembrance of popular manners and folklore – an interpretation supported by the copious historical and personal notes appended to the novel by Aubert de Gaspé. In 1909, Camille Roy put forward the idea that *Les anciens Canadiens* was the first series of Aubert de Gaspé's later *Mémoires* (1866).[18] E. Margaret Grimes subsequently deprioritized the resolutions of the novel, writing that "The plot of the novel of *Les Anciens Canadiens* is the least interesting."[19] Similarly, Clara Thomas suggests that "The plot is only the skeleton of the book; the flesh of *Les Anciens Canadiens* is a wealth and a depth of incident, description, reminiscence, and folklore."[20] However, the events of *Les anciens Canadiens* outline a well-defined sociopolitical trajectory, making visible the progress of French Canada within British North America. Owing much to the theme of national reconciliation central to *Waverley*, narrative outcomes were an essential part of the lesson in community formation that made *Les anciens Canadiens* and other historical novels of the period so useful to French-Canadian authors and readers throughout the century.

The first chapter of *Les anciens Canadiens* is titled "The End of College Days" and the tale begins in April – a time for new beginnings. The transition that follows is from passive education to active participation, from the pranks and lessons of childhood to the acts and responsibilities of adulthood. The introduction of two protagonists allows Aubert de Gaspé to differentiate interlocking national histories. After the Battle of Culloden, the last of the Jacobite risings that attempted to reinstate a Stuart monarch on the throne of Britain, Scottish-born Archibald Cameron of Locheill is brought to Canada from France by Jesuits to attend a seminary in Québec. He becomes friends with Jules d'Haberville, the son of a prosperous *seigneur*, and spends his holidays with the d'Haberville family in the country. Around 1757, Archie joins the British army and Jules joins the French army; both leave Canada to begin their military careers. Jules is expected to return to New France – he is a *Canadien*. Archie, on the other hand, bids farewell to his classmates, "perhaps forever," for he is of "foreign birth."[21] The early differentiation of Jules and Archie along national lines plays out through the novel in different ways, but initially it allows for a contrast of national character. Archie is cold, practical, and logical; Jules is passionate, free-spirited, and comedic. Whereas Archie demonstrates shrewd calculation and physical daring to save Dumais, "Jules had no idea that his friend was trying to rescue Dumais. His highly sensitive nature had found the heartrending sight on the shore unbearable, and after one glance of unutterable compassion he had lowered his eyes and stared fixedly at the ground. It all seemed like a horrible dream to him."[22] The difference in character does not alter their love for each other – both are noble and generous. Yet Aubert de Gaspé repeatedly describes their differences, sometimes rather bluntly. Jules, for example, lamenting his upcoming departure from Canada, exclaims, "And to think I must leave all this – perhaps forever. Oh, Mother, Mother, what a separation!"[23] Archie responds by comforting his friend, then turns his attention to more practical interests, inquiring about the mechanism used to tap the trees of sap: "Wouldn't you say the trunks are like immense hydraulic tubes with taps ready to provide refreshment for a populous town?"[24] The animating force of this difference in character informs the depiction of modernization that follows.

Archie's practical way of thinking is integral to his own personal history, which speaks directly to French Canadians of their own national history: Archie lost his mother at the age of four; his father fought with Prince Charles Edward and died at Culloden. In other words, Archie has suffered loss, and his family was on the wrong side of history. But he escapes to France at the age of twelve and is eventually admitted to the Jesuit Collège of Québec. The lesson is that the Scot moves on, takes advantage of new situations, and although he looks back, embracing the past and his cultural origins, he does not take his eye off the present – past and future must be reconciled in the moment. Aubert de Gaspé then shifts toward a larger picture that connects the histories of Scotland and French Canada. Initially, he describes the events of Culloden as "the death rattle of a brave nation," but the following is quickly added: "Scotland, now part and parcel of one of the world's most powerful empires, has had no cause to regret defeat."[25] *Les anciens Canadiens* traces a similar history of war, loss, reconciliation, and ultimate prosperity for French Canada, informed further by the comparison of Scotland to Ireland: while "their brothers in green Erin, the warmhearted and generous Irish, still struggle against their chains, the people of Scotland enjoy their prosperity in peace."[26] The connection of personal fortunes to national histories is exactly the shift in perspective Aubert de Gaspé promotes in *Les anciens Canadiens*, situating the trajectory of the d'Haberville family and French Canada in relation to international history. The tale seems personal, especially as framed by the memories of an aging narrator, but the lessons are of national significance. Accordingly, Aubert de Gaspé's prescription is straightforward: "History provides the answer."[27] More accurately, at stake is the use of history to remake history, to cast aside the shadow of defeat and begin a new path of prosperity defined by the priorities of French Canadians situated within British North America.

Aubert de Gaspé's historification of French Canada begins with a portrait of the d'Haberville family firmly entrenched in the old ways. Each of the d'Haberville men begin the tale as inflexible, passionate, and unforgiving

152   Community lessons

advocates of New France: Jules "worked on the principle that one must never admit defeat"; Seigneur d'Haberville "rarely pardoned a real or even a supposed injury"; for Raoul, "The perfidious Britons had broken his leg at the taking of Louisbourg, and because of this he had been forced to give up his army career, a point on which he was very sensitive."[28] The underlying issue is an inability to meet the needs of the present. The curé brings up the approaching conflict with the British at the Plains of Abraham: "Do you realize, gentlemen, that New France's horizon is darkening with each day? Our English neighbours are busy with formidable preparations for the invasion of Canada, and there seems to be every indication that it will happen soon."[29] After listening to further practical observations regarding the lack of French military strength in Canada, Seigneur d'Haberville responds, "Which goes to show how confidently our beloved King Louis XV believes we have the courage to defend his colony."[30] In short, he is blinded by patriotism, which is fueled by ignorance. Archie's interruption signals the mistake in progress:

> Perhaps a young man like myself shouldn't take part in your grave discussion, but history makes up for my lack of experience. Be wary of the English and of a government that is always wide awake to its colonies' interests, and therefore the interests of the British empire. Beware a nation with the tenacity of a bulldog. If the conquest of Canada is a necessary goal, it will never lose sight of this objective, no matter at what sacrifice. Witness the fate of my unfortunate homeland.[31]

In reply to such a measured warning – based on personal experience and historical record – Raoul dismisses the Scot out of hand and Jules says, "You'll come back with me, brother Archie, and revenge yourself on the sassenachs this side of the Atlantic for everything you've suffered in your homeland."[32] Raoul is ignorant of the history recounted by Archie, and Jules's infatuation with juvenile tales of vengeance seems naïve in light of Archie's calculated response: "I'll serve as a volunteer in your company if I don't get a commission, and the simple soldier will be as proud of your feats as if he had a greater share in them."[33] Archie's practicality, along with that of the curé, which seems to go unnoticed and unappreciated in the face of present realities, is quickly effaced as enthusiasm mounts, drinking ensues, and Seigneur d'Haberville exclaims, "To the success of our arms! And may the glorious fleur-de-lys fly over all the citadels of New France till the end of time!"[34] Such colorful phrases provide a useful point of contrast, for *Les anciens Canadiens*, in the end, counters patriotism with the practical act of history-making. In defense of previous generations, Aubert de Gaspé writes: "You have long been misunderstood, my Canadian brothers of old! You have been falsely besmirched. Honour be to those who have restored your good name! Honour, a hundred times honour, be to our compatriot, Monsieur Garneau, who has torn back the veil that hid your exploits!"[35]

Community lessons 153

Contrary to appearances, this is not flag waving, but rather a call to build the foundation for such enthusiasm. The call to remember, specifically referencing French-Canadian historian François-Xavier Garneau, is an extension of the mission of *Club des Anciens* to remake cultural history, to create "the story of our heroic past" and thus establish the basis for a collective way forward.[36] First and foremost, the emphasis is on the hard work of remaking history. This means fostering an awareness of history from a French-Canadian perspective; the reader is admonished: "We were abashed at our ignorance of the history of the Assyrians, Medes, and Persians, yet we knew nothing of the history of our homeland."[37] It is a call to arms; the ammunition is education, and the intended outcome is self-interest. History provides the knowledge to make rational decisions in the present; French Canadians must move forward, initially at least, by walking backward.

In this sense, chapter twelve is a critical junction in the novel, for just as Aubert de Gaspé is about to describe the battle at the Plains of Abraham he stops to outline the benefits that resulted from the so-called Conquest, boldly stating that French Canadians "may have benefitted from the cession of Canada."[38] The benefits described include escaping the horrors of 1793 in France, gathering honors fighting under Britain's banners, and the preservation of cultural heritage. This leads to a call for collective bravery in the face of domination: "Be brave and stand together, O my compatriots!"[39] Patriotism here begins to take on a strategic look as Aubert de Gaspé provides a moderate, balanced tale of two battles on the Plains of Abraham – one victory for each side, both nations brave, resolute, fierce, and uncompromising. There is only one loser: "September 13, 1759 – a black day in the annals of France."[40] French Canada is thus nobly resituated between Britain's victory and France's loss. Here, then, is the power of the historical novel to remake history in action. The space between France and Britain, and especially between France and Québec, is reconstructed by Aubert de Gaspé's narrative of loss, victory, and abandonment, making possible a new beginning from a position of, if not strength, at least possibilities. The new home of the d'Haberville family is spare, pared down from the former extravagance of the manor house, and made of Canadian materials, with only a few remnants, or souvenirs, from France. Ultimately, the change is framed as a new start: "The house smelled so clean and fresh that one couldn't regret the lack of more sumptuous appointments."[41] The attitude of the French Canadians shifts with new realities, as do their actions. Aubert de Gaspé notes, "Of all the passions that torment the heart of man, jealousy and the desire for vengeance are the most difficult to conquer. Rarely can such feelings be rooted out."[42] Yet Jules, unlike his father, can say, "But then I've never been one to harbour a grudge"; he even gives Archie the following advice: "You should put the past behind you now, satisfied that you acted honourably in carrying out a soldier's inescapable duties. . . . We've recovered most of our losses, and our life is more peaceful under British rule than under French domination."[43] Poise and practicality have replaced enthusiasm and

154 *Community lessons*

passion; Jules speaks not of revenge but to economic prosperity and political security. Seigneur d'Haberville's position for most of the novel is clear: "you know I never forget an injury. I can't help it: that's my nature. If it's a sin, God hasn't seen fit to bless me with the ability to overcome it."[44] But after the war, when he meets Archie, the man who burned down his estate and caused the ruin of his family, Seigneur d'Haberville walks away, ponders the situation, and is then able to forgive: "And with this he cordially pressed Locheill's hand. The lion was tamed."[45] Even Raoul, who repeatedly rails against the English, accepts Jules's English wife and embraces their son: "He'll have the fiery courage of the d'Habervilles combined with the tenacity and independence of the proud islanders on his mother's side."[46] Post-war reconciliation is under way. As with Scotland, French Canada will survive union; fortune will depend on the selective re-embedding of social relationships. The question is, how will the feudal past of New France be reconciled with the realities of modern Canada?

Les anciens Canadiens advocates the cultivation of political power and cultural independence under British administration. Aubert de Gaspé emphasizes the preservation of class structures; as Maurice Lemire writes, "The standpoint of Aubert de Gaspé in his novel aims to justify the seigneurs at the time they held power."[47] Although officially ended in 1854, the seigneurial system is depicted by Aubert de Gaspé, first as part of a pristine feudal past, and second as re-established in a revised form. This representation actually ran counter to prevailing views; Lemire writes, "The new public discourse not only devaluated the social role of the seigneur, but treated him as a profiteer. By taking up his case, Gaspé seeks less to make a review of the customs and habits of old than to rehabilitate the domination of the seigneurs."[48] As Enn Raudsepp concludes her own analysis: "Thus, far from being a faithful depiction of French Canadian life, free of didactic purpose, *Les Anciens Canadiens* must, in the final analysis, be seen as a polemical work which is historically valid only in so far as it casts light on the motives and aspirations of the Québec gentry."[49] Aubert de Gaspé's aim was to replace one history with another. He does not aim for verisimilitude so much as the reinvention of Canadian progress defined by his own view of French Canada. Community-specific continuity plays out in several ways, of which the preservation of class structures is only one, and in the end, perhaps not the most important means of fostering political power and cultural differentiation. Again, the comparison to Scotland is instructive. As a commissioned officer in the British army, the French refer to Archie as Monsieur l'Anglais. Archie, however, is of course a Scotsman; on the battlefield, he too must bend to the will of his British superiors. He must, for example, sacrifice his personal attachment to the d'Haberville family and follow state orders. Notably, whereas Archie falls in line and carries out his duty, thus ensuring his later promotion, he is also able to find common ground with French Canadians, not only due to his knowledge of the French language, but because he is Catholic. Politically, he acts within and

Community lessons 155

furthers the British power structures that enable professional achievement; culturally, he maintains a sense of difference from the English. This is the awkward compromise that Aubert de Gaspé lays out for French Canada. Seigneur d'Haberville will not serve the new government or fight against France, but he agrees to let Jules, "who is just starting out in life," "devote his talents and energy to the service of his Canadian countrymen."[50] Having paid his debt to his ancestors and able to retire from military service with honor, the father recommends that the son take the oath to the British crown. Only a few years before, an alliance with the British was unthinkable. Just as important is the basis of the decision: "he was too fair-minded to ruin his son's future for the sake of an extreme sensitivity."[51] As descriptive of a signal shift from fiery, unforgiving, and rash (college days) to thoughtful, generous, and prudent (adulthood), *Les anciens Canadiens* is a lesson in community building, ostensibly in the form of a *bildungsroman*, that aims, above all else, to bridge the gap between past and future, in this case, with an eye to French-Canadian interests. The act of history-making to advance a vision of French-Canadian progress takes precedence over fidelity to the facts of historical record. Furthermore, it does not rule out the cultivation of cultural difference.

The romance of progress in the aftermath of war depends on a conscious juxtaposition of cultural independence and economic prosperity. Cultural survival is most dramatically depicted by Jules's marriage to an unnamed English woman and Blanche's refusal of Archie. Marriage provides the means to sketch a way forward; as Raudsepp writes, "Aubert de Gaspé's handling of the 'ever after' life of the two d'Haberville children, Jules and Blanche, seems almost to have been designed to provide a blueprint for the conduct of Québécois men and women under British rule."[52] Jules's marriage brings others into French-Canadian social structures: "Jules' wife is absorbed into his family and will be guided by his traditions in the socialization of their children."[53] As Gerson puts it, "Such a union predicates the absorption of the female partner into the dominant culture of the male, the sexual submission of the individual symbolizing the political submission of the group."[54] Patriarchal incorporation is a means to maintain social structures and a sense of national continuity in the midst of transformation. French Canada cannot exclude British influence – the point is to manage the situation, that is, to engineer the existence of a strong French-Canadian community. Blanche's refusal of Archie's proposal is an extension of Jules's marriage to an English woman; as Nicole Deschamps writes, "By her refusal, Blanche d'Haberville prefigures the French-Canadian mother, fertile and sacrificial."[55] Blanche encourages cross-cultural relationships in light of political realities: "Since the French and Anglo-Saxon races now share the same homeland after centuries of hatred and warfare, it's only natural and even desirable that they should be governed by the same laws and establish closer ties through such intimate relationships."[56] However, the nature of Blanche's sacrifice determines the "closer ties" in question. As

156 *Community lessons*

Raudsepp suggests, "She becomes, in essence, a role model for all succeeding generations of Québec women, for whom, along with religion, language and land, the family is to be one of the inviolable cornerstones upon which the survival of French Canada is based."[57] But the construction of that family is particular. After much talk of old times, Archie proposes. Blanche's response is definitive: "No d'Haberville woman will ever consent to such humiliation."[58] To describe marriage to Archie as shameful is to express the deepest regrets and fears of a nation, but the refusal also constitutes French-Canadian identity in practical terms: "Archie, you had everything to captivate a girl of fifteen. . . . But now, Captain Archibald Cameron of Locheill, there is a gulf between us that I will never cross."[59] A French-Canadian woman (like a French-Canadian man) cannot submit to the British; as a Captain in the British military, Archie is no longer a childhood friend from Scotland. Ironically, although *Les anciens Canadiens* teaches French Canadians to follow the example of Scotland, the lesson learned requires the rejection of a Scot. The romantic flirtations of youth are over; like Jules, Seigneur d'Haberville, and Raoul, Blanche must come of age and play her role in an adult world requiring personal decisions of national consequence. Archie asks if he may hope, but Blanche's answer, however endearing, is emphatic: "Never. Never, my dear Archie."[60] National interest trumps individual inclination.

In this anti-romance of progress, patriarchal social formation remains central, but women, representative of production in a double sense, as mothers and teachers, have an important political role to play in community formation. The lesson seems to be, as Dennis Duffy describes, that "A patriarchal model of society can handle the threat of dilution when it comes from the female side, for Jules' English wife, like all good wives, will be absorbed into her husband's ways. The outsider male cannot be as easily accommodated."[61] Yet women are active agents in a process of cultural differentiation that defines the basis of national progress. As Duffy also notes, Blanche's *grand refus* does not indicate sterility, but rather "an affirmation of a culture richly evolved and complete in itself."[62] It is, in other words, a complete refusal of Durham's *Report*, which described French Canadians as an inferior race.[63] Archie perseveres but his passion cannot overcome Blanche's cold confidence – another stark example of the character reversal that takes place over the course of the novel. Marriage is constituted by new circumstances. Jules conquers (by marrying an English woman) and the d'Haberville family grows, whereas Blanche maintains a sense of purity, protecting her name and stopping the penetration of her family by a foreigner, a conqueror: "Am I, a d'Haberville, to set the example to the noble daughters of Canada by being twice conquered?"[64] In both ways, marriage demonstrates that the Conquest ended on the Plains of Abraham. Jules not only accepts Blanche's decision but adds, "Your soul is sublime!"[65] The future of the nation depends not only on the advantages of a strong economic state but also on the perpetuation of community priorities at the level of individuals and families; in this way, all French Canadians have the

Community lessons   157

power to remake French Canada in their own image. Contrary to the folksy descriptions of days gone by, the call to remember, like the novel's resolution, is practical rather than romantic; as the so-called "good gentleman" tells Jules, "the survivor inherits all."[66] On the eve of Confederation, it is the romance of self-interest that dominates this historification of French-Canadian progress.

Canadian tales of national progress were not neutral. From a French-Canadian perspective, positive representation required the imagination of things otherwise, which did not begin or end with *Les anciens Canadiens*, and took a variety of forms. Patrice Lacombe's *La terre paternelle* (1846) was an influential early predecessor in this respect.[67] Perron usefully identifies a fundamental concern in French-Canadian novels that emerge after *La terre paternelle* as "the articulation of humanized topoi in which socialized and historical subjects can realize their potential with respect to the survival, the continuation, and the development of the group, the race, and the nation."[68] This description suits *The Manor House, Les anciens Canadiens*, and other historical novels of the 1860s, however differently, in part because it is a broad definition, but also because it gestures to an important question: what, beyond the longstanding conflict between the French and the English, conditioned new representations of modernity specific to the interests of French-Canadian readers? *La terre paternelle* was published just after Durham posed the following question: "by what race is it likely that the wilderness . . . in which the French Canadians are located, is eventually to be converted into a settled and flourishing country?"[69] Coming from Durham, it was a rhetorical question. *La terre paternelle*, in contrast, projected the continuity of French-speaking communities in Canada as a historical project of empowerment grounded by the relationship between people and the land. Although *Les anciens Canadiens* was the more popular novel, by modernizing Lacombe's representation, Antoine Gérin-Lajoie's *Jean Rivard* (1862–64) provided a tale of progress that, in retrospect at least, seems no less important to the historification of French Canada, as both a response to British colonialism and a lesson aimed at French Canadians.

In 1877, Lesperance described *Jean Rivard* as "a gossipy account of pioneer life in the Townships."[70] Camille Roy was more accurate when forty years later he described it as a "novel of the colonist."[71] The first part of *Jean Rivard* follows directly on the heels of *La terre paternelle*, but overall, the more informative and timely contrast is to *Les anciens Canadiens*. As historical accounts, both *Les anciens Canadiens* and *Jean Rivard* accept a British framework to varying degrees; these are not novels of outright revolt but instead historical interventions to set forth a localized view of prosperity dependent on the use of modernized social structures. The difference is that *Jean Rivard* provides a step-by-step plan for settlement and community formation that begins with reclamation of the land, includes the possibility of governance by an upwardly mobile working class, and most importantly, results in a recognizably modern community. Like other novels of the

158   *Community lessons*

period, *Jean Rivard* is not concerned with Aboriginal rights; to use the land is to clear the trees and build a home. Yet, rather than a simple agrarian novel of making hay in the wilderness, *Jean Rivard* is a two-part manual describing not only how to settle but also how to build modern communities, as alluded to by the subtitles of each part of the novel: *le défricheur'* (settler) and *économiste* (economist).

Self-education is central to Gérin-Lajoie's depiction of French-Canadian independence; the lessons required, however, are of modernity as experienced across the Western world. Modern practices such as agriculture, industry, organization, efficiency, and cleanliness must be learned: "The science of government is not acquired by magic."[72] During the settlement phase, Rivard repeatedly reads *Robinson Crusoe, The History of Napoleon, Don Quixote*, and *The Imitation of Christ*; each text has a singular purpose: "Robinson Crusoe taught me to be industrious, *Napoleon* taught me to be active and courageous, Don Quixote made me laugh in my moments of deepest despair, *The Imitation of Christ* taught me submission to the will of God."[73] *Jean Rivard* is no less instructive. As a settler, Rivard is heroic, carving out his own plot of land from the wilderness. More importantly, the longer process of establishing a new, modern community depends on continuing education and expert management: once the land is cleared, the farm prospers, in part due to hard work, but also because Rivard keeps a journal, account books, an office, and a library in his home. He reads instructive, middle-class literature – religion, classics, history, science, agriculture, languages, law, and politics – emphasizing the pillars of this new world. The message is as Perron notes in his study of the agrarian novel in Québec: "Positively invested agents can realize and fulfil their destiny from a social, political, ethical, and religious perspective only within a specific space."[74] As opposed to the first agrarian novel in Canada, *La terre paternelle*, in *Jean Rivard*, the space in question is that of modernity, and thus international in important respects; the destiny acted out in the second volume is that of the middle-class nation-state. Jeanie Deans and Mabel Dunham would thrive in Rivardville, which is described in a final tour of the model farm, house, garden, and town. It is Voltaire's garden in the age of modernity, or a French-Canadian Knocktarlitie. However it might be described, although the instruction manuals originated elsewhere, this garden was built with French-Canadian hands; similarly, although a community situated by the wider reaches of modernity, the particularities of the Canadian context remain visible: at Rivard's house, "Two big flags hung from the windows: the British flag and the national flag. On the latter was inscribed, in large letters, on one side, Religion, Homeland, Liberty, and on the other, Education, Agriculture, Industry. These words by themselves explained Jean Rivard's entire politics."[75] Rather than marriage, Rivardville itself is the blueprint for a bi-cultural Canada constituted by (and constitutive of) modernity.

In English Canada, although the historical novel was used to consider the political history of French-English relations, novels after Confederation also took up different concerns. For example, Lesperance's *The Bastonnais: Tale of the American Invasion of Canada in 1775–76* (1877) is a typical story of upper-class marriage embellished with the description of local customs and legends, but the outcome is specific to circumstances of production and reception. The British soldier Roderick Hardinge marries the exotic French-Canadian beauty Zulma and the American soldier Cary Singleton marries Frenchwoman Pauline Belmont. The British and the Americans are equal: Roderick wins one battle; Cary wins another. Moreover, the son of Roderick and Zulma marries the daughter of Cary and Pauline, and the novel concludes: "Thus, at last, the blood of all the lovers had mingled together in one."[76] Nevertheless, patriarchy ensures that the British and American family names will continue – dominant political and social spheres from north and south subsume the French-Canadian women. The use of marriage to resolve larger social issues by the maintenance of patriarchal, elitist class structures is reminiscent of *Les anciens Canadiens*, yet the frame of reference shifts to America, with the attempt by American forces to capture Québec in 1775–76 forming the historical backdrop and shaping the resolutions. In general, the problem addressed by the historical novel in Canada, as elsewhere, was how to maintain order during a period of unprecedented social transformation; proposed solutions, in English Canada as in French Canada, were always contextual, and no less a matter of self-interest. English historical novels tended to focus on the maintenance of colonial power structures rather than pose a challenge to the status quo, although as the century progressed, the two often coincided uneasily in the same novel. The romanticization of New France and the Conquest was popular throughout the period, as in William Kirby's *The Golden Dog* (1877) and Gilbert Parker's *The Seats of the Mighty* (1896), both of which offer an Anglophone interpretation of French-Canadian history.[77] The historical novel, however, remained a genre readily adapted to changing circumstances and the related interests of readers. The cultivation of British values in the face of external threats, especially the rise of American power, led to new representations of cultural reference; for example, Robert Sellar's *Hemlock: A Tale of the War of 1812* (1890) upholds British virtues against American self-interest.[78] The negotiation of national identity, still from an Anglophone perspective, also took up modernization from social, geographic, and political angles: Francis Grey's *The Curé of St Philippe: A Story of French-Canadian Politics* (1899) applies British social realism to Québec; *Lords of the North: A Romance of the North-West* (1900) was the first of many novels by Agnes Laut to address the expansion of Canadian territory; and William Wilfred Campbell's *A Beautiful Rebel: A Romance of Upper-Canada in Eighteen Hundred and Twelve* (1909) looks at the impact of civil war on Canada-US relations.[79] In short, tales of national progress remained in fashion, but representation changed as informed by authorial interests and the circumstances of reception.

The historical novel was used to address the internal dynamics of a modernizing nation-state. A major development in this regard was the use of the

160 *Community lessons*

historical novel to consider everyday life from the perspective of common people. The treatment of industrialization and the plight of working-class people in novel form had a longer history elsewhere with, for example, Chartist novels in Britain, novelistic commentaries on the gilded age in America, and socialist novels in France. The integration of national print markets ensured that Canadians had access to foreign literature about labor relations, capitalist economics, and the experiences of the proletariat.[80] Writers from or writing in Canada also took up the consequences of modernization in their own way. Whereas French-Canadian historical novels of the early 1860s aimed to guide the future prosperity of French Canada within an emerging bi-cultural nation-state, post-Confederation historical novels in English started to pay more attention to industrialization, which took effect earlier in English Canada.

A relatively unknown early example of working-class fiction in Canada is *My Own Story: A Canadian Christmas Tale* (1869) by "Grodenk," a first-person account of "Canadian every day life" in nineteenth-century Canada.[81] Poverty, factories, political economy, and trade unions are absent. Still, only two years after Confederation, the opening chapter situates this tale within the context of early industrialization in Canada by describing the transition from hunting to the hum of machinery, the extensive use of steamboats and locomotives, and increased literacy and education in new towns and busy cities. The story begins with a description of the narrator's poor father, an officer in the British army who served in India before receiving a grant of land in western Canada from the government. Accompanied by a small group including mechanics and farm laborers, he sets up in unsettled territory. From the birth of the narrator to the writing of his story, the Canadian frontier flourishes – agriculture takes root and manufacturing begins to boom. As the story unfolds, the maturation of the narrator speaks to the transformation of the nation, outlining a personal, collective, and colonial trajectory germane to the modernization of Canada. The details of this transformation are lacking, but other novels took up the consequences of modernity more directly.

Ginx's Baby (1871) by John Edward Jenkins, who was born in India and came to Canada with his parents early in life, is set in England and framed as a satire of modern life, depicting problem-solutions relevant to the experience of modernization by working-class people in Canada.[82] The preface is noteworthy: "Critic: I never read a more improbable story in my life. Author: Notwithstanding, it may be true." The situation depicted was not uncommon: Ginx's wife has twelve children, his family lives in dire poverty, and he is ignorant of government, law, and much else besides. Ginx takes his newborn baby, his thirteenth, from the mother's arms and heads for the bridge convinced that he cannot support another child. An officer threatens the law before two gentlemen come along, one of which is a philosopher who questions Ginx, asking why he has so many children, and why he married at all if he is unable to support a family. The philosopher

Community lessons 161

addresses the crowd directly: "Ought you not to act more like reflective creatures and less like brutes? As if breeding were the whole object of life!"[83] As might be expected, the working-class crowd is neither convinced by the arguments nor pleased with the admonitions. A stonemason steps in to take up the fight, which pits upper-class rationality against the natural rights of common people, and states: "I think a statesman ought to make something out of what's nateral to human beings, and not try to change their naturs."[84] The stonemason, who speaks eloquently and thoughtfully, is the hero of the moment and of the people. A nun then appears and offers to take the baby from Ginx, who is happy to give him up. This leads to the many twists and turns of the child's life as Catholics and Protestants, parishes, clubs, and institutions fight to impose their own views upon the child. Ginx's baby is passed around, left on doorsteps and, more often, to himself, until he lands at the Radical Club, where the lightly disguised focus of the novel becomes clear. At the Club, the poor, economics, emigration, health, and other aspects of society are considered, with contrasting humanitarian and libertarian views represented. The central figure is Sir Charles Stirling, who outlines a progressive social agenda "nearer to communism than our present form of society,"[85] calling for "practical Christianity" resulting in "a community of goods."[86] Discussion at the Club continues with a more detailed search for solutions, including repeal of the Poor Laws, the advancement of trade unions and cooperative manufactures, laws against eviction, and the use of waste lands in the kingdom. Stirling's main point is that the circumstances of a child's upbringing must be improved; the application of temporary, after-the-fact solutions such as poorhouses and prisons are reactionary means of dealing with symptoms that often aggravate the situation. The primary conflict between private influence and public intervention may be read as a broad response to the symptoms of modernity. But as with *Jean Rivard*, Jenkins offers a historically sensitive picture of progress in the modern world. In general, *Ginx's Baby* supports centralized, inclusive forms of improvement, but Stirling's list of proposed changes is detailed, including expatriation to reduce competition; removal of those incapable of work to humane workhouses; banning weak men from marrying and propagating weakness; legislation of the improvement of workmen's dwellings; improved legislation of and access to health care and education, especially for women and children; and the provision of museums, libraries, and clubs for the poor.[87] The implementation of such measures is not pursued further, although they do point to Jenkins's later career as a politician: he was appointed the first agent-general for Canada in London in 1874, and from 1874 to 1880, he represented Dundee as a radical in the British House of Commons.[88] Ginx's unnamed baby sneaks off from the Club with some clothes and silverware and is never heard from again. His fate, as with that of the anonymous masses, remains unresolved. Regardless, this historical novel represents an important shift in public discourse, from the resolution of national conflict and the development of modern communities to coping

162 *Community lessons*

mechanisms that respond to the consequences of industrial capitalism at the heart of the nation-state.

As *My Own Story* and *Ginx's Baby* describe, the novel in English Canada was used to tackle contemporary social issues. *Roland Graeme: Knight: A Novel of Our Time* (1892), by social reformer Agnes Maule Machar,[89] was one of the first Canadian novels to address labor reform. Based loosely on the program and cause of the Knights of Labor, an American-based organization that worked to further economic cooperation and social justice in Canada, *Roland Graeme* also dealt more specifically with issues such as temperance.[90] Accordingly, it was an important early contribution to the exploration of widespread problems and possible solutions of direct significance to the working classes, yet the application of socially oriented Christianity was far from suggesting the necessity of systemic change. Other novels of the period took a different approach to the representation of modernization in Canada. In the wake of American Edward Bellamy's popular socialist novel *Looking Backward: 2000–1887* (1888), some novelists began to look to the future to reconsider options in the present. This was the historical novel in another form; the purpose – to educate – remained the same. To cite one example of the influence in Canada, John Galbraith's *In the New Capital: A Nineteenth-Century View of Ottawa in the Twenty-First Century* (1897) explores contemporary social conditions and potential means of reformation applicable to industrial Canada at the end of the nineteenth century in two ways, the methods – history and romance – separated into parts.[91] Part one is a series of interviews with common people on various aspects of daily life: for example, with a French Canadian on his unemployment; a colored gentleman on machinery; farmer Jones on hard times, machinery, and taxation; Paddy Hogan on socialism; and Nelly Jones on misfortune at home. The first part is the realistic ground for the projection that follows in part two, which is subtitled "A dream of the city of Ottawa, in the year 1999 illustrating what it would be if certain social conditions which are now advocated were put in force"; in this novel, by 1999, society becomes cooperative, unselfish, and based on social equality. In typically Canadian fashion, the changes come about through a Royal Commission and legislation, resulting in shorter working hours; the end of profiteering from the sale of liquor through individual taxation; a single tax on land; free trade among English-speaking nations; the end of monopolies; work farms for idle citizens; the abolition of religious instruction at public schools; an immigration policy excluding males under sixteen not accompanied by an adult, females under fourteen not accompanied by an adult, and people over sixty; reduction of the House of Commons, the Senate, and the salary of each member; an increase in the volume of money each decade relative to population growth; and legislation to make Canada an autonomous nation. The info dump approach to the communication of suggestions for social reform continues; there is little attempt to "fill up and round the sketch with the colouring of a warm and vivid imagination."[92] The more important point is that the historical novel continued to act as a manual of modernity, in this case by instructing readers, point-by-point, as to how best ameliorate the consequences of modernization. At the end of the century, such instruction manuals were not concerned with "roughing it in the bush";[93] with the passing of the settlement phase in Canadian history, more and more novels took up the implementation of social theories that responded to the concerns of an urban population, although often from the perspective of the middle-class social reformer.

Although the historical novel was adapted to new circumstances, in some ways, the more things changed the more they stayed the same. As in *Les anciens Canadiens*, *Jean Rivard*, and *Roland Graeme*, Albert Carman's *The Preparation of Ryerson Embury: A Purpose* (1900) once again links the education of a *Waverley*esque young man to the fortunes of a nation, but in this case the question of labor is front and center.[94] The first seven chapters describe Ryerson's time studying law, reading theology, and questioning religion in the college town of Ithaca, Ontario. The focus of the work emerges more clearly in the eighth chapter when talk turns to a possible strike, the union, demands for higher wages, and the troubled relationship between Capital and Labor in Canada. Initially at least, as in so many social problem novels of the nineteenth century, labor troubles amount to conflict between masters and men. Despite his membership in the Free Thought Club, Ryerson's initial reaction echoes that of the masters: "The riotous beggars!"[95] Consumed by his individual studies, "he only thought of it to wonder at the stupidity of men who would not work when they could, preferring rather to let their families go hungry."[96] Ryerson follows the laissez faire theory advocated by both the industrialist, Mr Masterson, and the preacher, Dr Holden – that is, mainstays of the community; as his textbooks no doubt suggested, wages supposedly result from the laws of Political Economy, a mystical view of economics derived from a limited reading of Adam Smith's "invisible hand" of the market, popularized in the 1830s by the didactic fiction of Harriet Martineau, among others.[97] In this light, not much could be done. Importantly, Ryerson's attitude changes as the strike touches his own life in several ways. First, he takes a position in a law firm vacated by a young man, Allan, who returns home because of his father's involvement in the strike. Second, he overhears the ambitious young preacher say, "I think you are right, Christian people are not bound to extend charity to the families of men who can work but will not. What does the Book say? – 'If any could not work, neither should he eat.' I don't think we are bound to support the striking class."[98] Ryerson and friends visit Allan, whose father has mortgaged his property to support the union. This is where Ryerson, like Waverley, ventures off into his own version of the Highlands – the preparation of Ryerson Embury begins when Allan offers a perspective on the material condition of the working classes that is new to Ryerson: "The best workmen do get their heads above the water a bit and begin to cherish some ambitions. But for the rest, there is nothing."[99]

164   *Community lessons*

The lesson that follows is more specific, however; Allan describes the conditions that led to the strike and the unethical position of capitalists who take a holiday in Montréal while many workers struggle, some starving. In this light, the matter at hand is no longer that of disgruntled workers ignorant of abstract economic principles but one of social justice based on material realities. Ryerson attends a meeting of young men who discuss the strike, charity – which is referred to by one participant as "the chloroform that the rich administer to their victims"[100] – and the nationalization of land and resources. Ryerson understands little of the discussion, indicating a divide between college theory and working-class reality; as a result, however, he reads Henry George's *Progress and Poverty: An Inquiry into the Cause of Industrial Depressions and of Increase of Want with Increase of Wealth: The Remedy* (1879) and concludes that "The succour of the poor – the lifting of man out of brutalising environment – was surely the work God would have men do."[101] Overall, the response remains conservative as tied to Christian socialism; Ryerson asks, for example, "Was Christ, after all, a social reformer?"[102] Regardless, the lesson is suited to circumstances, and the picture of self-education is not so different from that of Jean Rivard sitting in his rustic cottage reading his own manuals of modernity. Ryerson does not read *Don Quixote* or of Napoleon; instead, he continues his education by reading a British social problem novel, George Eliot's *Felix Holt, the Radical* (1866), which features another *Waverley*esque figure at the heart of labor troubles in the modern world.[103] His ideas of social justice continue to evolve within a limited sphere of Christian-minded activism. Ryerson brings up the strike at the Free Thinkers Club and suggests that the Club support the strikers because the Church (backed by the industrialists) refuses to do so. He fails to convince; the survival of the fittest argument wins out. In this way, Ryerson's actions are framed as a radical challenge to authority and common practice, although in retrospect, and in relation to contemporary socialist agitation that sought no mediation between capitalists and the proletariat, the presentation seems misleading. True to *Waverley*, *Ryerson Embury* may be read as a civil war novel, in this case, presenting nation building as dependent on the reconciliation of class interests. Carman, who was a Methodist minister, educator, and administrator,[104] treats labor as an extension of the establishment, meaning the management of industrialization by and for capitalists. Labor disputes were often international in scope, but the problem at home, certainly from the perspective of those in power, was how to smooth the internal politics of the nation-state and further progress, or profit. As in *Les anciens Canadiens* and *Jean Rivard*, the solution offered by the protagonist is practical:

> I believe in Trades Unions as a war measure; and labour is always at war with its oppressors. But you must know who your oppressors are, and how to get at them. . . . I know strikes are good things very often; they've done much for labour. But I must take courage to tell you that

if a man had a thousand loaves of bread in his pantry and I had none, I wouldn't sit down to beat that man by starving him out.[105]

Pragmatism here belies a singular view of progress. Ryerson tells the men they must redistribute the land through tax legislation, cultivate the land, and profit from the sale of goods produced, all of which is supposed to lower the industrial working population, resulting in higher wages. His speech incites the crowd to march upon the town, which seems odd given the moderate nature of Ryerson's proposal. Regardless, nothing comes of the workers' foment. Where does this leave Ryerson? He has turned from the path supported by his family, friends, and colleagues. Yet he has done so without supporting revolutionary change. Like Étienne in *Germinal*, he is placed, momentarily at least, at the center of the "great modern struggle,"[106] between Capital and Labor, and it is here that he finds a purpose. Still wavering, he comes close to choosing compassion for the poor rather than fellowship with them, but ultimately returns to address the strikers and thus participate in their struggle. However, based on the events that follow, Ryerson seems to infiltrate a community of workers of which he has never been a part and remains only ambiguously attached to *their* cause. Addressing the workers in the role of consultant, he advocates tax reform and condemns landlordism, and calls for "a fight with the ballot."[107] Ultimately, then, he advocates a law-abiding, incremental form of progress that was in line with moderate socialist activity in Canada in the 1890s.[108] In this sense, Carman's portrayal of middle-class activism remains unconvincing, in part because Ryerson has nothing to lose, and in the end, moves on. The strike ends and the union prepares for larger battles ahead, asking Ryerson "to come back later in the winter and address their Union again on lines of practical political work."[109] At a time when the Knights of Labor had essentially folded and the more moderate American Federation of Labor began to represent the rights of workers through collective bargaining, radical calls for systemic change play no role in the novel's resolution. Although dismissed by his firm, a partner sympathetic to his support of the union provides a letter of introduction to a Montréal lawyer, "an old schoolmate boasting a labour *clientèle*."[110] There is no question of this protagonist ending up on the streets or turning to manual labor. Cronyism and reform allow Ryerson to carry on as before, although with a sympathetic eye to the well-being of those (clients) a station or two below. The result, then, as far as reform goes, is inconclusive and thus hardly radical. With respect to use of the novel, Ryerson, like Jules, Jean, and Roland before him, finds his way in this new world, which required new community lessons on a regular basis.

Throughout the nineteenth century, the historical novel was used to describe problem-solutions of relevance to Canadian readers situated by the consequences of modernity. However, historification depended on the self-interest of cultural producers and their respective communities. As a result, the ramifications of the localization of community lessons were especially

166 *Community lessons*

acute for those without a voice. For example, historical novels of the 1860s tended to romanticize the lower classes, when they were included at all. In *Les anciens Canadiens*, lower-class characters play no significant role and have no aspirations; José, who lost his right hand in battle, says, "Well, it's all for the best – what would I do with a right hand, now that the fighting's done?"[111] He seems content with an ironic combination of revenge and peace; he explains how he killed the Highlander who took his hand, making them even, and adds that with the British in control, "there's not so much as a whiff of war."[112] In contrast, the depiction of Jean Rivard as mayor of a thriving new community seems an enlightening representation, and yet this story of upward mobility has nothing to say of the workers who toil in fields and factories to manufacture the economic prosperity of Rivardville. The priorities of Aubert de Gaspé and Gérin-Lajoie were of the moment and specific to their community interests. History-making was selective and self-centered. There were, then, ethical limits to cultural production, and in relation, to the representation of progress. Point of view was no less relevant to use of the historical novel in English Canada. For the most part, social problem novels in English Canada were written by and for middle-class readers. Not merely instructive, they were often downright moralistic novels concerning conditions faced by others. Top-down, philanthropic applications of bourgeois values to lower-class problems were common throughout the nineteenth century, originating from Canada and elsewhere. Novels that listed legislative changes or otherwise addressed social issues acted, often sympathetically, upon the need for reform; yet few such novels were radical enough to directly challenge the capitalist system or industrialization, which would have meant questioning the nation-state itself, and likely also undermining the privileged status of the author. Instead, as in *Ryerson Embury*, the uncomfortable tension between social transformation and the maintenance of order plays itself out to a stalemate that leaves the workers where they began, although readers may have benefitted from a better understanding of the relationship between Capital and Labor. On the one hand, reform novels often returned middle-class readers to a safe space where they could breathe a little easier. On the other hand, the journey often involved knowledge generation that contributed to the self-reflexive examination of the practices of everyday life.

Notes

1 *Historica Canada*, s.v. "Quebec Act," www.thecanadianencyclopedia.ca/en/article/quebec-act/.
2 *Historica Canada*, s.v. "Constitutional Act 1791," www.thecanadianencyclopedia.ca/en/article/constitutional-act-1791/.
3 John George Lambton Durham, *Lord Durham's Report: An Abridgement of Report on the Affairs of British North America*, ed. Gerald M. Craig (Toronto: McClelland and Stewart, 1963), 126–74.

Community lessons   167

4 *Historica Canada*, s.v. "Act of Union," www.thecanadianencyclopedia.ca/en/article/act-of-union/.

5 Rosanna Mullins Leprohon, *The Manor House of De Villerai: A Tale of Canada Under the French Dominion*, ed. Andrea Cabajsky (Peterborough, ON: Broadview Press, 2015). The question of first Canadian historical novel seems to me a distracting and largely unproductive one, but a timeline of well-known predecessors might include Frances Brooke, *The History of Emily Montague* (1769); Julia Catherine Beckwith, *St Ursula's Convent; or, The Nun of Canada* (1824); John Richardson, *Wacousta; or, The Prophecy: A Tale of the Canadas* (1832); James Russell, *Matilda; or, The Indian's Captive: A Canadian Tale Founded on Fact* (1833); Philippe-Agnace-François Aubert de Gaspé, *L'influence d'un livre: roman historique* (1837); Joseph Doutre, *Les fiancés de 1812: essai de littérature canadienne* (1844); and Georges Boucher de Boucherville, *Une de perdue, deux de trouvées* (1849–51).

6 Andrea Cabajsky, introduction to *The Manor House of De Villerai: A Tale of Canada Under the French Dominion*, by Rosanna Mullins Leprohon, ed. Andrea Cabajsky (Peterborough, ON: Broadview Press, 2015), 17–18.

7 Cabajsky, "A Note on the Text," in *The Manor House of De Villerai: A Tale of Canada Under the French Dominion*, ed. Andrea Cabajsky (Peterborough, ON: Broadview Press, 2015), 37.

8 Cabajsky, "Appendix A: Contemporary Reception of Leprohon's Works," in *The Manor House of De Villerai: A Tale of Canada Under the French Dominion*, ed. Andrea Cabajsky (Peterborough, ON: Broadview Press, 2015), 212, note 2.

9 Cabajsky, introduction to *Manor House*, 11.

10 Gerson, *Purer Taste*, 136. Catharine Parr Traill, *Canadian Crusoes: A Tale of the Rice Lake Plains* (London: Arthur Hall, Virtue, 1852).

11 Cabajsky, introduction to *Manor House*, 17.

12 Michel Bibaud, *Histoire du Canada sous la domination française* (Montréal: John Jones, 1837); *Histoire du Canada et des Canadiens sous la domination anglaise* (Montréal: Lovell and Gibson, 1844). François-Xavier Garneau, *Histoire du Canada depuis sa découverte jusqu'à nos jours* (Québec: Napoléon Aubin, 1845–52).

13 Philippe Aubert de Gaspé, *Les anciens Canadiens*, trans. Jane Brierley, *Canadians of Old: A Romance* (Montréal: Véhicule, 1996). Note: All translations of *Les anciens Canadiens* are by Brierley.

14 Paul Perron, *Narratology and Text: Subjectivity and Identity in New France and Québécois Literature* (Toronto: University of Toronto Press, 2003), 137.

15 Hayne, "Historical Novel," 77.

16 Jane Brierley, introduction to *Canadians of Old: A Romance*, by Philippe-Joseph Aubert de Gaspé, trans. Jane Brierley (Montréal: Véhicule, 1996), 10.

17 Aubert de Gaspé, *Canadians of Old*, 20.

18 Camille Roy, "Philippe Aubert de Gaspé d'âpres les Anciens Canadiens," *La Nouvelle-France* 8, no. 4 (April 1909): 158–68.

19 E. Margaret Grimes, "Philippe Aubert de Gaspé, Historian and Biographer of Canadians of Former Days," *The French Review* 11, no. 1 (October 1937): 14, www.jstor.org/stable/379238.

20 Clara Thomas, introduction to *Canadians of Old*, by Philippe-Joseph Aubert de Gaspé, trans. Charles G. D. Roberts (Toronto: McClelland and Stewart, 1974), ix.

21 Aubert de Gaspé, *Canadians of Old*, 25, 23.

22 Ibid., 67.

23 Ibid., 94.

24 Ibid.

25 Ibid., 27

168   *Community lessons*

26 Ibid.
27 Ibid., 28.
28 Ibid., 28; 95; 99.
29 Ibid., 140.
30 Ibid., 141.
31 Ibid., 141–42.
32 Ibid., 142.
33 Ibid.
34 Ibid., 143.
35 Ibid., 151.
36 Ibid.
37 Ibid.
38 Ibid.
39 Ibid., 152.
40 Ibid., 177.
41 Ibid., 207.
42 Ibid., 201.
43 Ibid., 228; 238–39.
44 Ibid., 198.
45 Ibid., 206.
46 Ibid., 248.
47 Maurice Lemire, introduction to *Les Anciens Canadiens*, by Philippe-Joséph Aubert de Gaspé, ed. Aurélien Boivin (Montréal: Les Presses de L'Université de Montréal, 2007), 43. Note: All translations of Lemire are my own.
48 Lemire, introduction to *Les Anciens Canadiens*, 52.
49 Enn Raudsepp, "Patriotism and Class Interest in *Les Anciens Canadiens*," *Journal of Canadian Fiction* 30 (1980): 112.
50 Aubert de Gaspé, *Canadians of Old*, 212, 213.
51 Ibid.
52 Raudsepp, "Patriotism," 111.
53 Ibid., 112.
54 Gerson, *Purer Taste*, 120.
55 Nicole Deschamps, "Les 'Anciens Canadiens' de 1860: une société de seigneurs et de va-nu-pieds," *Études françaises* 1, no. 3 (October 1965): 12, doi: 10.7202/036198ar. Note: All translations of Deschamps are my own.
56 Aubert de Gaspé, *Canadians of Old*, 241.
57 Raudsepp, "Patriotism," 112.
58 Aubert de Gaspé, *Canadians of Old*, 217.
59 Ibid., 218.
60 Ibid., 219.
61 Dennis Duffy, *Sounding the Iceberg: An Essay on Canadian Historical Novels* (Toronto: ECW Press, 1986), 6.
62 Ibid.
63 Durham, *Report*, 147.
64 Aubert de Gaspé, *Canadians of Old*, 241.
65 Ibid., 242.
66 Ibid., 125.
67 Patrice Lacombe, *La terre paternelle* (Montréal: Fides, 1981).
68 Perron, *Narratology and Text*, 153.
69 Durham, *Report*, 146.
70 John T. Lesperance, "The Literary Standing of the Dominion," in *The Manor House of De Villerai: A Tale of Canada Under the French Dominion*, ed. Andrea Cabajsky (Peterborough, ON: Broadview Press, 2015), 225.
71 Camille Roy, *Nouveaux essais sur la littérature Canadienne* (Québec: Imp. de L'Action Sociale Limitée, 1914), 84. Note: All translations of Roy are my own.

72 Antoine Gérin-Lajoie, *Jean Rivard*, trans. Vida Bruce (Toronto: McClelland and Stewart, 1977), 208. *Jean Rivard* first appeared in two parts: *Jean Rivard, le défricheur canadien*, in *Les Soirées canadiennes* 2 (1862): 65–319; *Jean Rivard, économiste*, in *Le Foyer canadien* 2 (1864): 15–371. Note: All translations of *Jean Rivard* are by Bruce.

73 Gérin-Lajoie, *Jean Rivard*, 256.

74 Perron, *Narratology and Text*, 152.

75 Gérin-Lajoie, *Jean Rivard*, 231.

76 John Lesperance, *The Bastonnais: Tale of the American Invasion of Canada in 1775–76* (Toronto: Belford, 1877), 359, https://archive.org/details/cihm_08977.

77 William Kirby, *The Golden Dog: (Le chien d'or): A Romance of the Days of Louis Quinze in Quebec* (New York: Lovell, Coryell, 1877), https://archive.org/details/cihm_48126. Gilbert Parker, *The Seats of the Mighty; Being the Memoirs of Captain Robert Moray, Sometime an Officer in the Virginia Regiment, and Afterwards of Amherst's Regiment* (Toronto: McClelland and Stewart, 1971).

78 Robert Sellar, *Hemlock: A Tale of the War of 1812* (Montreal: F. E. Grafton and Sons, 1890).

79 Francis Grey, *The Curé of St Philippe: A Story of French-Canadian Politics* (Toronto: McClelland and Stewart, 1970). Agnes Laut, *Lords of the North: A Romance of the North-West* (Toronto: Ryerson Press, 1920). William Wilfred Campbell, *A Beautiful Rebel: A Romance of Upper-Canada in Eighteen Hundred and Twelve* (Toronto: Westminster, 1909).

80 See Frank W. Watt, "The Growth of Proletarian Literature in Canada, 1872–1920," *Dalhousie Review* 40, no. 2 (Summer 1960): 157–73; and "Literature of Protest," in *Literary History of Canada: Canadian Literature in English*, ed. Carl F. Klinck (Toronto: University of Toronto Press, 1965), 457–73.

81 Grodenk, *My Own Story: A Canadian Christmas Tale* (Toronto: A. S. Irving, 1869), https://archive.org/details/cihm_06368.

82 John Edward Jenkins, *Ginx's Baby* (N.p.: n.p., 1871), https://archive.org/details/cihm_07434.

83 Ibid., 40.

84 Ibid., 42.

85 Ibid., 144.

86 Ibid., 145.

87 Ibid., 153–54.

88 *L'Encyclopédie de l'histoire du Québec/The Quebec History Encyclopedia*, s.v. "John Edward Jenkins," http://faculty.marianopolis.edu/c.belanger/quebechistory/encyclopedia/JohnEdwardJenkins-QuebecHistory.htm.

89 Agnes Maule Machar, *Roland Graeme: Knight: A Novel of Our Time* (Nepean, ON: Tecumseh Press, 1996).

90 Regarding the Knights of Labor in Canada, see Bryan D. Palmer, *Culture in Conflict: Skilled Workers and Industrial Capitalism in Hamilton, Ontario, 1860–1914* (Montreal: McGill-Queen's University Press, 1979); and Gregory S. Kealey and Bryan D. Palmer, *Dreaming of What Might Be: The Knights of Labor in Ontario, 1880–1900* (New York: Cambridge University Press, 1983).

91 John Galbraith, *In the New Capital: A Nineteenth-Century View of Ottawa in the Twenty-First Century*, ed. R. Douglas Francis (Manotick, ON: Penumbra Press, 2000).

92 Scott, *Waverley*, 124.

93 The reference is to Susanna Moodie, *Roughing It in the Bush, or, Life in Canada* (London: R. Bentley, 1852), one of many books published on the experience of settlement.

94 Albert Carman, *The Preparation of Ryerson Embury: A Purpose* (Toronto: Publishers' Syndicate, 1900), https://archive.org/details/cihm_03840.

95 Ibid., 105.

170 Community lessons

96 Ibid., 106.
97 See, for example, Harriet Martineau, *A Manchester Strike*, in *Illustrations of Political Economy: Selected Tales*, ed. Deborah Anna Logan (Peterborough, ON: Broadview Press, 2004), 137–216.
98 Carman, *Ryerson Embury*, 113.
99 Ibid., 130.
100 Ibid., 142.
101 Henry George, *Progress and Poverty: An Inquiry into the Cause of Industrial Depressions and of Increase of Want with Increase of Wealth: The Remedy*, author's ed. (San Francisco, CA: W. M. Hinton, 1879). Carman, *Ryerson Embury*, 158.
102 Carman, *Ryerson Embury*, 159.
103 George Eliot, *Felix Holt, the Radical*, ed. William Baker and Kenneth Womack (Peterborough, ON: Broadview Press, 2000).
104 *Dictionary of Canadian Biography*, s.v. "Albert Carman," www.biographi.ca/en/bio/carman_albert_14E.html.
105 Carman, *Ryerson Embury*, 175.
106 Ibid., 190.
107 Ibid., 237.
108 For more information on early socialism in Canada, see A. Ross McCormack, *Reformers, Rebels, and Revolutionaries: The Western Canadian Radical Movement, 1899–1919* (Toronto: University of Toronto Press, 1977); Gregory S. Kealey, *Workers and Canadian History* (Montreal: McGill-Queen's University Press, 1995); and Ian McKay, *Reasoning Otherwise: Leftists and the People's Enlightenment in Canada, 1890–1920* (Toronto: Between the Lines, 2008).
109 Carman, *Ryerson Embury*, 245.
110 Ibid., 244.
111 Aubert de Gaspé, *Canadians of Old*, 211.
112 Ibid.

9 History in action
Dramatizations at Montréal, Paris, New York, and London

> Building on our knowledge of these social phenomena, it seems both possible and necessary to determine the *use* to which they are put by groups or individuals.
>
> – Michel de Certeau, *The Practice of Everyday Life*, xii

The historical novel was only one of many acts of modernity in the nineteenth century used to address the development of the nation-state. Whereas previous chapters in this book have focused on the literary and material reinvention of the historical novel in print, this chapter reconsiders meaning-as-use with respect to the dramatization of popular historical novels at Montréal, Paris, New York, and London. By returning to *Les anciens Canadiens*, *Le père Goriot*, *The Spy*, and *The Heart of Mid-Lothian*, the aim is to learn something new about use of the historical novel to effectively communicate about and contribute to modernity. Moreover, by shifting the emphasis from downmarket print to stage adaptation, this chapter resituates the historical novel in relation to a broader media landscape, which enabled people on both sides of the Atlantic to repeatedly engage with representations of modernity.

The impact of the historical novel was perhaps more pronounced in French Canada than it was in English Canada. As Micheline Cambron and Carole Gerson write, "From its earliest days, the existence of a national literature was important to Lower Canada. It was a matter of being not just a writer but a *canadien* writer, the term used until Confederation, after which writers gradually began calling themselves French-Canadian."[1] As a measure of the past used to sketch paths forward, the historical novel was well-placed to contribute to the unique social identity of *Canadiens*. And yet, although seemingly a singular expression of French-Canadian interests, the first English translation of *Les anciens Canadiens* was published only one year after the initial French publication.[2] Editions over the next half century involved various forms of adaptation. Whereas French reprints by Coté, Cadieux and Derome, and Beauchemin kept the original title,[3] English titles changed. The cover of the 1890 Appleton's Town and Country Library edition included

172   *History in action*

the phrase "An Historical Romance," which became the subtitle of Hart's 1891 reprint.[4] In 1905, new editions of the Charles G. D. Roberts translation by Copp, Clark, and Page were retitled *Cameron of Lochiel* and *Cameron of Locheill*, respectively, and added a new front by H. C. Edwards.[5] In 1929, Musson of Toronto published *Seigneur d'Haberville (The Canadians of Old): A Romance of the Fall of New France.*[6] Further, the English translations of *Les anciens Canadiens* did not include the explanatory notes of the original French edition. As such, English readers did not read the historical facts, stories, and opinions that situated the popular tale within a longer history of the people and culture of New France. The primary reason might have been financial; shorter books cost less to produce. In addition, as later subtitles suggest, readers of popular fiction in English were perhaps more interested in the exotic representation of Old Québec than the cultural history of French Canada. For instance, William Kirby makes ample use of the romanticization of the fall of New France in *The Golden Dog*, subtitled "A Romance of the Days of Louis Quinze in Quebec," as did other popular novelists, such as Gilbert Parker.[7] Eliminating the back matter from *Les anciens Canadiens* similarly limits the social complexities of the work for an English-Canadian readership more inclined to see French-Canadian history as quaint and romantic rather than raw, contentious, or potentially subversive. In contrast, members of *Club des Anciens*, such as François-Xavier Garneau and Philippe Aubert de Gaspé, worked to define French-Canadian history and culture within (and against) the wider context of British North America. Community interests were not always or in all ways exclusive to English or French Canadians, though decisive differences were often constructed.[8] The particularities of this bi-cultural publishing history coincided with similarly situational reuse on stage. As a novel, *Les anciens Canadiens* is a prime example of the politics of cultural production; dramatizations of this popular novel were used to further the timely communication of political priorities.

Development of the theatre in late-nineteenth-century Canada was common to English and French Canada but also attuned to cultural context. As Richard Plant describes, in English Canada, most towns had a theatre of some sort by 1870 and new halls, stages, and theatres were built over the next thirty years: "approximately forty theatres with a capacity of 1,000 or more were opened between 1873 and 1892."[9] Early on, touring companies dominated by American and British troupes performed "well-tried plays from abroad as the standard repertoire."[10] However, eventually, "Many original Canadian farces, comic operas, and melodramas were written and produced in the nineteenth century, and they offered audiences an alternative to the standard British fare favoured by the relentless touring companies from Great Britain and the United States."[11] A similar process of localization occurred in French Canada, where theatre also emerged as a prominent cultural force in the nineteenth century. Due to linguistic and cultural factors, French-Canadian theatre was less directly affected by British and American theatre, and more so by works originating in France. For example, following a hiatus during the Seven Years' War, "College theatre returned in the 1770s, with ambitious semi-public performances of works chosen from the large repertory of French school classics."[12] At the same time, increases in population growth and urbanization encouraged development of the theatre in Montréal and Québec, where performances, especially at secondary institutions, increasingly reflected the interests of local audiences. Leonard Doucette, for instance, notes that Antoine Gérin-Lajoie's *Le jeune Latour: tragédie en trois actes*, first performed in 1844 at the Collège de Nicolet, was based on Michel Bibaud's *Histoire du Canada sous la domination française* (1837) and that as "A historical tragedy in verse on a Canadian topic" it was "the first of its kind."[13] As with French-Canadian novels, the stage was used effectively for political purposes, and in many instances, quite explicitly to instruct. Under the supervision of the Church, dramas produced at schools appealed to a young, educated class of men preparing to enter elite society. According to Doucette, religious-pedagogic theatre, at once socially conservative and patriotic, reached "a culmination in college theatre with *Archibald Cameron of Locheill*,"[14] a melodrama in three acts adapted by Fathers Joseph-Camille Caisse and Pierre-Arcade Laporte, first performed at the Collège de l'Assomption (located just north of Montréal) on January 19, 1865, later published in 1894 as *Les anciens Canadiens*. A closer look at this dramatization reveals how *Les anciens Canadiens*, already a rather singular vision of French Canada, could be further refined according to interests and circumstances.

In *Archibald Cameron*, Caisse and Laporte highlight a dramatic twenty-four-hour period from the original novel, beginning in the French camp the night before the Battle of the Plains of Abraham. As expected, the two protagonists are Jules d'Haberville and Archibald Cameron of Locheill. Following the orders of his commanding officer, Major Montgomery, Archie has burned down French-Canadian houses, including the d'Haberville family home. Both Archie and Jules distinguish themselves in battle and after a chance meeting are reconciled. In this respect, the play is balanced, and in general, dramatic events follow the plot of the novel. However, all female characters are removed; the complexities of the resolution in *Les anciens Canadiens* are thus absent. In this and other ways, adaptation was used to communicate a singular message. Caisse and Laporte, both instructors at the Collège de l'Assomption, isolate the reconciliation of Jules and Archie, hence French and English Canada, creating a socially conservative view of progress in line with nationalist prerogatives that would stir partisan sentiment. In other words, the communication situation was essential to the production. An anonymous account of the initial stage performance in the *Bulletin des recherches historiques* (1903) highlights the patriotic feeling associated with *Les anciens Canadiens* and the memory of New France.[15] As Doucette explains, "A 'national drama' was indeed what the play seemed to represent, and that is part of its success."[16] Patriotism played well, but given

174   *History in action*

the temporal proximity to Confederation, the situation was more particular. Adding to the sense of national fervor, Aubert de Gaspé was in attendance at the initial performance, where he received a medal of honor and gave a short speech: "With the first appearance of M. de Gaspé in the room, the spectators, who waited with anxiety, yielded to the dashes of their hearts and accepted it with a dazzling volley of applause."[17] The dramatization itself, and accounts of reception, point to highly selective, politicized use of a novel that offered a far more complex investigation of the continuities and compromises required for French Canada's successful transition from dependence on New France to cultural independence and economic prosperity under British administration. Regardless, in line with the intensification of political debate in Canada throughout the 1860s, *Archibald Cameron* was repeated dozens of times on college stages,[18] that is, at all-male schools providing leadership within the French-Canadian community. Just as *Les anciens Canadiens* appeared when historiography and the historical novel became prominent aspects of French-Canadian literature, *Archibald Cameron* hit the stage when the dramatization of history began to impact theatre and politics in French Canada. That the space of reinvention was French Canada mattered, and so too did the timing; adaptation, context, and reception informed each other.

Although outside the timeframe of this study, Georges Monarque's *Blanche d'Haberville; drame en cinq actes en vers* (1931) provides a point of comparison to describe further the chronotopic use of *Les anciens Canadiens*.[19] Whereas *Archibald Cameron* removes Blanche entirely, *Blanche d'Haberville* puts Aubert de Gaspé's figure of sacrifice front and center. Both are nationalistic dramatizations, but they were also timely productions, which led to significant differences in representation. Monarque's adaptation fits in with French-Canadian grievances and nationalistic sentiments common to the period, which resulted in part from the economic and social impact of the Great Depression and lingering resentment from the 1918 Conscription Crisis. Regardless, to leave out Blanche in the interwar period would have been strange indeed. Although women in Québec did not have the right to vote until 1940, women in other Canadian provinces did, and all Canadian women could vote in federal elections as of January 1, 1919. In short, acts of historification continued, resulting in portrayals of French Canada designed to communicate effectively in new communication situations.

Although the dramatizations of *Les anciens Canadiens* were specific to time and place, the politics of stage reproduction had a longer history elsewhere. In *Le père Goriot*, the theatre is a place where important things happen. For example, Madame de Beauséant takes Rastignac to the Italiens, where he is introduced to Delphine; they continue to meet at the theatre on Tuesdays, Thursdays, and Saturdays. As George Raser notes, "The boulevard des Italiens is one of the great meeting-places of characters of the *Comédie Humaine*, as it was in truth in the Paris of the Restauration and the reign of Louis-Philippe."[20] The Italiens was a fashionable place for people to show themselves, to meet lovers, and to do business. Balzac's depiction is thus historically accurate. Just as important, however, is that the theatre itself distinguishes between characters. For example, contrary to Rastignac and Delphine, Vautrin and Madame Vauquer go to the downmarket Théâtre de la Gaîté to see *Le mont sauvage, ou le solitaire*, a melodrama in three acts published in 1821 by the prolific playwright René-Charles Guilbert de Pixerécourt. In *Le père Goriot*, the theatre is a means of reaffirming the differentiation of social circumstances; in relation, successful adaptation for the theatre depended on sensitivity to the particularities of venue and audience. Historical novels in France were acts of modernity that shaped and were shaped by conditions of production and reception. As a form of popular communication, the theatre played a similar role in fostering community in nineteenth-century Paris. As indicated by Balzac's use of the theatre in *Le père Goriot*, theatres were places for social engagement, among the aristocracy and artists, but also among the middle and working classes at downmarket theatres. In either case, plays entertained and informed, often mirroring the priorities of the audience.

An author in tune with venue could profit from the popularity of the theatre; for example, "The fiction and stage adaptations of Charles-Antoine-Guillaume Pigault-Lebrun and François Guillaume Ducray-Duminil, like the melodramas of Pixerécourt (whose *Coelina* was staged 1,500 times in his lifetime), made their authors rich."[21] A bestselling novel rarely netted 5,000 francs, and most editions were of 1,000 copies or less and published only once, whereas a long-running play could earn 15,000 francs for the author.[22] Not surprisingly, then, literary works in France often crossed from one medium to another: in general, "After receiving money for his novel from, first, a newspaper and then a publisher, a writer could obtain some extra remuneration by allowing a professional to adapt his work for the stage, or he could collaborate with such a writer in producing a stage version."[23] Many of Balzac's contemporaries, such as Victor Hugo and Alexandre Dumas, took advantage of the financial possibilities afforded by writing for the theatre.[24] Drama would seem to have been a form well suited to Balzac; as David Coward writes, "During the Restoration, when political subjects remained taboo, comedy returned to its traditional assault on manners: money, marriage and social ambition."[25] Further, John McCormick remarks that "After 1830 many writers of melodrama began to aim at an increasingly middle-class public and preferred to refer to their works as 'drames' ... The historical melodrama and the 'drame romantique' in prose, with a historical theme or setting, had become virtually indistinguishable."[26] *Le père Goriot*'s literary integration of historical representation, colorful characters, and dramatic action seems primed for adaptation. More directly, Balzac refers to theatre projects in his letters of 1834,[27] and the motive is clear enough in a letter the following year: "To sell off this appalling production of books, which involved so many experiments, is not enough. It is necessary to come to the *theatre*, where the incomes are enormous compared to what the books make us."[28]

176 History in action

Balzac made repeated attempts to write for the stage, especially in the 1840s, but unlike Hugo and Dumas, "He had few real successes in the theatre during his lifetime, two real fiascos, wrote a few plays which he could not get performed, and a large number of skeletons or scenarios he intended to fashion into regular plays."[29] His own dramatization of *Le père Goriot*, *Vautrin, drame en cinq actes, en prose*, was first performed on March 14, 1840 at Théâtre de la Porte Saint-Martin, published on March 23, 1840 by Delloye, Tresse, and reprinted in April, May, and July of the same year.[30] However, it does not appear to have been a great success. Raser notes problems with the first performance, a cool reception, and political hostilities as contributing factors.[31] Nevertheless, Balzac's adaptation of *Le père Goriot* was not actually the first. *Le père Goriot: drame-vaudeville en 3 actes* by Emmanuel Théaulon, Alexis Decomberousse, and Ernest Jaime was first performed at the Théâtre des Variétés on April 6, 1835.[32] During the 1830s and 1840s, the Variétés was one of the most popular theatres in Paris. It was a common meeting place for professionals, as opposed to primarily upper-class gatherings at the Opera and the Italiens. Marchant in Paris and Jouhaud in Brussels are listed as publishers on the title page of the twenty-page publication, which sold for forty centimes. The advertisement following the text describes *Le père Goriot* as the last title of the first volume in the second year of *Le magasin théâtral, choix de pièces nouvelles jouées sur tous les théâtres de Paris*. In the first year, there were four volumes, each volume containing twenty-five titles, which suggests demand for dramatizations in print, at least among those able to pay the price of five francs for each volume. Théaulon was adept at the stage adaptation of popular works; his other productions include *L'Auberge du grand Frédéric, comédie-vaudeville en 1 acte* (1821, adapted from La Fontaine) and *Faust, drame lyrique en 3 actes* (1827, adapted from Goethe).[33] His adaptation of *Le père Goriot* provides an interesting example of the flexibility afforded stage adaptation and the negotiation of production and reception relative to medium and audience.

The scene is Paris: the first act is set in the back room of Goriot's business; the second in a middle-class boarding house; and the third in a nursing home. Théaulon starts with a realistic opening act focused on the ambitious rise of the *nouveaux riches* (with scenes that do not exist in the novel), then follows the novel closely in the second act (e.g., with speeches from Vautrin and Rastignac), and finally concludes with a seemingly reinvigorated Goriot, who rejects his legitimate daughters and finds solace in the union of his rediscovered, illegitimate daughter and a benign, unambitious Rastignac. This ending is, of course, completely different from the novel. The critical discrepancy is that in the play Rastignac sides with a lower-class girl and her working-class father, although other alterations are not unimportant. For example, memorable characters are reformulated to comment on social behavior. Vautrin never threatens to kill anyone, he is never revealed to be a criminal, and he ultimately proves rather helpful. Goriot does not

History in action 177

allow his passion for his daughters to overcome him and seems quite happy to embrace Rastignac and Victorine instead; in short, he is quite practical. Moderation seems to be the word of the day. The real villain, although not fully developed, is Nucingen, and to a lesser extent Goriot's daughters, who seem spoiled and greedy, without exactly being wicked. The adaptation, in other words, is rather tame, and probably suited to venue and audience; in general, it sets forth an opening that the audience can relate to (e.g., including lawyers, marriage), redeploys the most dynamic characters and phrases from the literary source, and then sends the audience home with an ending that depicts the triumph of good over evil. More specifically, it is sympathetic to the working-class and critical of extreme exploitation, reaffirming a moral center recognizable to the professional classes in attendance. In short, as designed for the Théâtre des Variétés, this *dramevaudeville* is socially aware and politically astute – another notable example of the situation-specific socialization of downmarket literary adaptation that occurred on both sides of the Atlantic.

The records describing stage performances in early America are far from complete; in many cases, scripts were not retained and at best titles can be recovered. But we do know that the theatre played a substantial role in the cultural life of early America and also that the works of James Fenimore Cooper were integral to such developments.[34] As with American reading, drama in colonial America depended on British content, but it was not long before the American theatre adapted British themes for American purposes.[35] This involved the emergence of a theatrical discourse to represent American views of modern history in the so-called New World.[36] As a democratic form of communication, that is, as independent of literacy or access to upmarket print, theatre was a valuable means to represent American identity in front of diverse audiences.[37] Much to Cooper's advantage, American theatres took root on the East Coast in the decade preceding his rise to prominence as a historical novelist. According to Edward Harris, "Cooper holds the distinction of writing the first American novel to be dramatized."[38] Charles Powell Clinch's adaptation of *The Spy* was produced at the Park Theatre in New York on March 1, 1822 – less than ten weeks after publication of the novel; it quickly rivaled local popularity of the novel itself, traveling to Philadelphia, Baltimore, and Washington.[39] The play may be said to follow the novel in important respects, but it is also an example of the sort of patriotic presentation of American history that depended on selective reinterpretation.[40] George Washington makes no appearance in the play, but he is, by repeated reference, the god-like father of American republicanism behind the action, which culminates with the revelation that Harvey Birch, the enigmatic peddler-spy, has actually been working for American independence all along. Poorly developed romantic plots sit awkwardly next to repeated clashes between Royalists, Republicans, and a group of vagabond skinners intent on loot. And yet, Eugene Page notes the popularity of the play into the 1850s.[41] At first, this seems difficult to account for given

178   *History in action*

that neither plot nor characterization seems to merit such appreciation. In print, at least, the transition from one scene to another lacks coherence; the several comic characters are notable, but all are stereotypes typical of melodrama. However, the combination of pursuit, mystery, and patriotism might explain repeated performance. Further, the first staging in 1822 coincided with popular reception of the novel, as well as Cooper's rise to fame in the 1820s, and followed closely on the recent development of independent American theatre. Although Cooper's novel is more ambiguous, particularly as it avoids the reification of Washington, Clinch's dramatization effectively translated the historical novel for local audiences.

The impact of Cooper's popularity on American theatre was significant; his early novels, and adaptations of them, contributed to the "Military, patriotic, and period adventure (Indians and pirates) themes [that] were often portrayed on the early stage."[42] Additionally, just as the Leatherstocking novels traveled to Europe, so too did dramatizations of those novels. In fact, American themes appear to have been even more popular on stages across the Atlantic: "Except for a few adaptations, Cooper fared dramatically much better in Europe than at home in America: there were more offerings of his works on foreign stage and these adaptations had longer runs [ie: were more successful] than their American counterparts."[43] All the same, Eric Partridge points to the ultimately limited appeal of what amounted to the static repetition of a singular American theme: "The American novelist [Cooper in France], in short, was popular in the theatres for about twelve years, but the sameness of his stories caused him soon to be exhausted as a 'mine à exploiter.'"[44] There are two points of interest here: first, that a novel like *The Spy* was quickly exploited both at home and abroad to communicate representations of frontier life in America; and second, that the apparent narrowness of the adaptations noted by critics seems to reflect on Cooper rather than the process of adaptation itself. The first point may underestimate the complexities of localization; despite the speed of adaptation for popular theatres, melodramatic adaptations were specific to context, venue, and audience. The second likely points to the priorities of critics, who were always more likely to read literarily (i.e., for their own purposes). Regardless, the use of Cooper in Europe undoubtedly had more to do with the timely exploitation of the exoticism of the frontier, which might also explain its limited shelf life; in contrast, it is easier to imagine audiences in America, using American literature and theatre to shape their own sense of self, as identifying character types and local scenes relevant to the everyday experience (or imagination) of American life – past or present. Nevertheless, whether depicting frontiersmen, pirates, or sailors – in America or Europe – dramatizations of Cooper, and the critical appreciation of them, seem to have pegged him as a writer of adventure novels, a distinction that was undoubtedly exaggerated by the popularity of his early novels and even more so the later downmarket adaptations, especially dime novels. Others have pointed to similarly selective thematic repetition in early

History in action 179

American theatre, for example with respect to the presentation of heroic figures and values.[45] Overall, however, the larger point is that, as in Canada and France, adaptation for the American stage responded to communication situations. The American historical novel was valuable source material, but it did not dictate any specific outcome on the stage. The timing and subject matter of *The Spy* meant that the extensive reinvention of Cooper for opera, ballet, songs, and the stage,[46] in addition to the many downmarket print editions, could be used variously to cultivate cultural memory and communicate political messages during a period critical to the development of American theatre and the related representation of America.

Both the selective manipulation and potential consequences of remediation are nowhere more evident than in the dramatizations of the Waverley novels, which were among the works most often and most successfully transformed for the stage in nineteenth-century Britain. Melodramatic adaptations of *The Heart of Mid-Lothian* successfully played upon genre stereotypes such as the undivided, externally oriented character and clear-cut results, but the real power of dramatic adaptation lay in the integration of diverse cultural forms of representation in the lives of working-class people. The history of *The Heart of Mid-Lothian*'s dramatization in the national capital, north and south of the Thames, demonstrates how political and socioeconomic factors participate appreciably in the production and reception of melodramatic adaptation for upmarket and working-class audiences. H. Philip Bolton records thousands of performances at legitimate and illegitimate theatres based on the prose works of Scott, in London at the Theatres Royal and at numerous minor theatres, not least the Surrey and the Coburg on the south bank of the Thames, in addition to many others throughout Britain. He lists over 300 productions of *The Heart of Mid-Lothian*, adding that it "ranks fourth among Scott's long prose narratives for its ability to inspire the commercial playwrights of the nineteenth century: only *Rob Roy*, *Guy Mannering*, and *Bride of Lammermoor* come before it."[47] He further reports "twenty-one publications of plays from *Heart of Mid-Lothian* – a number exceeded only by those published dramas derivative from *Ivanhoe* (42), and *Kenilworth* (27)."[48] *The Heart of Mid-Lothian* was a favorite with audiences in Britain with at least sixty-four distinct productions of six dramatic versions produced in London, at least fifty-three in Edinburgh by 1900, thirty-two for the Glasgow region, and many others of the provincial variety throughout England and Scotland.[49] As with the popular dissemination of Waverley novels in print, the repeated reinvention of *The Heart of Mid-Lothian* for the stage provides further insight into the complexities of adaptation as a contributor to identity formation.

The first dramatization was *The Heart of Mid-Lothian; or, The Lily of St. Leonard's: A Melo-Dramatic Romance, in Three Acts* by Thomas Dibdin at the Surrey Theatre in London on January 13, 1819; there were at least seventy-two performances in its first season, and it was successful enough to be revived, including versions at the Pantheon Theatre in Edinburgh and

180 *History in action*

at Newcastle, York, as well as many other provincial sites.[50] The advertisement to the first print edition of Dibdin's melodrama provides some insight into the process of adaptation by describing circumstances of production. Dibdin refers to criticism suggesting "it required little more than an amanuensis to construct it"; he responds, "[I] avoided giving any but the original language of the Romance, wherever I could introduce it," but goes on to note that "some little difficulty, must, however, be allowed, in transferring nearly every leading incident from four duodecimo volumes to the following few pages, especially with the very limited means of a Minor Theatre to complete the task."[51] Clearly, this is a reminder to the literary reader that the difficulties of adaptation, from four volumes to a "few pages," historical romance to "melo-dramatic romance," the drawing room to a "Minor Theatre," must be taken into account. Dibdin openly admits to the speed involved in the process, claiming to have worked "fourteen out of every twenty-four hours," looked at the prototype only "Thursday the last day of the late Year," with the manuscript "finished and read in the Green-room on the succeeding Wednesday, January 6th," only one week prior to the first performance.[52] Dibdin further acknowledges "Members of an Establishment" for their "liberal and decided reception of it" and "Company, (Family I had nearly said)" while noting audience reception: "tears and laughter testified."[53] In his own way, he thus outlines four aspects of dramatic production and reception: topicality, censorship, performance, and audience. In doing so, he openly sets out an understanding of the process of dramatization for the print reader, although not just any reader. Dibdin's description of the transition from print to stage is even more explicit as he mentions the impossibility of adhering to unities of time and space, "particularly in the Last Act."[54] A reader able to pay two shillings and sixpence for a copy of Stodart's publication, perhaps not familiar with a working-class theatre south of the Thames, might have read a drama that does not conform to Aristotelian expectations as inadequate. Dibdin, then, caters to a subset of the reading population. In relation, accompanying the text are the terms for subscribers and non-subscribers to a circulating library, which would have been inaccessible to most working-class readers. The advertisement to the print edition of this popular melodrama frames an attempt to bridge a gap between the expensive literary novel (32s.) and a seat at an illegitimate theatre (6d.) with a dramatization in print (2s. 6d.). In this way, access to first editions and downmarket reprints, tragedy and burletta, Theatres Royal and minor theatres – forms, genres, and venues – articulated and reproduced class differences.

Dibdin's melodramatic adaptation succeeded for many reasons. At the most respected of minor theatres, the genre of historical romance acted as an intellectual pretext for topical exploration, and anything by the "Author of *Waverley*" was of interest. As a recognizable form well-suited to quick adaptation, melodrama spoke to the present such that "illegitimate theatre became the dramatic newsreel of the modern metropolis."[55] More

History in action   181

particularly, Dibdin's adaptation adheres to the expectations of melodrama while also making accommodations for performance at the Surrey Theatre. In the opening scene, Dibdin quickly introduces Effie (conflicted) and Jeanie (good), their father (lamenting), a stranger (evil), Dumbiedikes (comical), Butler (Jeanie's lover), and a situation that suggests family tension, illness, mystery, and wrongdoing. In melodrama adapted for the stage, there is little time for the character development, plot progression, and integration of historical background typical of a Waverley novel. Within a single page (a few moments on the stage), many of the archetypal confrontations common to melodrama are in place, or at least in motion, and the situation is spelled out so as not to leave those with no knowledge of the story behind. Once the stock characters (i.e., suffering heroine, old man/father, villain, comical figure) and the key oppositions between good and bad, religion and money, lower and upper class are established, the play proceeds without delay, fluctuating between high drama and comic relief. In the second scene, the dramatic opportunities afforded by Scott's minor characters become obvious. Dibdin introduces Ratcliffe and Sharpitlaw, a likeable convict opposite a hard-nosed deputy, who together track down the outlaw Robertson. The popular Madge Wildfire enters, fantastically dressed, speaking madly of murder in an identifiably Scottish dialect. Dramatic scenes from the novel are redeployed in similarly exaggerated fashion for performance purposes. The final scene of the first act ends when Effie, condemned because Jeanie refuses to commit perjury, is taken in a procession through the streets complete with the town guard wielding Lochaber axes. Jeanie falls at her father's knees and exclaims, "O! Father, I – I have killed her."[56] She faints. Effie then kneels to her father, but he turns away. Effie moves toward the Tolbooth; Jeanie recovers and runs to her but is repelled. Effie breaks from her kneeling sister and says, "A word would have saved me, and she would not speak it!"[57] Jeanie falls to the ground and swears she will save her sister yet. Produced for large theatres built for audiences of several thousand, dramatic productions often made use of large displays, extensive props, pantomime, exaggerated language, and affected action. The content of the play was similarly designed to enhance communication. References to money, for example, provide a repeated and effective means of grounding the play in a socioeconomic reality that likely rung true for a chiefly working-class audience at an illegitimate theatre. Comedy and songs are offset by darker plot twists that play upon popular forms and themes. Dibdin's creative insertion of witty words, show tunes, and physical comedy is followed by the entrance of Black Frank and Tom Tyburn, two roadside bandits from the novel. The introduction of shadier characters such as Frank and Tom, who sing a duet in the play, followed by the more flamboyantly named "Mother Murder-Love" (i.e., Madge's mother Margery), affords a view of the outlaw way of life, a common theme in popular fiction of the Romantic period. Overall, the juxtaposition of lower-class characters and high-born figures points to an effort on Dibdin's part to highlight popular characters and

182   *History in action*

situations from the novel. Just as important to effective communication, Effie is found to be innocent because Jeanie Deans succeeds – against all odds; despite challenges, change is in the hands of common individuals, a stance not inappropriate to the venue and in line with contemporaneous agitation for reform in London and other parts of Britain.

Daniel Terry's near simultaneous production of *The Heart of Mid-Lothian, A Musical Drama* takes a decidedly different approach.[58] Terry deviates from the original to a greater degree than Dibdin, taking liberties with plot and character to emphasize action, sentiment, comedy, and high drama, and more importantly, to reflect the social priorities associated with performance at a Royal Theatre. Whereas Dibdin opens with a meeting of sisters next to a rural cottage, Terry begins in the shadows of spectacle: in the High Street of Edinburgh with a view of the Tolbooth, a door is burnt down, and the shouts of armed rioters returning from the Porteous lynching fill the stage. In short, respectable people are at risk. Strikes, protests, and demonstrations were common in the period. In relation, it is hard to ignore the likely impact of wider social fears among both upper-class theatre goers and government censors on Terry's reshaping of Scott's novel. Laird Dumbiedikes is trapped in the Grassmarket all night with the rioters. As the mob approaches, Saddletree shuts his window. Tensions ease when Robertson and Ratcliffe force the mob to release Dumbiedikes and soldiers are heard coming from the castle. Order is restored, which is the thrust of Terry's adaptation. Minor characters may be said to have been employed appropriately with respect to the expectations of melodrama: the portrayal of Madge seems sympathetic; Dumbiedikes is used for comedic effect. More to the point, this is not a play that questions authority – just the opposite. The Earl of Oakdale, Special Commission from King and Parliament to settle the Porteous job, plays an especially important role in this adaptation. First, he is central to the plot. He speaks to Wilmot (servant) of public duty and laments the loss of his son. Wilmot suggests that if his son were to return he may prove worthy to bear his name. In a reprisal of the old man/father role usually reserved for Deans, Oakdale replies, "Never, Wilmot, never! – early indulgence – uncontrolled passions – the power of disposing of his mother's independent fortune, early ruined the blooming boy, who was once, all that a father could hope."[59] Later, Oakdale blocks the passage Robertson must pass through. Robertson says, "Let me pass, or call your sentinels! – A father and a husband in my circumstances is a desperate man"; Oakdale answers, "Pass on! pass on! – our fates too closely resemble each other."[60] Oakdale offers money, but it is refused with high language. As Robertson disappears, Oakdale guesses at the stranger's identity – Robertson the outlaw is Staunton, his own high-born son.

Second, the character of Oakdale seems to combine three characters from the novel: Mr. Middleburgh the Edinburgh magistrate, the Rector of Willingham (also a justice of the peace), and Queen Caroline. As representative of King and Parliament, Oakdale stands in place of local Scottish

History in action 183

representation and religious authority. Appropriately, then, the resolution plays out in a state apartment in Holyrood Palace. Oakdale questions Jeanie and, as in the novel, she denies any knowledge of Effie's condition. Effie responds, "She has killed me – she might have saved me, and would not!"[61] Jeanie makes a similar speech to Oakdale as she does to the Queen in both Scott's novel and Dibdin's melodrama, concluding, "Save an unhappy girl, not eighteen years of age, from an early and dreadful death!"[62] Staunton enters, introducing himself as "The husband of this unfortunate! – the father of her infant! – come to vindicate her innocence at the price of my own life!"[63] Oakdale and Staunton recognize each other. Oakdale condemns his own son, but Staunton claims no part in the consequences of the riots; the father sees hope. Staunton holds Effie's hand, refuses to let her go, and exclaims, "Mine! in weal and woe! and, if I cannot save her, I will share her ruin!"[64] Rat enters, states that he has found the infant, and reveals that Effie had said nothing of her nurse, now revealed to be Madge, to protect Staunton. Oakdale asks, "What motive could induce this woman to steal the infant?" Staunton replies, "Alas! my Lord, her motives are not within the rule of reason. – Some wild fancy, probably, of wounded affections – the source, poor creature! of her malady."[65] This statement, although hinting at the truth, conveniently obscures Staunton's previous involvement with Madge. Deans takes Effie back and Staunton claims to have overcome "the ungoverned wildness of youth" by Effie's "simple loveliness."[66] In the presence of an English magistrate, through carefully worded deception and the actions of a convict turned state employee (Rat), order is restored. As evidenced by the early scenes of Terry's drama, entertainment was no less important at a Royal Theatre than it was at an illegitimate theatre, but the moral straightjacket used to wrap things up is specific to both the conditions of production and the communication situation. In a Royal Theatre, the play ends with a song featuring the God-fearing Jeanie, Rat the savior, and finally, Effie redeemed. Terry does not simply change the plot to please; historification, in this situation, required plotting and characterization designed to comfort a Covent Garden audience, or at least the censor that vetted the pre-performance version of the play.

Two further points of difference between novel and dramatization are noteworthy. First, Terry's elimination of Jeanie's journey from Scotland to London negates spatial, cultural, and political questions central to Scott's novel. By leaving Jeanie in Scotland and sending Oakdale from London, Terry not only reaffirms London as the political center of Britain, for the move also suggests that Scotland is merely a subordinate provincial region. Further, without Jeanie's efforts to save her sister, the play seems to remove the agency of a lower-class woman. It is, perhaps, the exclusion of the journey that most explicitly points to the shaping influence of audience expectations and pre-performance censorship. Second, in the novel, Scott refers to Madge as "insane" or "crazy" numerous times, but his portrayal is ultimately sympathetic; her "malady" is the result of tragic circumstances

184   *History in action*

beyond her control (e.g., the loss of her child).[67] Thus, "poor Madge" is not a "raging lunatic" but possessed of "a doubtful, uncertain, and twilight sort of rationality."[68] In the fourth volume, Jeanie calls for Madge, "the poor maniac," to be saved, saying that "She is mad, but quite innocent";[69] the deathbed scene that follows is heart-wrenching.[70] Dibdin treats Madge similarly, that is, as a person of unsure mental stability, mainly due to imposed circumstances, and worth saving. Terry, on the other hand, despite a sympathetic opening and comical interludes, ultimately frames Madge as a disillusioned outcast. She is demented, pitiful, and finally disappears, fitting in with a stereotype of vagrants, gypsies, bohemians, and foreigners as disreputable and basically forgettable. Terry's discarding of Madge also mirrors his removal of Caroline, a figure of sympathy to lower-class Londoners. Dibdin emphasizes this sense of sympathy; Terry stresses legal authority and class isolation. That Bolton finds most provincial productions were derived from Dibdin's version is not unexpected.[71]

Stage adaptations of *The Heart of Mid-Lothian* continued to evolve. George Dibdin Pitt's popular spin-off *The Whistler; or, The Fate of the Lily of St. Leonard's* (1833) is an interesting innovation in that it begins with the final scenes of volume four and goes on to describe Jeanie married and Effie's child grown up.[72] But Thomas Hailes Lacy's *The Heart of Mid-Lothian; or, The Sisters of St. Leonard's* (1863) offers a better view of how the novel itself was re-invented.[73] This broad-ranging pastiche provides two points of emphasis. First, the court scene is drawn out; the examination of Jeanie is taken up with care, including lengthy exchanges between judge, counsel, and defense concerning the nature of guilt and innocence, as well as the worth of a statute that does not depend on proof of the act prior to the verdict. Second, Lacy takes the high drama of previous adaptations to new heights, as the following summary indicates: Madge descends to the bridge and says that although she does not like Effie, Jeanie was good to her: "she aye gae me a drink of milk and was unco kind to me – and maybe, they shall no hang her sister Effie."[74] Staunton asks what she means; Madge removes her plaid to reveal the child. Staunton causes Madge to look into the distance, then snatches the baby from her arms and dashes away. Jeanie is on her way back to Edinburgh, hurrying to save her sister from the impending death sentence, when she meets Margery (Madge's mother), who attempts to stop Jeanie from reaching her sister in time. Margery tries to take the pardon from Jeanie, but she struggles and gets away. Margery aims a pistol at her and says, "Another step and I pull the trigger!"[75] Madge steps in, telling her, "Dinna fear, Jeanie, I will na let her hurt ye!"[76] Margery continues to threaten; just as she fires, Madge jumps to stop her and tells Jeanie to run. Margery is furious, screaming, "Ah! My bairn! I hae killed my ane bairn!"[77] She runs to Jeanie, grasping her by the throat. Margery screeches, "Revenge! – double revenge! – your life and the pardon, both!"[78] She is just about to overpower Jeanie when two officers enter and take her off. Jeanie runs from the bridge. At the Tolbooth, another mob

History in action   185

threatens as Sharp [*sic*] and Rat [*sic*] await the execution of Effie. Deans prays, Effie cries, Sharp watches the clock, soldiers enter to take Effie, the crowd breaks through the gates, flames spring up, parts of the wall topple down, the people rush to protect Effie, the soldiers level their guns at the people, Dumbie [*sic*] runs in shouting not to cut her down, and finally, Jeanie runs in waving the pardon, saying, "Effie – Effie, the word is spoken. I bring ye pardon – life and happiness; your child lives, and a repentant husband kneels to you for pardon."[79] Staunton, holding the child up to her, says, "Yes, dear Effie – repentance for me – pardon and happiness for you."[80] In 1819, Terry certainly did not feel it necessary to follow the novel too closely, but by 1863, as the subtitle suggests, Lacy could compile a representative sampling of dramatic scenes from various versions stretching back over forty years. Lacy essentially juxtaposed a general knowledge of *The Heart of Mid-Lothian* (which was available to all classes by this time, in print and on stage) with the popularity of melodrama, sensation novels, and other forms of entertainment. Lacy's emphasis on Jeanie also reflects a trend beginning about 1860 with Dion Boucicault's *Jeanie Deans* (also, *The Trial of Effie Deans; or, The Heart of Mid-Lothian*), which opened in 1863 at Astley's (Theatre Royal), London.[81] From here on, Jeanie and Effie take center stage more regularly until the turn of the century, when the title of the drama is often just *Jeanie Deans* or *The Trial of Effie Deans*. Such adjustments likely reflect the changing role and increasing prominence of women in Victorian Britain, not least in relation to the suffrage move-ment that gained momentum at the end of the nineteenth century, as well as the interest of women in theatre itself. Also, as Gillen D'Arcy Wood suggests: "As the importance of literary originality on the London stage diminished, attention turned to innovations in stage performance and the actors' interpretation of well-known roles."[82] As playbills from the period indicate, stars as much as plays were often used to attract an audience; actors known for their ability – through voice, gesture, and presence – to bring well-known characters to life in new and interesting ways could increase ticket sales. Further experimentation with the dramatization of Scott's novel came in several forms. The year 1863 marks the first instances of burlesque (*Jeanie Deans; or, Any Other Gal*, at Britannia, London) and travesty (*The Heart of Mid-Lothian; or, A New Trial of Effie Deans*, at Victoria, London).[83] After so many performances within a relatively short time frame, there was no doubt some strain put upon the story as theatre managers competed with a multitude of venues, plays, and publications. Clearly, greater liberties were taken, likely as adaptation proceeded more by way of earlier dramatizations and downmarket adaptations rather than the novel itself, and in relation to sensational newspapers of the period. David Worrall writes that "By the late 1810s drama was the primary liter-ary form mediating between the British people and national issues."[84] Over the next fifty years, the dramatization of Waverley novels such as *The Heart of Mid-Lothian* played no small role in this mediation.

186 *History in action*

The historical novel provided a foundation for localized dramatizations designed to communicate effectively with upmarket and downmarket audiences in different national contexts throughout the century. The potential for further consideration of the connections between the historical novel and theatrical adaptations is great. In studies of the novel, however, the boundaries of inquiry too often hinge solely upon the close reading of novels. This, I would argue, has more to do with academic norms and the practicalities of research and publishing than with the accurate representation of communication practices. Recent investigations of literary afterlives have begun to contribute to better understanding of the wider impact of the adaptation of novels on cultural production and reception. Yet much remains to be learned about how people encountered and made sense of the many forms of communication available in the nineteenth century. Although beyond the scope of this study, it is worth reiterating that historical novels of the nineteenth century were produced and received, reinvented and experienced as one part of an evolving, varied mediascape. This was true – differently – on both sides of the Atlantic. Just as readers read historical novels for their own purposes, theatre goers, whether at the Surrey in London or the Park in New York, encountered the dramatization of history both in their own way and as integrated within a local field of communication practices. Forms of communication, in this case the novel and the play, informed each other, as well as readers and audiences; the interdisciplinary work to recover such connections in the nineteenth century, and to then trace related outcomes up to the present, is just beginning.

Notes

1 Micheline Cambron and Carole Gerson, "Literary Authorship," in Lamonde, Fleming, and Black, *1840–1918*, 121.
2 Philippe Aubert de Gaspé, *Les anciens Canadiens* (Québec: Desbarats and Derbishire, 1863); *Les anciens Canadiens*, 2nd ed. (Québec: G. and G. E. Desbarats, 1864); *The Canadians of Old*, trans. G. M. Ward (Quebec: G. and G. E. Desbarats, 1864); *Les anciens Canadiens*, 2nd ed., rev. and corr. by the author (Québec: G. and G. E. Desbarats, 1864).
3 Philippe Aubert de Gaspé, *Les anciens Canadiens*, new ed. (Québec: Augustin Coté, 1877); *Les anciens Canadiens* (Montréal: Cadieux and Derome, 1886); *Les anciens Canadiens* (Montréal: Librairie Beauchemin, 1899); *Les anciens canadiens*, 21st ed. (Montréal: Librairie Beauchemin, 1899); *Les anciens Canadiens* (Montréal: Beauchemin, 1913); *Les anciens Canadiens* (Montréal: Librairie Beauchemin, 1925); *Les anciens Canadiens* (Montréal: Librairie Beauchemin, 1931).
4 Philippe Aubert de Gaspé, *The Canadians of Old*, trans. Charles G. D. Roberts (New York: D. Appleton, 1890), Appleton's town and country library, no. 62; *The Canadians of Old: An Historical Romance*, trans. Charles G. D. Roberts (Toronto: Hart, 1891).
5 Philippe Aubert de Gaspé, *Cameron of Lochiel*, new ed., trans. Charles G. D. Roberts (Toronto: Copp, Clark, 1905); *Cameron of Locheill*, new ed., trans. Charles G. D. Roberts (Boston: Page, 1905).

History in action 187

6 Philippe Aubert de Gaspé, *Seigneur d'Haberville (The Canadians of Old): A Romance of the Fall of New France* (Toronto: Musson Book, 1929).

7 Kirby, *Golden Dog*. By Gilbert Parker, see *Seats of the Mighty*.

8 See, for example, Robert David Stacey, "Romance, Pastoral Romance, and the Nation in History: William Kirby's *The Golden Dog* and Philippe-Joséph Aubert de Gaspé's *Les Anciens Canadiens*," in Blair et al., *ReCalling Early Canada*, 91–116. Stacey argues that *The Golden Dog* and *Les anciens Canadiens* "express radically divergent views of historical process and the role of the nation within that process" (ibid., 96).

9 Richard Plant, "Drama in English," in *The Oxford Companion to Canadian Theatre*, ed. Eugene Benson and Leonard W. Connolly (Toronto: Oxford University Press, 1989), 152.

10 Eugene Benson and Leonard W. Connolly, *English-Canadian Theatre* (Toronto: Oxford University Press, 1987), 11.

11 Ibid., 14.

12 Leonard E. Doucette, "Drama in French," in *The Oxford Companion to Canadian Theatre*, ed. Eugene Benson and Leonard W. Connolly (Toronto: Oxford University Press, 1989), 171.

13 Ibid., 172. Antoine Gérin-Lajoie, *Le jeune Latour: tragédie canadienne en trois actes* (Montréal: n.p., 1845). Bibaud, *Histoire du Canada*.

14 Doucette, "Drama in French," 172. All references are to Joseph Camille Caisse, *Les anciens Canadiens: drame en trois actes tire du roman populaire de P.A. de Gaspé* (Montréal: Beauchemin, 1894), CIHM Microfiche series, no. 02434. Note: All translations of *Les anciens Canadiens* (1894) are my own.

15 "Les 'Anciens Canadiens,'" *Bulletin des recherches historiques* 9, no. 8 (August 1903): 252, https://archive.org/details/lebulletindesrec09archuoft. Note: All translations of *Bulletin* are my own.

16 Leonard E. Doucette, *Theatre in French Canada: Laying the Foundations 1606–1867* (Toronto: University of Toronto Press, 1984), 151.

17 "'Anciens Canadiens,'" 252.

18 Doucette, *Theatre in French Canada*, 148.

19 Georges Monarque, *Blanche d'Haberville; drame en cinq actes en vers* (Montréal: Librairie d'Action canadienne-française, 1931).

20 George Bernard Raser, *The Heart of Balzac's Paris* (Choisy-le-Roi: Imp. de France, 1970), 28.

21 Coward, *French Literature*, 203.

22 Allen, *Popular French Romanticism*, 91.

23 Lough and Lough, *Nineteenth Century France*, 270.

24 For example, plays by popular fiction writers of the period include *Hernani, ou, l'honneur castillan drame* (1830), *Marion de Lorme: drame en cinq actes* (1831), and *Lucrèce Borgia, drame* (1833) by Victor Hugo; and *Henri III et sa cour, drame en cinq actes* (1829) and *Antony: drame* (1831) by Alexandre Dumas.

25 Coward, *French Literature*, 246.

26 John McCormick, *Theatre in Focus: Melodrama Theatres of the French Boulevard* (Cambridge: Chadwyck-Healey, 1982), 55. *Drame*: "A form of play between tragedy and comedy originating in the eighteenth century, comparable to the modern serious, problem play" (Allen, *Popular French Romanticism*, 252).

27 Vachon, *Travaux*, 143–44.

28 Honoré de Balzac, *Lettres à Madame Hanska*, ed. R. Pierrot, vol. 1 (Paris: 1967), 354, qtd. in Lough and Lough, *Nineteenth Century France*, 270. Note: This translation is my own.

29 Raser, *Balzac's Paris*, 67. Raser also notes that Balzac wrote or started at least six plays between 1838 and 1848: *Les employés* (*La femme supérieure*) (1838);

188   *History in action*

L'école des ménages (1839); *Vautrin* (1839); *Les ressources de Quinola* (1842); *Pamela Figaud* (1843); and *La marâtre* (1848) (ibid.).

30 Vachon, *Travaux*, 191–92.

31 Raser, *Balzac's Paris*, 53. *Vautrin* was published in 1852 (dated 1853) as part of a collection of plays: Honoré de Balzac, *Théâtre* (n.p.: Girard and Dagneau, 1853); see Vachon, *Travaux*, 289.

32 Emmanuel Théaulon, Alexis Decomberousse, and Ernest Jaime, *Le père Goriot: drame-vaudeville en 3 actes/par MM. Théaulon, Al. Decomberousse et [E.] Jaime. . . .* (Paris: Marchant; Brussels: Jouhaud, 1835), http://gallica.bnf.fr/ark:/12148/bpt6k104328x.

33 Emmanuel Théaulon, *L'auberge du grand Frédéric, comédie-vaudeville en 1 acte, de MM. Lafontaine et Léon . . .* (Paris: Huet, 1821); *Faust, drame lyrique en 3 actes, par E. Théaulon . . .* (Paris: Duvernois, 1827).

34 See, for example, George Clinton Densmore Odell, ed., *Annals of the New York Stage*, 15 vols. (New York: Columbia University Press, 1927–49).

35 See Jeffrey H. Richards, *Drama, Theatre, and Identity in the American New Republic* (Cambridge: Cambridge University Press, 2005).

36 See Jeffrey H. Richards, *Theatre Enough: American Culture and the Metaphor of the World Stage, 1607–1789* (Durham, NC: Duke University Press, 1991).

37 See Jason Shaffer, *Performing Patriotism: National Identity in the Colonial and Revolutionary American Theatre* (Philadelphia: University of Pennsylvania Press, 2007).

38 Edward Harris, "Cooper on Stage," in *James Fenimore Cooper Society Website*, ed. Hugh C. Macdougall (webmaster) (Oneonta: State University of New York College, n.d.), http://external.oneonta.edu/cooper/drama/stage.html.

39 Eugene R. Page, introduction to "The Spy, a Tale of the Neutral Ground," in *Metamora and Other Plays*, ed. Eugene R. Page (Princeton, NJ: Princeton University Press, 1941), 59.

40 For a detailed comparison of *The Spy* and Clinch's adaptation, see Carol Anne Ryan Pagel, "A History and Analysis of Representative American Dramatizations from American Novels 1800–1860" (PhD diss., University of Denver, 1970), see esp. chp. 4.

41 Page, introduction to "The Spy," 59.

42 See Harris, "Cooper on Stage," n. pag.

43 Ibid.

44 Eric Partridge, "Fenimore Cooper's Influence on the French Romantics," *Modern Language Review* 20, no. 2 (April 1925): 177, doi: 10.2307/3714204.

45 Blanche Elizabeth Davis, "The Hero in American Drama 1787–1900: A Critical Appraisal of American Dramas Through a Consideration of the Hero" (PhD diss., Columbia University, 1950).

46 Harris, "Cooper on Stage," n. pag.

47 Bolton, *Scott Dramatized*, 259.

48 Ibid.

49 Ibid., 260.

50 Ibid., 259.

51 Dibdin, *Heart of Mid-Lothian*, v.

52 Ibid.

53 Ibid., v–vi.

54 Ibid., vi.

55 Jane Moody, *Illegitimate Theatre in London, 1770–1840* (Cambridge: Cambridge University Press, 2000), 7.

56 Dibdin, *Heart of Mid-Lothian*, 23.

57 Ibid.

History in action 189

58 Terry, *Heart of Midlothian.* Terry's dramatization was produced sixteen times at the Theatre Royal Covent Garden (Bolton, *Scott Dramatized*, 263).
59 Terry, *Heart of Midlothian*, 42.
60 Ibid., 44.
61 Ibid., 60.
62 Ibid.
63 Ibid., 61.
64 Ibid., 62.
65 Ibid., 64.
66 Ibid., 65.
67 Scott, *Heart of Mid-Lothian*, 265.
68 Ibid., 271.
69 Ibid., 363.
70 Ibid., 365–66.
71 Bolton, *Scott Dramatized*, 259.
72 Ibid., 276.
73 Thomas Hailes Lacy, *The Heart of Mid-Lothian; or, The Sisters of St. Leonard's. A Drama . . . in Three Acts. Adapted from Sir Walter Scott's . . . Novel, with Introductions from T. Dibdin's Play, W. Murray's Alteration of the Same, Eugene Scribe's Opera, and Dion Boucicault's Amalgamation of the Above, Colin Hazlewood's Adjustment and Re-Adjustment, J. B. Johnstone's Appropriation, and Other Equally Original Versions, Together with a Very Small Amount of New Matter, by T. H. Lacy* (London: Lacy, 1863).
74 Ibid., 39.
75 Ibid., 41.
76 Ibid.
77 Ibid.
78 Ibid.
79 Ibid., 44.
80 Ibid.
81 Bolton, *Scott Dramatized*, 289.
82 Gillen D'Arcy Wood, "Visual Pleasures, Visionary States: Art, Entertainment, and the Nation," in *A Concise Companion to the Romantic Age*, ed. Jon Klancher (Chichester: Wiley-Blackwell, 2009), 241.
83 Bolton, *Scott Dramatized*, 290.
84 Worrall, *Theatric Revolution*, 274.

Conclusion
Working the historical novel

> We construct our texts as we go: they are not given to us in advance of the
> operations by which we contextualize them.
>
> — Roy Harris, *Integrational Linguistics*, 104

The histories of representation and remediation in this book describe chronotopic uses of the historical novel as acts of modernity. As Anthony Giddens explains, the dynamism of modernity stems from "the *reflexive ordering and reordering* of social relations in the light of continual inputs of knowledge affecting the actions of individuals and groups."[1] The combination of history and romance in the nineteenth-century historical novel facilitated the important work of continually re-determining how the present differed from the past. Ostensibly always looking backward, it was used to outline the consequences of modernity as problem-solutions relevant to the reconstruction of community practices on both sides of the Atlantic. As a popular form of reading, it was also creatively and profitably adapted for new modes of communication accessible to downmarket readers and theatre audiences. To highlight the historicity of meaning-making, I conclude this book by first relating Walter Scott's accounts of the production of *Ivanhoe* as a form of popular translation, and then by describing the remediation of *Ivanhoe* as opera, comic book, study guide, and film. Beyond offering sketches of a history of literary reinvention that continues to the present, my aim is to point to reading practices and research trajectories available to those who take up the historical novel or other forms of print culture at the intersection of close reading, effective semiotics, book history, and new media.

Ivanhoe begins with a dedicatory epistle from Laurence Templeton, the supposed author of *Ivanhoe*, to his antiquarian friend the Rev. Dr Dryasdust, F.A.S. The immediate concern is with genre expectations; Templeton worries that the "grave antiquary will perhaps class [*Ivanhoe*] with the idle novels and romances of the day."[2] As such, the novel opens by responding to ongoing criticism of the genre as an unwieldy, popular mixture of history and romance. As becomes clear, however, Templeton is preoccupied with the popularization of history rather than the supposed threat of popular

Conclusion   191

reading. Templeton, for instance, discusses how the author of historical fiction would "work a mine" of "antiquarian stores."[3] Of course, the "stores" are not the same north and south of the Tweed. Scotland offered the recent past, "a body whose limbs had recently quivered with existence," readily accessible to the "Scottish magician"; the English author, in contrast, was left with the "dust of antiquity."[4] Conditions impact production, but the expectations of readers even more so. The question is, could the English reader be convinced that the past differed so much from the present? Templeton argues that "with more labour in collecting, or more skill in using" it is possible to write of the English as well as the Scottish past in the same manner, that is, as popular history.[5] He refers to Horace Walpole's "goblin tale" and George Ellis's "Abridgement of the Ancient Metrical Romances" as precedents.[6] What manner of precedent is important; both Walpole and Ellis were known for imaginative reinventions. Templeton does not pretend to "complete accuracy."[7] This might be read as targeting the authority of history. More directly, the case is for a form of historification sensitive to the reading practices and political interests of the emerging nation of readers.[8] As Templeton notes, "It is necessary, for exciting interest of any kind, that the subject assumed should be, as it were, translated into the manners, as well as the language, of the age we live in."[9] The act of translation here described is history-making suited to a particular communication situation, for which there were well-known examples. Galland's translation of the "Arabian Tales," Templeton notes, "though less purely Oriental than in their first concoction, were eminently better fitted for the European market" as "familiarized to the feelings and habits of the western reader."[10] As a point of comparison, he also criticizes the antiquarian Joseph Strutt's novel *Queenhoo-Hall* (1808),[11] which Scott completed following Strutt's death in 1802, for sticking too closely to chronology.[12] If, then, filling in the gaps of history is necessary to the successful translation of history, how does a modern author go about doing so? The claim is that the affections and feelings of those in the distant past cannot have been all that different from those in the present. The related argument is for the "license" to historify the past in terms that will prove popular among contemporary readers.[13] There are restrictions; for example, the author "must introduce nothing inconsistent with the manners of the age."[14] But this toeing the line between history and fiction is another form of situational communication – with an eye to appeasing the ever-vigilant Dryasdust. Templeton notes his own errors against historical record, citing the difficulty of execution, but his point is more broadly that meaning depends on use, and that the effective translation of history in the modern era of popular print and mass reading requires attention to community-specific methods of historification. The dedicatory epistle ends with several telling references: first, to a source text, a conveniently Anglo-Norman manuscript, which gestures to a sense of authenticity as well as shared cultural origins; second, and more importantly, to historical artefacts recently dug up; to the destruction of a local statue; and to the

192   *Conclusion*

new Secretary to the Society of Antiquaries of Scotland, who is a drafts-man, and therefore expected to delineate "specimens of national antiquity, which are either mouldering under the slow touch of time, or swept away by modern taste."[15] Templeton points to acts of recovery, effacement, and reinvention, thus providing a symbolic, three-pronged cap to an introduction focused on the chronotopic processes of history-making.

Reprints, translations, dramatizations, and chapbook versions of *Ivanhoe* followed quickly and repeatedly.[16] Of especial interest here are the operas that reworked the original novel freely. For example, in Gioacchino Rossini's *Ivanhoé* (first performed Paris, 1826), Rebecca becomes Léila and Isaac becomes Ismael – and they are introduced as Muslims.[17] In the first act, Ismael is revealed to be French King Philippe's treasurer. Follow-ing an attack on the chateau, Bois [sic] takes Léila away. The second act focuses on the relationship of Bois and Léila. Léila is put on trial for send-ing messages to King Philippe (i.e., treason) and inciting conflict between Saxons and Normans. In the third act, Léila is revealed to be Édith, the daughter of a Saxon nobleman, Olric, descendent of King Alfred. Ivanhoé wins his duel with Bois and proposes to Édith. Philippe's army approaches and the Saxons prepare for battle. *Ivanhoé*, in sum, begins with a clever disguise to draw the attention of viewers, and likely to avoid the nega-tive depiction of Jewish characters, but ultimately concludes to please an audience ready to applaud a Christian union featuring Ivanhoe and Rebecca – albeit under different names – and a Saxon-Norman war, which was unlikely to go out of fashion any time soon. The personal relation-ships and national conflicts of Scott's *Ivanhoe* were used to stage problem-solutions specific to community concerns of the moment. As Templeton argues in his dedicatory epistle, more important than staying true to an original manuscript was the appropriateness of the adaptation to the con-ditions that favored popular reception. Put more bluntly, stage success depended on sales, which could only be achieved by generating interest. Accordingly, although Christian and Jew are not united, Heinrich Marsch-ner's *Der Templar und die Jüdin* (first performed Leipzig, 1829) focuses on the historically unlikely yet endlessly popular relationship between the Templar Boisguilbert and the Jewess Rebecca.[18] However, as with Rossini's more adventurous adaptation, the incentive to popularize the novel by ensuring that Ivanhoe and Rebecca marry seems to have been difficult to resist. For instance, in Giovanni Pacini's *Ivanhoe* (first performed Venice, 1832), Rowena turns out to be Ivanhoe's sister and Rebecca a Saxon, thus paving the way for the union desired by readers and theatre-goers alike.[19] Such adaptations represent a form of the "license" referred to by Temple-ton in his argument for the need to "translate" history for contemporary readers, or in this case, viewers. The historification of England's past, and of Scott's version of it in *Ivanhoe*, depended upon production adapted to situation. There was no such thing as a reading-in-general of *Ivanhoe* at the opera house.[20]

Conclusion 193

Following the frequent adaptation of *Ivanhoe* in the 1820s, in the 1830 introduction to *Ivanhoe* for the collected edition of his Waverley novels, Scott again addressed his own use of fiction to make history. He points out that the contrast between Normans and Saxons in the novel derives from Logan's tragedy of Runnamede, and that the title *Ivanhoe* itself was derived from ancient sources.[21] More interestingly, Scott sets out a complex description of the fictional sources for the meeting of King Richard and Friar Tuck in *Ivanhoe*. He refers to Eastern tales, Scottish tradition, French minstrelsy, Norman precedents, and popular ballads in England, before noting that his version depends on sources that go back another two centuries, to a "curious record of ancient literature," which was recorded in a periodical called the *British Bibliographer*, then transferred to a volume titled "Ancient Metrical Tales," where it is called the "Kyng and the Hermite."[22] Scott retells the "original legend" in some detail.[23] In doing this, he points to a history of communication from feudal to modern times – from oral storytelling, to bibliographical preservation of those stories, to the modernized romance epitomized by the Waverley novels. This history reflects his own antiquarian work collecting ballads in the Scottish countryside, which led to his preservation of oral poetry in print collections, and then his reinvention of historical record in popular narrative poems.[24] In this way, the 1830 introduction and the dedicatory epistle combine to frame *Ivanhoe* as an instance of history-making dependent on reading practices rather than the recovery of history itself. The concurrent adaptation of *Ivanhoe* in print and on stage might be said to have driven home the point, which has been made repeatedly in different media over the last 200 years.

In the 1940s, the emergent comic book industry played an important role in placing *Ivanhoe* at the forefront of popular culture in twentieth-century America. Following *The Three Musketeers*, the second issue of *Classic Comics* published in New York by Gilberton in 1941 was an adaptation of *Ivanhoe*.[25] The educational intent of the series set it apart from other comic books of the period. This was the so-called Golden Age of comics in America, when Superman, Batman, Wonder Woman, and Captain America exploded on to the scene (Superman was introduced in *Action Comics*, no. 1, 1938). In contrast, the front cover of every issue of *Classic Comics* framed the content as literature worth reading, "Featuring Stories by the World's Greatest Authors." The intent was to introduce young readers to great books; the first edition of *Classic Comics* included a letter from the publisher outlining the aim "to create an active interest in those great masterpieces and to instill a desire to read the original text."[26] Rather than worrying about the impact of adventure stories and superheroes on impressionable young minds, parents might rest easier knowing that *Classic Comics* was a gateway to better things for their children. Although the figures are not precise, to say that *Classic Comics* was successful is clearly understating the case. The low price (starting at ten cents) and content (i.e., well-known tales) contributed to frequent reprints.[27] But against the

194 *Conclusion*

backdrop of superhero comics, and even more, the subsequent diversification of the industry to include genre comics (e.g., horror, science fiction, and fantasy), the educational frame was essential to continued success. Comics, widely recognized as both popular and fantastic, were considered (by some) a threat to social norms. *Classic Comics* became *Classics Illustrated* in 1947, removing the unsavory association with a disreputable form of reading that was, importantly, not incorporated by the education system. Comic books came under increasing scrutiny in the 1950s. A United States Senate Subcommittee was established in 1953 to investigate the problem of juvenile delinquency; public hearings in 1954 included the questioning of EC Comics publisher William Gaines, who responded to questions about editorial practices and good taste. In the moderately popular but influential book *Seduction of the Innocent: The Influence of Comic Books on Today's Youth* (1954), Fredric Wertham argued that the depiction of violence in comics adversely impacted children.[28] In response to such high-profile disparagement, the Comics Magazine Association of America attempted to self-regulate the industry by creating the Comics Code Authority in 1954. In this context, *Classics Illustrated*, relative to more sensational comic books, could at least be positioned as a lesser evil. Yet, despite wide circulation, the printing of new titles stopped in 1962, following on F. W. Woolworth's decision to discontinue the sale of comic books and Gilberton's failure to renew the second-class postage permit, both of which negatively impacted distribution.[29] In addition, the popularity of cheap paperbacks and television provided competition, and the introduction of study aids such as *CliffsNotes* (1958) for use by secondary and post-secondary students pointed to new ways of making classic literature available to subsequent generations. In this context, the use of *Ivanhoe* changed again, both within and beyond the comic book industry.

In 1991, *Classics Illustrated* gave *Ivanhoe* a makeover.[30] The scenes are familiar but the comic is redrawn with watercolors, thus establishing a clear aesthetic difference from 1940s renditions. Still marked out as an introduction to the world of great literature, this edition was also supported by the Literacy Volunteers of America, as indicated on the back cover, and thus framed as reading material for students of English. Besides the standard inclusion of an introduction to the novel and a biography of Scott, the glossy front image is produced on stiffer cardboard and the volume's size is reduced, giving it the feel of a book rather than a comic – a more durable product that might be transported in a backpack to and from school or find a place on a shelf. More directly, advertisements for dictionaries, a grammar guide, and a thesaurus target students of language and literature. Such modifications solidified the educational intent of *Classics Illustrated*. The classic as comic became, literally, a classic illustrated; the comic was no longer just a path to the novel but a means to supplement pedagogical priorities. In this way, reinventions of the novel were repositioned by publishers with an eye to the education market.[31]

Conclusion   195

In 1997, the Acclaim Books version of *Ivanhoe* aimed to capitalize on the market for the abridged, annotated versions of school reading that were beginning to make their presence felt on the Internet.[32] Although still "Your Doorway to the Classics," following on *Classic Comics* and earlier editions of *Classics Illustrated*, at the end of Acclaim's "Classics Illustrated Study Guide" is an "essay" by Susan Shwartz, PhD. An information box on the last page highlights her credentials as an expert: MA and PhD from Harvard; studied at Trinity College, Oxford; author of several books; taught at Ithaca College and Harvard University.[33] In an interview, series editor Madeleine Robins described the aim of the study guide supplements: "We try to put back what was left out."[34] In other words, the aim was to overcome the reduction of a novel to a singular plot line devoid of context and complexity. In the case of *Ivanhoe*, at least, the result is an excellent example of meaning-as-use. Shwartz begins her essay by noting that for contemporary readers, *Ivanhoe* may cause dismay, not least because it is "Required Reading."[35] Importantly, we are already at school. According to Shwartz, we read with "modern romantic sensibilities."[36] As in many classrooms, reading practices are not so much open to interpretation as designed to close down the production of meaning: for example, we are to read Scott as representing "Moors, Saracens, Muslims, or whatever you want to call them, not as people but as The Other, exotic, dangerous, and above all, *wrong*: a sure sign that a character is questionable is exposure to Arab culture."[37] The reader should be worried at this point, says Shwartz, for "what's worse, we suspect that he's missing important details of correctness with respect to history and costume."[38] Dryasdust would not be pleased. Regardless, given such a negative critique, why bother with *Ivanhoe* at all? Two reasons, says Shwartz: excitement and enthusiasm; the plot is full of twists and turns, and despite Scott's faults, what still comes shining through is his "love and energy."[39] This hardly seems a resounding endorsement, so what, then, did Scott give us with *Ivanhoe*? Apparently, only what people wanted – he recreated the Age of Chivalry, that is, "a sense and feeling of that time – not as it was, perhaps, but as people enjoy perceiving it."[40] Scott is castigated for the historification that made the novel popular, a stance derivative of the nineteenth-century criticism of Thomas Carlyle. Her subsequent reference to A. N. Wilson to frame Scott as a writer of fantasy leads to the more important point: if you acknowledge that *Ivanhoe* is not real literature, then it is likely safe to proceed. Romance has been thus denigrated for centuries; Harlequin and other forms of popular romance still get the same treatment.[41] But the limited appreciation of *Ivanhoe* as fantasy was unlikely to convince students or appease wary parents, so it was necessary to strengthen the educational framework. What follows is exactly what one would expect from study aids aimed at high school and post-secondary students: a list of character descriptions; insets on Templars, knights and jousting, and Jewish history; plot summary; and themes, including a prominent section on "The Middle Ages as Scott Dreamed Them," in which Shwartz describes *Ivanhoe*

196 *Conclusion*

as a form of wish fulfillment and compares Scott to "modern fantasists like Le Guin and Tolkien."[42] In practical terms, Shwartz helps students with exam preparation while trying to persuade them that it is possible to be a fan, to read Scott for his "world-building fantasies."[43] To bring home this last point, Shwartz again draws upon stereotypes that locate Scott as a writer clinging to the lower rungs of popular fiction; whereas J. R. R. Tolkien spent years "working and reworking his material," Scott "let it flow out fast, with total conviction, from what our current, psychologically-aware age might well call the subconscious."[44] The result was the "sheer magic" of *Ivanhoe*.[45] As a second-rate fantasy, Shwartz can then recommend "reading it in great gulps."[46] She asks if such reading is copping out, which seems to be asking if it is satisfactory to read in such a common way. It is acceptable, she claims, if we see something of ourselves or nature in the text, which brings her full circle, back to modern romantic sensibilities – the bell rings, class is out. The end of the Acclaim Books Study Guide series came after issuing only sixty-two titles; publication was suspended in April 1998.[47] As William Jones notes, the difficulty marketing works that defied categorization likely played a role in their demise.[48] The low quality and didactic purpose of the educational supplement may also have contributed. Less obviously, perhaps, the emergence of media better suited to reinterpret *Ivanhoe* for new generations – namely, film – was likely a factor.

Although *Ivanhoe* was first adapted for film in 1913,[49] it was not until the 1950s that *Ivanhoe* reached wider audiences on the big screen. Early adaptations were relatively faithful interpretations of the original novel, although not without important modifications relevant to historical context. Richard Thorpe's *Ivanhoe* (1952) starring Elizabeth and Robert Taylor opens by establishing the relationship between Ivanhoe and Isaac the Jew, who cooperate to free King Richard and defeat Prince John.[50] Isaac's daughter Rebecca supplies jewels to pay for Ivanhoe's horse and armor. Later in the film, Isaac must choose between Richard and his daughter, and this being a patriotic film, he chooses the King. In the aftermath of the Holocaust, the representation of Jewish characters, although not without limitations, is largely positive – a significant change from some nineteenth-century adaptations. Yet the film does not take the sort of narrative liberties familiar to early operas. As in so many reproductions of *Ivanhoe*, Rebecca is the dominant character in a love triangle that also includes Ivanhoe and Rowena. Although she whispers her love to a sleeping Ivanhoe, she relinquishes him to Rowena; as in the novel, the historical divide between Jews and Christians is not overcome. Jewish character is thus represented as exemplary in another way: Rebecca is at once humane (capable of love) and noble (willing to sacrifice for others). Audiences were likely pleased by recognition of the love between Rebecca and Ivanhoe, sympathetic to her silent anguish, and perhaps not unhappy that a cross-cultural union did not challenge their notions of propriety – however dull, Ivanhoe is supposed to marry Rowena, and that is what happens. The post-WWII context also contributed to the politics of cultural representation

Conclusion 197

in other ways. Much like dramatizations of *Ivanhoe* in the 1820s, the conflict between Normans and Saxons could be used to stimulate patriotism and represent the overcoming of social divisions. In the final scene of Thorpe's film, Richard calls on all to rise as one for England, and Rebecca's father, Isaac, is no exception. In the 1820s and 1830s, melodramatic adaptations of *Ivanhoe* were either relatively faithful accounts or wildly permissive rewrites. Thorpe's *Ivanhoe* is essentially a film version of *Classics Illustrated*, intended to further a familiarly conservative story in a new medium – Rebecca does not become a Saxon princess or die at Ivanhoe's feet; all unite under an English flag. Douglas Camfield's *Ivanhoe*, which was made for television and originally aired by CBS in America in 1982, is a similarly conventional rendition of a classic.[51] Tellingly, the film begins with a voiceover narrating a universal story of "love, prejudice, and hatred" that is "ever new." Again, strong emphasis is placed on the historical divide between Christians and Jews that keeps Ivanhoe and Rebecca apart – history will not be violated – and in the end, Richard calls for a close union of Saxons and Normans. Given the use of it, *Ivanhoe* seems to have been easily redeployed to align with Cold War sensibilities. Yet the proliferation of Crusader histories, medieval adventure-fantasies, and Robin Hood spin-offs suggests that experimentation to meet and cultivate the formal and thematic preferences of contemporary audiences has continued in other ways.[52] As the best-known Crusader in history, Ivanhoe has been an indirect source for many Crusader films. Scott's later series of novels, *Tales of the Crusaders*, including *The Betrothed* (1825) and *The Talisman* (1825), contributed more directly to films such as *The Crusades* (1935), *King Richard and the Crusaders* (1954), and *Kingdom of Heaven* (2005).[53] The exoticism of the Orient was of great interest to nineteenth-century readers. Today, conflict in the Middle East and recent interventions in Iraq, Afghanistan, and Syria continue to provoke interest in East-West relations, modern forms of Orientalism, and responses to it. Although not often recognized, at the heart of many contemporary fantasy fictions, action films, and role-playing games, Scott's Crusader novels (and derivatives of them) continue to contribute to the historification of the past for new generations. As Scott himself realized, sensitivity to the formal and thematic requirements of popular reception is essential to successful translation.

The multimedia history of *Ivanhoe* points to a productive dilemma for contemporary scholars of historical fiction. On the one hand, a record of remediation over two centuries documents varied production, circulation, and reception over time. On the other hand, such records should lead to better understanding of the processes and outcomes of meaning-making. Therein lies the challenge to contemporary scholars: to uncover and then make use of the histories of historical fiction to generate concrete knowledge of communication practices. Rather than falling into the assertion of a sliding scale of appreciation, the uses of *Ivanhoe*, for example, might be reconsidered as historical cases of meaning production. Through the dedicatory epistle and the 1830 introduction to *Ivanhoe*, Scott provided an overview of

198   *Conclusion*

the historification central to his popularization of history. Histories of *Ivanhoe*, in turn, are further evidence that, if there is a lesson to be learned, it is that "We construct our texts as we go: they are not given to us in advance of the operations by which we contextualize them."[54] How exactly do we construct our texts? Under what conditions? For what purposes? Answering such questions requires further attention to the case-by-case working of the historical novel to make meaning. In this light, perhaps *Acts of Modernity*, as a study of communication practices, has something to offer not only to scholars of the historical novel but also to those who find themselves asking today, what does it mean to be modern? This was the question that prompted the many uses of the historical novel discussed in this book, and it is one that will remain relevant for the foreseeable future.

Notes

1 Giddens, *Consequences of Modernity*, 17. Giddens also describes the dynamics of modernity as dependent on "the *separation of time and space* and their recombination in forms which permit the precise time-space 'zoning' of social life; [and] the *disembedding* of social systems" (ibid., 16–17).
2 Scott, *Ivanhoe*, 13.
3 Ibid., 14.
4 Ibid., 15.
5 Ibid., 16.
6 Ibid., 17. Horace Walpole, *The Castle of Otranto* (London: Tho. Lownds, 1764). George Ellis, *Specimens of Early English Metrical Romances, Chiefly Written During the Early Part of the Fourteenth Century: To Which Is Prefixed an Historical Introduction Intended to Illustrate the Rise and Progress of Romantic Compositions in France and England*, 3 vols. (London: Longman, Hurst, Rees, and Orme, 1805).
7 Scott, *Ivanhoe*, 17.
8 The term "nation of readers" refers to increased access to and interest in print communication across diverse reading communities in Britain.
9 Scott, *Ivanhoe*, 17–18.
10 Ibid., 18.
11 Joseph Strutt, *Queenhoo-Hall, a Romance: And Ancient Times, a Drama*, 4 vols. (London: John Murray; Edinburgh: Archibald Constable, 1808).
12 Scott, *Ivanhoe*, 18.
13 Ibid.
14 Ibid., 21.
15 Ibid., 23.
16 See Graham Tulloch, "Essay on the Text," in Walter Scott, *Ivanhoe*, ed. Graham Tulloch (Edinburgh: Edinburgh University Press, 1997), 403–62; Barnaby, "Timeline," xxiv–lxxiv; Bolton, *Scott Dramatized*, 342; and Parsons, "Chapbook Versions," 202–5.
17 Mitchell, *Walter Scott Operas*, 146–56. Gioacchino Rossini, *Ivanhoé*, libretto by Émile Deschamps and Gustave de Wailly (1826). Note: Mitchell provides more detailed description of each of the operas mentioned in this paragraph.
18 Mitchell, *Walter Scott Operas*, 156–66. Heinrich Marschner, *Der Templar und die Jüdin*, libretto by W. A. Wohlbrück, adapted by John P. Jackson (1829).
19 Mitchell, *Walter Scott Operas*, 166–71. Giovanni Pacini, *Ivanhoe*, libretto by Gaetano Rossi (1832).

Conclusion 199

20 For more on Scott operas, see Mitchell, *Walter Scott Operas*; and *More Scott Operas*.

21 Scott, *Ivanhoe*, 5, 11.

22 Ibid., 7–8.

23 Ibid., 11.

24 See, for example, Scott, *Minstrelsy*; *Lay of the Last Minstrel*.

25 *Ivanhoe*, *Classic Comics*, no. 2 (New York: Gilberton, 1941).

26 William B. Jones, Jr., *Classics Illustrated: A Cultural History*, 2nd ed. (Jefferson, NC: McFarland and Company, 2011), 12.

27 One collector suggests that the second issue featuring *Ivanhoe* went through twenty-five different printings over a period of thirty years; see King-collect, "Classics Illustrated Comics: Identifying Reprints," *Ebay*, December 2, 2005, www.ebay.com/gds/CLASSICS-ILLUSTRATED-comic-books-IDENTIFYING-REPRINTS-/10000000000084872/g.html.

28 Frederic Wertham, *Seduction of the Innocent: The Influence of Comic Books on Today's Youth* (New York: Rinehard, 1954).

29 Jones, *Classics Illustrated*, 238.

30 Mark Wayne Harris and Ray Lago, *Ivanhoe*, in *Classics Illustrated*, no. 25 (New York: Berkley; Chicago: First Publishing, 1991).

31 Examples I have seen are Michael West, *Ivanhoe*, new ed. (London: Longman, 1967); Ed Teeling and Paula Teeling, *Ivanhoe* (Long Island, NY: EDCON, 1993); Malvina G. Vogel and Pablo Marcos Studios, *Ivanhoe* (New York: Baronet Books, 1994); and Marianne Mayer and John Rush, *Sir Walter Scott's Ivanhoe* (San Francisco, CA: Chronicle Books, 2004).

32 Madeleine Robins, ed., *Classics Illustrated: Sir Walter Scott: Ivanhoe* (New York: Acclaim Books, 1997).

33 Susan Shwartz, "Ivanhoe: Sir Walter Scott," in *Classics Illustrated: Sir Walter Scott: Ivanhoe*, ed. Madeleine Robins (New York: Acclaim Books, 1997), n. pag.

34 Robins, qtd. in Jones, *Classics Illustrated*, 292.

35 Shwartz, "Ivanhoe," n. pag.

36 Ibid.

37 Ibid.

38 Ibid.

39 Ibid.

40 Ibid.

41 See, for example, Juliette Woodruff, "A Spate of Words, Full of Sound and Fury, Signifying Nothing: Or, How to Read in Harlequin," *Journal of Popular Culture* 19, no. 2 (Fall 1985): 25–32.

42 Shwartz, "Ivanhoe," n. pag.

43 Ibid.

44 Ibid.

45 Ibid.

46 Ibid.

47 Jones, *Classics Illustrated*, 293.

48 Ibid.

49 *Ivanhoe*, directed by Herbert Brenon (1913), film. *Ivanhoe*, directed by Leedham Bantock (1913), film. *Pimple's Ivanhoe*, directed by Fred Evans and Joe Evans (1913), film.

50 *Ivanhoe*, directed by Richard Thorpe (1952), film.

51 *Ivanhoe*, directed by Douglas Camfield (1982), film. See also, *Ivanhoe*, directed by HSB Coote (1958–59), tv series; and *Ivanhoe*, directed by Stuart Orme (1997), tv mini-series.

52 Examples of Robin Hood films are *Robin Hood*, directed by Ridley Scott (2010); *Robin Hood: Men in Tights*, directed by Mel Brooks (1993); *Robin Hood:*

200 *Conclusion*

Prince of Thieves, directed by Kevin Reynolds (1991); *Robin Hood*, directed by John Irvin (1991); *Robin and Marian*, directed by Richard Lester (1976); *Robin Hood*, directed by Wolfgang Reitherman (1973); *The Men of Sherwood Forest*, directed by Val Guest (1965); *The Story of Robin Hood and His Merrie Men*, directed by Ken Annakin (1952); and *The Adventures of Robin Hood*, directed by Michael Curtiz and William Keighley (1938). On the afterlives of *Ivanhoe*, see also Paul Barnaby, *The Walter Scott Digital Archive*, University of Edinburgh Library, www.walterscott.lib.ed.ac.uk/publications/criticism/worksindex.html#ivanhoe.

53 Walter Scott, [*The Betrothed*] *Tales of the Crusaders* (Edinburgh: Constable; London: Hurst, Robinson, 1825); [*The Talisman*] *Tales of the Crusaders* (Edinburgh: Constable; London: Hurst, Robinson, 1825). *The Crusades*, directed by Cecil B. DeMille (1935), film. *King Richard and the Crusaders*, directed by David Butler (1954), film. *Kingdom of Heaven*, directed by Ridley Scott (2005), film.

54 Harris, *Integrational Linguistics*, 104.

Bibliography

Adams, James Eli. "The Novel in Theory Before 1900." In *A Companion to the English Novel*, edited by Stephen Arata, Madigan Haley, J. Paul Hunter, and Jennifer Wicke, 241–55. Hoboken, NJ: Wiley-Blackwell, 2015.

Aimard, Gustave. *Aimard's Indian Tales: Author's Copyright Ed.* Edited by Percy Bolingbroke St. John. London: J. and R. Maxwell, 1877–79.

———. *The Bandit at Bay, or The Pirates of the Prairies.* Beadle's New York dime library, no. 20. New York: Beadle and Adams, 1879.

———. *Les bandits de l'Arizona.* Limoges: E. Ardant, 1882.

———. *The Frontiersmen: A Novel.* New York: F. M. Lupton, 1892. https://archive.org/details/frontiersmennove00aimarich.

———. *The Indian Scout: Being the Conclusion of "The Prairie Flower."* Revised and edited by Percy Bolingbroke St. John. Seaside library, no. 1740. New York: George Munro's Sons, 1893.

———. *Les pirates des prairies.* Paris: Amyot, 1858.

———. *The Pirates of the Prairies.* Revised and edited by Percy Bolingbroke St. John. Lovell's library, no. 1011. New York: Lovell, 1887.

———. *The Pirates of the Prairies: or, Adventures in the American Desert.* Translated by Lascelles Wraxall. Complete and unabridged ed. Aimard's novels, v. 2. Philadelphia: T. B. Peterson, 1862.

———. *The Prairie Pirates, or, The Hunter's Revenge.* Beadle's pocket novels, no. 218. New York: Beadle and Adams, 1869.

———. *Stronghand.* Revised and edited by Percy Bolingbroke St. John. Boys' dashaway series, no. 46. New York: George Munro, 1895.

———. *Works of Gustave Aimard.* Edited and revised by Percy Bolingbroke St. John. 8 vols. London, 1877–79.

Aimard, Gustave, and Frances Henshaw Baden. *The Frontiersmen: A Novel.* New York: F. M. Lupton, 1854.

Allemano, Marina. *Historical Portraits and Visions: From Walter Scott's* Waverley *to Michel Tournier's* Le Roi des Aulnes *and Thomas Pynchon's* Gravity's Rainbow. New York: Garland, 1991.

Allen, James Smith. *Popular French Romanticism: Authors, Readers, and Books in the 19th Century.* Syracuse, NY: Syracuse University Press, 1981.

Alves, Robert. "A Parallel Between History and Novel Writing." In Nixon, *Novel Definitions*, 181–82. First published in Robert Alves, *Sketches of a History of Literature.* Edinburgh: Chapman, 1794.

202 Bibliography

Anderson, Benedict. *Imagined Communities: Reflections on the Origin and Spread of Nationalism*. Revised and extended ed., 2nd ed. London: Verso, 1991.

Arata, Stephen, Madigan Haley, J. Paul Hunter, and Jennifer Wicke, eds. *A Companion to the English Novel*. Hoboken, NJ: Wiley-Blackwell, 2015.

Arch, Stephen Carl. "Cooper's Turn: Satire in the Age of Jackson." In vol. 2 of *Literature in the Early American Republic: Annual Studies on Cooper and His Contemporaries*, edited by Mathew Wynn Sivils and Jeffrey Walker, 173–201. New York: AMS Press, 2010.

———. "Romancing the Puritans: American Historical Fiction in the 1820s." *ESQ* 39, no. 2/3 (1993): 107–32.

Aubert de Gaspé, Philippe. *Les anciens Canadiens*. Montréal: Beauchemin, 1913.

———. *Les anciens Canadiens*. Montréal: Cadieux and Derome, 1886.

———. *Les anciens Canadiens*. Montréal: Librairie Beauchemin, 1899.

———. *Les anciens Canadiens*. Montréal: Librairie Beauchemin, 1925.

———. *Les anciens Canadiens*. Montréal: Librairie Beauchemin, 1931.

———. *Les anciens Canadiens*. Québec: Desbarats and Derbishire, 1863.

———. *Les anciens Canadiens*. Québec: Desbarats and Derbishire, 1863. Translated by Jane Brierley as Canadians of Old: A Romance . Montréal: Véhicule, 1996.

———. *Les anciens Canadiens*. 2nd ed. Québec: G. and G. E. Desbarats, 1864.

———. *Les anciens Canadiens*. 2nd ed., revised and corrected by the author. Québec: G. and G. E. Desbarats, 1864.

———. *Les anciens Canadiens*. 21st ed. Montréal: Librairie Beauchemin, 1899.

———. *Les anciens Canadiens*. New ed. Québec: Augustin Coté, 1877.

———. *Cameron of Locheill*. New ed. Translated by Charles G. D. Roberts. Boston: Page, 1905.

———. *Cameron of Lochiel*. New ed. Translated by Charles G. D. Roberts. Toronto: Copp, Clark, 1905.

———. *The Canadians of Old*. Translated by Charles G. D. Roberts. Appleton's town and country library, no. 62. New York: D. Appleton, 1890.

———. *The Canadians of Old*. Translated by G. M. Ward. Quebec: G. and G. E. Desbarats, 1864.

———. *The Canadians of Old: An Historical Romance*. Translated by Charles G. D. Roberts. Toronto: Hart, 1891.

———. *Seigneur d'Haberville (The Canadians of Old): A Romance of the Fall of New France*. Toronto: Musson Book, 1929.

Aubert de Gaspé, Philippe-Agnace-François. *L'influence d'un livre: roman historique*. Montréal: Boréal, 1996. First published Québec: W. Cowan, 1837.

Aubin, Penelope. Preface to *The Strange Adventures of the Count de Vinevil and His Family*. In Nixon, *Novel Definitions*, 66–67. First published in Penelope Aubin, *The Strange Adventures of the Count de Vinevil and his Family*, 2nd ed. London: E. Bell, J. Darby, A. Bettesworth, F. Fayram, J. Pemberton, J. Hooke, C. Rivington, F. Clay, J. Batley, and E. Symon, 1728 [1st ed.: 1721].

Auerbach, Erich. *Mimesis: The Representation of Reality in Western Literature*. Princeton, NJ: Princeton University Press, 1953.

Baguley, David. "*Germinal*: The Gathering Storm." In *The Cambridge Companion to Émile Zola*, edited by Brian Nelson, 137–51. Cambridge: Cambridge University Press, 2007.

Bakhtin, Mikhail M. "The *Bildungsroman* and Its Significance in the History of Realism (Toward a Historical Typology of the Novel)." In *Speech Genres and*

Bibliography 203

Other Late Essays, edited by Caryl Emerson and Michael Holquist, translated by Vern W. McGee, 10–59. Austin: University of Texas Press, 1986.

———. "Forms of Time and of the Chronotope in the Novel." In *The Dialogic Imagination: Four Essays*, edited by Michael Holquist, translated by Caryl Emerson and Michael Holquist, 84–258. Austin: University of Texas Press, 1981.

Baldick, Chris. "The Novel in Theory, 1900–1965." In Arata et al., *A Companion to the English Novel*, 256–70.

Balzac, Honoré de. *La comédie humaine, Œuvres complètes de M. de Balzac*. Paris: Furne, Dubochet, Hetzel and Paulin, 1842–48.

———. *Études de moeurs au XIXe siècle*. 12 vols. Paris: Béchet, 1834–37.

———. *Lettres à Madame Hanska*. Edited by R. Pierrot. 4 vols. Paris: 1967–71.

———. *La maison Nucingen*. In *La femme superieure, La maison Nucingen, La tophille*, 2 vols. Paris: Werdet, 1838. Translated by James Waring as *The Firm of Nucingen*. Champaign, IL: Project Gutenberg, 2013. www.gutenberg.org/ebooks/1294 .

———. *Œuvres illustrées de Balzac*. Paris: Marescq, 1851–53.

———. *Papà Goriot: storia parigina*. Translated by L. M. 2 vols. Milano: Pirotta, 1836.

———. *Le père Goriot*. In vol. 3 of *Oeuvres de H. de Balzac*. Bruxelles: Meline, Cans, 1837.

———. *Le père Goriot*. In vol. 7 of *Collection of Stories by Honoré de Balzac Extracted From the Revue de Paris, 1830–1835*. Paris: Au Bureau de la revue de Paris, 1830–35.

———. *Le père Goriot*. In *Revue de Paris*, December 1834 – February 35. Translated by Marion Ayton Crawford as *Old Goriot*. Harmondsworth: Penguin Books, 1983.

———. *Le père Goriot: histoire parisienne*. 2 vols. Bruxelles: J. P. Meline, 1835.

———. *Le père Goriot: histoire parisienne*. 2 vols. Paris: Werdet and Spachmann, 1835.

———. *Le père Goriot: par M. de Balzac*. Bruxelles: A. Wahlen, 1835.

———. *Le père Goriot, nouvelle édition revue et corrigée*. Paris: Charpentier, 1839.

———. Review of *The Pathfinder, or The Inland Sea*, by James Fenimore Cooper. In *Fenimore Cooper; The Critical Heritage*, edited by George Dekker and John P. McWilliams, 207–10. London: Taylor and Francis e-Library, 2003. First published in Revue Parisienne , July 25, 1840.

———. *Scènes de la vie parisienne: Le père Goriot*. Paris: Bureaux du "Siècle," 1856.

———. *Théâtre*. N.p.: Girard and Dagneau, 1853.

———. *Vater Goriot*. Stuttgart: Hallberger, 1835.

Barba, Preston A. *Cooper in Germany*. Bloomington: n.p., 1914.

Barbauld, Anna Letitia [Aikin]. "On the Origin and Progress of Novel-Writing." In Nixon, *Novel Definitions*, 361–69. First published in *The British Novelists; With an Essay, and Prefaces, Biographical and Critical*, edited by Anna Letitia [Aikin] Barbauld, 50 vols. London: F. C. and J. Rivington, 1810.

Barber, Giles. "Galignani's and the Publication of English Books in France from 1800 to 1852." *The Library*, 5th ser., 16 (1961): 267–86. http://library.oxford journals.org/content/s5-XVI/4/267.full.pdf.

Barbéris, Pierre. "L'amour: ambiguïtés et contradictions." In Gengembre, *Le père Goriot*, 439–41.

204   Bibliography

Barnaby, Paul. "Timeline of the European Reception of Sir Walter Scott, 1802–2005." In *The Reception of Sir Walter Scott in Europe*, edited by Murray Pittock, xxiv–lxxiv. London: Continuum, 2006.

———. *The Walter Scott Digital Archive*. University of Edinburgh Library, Edinburgh. www.walterscott.lib.ed.ac.uk/publications/criticism/worksindex.html#ivanhoe.

Barnes, Elizabeth. "Novels." In Gross and Kelley, *An Extensive Republic*, 440–49.

Bautz, Annika. *The Reception of Jane Austen and Walter Scott: A Comparative Longitudinal Study*. London: Continuum, 2007.

Baym, Nina. "How Men and Women Wrote Indian Stories." In *New Essays on the Last of the Mohicans*, edited by H. Daniel Peck, 67–86. Cambridge: Cambridge University Press, 1992.

Beard, James Franklin, ed. *The Letters and Journals of James Fenimore Cooper*. Vol. 2. Cambridge, MA: The Belknap Press of Harvard University Press, 2004.

Beattie, James. "On Fable and Romance." In Nixon, *Novel Definitions*, 347–50. First published in James Beattie, *Dissertations Moral and Critical*. London: W. Strahan, T. Cadell, and W. Creech, 1783.

Beckwith, Julia Catherine. *St Ursula's Convent; or, The Nun of Canada: Containing Scenes From Real Life*. Edited by Douglas Lochhead. Ottawa: Carleton University Press, 1991. First published Kingston, Upper Canada: H. C. Thomson, 1824.

Bell, Bill, David Finkelstein, and Alistair McCleery, eds. *Ambition and Industry 1800–80*. Vol. 3 of *The Edinburgh History of the Book in Scotland*, edited by Bill Bell. Edinburgh: Edinburgh University Press, 2007.

Bellos, David. *Honoré de Balzac, Old Goriot*. Cambridge: Cambridge University Press, 1987.

Benjamin, Walter. *Illuminations*. Edited by Hannah Arendt. Translated by Harry Zohn. New York: Schocken Books, 2007.

Benson, Eugene, and Leonard W. Connolly. *English-Canadian Theatre*. Toronto: Oxford University Press, 1987.

Berlatsky, Eric L. *The Real, the True, and the Told: Postmodern Historical Narrative and the Ethics of Representation*. Columbus: The Ohio State University, 2011.

Bibaud, Michel. *Histoire du Canada et des Canadiens sous la domination anglaise*. Montréal: Lovell and Gibson, 1844.

———. *Histoire du Canada sous la domination française*. Montréal: John Jones, 1837.

Bird, Montgomery. *Nick of the Woods, or, the Jibbenainosay: A Tale of Kentucky*. Philadelphia: Carey, Lea and Blanchard, 1837.

Black, Fiona A. "North America." In Bell, Finkelstein, and McCleery, *Ambition and Industry 1800–80*, 442–55.

Blair, Hugh. "Fictitious History." In Nixon, *Novel Definitions*, 343–46. First published in Hugh Blair, "Fictitious History," vol. 2 of *Lectures on Rhetoric and Belles Lettres*, 2 vols. London: W. Strahan, T. Cadell, and W. Creech, 1783.

Blair, Jennifer, Daniel Coleman, Kate Higginson, Lorraine York, and Carole Gerson, eds. *ReCalling Early Canada: Reading the Political in Literary and Cultural Production*. Edmonton: University of Alberta Press, 2005.

Bold, Christine. "Malaeska's Revenge; or, the Dime Novel Tradition in Popular Fiction." In *Wanted Dead or Alive: The American West in Popular Culture*, edited by Richard Aquila, 21–42. Urbana: University of Illinois Press, 1996.

———. *Selling the Wild West: Popular Western Fiction 1860–1960*. Bloomington: Indiana University Press, 1987.

Bolton, H. Philip. *Scott Dramatized*. London: Mansell, 1992.

Bibliography 205

Booth, Wayne C. *The Rhetoric of Fiction*. Chicago: University of Chicago Press, 1961.

Boucherville, Georges Boucher de. *Une de perdue, deux de trouvees*. Montréal: Beauchemin, 1955.

Brierley, Jane. Introduction to *Canadians of Old: A Romance*, by Philippe-Joséph Aubert de Gaspé, 9–18. Translated by Jane Brierley. Montréal: Véhicule, 1996.

Brooke, Frances. *The History of Emily Montague*. Edited by Laura F. E. Moss. Critical ed. Ottawa: Tecumseh Press, 2001. First published London: J. Dodsley, 1769.

Brooke, John L. "Print and Politics." In Gross and Kelley, *An Extensive Republic*, 179–90.

Brown, Charles Brockden. *Arthur Mervyn, or, the Memoirs of the Year 1793*. Philadelphia: H. Maxwell, 1799.

Brown, Dana. "Travel Books." In Gross and Kelley, *An Extensive Republic*, 449–58.

Brumm, Ursula. *Geschichte und wildnis in der Amerikanischen literatur*. Berlin: Schmidt, 1980.

Buchanan, David. "Popular Reception by Dramatic Adaptation: The Case of Walter Scott's *The Heart of Mid-Lothian*." *European Romantic Review* 22, no. 6 (November 2011): 745–63.

———. "Scott Squashed: Chapbook Versions of *The Heart of Mid-Lothian*." *Romanticism and Victorianism on the Net* 56 (November 2009): n. pag. http://id.erudit.org/iderudit/1001097ar.

Buchenau, Barbara. "'Wizards of the West'? How Americans Respond to Sir Walter Scott, the 'Wizard of the North.'" In *James Fenimore Cooper Society Website*, edited by Hugh C. Macdougall (webmaster), n. pag. Oneonta: State University of New York College, 1999. http://external.oneonta.edu/cooper/articles/suny/1997suny-buchenau.html. First published in *James Fenimore Cooper: His Country and His Art (No. 11)*, Papers from the 1997 Cooper Seminar (No. 11), edited by Hugh C. MacDougall, Oneonta: State University of New York College, 1997, 14–25.

Burney, Frances. *The Wanderer: or, Female Difficulties*. London: Longman, Hurst, Rees, Orme, and Brown, 1814.

Butler, Ronnie. *Balzac and the French Revolution*. London: Croom Helm, 1983.

Butterfield, Herbert. *The Historical Novel: An Essay*. Cambridge, UK: The University Press, 1924.

Buzard, James. *Disorienting Fiction: The Autoethnographic Work of Nineteenth-Century British Novels*. Princeton, NJ: Princeton University Press, 2005.

———. "Appendix A: Contemporary Reception of Leprohon's Works." In *The Manor House of De Villerai: A Tale of Canada Under the French Dominion*, edited by Andrea Cabajsky, 209–15. Peterborough, ON: Broadview Press, 2015.

Cabajsky, Andrea. Introduction to *The Manor House of De Villerai: A Ta le of Canada Under the French Dominion*, by Rosanna Mullins Leprohon, 9–32. Edited by Andrea Cabajsky. Peterborough, ON: Broadview Press, 2015.

———. "A Note on the Text." In *The Manor House of De Villerai: A Tale of Canada Under the French Dominion*, edited by Andrea Cabajsky, 37–41. Peterborough, ON: Broadview Press, 2015.

Caisse, Joseph Camille. *Les anciens Canadiens: drame en trois actes tire du roman populaire de P.A. de Gaspé*. Montréal: Beauchemin, 1894. CIHM Microfiche series, no. 02434.

Cambron, Micheline, and Carole Gerson. "Literary Authorship." In Lamonde, Fleming, and Black, *1840–1918*, 119–34.

206   Bibliography

Campbell, William Wilfred. *A Beautiful Rebel: A Romance of Upper-Canada in Eighteen Hundred and Twelve*. Toronto: Westminster, 1909.

Carlyle, Thomas. *Carlyle's Essay on Sir Walter Scott*. Edited by Arnold Smith. London: J. M. Dent, 1933. First published in *London and Westminster Review 6/28*, no. 6, 12–54, 55 (October 1837 – January 1838): 293–345.

Carman, Albert R. *The Preparation of Ryerson Embury: A Purpose*. 2nd ed. Toronto: Publishers' Syndicate, 1900. https://archive.org/details/cihm_03840.

Carnes, Mark C. *Novel History: Historians and Novelists Confront America's Past (and Each Other)*. New York: Simon and Schuster, 2001.

Carpenter, Kenneth. "Libraries." In Gross and Kelley, *An Extensive Republic*, 273–86.

Casper, Scott E., Jeffrey D. Groves, Stephen W. Nissenbaum, and Michael Winship, eds. *The Industrial Book, 1840–1880*. Vol. 3 of *A History of the Book in America*, edited by David D. Hall. Chapel Hill: University of North Carolina Press/American Antiquarian Society, 2007.

Chartier, Roger. "Labourers and Voyagers: From the Text to the Reader." In *The Book History Reader*, 2nd ed., edited by David Finkelstein and Alistair McCleery, 87–98. London: Routledge, 2002.

Charvat, William. *Literary Publishing in America, 1790–1850*. Philadelphia: University of Pennsylvania Press, 1959.

Chateaubriand, François-René. *Atala; René*. Translated by Irving Putter. Berkeley: University of California Press, 1980.

Child, Lydia Maria. *Hobomok: A Tale of Early Times*. Boston: Cummings, Hilliard, 1824.

———. *The Rebels, or, Boston Before the Revolution*. Boston: Cummings, Hilliard, 1825.

———. *A Romance of the Republic*. Edited by Dana D. Nelson. Lexington: University of Kentucky Press, 2014.

Cleland, John. Opening to *Memoirs of a Woman of Pleasure*. In Nixon, *Novel Definitions*, 71–72. First published in John Cleland, *Memoirs of a Woman of Pleasure*, 2 vols. London: G. Fenton, 1748–49.

Clinch, Charles Powell. "The Spy, a Tale of the Neutral Ground." In *Metamora and Other Plays*, edited by Eugene R. Page, 57–106. Princeton, NJ: Princeton University Press, 1941.

Colley, Linda. *Britons: Forging the Nation, 1707–1837*. New Haven, CT: Yale University Press, 1992.

Cooper, James Fenimore. *The American Democrat, or, Hints on the Social and Civic Relations of the United States of America*. Cooperstown, NY: H. and E. Phinney, 1838.

———. *The Bravo: A Tale*. Philadelphia: Carey and Lea, 1831.

———. *Cooper's "Leather-Stocking" Tales: Comprising, The Deerslayer, The Pathfinder, The Last of the Mohicans, The Pioneers, The Prairie*. London: George Routledge and Sons, 1887.

———. *Cooper's 'Leather-Stocking' Tales: Comprising, The Deerslayer, The Pathfinder, The Last of The Mohicans, The Pioneers, The Prairie*. 5 vols. London: G. Routledge and Sons, 1868.

———. *Cooper's Novels*. 18 vols. London: George Routledge and Sons, 1866–67.

———. *Cooper's Novels*. 32 vols. New York: Hurd and Houghton; Boston: E. P. Dutton, 1865.

Bibliography 207

————. *Cooper's Novels*. People's ed. 34 vols. New York: W. A. Townsend and Company [Stringer and Townsend], 1857–60.

————. *The Deerslayer, or, The First War-Path: A Tale*. Philadelphia: Lea and Blanchard, 1841.

————. *Gleanings in Europe, England*. Edited by James P. Elliott, Kenneth W. Staggs, and R. D. Madison. Albany: State University of New York Press, 1982.

————. *Gleanings in Europe, France*. Edited by Thomas Philbrick and Constance Ayers Denne. Albany: State University of New York Press, 1983.

————. *Gleanings in Europe, Italy*. An approved ed. Edited by Constance Ayers Denne. Albany: State University of New York Press, 1981.

————. *Gleanings in Europe, the Rhine*. Edited by Maurice Geracht, Thomas Philbrick, and Ernest Redekop. Albany: State University of New York Press, 1986.

————. *Gleanings in Europe, Switzerland*. Edited by Kenneth W. Staggs and James P. Elliott. Albany: State University of New York Press, 1980.

————. *The Headsman, or, The Abbaye des Vignerons: A Tale*. London: R. Bentley, 1833.

————. *The Heidenmauer: A Legend of the Rhine*. Paris: Baudry's Foreign Library, 1832.

————. *History of the Navy of the United States of America*. Philadelphia: Lea and Blanchard, 1839.

————. *Home as Found*. Philadelphia: Lea and Blanchard, 1838.

————. *Homeward Bound, or, The Chase: A Tale of the Sea*. Philadelphia: Carey, Lea and Blanchard, 1838.

————. *James Fenimore Cooper's Novels*. 31 vols. New York: D. Appleton, 1872–73.

————. *Le lac Ontario*. Translated by Auguste-Jean-Baptiste Defauconpret. Vol. 17 of *Œuvres*, 30 vols. Paris: Furne, 1830–52.

————. *Le lac Ontario*. Translated by Auguste-Jean-Baptiste Defauconpret. Vol. 17 of *Œuvres*, 30 vols. Paris: Furne, Pagnerre, Perrotin/Furne, Jouvet, Garnier frères, 1872.

————. *Le lac Ontario*. Translated by Auguste-Jean-Baptiste Defauconpret. Vol. 17 of *Œuvres de J. F. Cooper*, 17 vols. Paris: Furne, 1839–40.

————. *Le lac Ontario*. Translated by Auguste-Jean-Baptiste Defauconpret. Vol. 17 of *Œuvres de J.-F. Cooper*. Paris: Furne-Gosselin, 1840.

————. *Le lac Ontario, ou, le guide*. 2nd ed. 4 vols. Oeuvres complètes de M. James Fenimore Cooper, Américain. Paris, 1840.

————. *Le lac Ontario, ou, le guide*. Translated by Auguste-Jean-Baptiste Defauconpret. Paris: C. Gosselin, 1840.

————. *Le lac Ontario ou le guide*. Translated by Auguste-Jean-Baptiste Defauconpret. 3 vols. Bruxelles: Meline, Cans, 1840.

————. *The Last of the Mohicans: A Narrative of 1757*. London: R. Bentley, 1826.

————. *The "Leather-Stocking" Tales*. 5 vols. New York: D. Appleton, 1873.

————. *A Letter to His Countrymen*. New York: J. Wiley, 1834.

————. *The Letters and Journals of James Fenimore Cooper*. Edited by James Franklin Beard. 6 vols. Cambridge, MA: The Belknap Press of Harvard University Press, 2004.

————. *Lionel Lincoln; or, The Leaguer of Boston*. Edited by Donald A. Ringe and Lucy B. Ringe. Albany: State University of New York Press, 1984.

————. *The Monikins*. Philadelphia: Carey, Lea and Blanchard, 1835.

208 Bibliography

———. *Notions of the Americans: Picked Up by a Travelling Bachelor*. Philadelphia: Carey, Lea and Carey, 1828.

———. *The Novels and Romances of J. Fenimore Cooper: A New Edition in Thirteen Volumes*. 13 vols. London: Routledge, Warne and Routledge, 1864.

———. *Novels and Tales: By the Author of the Spy*. 2nd ser. 14 vols. Philadelphia: Carey and Lea, 1841.

———. *Novels and Tales: By the Author of the Spy*. 26 vols. Philadelphia: Carey and Lea, 1835–36.

———. *L'Ontario*. Translated by Emile de la Bédollière. Romans populaires illustrés. Paris: Barba, 1850.

———. *The Pathfinder*. Author's revised ed. New York: G. P. Putnam, 1853.

———. *The Pathfinder*. Vol. 1 of *The Novels and Romances of J. Fenimore Cooper*, 13 vols. London: Routledge, Warne, 1864.

———. *The Pathfinder*. Vol. 3 of *Cooper's Leather-Stocking Tales for Boys and Girls: With Illustrations*, 5 vols. in 1. London: G. Routledge and Sons, 1892.

———. *The Pathfinder*. Vol. 3 of *The Leather-Stocking Tales*, 5 vols. New York: Stringer and Townsend, 1854.

———. *The Pathfinder*. Vol. 3 of *'Leather-Stocking' Tales*, 5 vols. in 1. New York: Appleton, 1873.

———. *The Pathfinder*. Vol. 3 of *The Works of James Fenimore Cooper*, Mohawk ed., 33 vols. New York: G. P. Putnam's Sons, 1895.

———. *The Pathfinder*. Vol. 10 of *The Works of James Fenimore Cooper*, 10 vols. London: Richard Bentley, 1854.

———. *The Pathfinder*. Vol. 13 of *Cooper's Works*. New York: Stringer and Townsend, 1853.

———. *The Pathfinder; or, The Inland Sea*. London: Richard Bentley, 1840.

———. *The Pathfinder, or, The Inland Sea*. New York: James G. Gregory, 1864.

———. *The Pathfinder; or, The Inland Sea*. Philadelphia: Lea and Blanchard, 1840.

———. *The Pathfinder, or, The Inland Sea*. Edited by Richard Dilworth Rust. Approved ed. Albany: State University of New York Press, 1981.

———. *The Pathfinder, or, The Inland Sea*. Illustrated by Felix Octavius Carr Darley. New York: W. A. Townsend, 1860.

———. *The Pathfinder, or, The Inland Sea*. Illustrated ed. London: Frederick Warne, ca. 1900.

———. *The Pathfinder, or, The Inland Sea*. Introduction by Susan Fenimore Cooper. Household ed. Vol. 3 of *The Leatherstocking Tales*, 5 vols. Boston: Houghton, Mifflin; Cambridge: Riverside, 1876.

———. *The Pathfinder, or, The Inland Sea*. Vol. 3 of *Cooper's Leather Stocking Tales*, 5 vols. New York: Hurd and Houghton, 1869.

———. *The Pathfinder, or, The Inland Sea*. Vol. 4 of *The Choice Works of Cooper: Revised and Corrected Series: With New Introductions, Notes, etc.*, 34 vols. New York: Stringer and Townsend, 1856.

———. *The Pathfinder, or, The Inland Sea*. Vol. 6 of *The Works of J. Fenimore Cooper*, 12 vols. New York: George P. Putnam, 1851.

———. *The Pathfinder, or, The Inland Sea*. Vol. 7 of *Cooper's Novels*, 32 vols. Illustrated by Felix Octavius Carr Darley. New York: James G. Gregory (successor to W. A. Townsend), 1864.

Bibliography   209

———. *The Pathfinder, or, The Inland Sea.* Vol. 10 of *Cooper's Novels*, 18 vols. London: George Routledge and Sons, 1866.

———. *The Pathfinder, or, The Inland Sea.* Vol. 13 of *Cooper's Works*, 33 vols. New York: Stringer and Townsend, 1852.

———. *The Pathfinder, or, The Inland Sea, a Tale.* Introduction by Susan Fenimore Cooper. Riverside ed. Vol. 3 of *The Leatherstocking Tales*, 5 vols. Boston: Houghton, Mifflin, 1898.

———. *The Pathfinder, or, The Inland Sea. By the Author of "The Pioneers" etc.* Standard novels, no. 90. London: Richard Bentley, 1843.

———. *The Pathfinder, or, The Inland Sea: By the Author of "The Pioneers" etc.* London: G. Routledge, 1855.

———. *The Pathfinder, or, The Inland Sea: By the Author of "The Pioneers" etc.* London: Frederick Warne, 1867.

———. *The Pathfinder, or, The Inland Sea: By the Author of "The Pioneers" etc.* Warne's "Crown" library, no. 18. London: Frederick Warne, 1887.

———. *The Pathfinder, or, The Inland Sea: By the Author of "The Pioneers" etc.* New York: James G. Gregory, 1863.

———. *The Pathfinder, or, The Inland Sea: By the Author of 'The Pioneers,' 'The Last of the Mohicans,' 'The Prairie,' &C.* Standard novels, no. 90. London: R. Bentley, 1850.

———. *The Pathfinder, or The Inland Sea: Complete in 1 Vol.* New York: Putnam, 1852.

———. *The Pioneers, The Last of the Mohicans: The Prairie; The Pathfinder.* London: Routledge, 1867.

———. *The Prairie: A Tale.* Philadelphia: Carey, Lea and Carey, 1827.

———. *Precaution: A Novel.* New York: A. T. Goodrich, 1820.

———. *The Spy: A Tale of the Neutral Ground.* New York: Wiley and Halsted, 1821.

———. *The Wept of Wish-ton-Wish: A Tale.* Philadelphia: Carey, Lea and Carey, 1829.

———. *The Works of James Fenimore Cooper.* 32 vols. New York: Hurd and Houghton, 1868–72.

Cottin, Madame (Sophie). *Elizabeth, or, The Exiles of Siberia: A Tale Founded upon Facts: From the French of Madame Cottin.* 3rd ed. London: S. A. and H. Oddy, 1809.

Coward, David. *A History of French Literature: From* Chanson de geste *to Cinema.* Oxford: Blackwell, 2002.

———. "Popular Fiction in the Nineteenth Century." In *The Cambridge Companion to the French Novel: From 1800 to the Present*, edited by Timothy A. Unwin, 73–92. Cambridge: Cambridge University Press, 1997.

Crane, Ronald S. *Critics and Criticism: Essays in Method.* Abridged ed. Chicago: University of Chicago Press, 1957.

Crawford, Marion Ayton. Introduction to *Old Goriot*, by Honoré de Balzac, 5–24. Translated by Marion Ayton Crawford. Harmondsworth: Penguin Books, 1983.

Criminal Trials: Illustrative of the Tale Entitled 'The Heart of Mid-Lothian' Published from the Original Record, With a Prefatory Notice, Including Some Particulars of the Life of Captain John Porteous. Edinburgh: Constable, 1818.

Croker, John Wilson. Review of *Waverley, or 'Tis Sixty Years Since*, by Walter Scott. In Howard, *Waverley*, 481–83. First published in *Quarterly Review*, July 1814.

210 *Bibliography*

Croxall, Samuel. Preface to *A Select Collection of Novels*. In Nixon, *Novel Definitions*, 224–25. First published in *A Select Collection of Novels*, 6 vols. London: John Watts, 1720–22.

Darwin, Erasmus. "Polite Literature." In Nixon, *Novel Definitions*, 245–47. First published in Erasmus Darwin, *A Plan for the Conduct of Female Education, in Boarding Schools*. Derby: J. Drewry and J. Johnson, 1797.

Davidson, Cathy N. *Revolution and the Word: The Rise of the Novel in America*. New York: Oxford University Press, 1986.

Davis, Blanche Elizabeth. "The Hero in American Drama 1787–1900; A Critical Appraisal of American Dramas Through a Consideration of the Hero." PhD diss., Columbia University, 1950.

De Certeau, Michel. *The Practice of Everyday Life*. Translated by Steven Rendall. Berkeley: University of California Press, 1988.

Defoe, Daniel. Preface to *The Farther Adventures of Robinson Crusoe*. In Nixon, *Novel Definitions*, 65–66. First published in Daniel Defoe, *The Farther Adventures of Robinson Crusoe, Being the Second and Last Part of His Life*. London: W. Taylor, 1719.

———. Preface to *Robinson Crusoe*. In Nixon, *Novel Definitions*, 65. First published in Daniel Defoe, *The Life and Strange Surprizing Adventures of Robinson Crusoe, of York, Mariner*. London: W. Taylor, 1719.

De Groot, Jerome. *The Historical Novel*. London: Routledge, 2010.

Dekker, George. *The American Historical Romance*. Cambridge: Cambridge University Press, 1987.

———. *James Fenimore Cooper: The American Scott*. New York: Barnes and Noble, 1967.

———. *James Fenimore Cooper: The Novelist*. London: Routledge and Kegan Paul, 1967.

Deschamps, Nicole. "Les 'Anciens Canadiens' de 1860: une société de seigneurs et de va-nu-pieds." *Études françaises* 1, no. 3 (October 1965): 3–15. doi: 10.7202/036198ar.

Devey, Joseph. *A Comparative Estimate of Modern English Poets*. London: E. Moxon, Sons, and Co., 1873. https://archive.org/details/comparativeestim00deveuoft.

Devine, Tom M. *The Scottish Nation, 1700–2000*. 1st American ed. New York: Penguin Books, 2001.

Dibdin, Thomas. *The Heart of Mid-Lothian; or, The Lily of St. Leonard's: A Melo-Dramatic Romance, in Three Acts. From 'Tales of My Landlord.' First Performed at the Surrey Theatre, on Wednesday, January 13, 1819. By T. Dibdin, Author of the Metrical History of England, and Many Dramatic Pieces*. 2nd ed. London: Robert Stodart, 1819.

Dickenson, Donna. Introduction to *The Miller of Angibault*, by George Sand, vii–xvii. Translated by Donna Dickenson. Oxford: Oxford University Press, 1995.

Doležel, Lubomír. *Possible Worlds of Fiction and History: The Postmodern Stage*. Baltimore, MD: Johns Hopkins University Press, 2010.

Doucette, Leonard E. "Drama in French." In *The Oxford Companion to Canadian Theatre*, edited by Eugene Benson and Leonard W. Connolly, 169–82. Toronto: Oxford University Press, 1989.

———. *Theatre in French Canada: Laying the Foundations, 1606–1867*. Toronto: University of Toronto Press, 1984.

Bibliography   211

Doutre, Joseph. *Les fiancés de 1812: essai de littérature canadienne*. Montréal: Réédition-Québec, 1969.

Dramatic Tales and Romances: Pantomimes. London: J. Duncombe, n.d., ca. 1817–36.

Dubosq, Emmanuel. "Aventure, idéologie et représentation du monde indien chez Gustave Aimard." MA thesis, Université de Caen, 2003. http://docplayer.fr/14464392-Aventure-ideologie-et-representation-du-monde-indien-chez-gustave-aimard.html.

Duffy, Dennis. *Sounding the Iceberg: An Essay on Canadian Historical Novels*. Toronto: ECW Press, 1986.

Duncan, Ian. *Modern Romance and Transformations of the Novel: The Gothic, Scott, Dickens*. Cambridge: Cambridge University Press, 1992.

———. *Scott's Shadow: The Novel in Romantic Edinburgh*. Princeton, NJ: Princeton University Press, 2007.

———. "The Trouble with Man: Scott, Romance, and World History in the Age of Lamarck." In *Romantic Circles Praxis Series: Romantic Frictions*, edited by Theresa M. Kelley (September 2011): n. pag. www.rc.umd.edu/praxis/frictions/HTML/praxis.2011.duncan.html.

———. "*Waverley* (Walter Scott, 1814)." In *Forms and Themes*, edited by Franco Moretti, 173–80. Vol. 2 of *The Novel*, edited by Franco Moretti. Princeton, NJ: Princeton University Press, 2006.

Durand. *De la condition des ouvriers de Paris, de 1789 jusqu'en 1841, avec quelques idées sur la possibilité de l'améliorer*. Paris: J. B. Gros, 1841. http://gallica.bnf.fr/ark:/12148/bpt6k6465840n/f1.image.r=histoire%20des%20ouvriers.

Durham, John George Lambton. *Lord Durham's Report: An Abridgement of Report on the Affairs of British North America*. Edited by Gerald M. Craig. Toronto: McClelland and Stewart, 1963.

Eliot, George. *Felix Holt, the Radical*. Edited by William Baker and Kenneth Womack. Peterborough, ON: Broadview Press, 2000.

Ellis, Edward. *Seth Jones, or, The Captive of the Frontier*. Beadle's dime novels, no. 8. New York: Beadle, 1860.

Ellis, George. *Specimens of Early English Metrical Romances, Chiefly Written During the Early Part of the Fourteenth Century: To Which Is Prefixed an Historical Introduction Intended to Illustrate the Rise and Progress of Romantic Compositions In France and England*. 3 vols. London: Longman, Hurst, Rees, and Orme, 1805.

Ferris, Ina. *The Achievement of Literary Authority: Gender, History, and the Waverley Novels*. Ithaca, NY: Cornell University Press, 1991.

Ferry, Gabriel. *Le coureur des bois, ou, les chercheurs d'or*. New ed. Paris: Librairie illustrée, 1850.

Feuchtwanger, Lion. *The House of Desdemona; or, The Laurels and Limitations of Historical Fiction*. Translated by Harold A. Basilius. Detroit, MI: Wayne State University Press, 1963.

Finley, C. Stephen. "Scott, Ruskin, and the Landscape of Autobiography." *Studies in Romanticism* 26 (Winter 1987): 549–72.

Fleishman, Avrom. *The English Historical Novel: Walter Scott to Virginia Woolf*. Baltimore, MD: Johns Hopkins Press, 1971.

Fluck, Winfried. "The Nineteenth-Century Historical Novel." In *Cambridge History of the American Novel*, edited by Leonard Cassuto, Clare Eby, and Benjamin Reiss, 117–34. New York: Cambridge University Press, 2011.

212   Bibliography

Ford, Ford Madox. *The English Novel*. Philadelphia: J. B. Lippincott, 1929.

Fortassier, Rose. Introduction to *Le père Goriot*, by Honoré de Balzac, 3–36. In vol. 3 of *La comédie humaine*, edited by Pierre-George Castex. Paris: Gallimard, 1976.

Frappier-Mazur, Lucienne. "Les échecs: jeu et société." In Gengembre, *Le père Goriot*, 323.

Frank, Armin Paul. "Writing Literary Independence: The Case of Cooper-the 'American Scott' and the Un-Scottish American." *Comparative Literature Studies* 34, no. 1 (1997): 41–70.

Franklin, Wayne. Introduction to *The Pathfinder*, by James Fenimore Cooper, ix–xxvi. Edited by Wayne Franklin. Cambridge, MA: Belknap Press of Harvard University Press, 2014.

———. "James Fenimore Cooper, 1789–1851: A Brief Biography." In *A Historical Guide to James Fenimore Cooper*, edited by Leland S. Person, 27–57. Oxford: Oxford University Press, 2007.

———. "James Fenimore Cooper and the Invention of the American Novel." In Samuels, *American Fiction*, 411–24.

"From the Periodical Archives: Ann S. Stephens's 'The Jockey Cap' – The First Version of 'Malaeska.'" *American Periodicals* 18, no. 1 (2008): 101–6.

Frye, Northrop. *Anatomy of Criticism: Four Essays*. Princeton, NJ: Princeton University Press, 1957.

Galbraith, John. *In the New Capital: A Nineteenth-Century View of Ottawa in the Twenty-First Century*. Edited by R. D. Francis. Manotick, ON: Penumbra Press, 2000.

Gamer, Michael. *Romanticism and the Gothic: Genre, Reception, and Canon Formation*. Cambridge: Cambridge University Press, 2000.

Gardiner, William H. "Review of *The Spy*, by James Fenimore Cooper." *North American Review* 15 (July 1822): 250–82. www.jstor.org/stable/25109145.

Garneau, François-Xavier. *Histoire du Canada depuis sa découverte jusqu'à nos jours*. Québec: Napoléon Aubin, 1845–52.

Garside, Peter D. "Scott and the 'Philosophical' Historians." *Journal of the History of Ideas* 36, no. 3 (September 1975): 497–512.

———. "Walter Scott and the 'Common' Novel, 1808–1819." *Cardiff Corvey: Reading the Romantic Text* 3 (September 1999): n. pag. www.romtext.org.uk/articles/cc03_n02/.

———. "*Waverley* and the National Fiction Revolution." In Bell, Finkelstein, and McCleery, *Ambition and Industry 1800–80*, 222–31.

Garside, Peter D., Ruth M. McAdams, Paul Barnaby, Bill Bell, and Andrew Grout. *Illustrating Scott*. Edinburgh: University of Edinburgh, 2009. http://illustrating scott.lib.ed.ac.uk/index.html.

Gengembre, Gérard. "Upstairs, Downstairs." In Gengembre, *Le père Goriot*, 133.

———, ed. *Le père Goriot*. Paris: Magnard, 1985.

George, Henry. *Progress and Poverty: An Inquiry into the Cause of Industrial Depressions and of Increase of Want with Increase of Wealth: The Remedy*. Author's ed. San Francisco, CA: W. M. Hinton, 1879.

Gérin-Lajoie, Antoine. *Jean Rivard*. Translated by Vida Bruce. Toronto: McClelland and Stewart, 1977.

———. "Jean Rivard, économiste." In *Le Foyer canadien* 2 (1864): 15–371.

Bibliography 213

———. "Jean Rivard, le défricheur canadien." In *Les Soirées canadiennes* 2 (1862): 65–319.

———. *Le jeune Latour: tragédie en trois actes*. Montréal: n.p., 1845.

Gerson, Carole. *A Purer Taste: The Writing and Reading of Fiction in English in Nineteenth-Century Canada*. Toronto: University of Toronto Press, 1989.

Giddens, Anthony. *The Consequences of Modernity*. 1st paperback ed. Cambridge: Polity Press, 1991.

———. *A Contemporary Critique of Historical Materialism*. 2nd ed. Houndmills: Palgrave Macmillan, 1995.

Giles, Paul. "Transatlantic Currents and the Invention of the American Novel." In *Cambridge History of the American Novel*, edited by Leonard Cassuto, Clare Eby, and Benjamin Reiss, 22–36. New York: Cambridge University Press, 2011.

Gilmore, Michael T. Introduction to *Early American Literature: A Collection of Essays*, edited by Michael T. Gilmore, 1–10. Englewood Cliffs, NJ: Prentice Hall, 1980.

Godwin, William. *Caleb Williams*. Edited by Gary J. Handwerk and Arnold A. Markley. Peterborough, ON: Broadview Press, 2000. First published as *Things as They Are; or, The Adventures of Caleb Williams*. London: B. Crosby, 1794.

———. "Of History and Romance." In *Caleb Williams*, edited by Gary Handwerk and Arnold A. Markley, 453–67. Peterborough, ON: Broadview Press, 2000.

———. *St. Leon: A Tale of the Sixteenth Century*. Edited by William D. Brewer. Peterborough, ON: Broadview Press, 2006. First published London: G. G. and J. Robinson, 1799.

GoGwilt, Christopher. "The Novel and the Nation." In *A Companion to the English Novel*, edited by Stephen Arata, Madigan Haley, J. Paul Hunter, and Jennifer Wicke, 441–55. Hoboken, NJ: Wiley-Blackwell, 2015.

Goldsmith, Oliver. *Deserted Village: A Poem*. 5th ed. London: W. Griffin, 1770.

Gordon, Catherine. "The Illustration of Sir Walter Scott: Nineteenth-Century Enthusiasm and Adaptation." *Journal of the Warburg and Courtauld Institutes* 34 (1971): 297–317.

Gould, Philip. *Covenant and Republic: Historical Romance and the Politics of Puritanism*. Cambridge: Cambridge University Press, 1996.

Green, James N. "The Rise of Book Publishing." In Gross and Kelley, *An Extensive Republic*, 75–127.

Green, Sarah. Preface to *Romance Readers and Romance Writers*. In Nixon, *Novel Definitions*, 96–98. First published in Sarah Green, *Romance Readers and Romance Writers: A Satirical Novel*, 3 vols. London: T. Hookham, Junior and E. Hookham, 1810.

Grey, Francis. *The Curé of St Philippe: A Story of French-Canadian Politics*. Toronto: McClelland and Stewart, 1970.

Grimes, E. Margaret. "Philippe Aubert de Gaspé, Historian and Biographer of Canadians of Former Days." *The French Review* 11, no. 1 (October 1937): 12–24. www.jstor.org/stable/379238.

Grodenk. *My Own Story: A Canadian Christmas Tale*. Toronto: A. S. Irving, 1869. https://archive.org/details/cihm_06368.

Gross, Robert A. "Introduction: An Extensive Republic." In Gross and Kelley, *An Extensive Republic*, 1–50.

Gross, Robert A., and Mary Kelley, eds. *An Extensive Republic: Print, Culture, and Society in the New Nation, 1790–1840*. Vol. 2 of *A History of the Book*

214   Bibliography

in America, edited by David D. Hall. Chapel Hill: University of North Carolina Press, 2010.

Groves, Jeffrey D. "Trade Communication." In Casper et al., *The Industrial Book, 1840–1880*, 130–39.

Guilds, John Caldwell. "The 'Untrodden Path': *Richard Hurdis* and Simms's Foray into Literary Realism." In *William Gilmore Simms and the American Frontier*, edited by John Caldwell Guilds and Caroline Collins, 47–54. Athens: University of Georgia Press, 1997.

Hamm, Jean-Jacques. "De Télémaque à Rastignac (suite)." In Gengembre, *Le père Goriot*, 319.

Hamnett, Brian R. *The Historical Novel in Nineteenth-Century Europe: Representations of Reality in History and Fiction*. Oxford: Oxford University Press, 2011.

Harris, Edward. "Cooper on Stage." In *James Fenimore Cooper Society Website*, edited by Hugh C. Macdougall (webmaster), n. pag. Oneonta: State University of New York College, 1999. http://external.oneonta.edu/cooper/drama/stage. html. Originally issued on disk as *James Fenimore Cooper Society Miscellaneous Papers*, Electronic series, no. 1.

Harris, Mark Wayne, and Ray Lago. *Ivanhoe*. In *Classics Illustrated*, no. 25. New York: Berkley; Chicago: First Publishing, 1991.

Harris, Roy. *Introduction to Integrational Linguistics*. 1st ed. Kidlington, Oxford, UK: Pergamon, 1998.

———. *The Linguistics of History*. Edinburgh: Edinburgh University Press, 2004.

———. *Signs, Language and Communication. Integrational and Segregational Approaches*. London: Routledge, 1996.

Hart, James D. *The Popular Book: A History of America's Literary Taste*. New York: Oxford University Press, 1950.

Harthorn, Steven P. "*The Pathfinder* and Cooper's Return to Popular Literature." In *Leather-Stocking Redux, or, Old Tales, New Essays*, edited by Jeffrey Walker, 193–224. New York: AMS Press, 2011.

Harvie, Christopher. *Scotland and Nationalism, Scottish Society and Politics: 1707–1994*. 2nd ed. London: Routledge, 1994.

Hayne, David M. "The Historical Novel and French Canada." MA thesis, University of Ottawa, 1945. Microfilm.

Haynes, Christine. *Lost Illusions: The Politics of Publishing in Nineteenth-Century France*. Cambridge, MA: Harvard University Press, 2010.

Haywood, Eliza. Preface to *The Fortunate Foundlings*. In Nixon, *Novel Definitions*, 70–71. First published in Eliza Haywood, *The Fortunate Foundlings: Being the Genuine History of Colonel M – rs, and His Sister, Madam Du P – y, the Issue of the Hon. Ch – es M – rs, Son of the late Duke of R – l – d*. London: T. Gardner, 1744.

The Heart of Mid-Lothian. Alnwick: W. Davison, n.d.

The Heart of Mid-Lothian; or, The Lily of St. Leonard's. Edinburgh: Caw and Elder; Alex. Peat, n.d., ca. 1819?.

The Heart of Mid Lothian; or The Lily of St. Leonard, a Caledonian Tale of Great Interest. London: Company of Booksellers, 1822.

Helsinger, Elizabeth K. *Ruskin and the Art of the Beholder*. Cambridge, MA: Harvard University Press, 1982.

Henderson, Andrea K. *Romantic Identities: Varieties of Subjectivity, 1774–1830*. Cambridge: Cambridge University Press, 1996.

Bibliography 215

Henderson, Harry B. *Versions of the Past: The Historical Imagination in American Fiction*. New York: Oxford University Press, 1974.

Hewitt, David, ed. *Edinburgh Edition of the Waverley Novels*. Edinburgh: Edinburgh University Press, 1993–2012.

Hewitt, David, and Alison Lumsden. "Essay on the Text." In *The Heart of Mid-Lothian*, edited by David Hewitt and Alison Lumsden, 471–528. Edinburgh: Edinburgh University Press, 2009.

Hobsbawn, E. J. *The Age of Revolution: Europe, 1789–1848*. London: Weidenfeld and Nicolson, 1962.

Hoggart, Richard. *The Uses of Literacy: Aspects of Working Class Life, With Special Reference to Publications and Entertainments*. Harmondsworth: Penguin Books, 1957.

Holman, C. Hugh. "The Influence of Scott and Cooper on Simms." In *The Roots of Southern Writing: Essays on the Literature of the American South*, 50–60. Athens: University of Georgia Press, 1972.

———. "The Status of Simms." *American Quarterly* 10 (Summer 1958): 181–85.

Horkheimer, Max, and Theodor W. Adorno. *Dialectic of Enlightenment*. Translated by John Cumming. New York: Continuum, 2000.

Howard, Susan Kubica, ed. *Waverley, or 'Tis Sixty Years Since*, by Walter Scott. Peterborough, ON: Broadview Press, 2010.

Huet, Pierre-Dabiel. From *The History of Romances*. Translated by Stephen Lewis. In Nixon, *Novel Definitions*, 336–42. First published in Pierre-Dabiel Huet, *The History of Romances. An Enquiry into their Origins; Instructions for Composing Them; An Account of the Most Eminent Authors; With Characters, and Curious Observations upon the Best Performances of that Kind*, translated by Stephen Lewis. London: J. Hooke and T. Caldecott, 1715.

Ivanhoe. In *Classic Comics*, no. 2. New York: Gilberton, 1941.

Jeanie Deans, and the Lily of St Leonard's. London: Webb, Millington, n.d.

Jeffrey, Francis. "Review of *Waverley, or 'Tis Sixty Years Since*, by Walter Scott." In *Walter Scott: The Critical Heritage*, edited by John O. Hayden, 79–84. New York: Routledge, 1995. First published in Francis Jeffrey, "Review of Scott, *Waverley*," *Edinburgh Review* 24 (November 1814): 208–43.

Jenkins, John Edward. *Ginx's Baby*. N.p.: n.p., 1871. https://archive.org/details/cihm_07434.

Johannsen, Albert. *The House of Beadle and Adams and Its Dime and Nickel Novels: The Story of a Vanishing Literature*. 1st ed. 3 vols. Norman: University of Oklahoma Press, 1950.

John, Richard R. "Expanding the Realm of Communications." In Gross and Kelley, *An Extensive Republic*, 211–20.

Johnstone, Christian Isobel. *Clan Albin: A National Tale*. Edited by Andrew Monnickendam. Glasgow: Association for Scottish Literary Studies, 2003.

Jones, William. "On Novels." In Nixon, *Novel Definitions*, 240–41. First published in William Jones, *Letters from a Tutor to his Pupils*. London: G. Robinson, 1780.

Jones, William B., Jr. *Classics Illustrated: A Cultural History*. 2nd ed. Jefferson, NC: McFarland and Company, 2011.

Kanes, Martin. *Père Goriot: Anatomy of a Troubled World*. New York: Twayne, 1993.

Karcher, Carolyn. *The First Woman in the Republic: A Cultural Biography of Lydia Maria Child*. Durham, NC: Duke University Press, 1994.

216   Bibliography

Kaser, David. *Messrs. Carey & Lea of Philadelphia; A Study in the History of the Booktrade*. Philadelphia: University of Pennsylvania Press, 1957.

———. "*Waverley* in America." *Papers of the Bibliographical Society of America* 51 (1957): 163–67.

Kealey, Gregory S. *Workers and Canadian History*. Montreal: McGill-Queen's University Press, 1995.

Kealey, Gregory S., and Bryan D. Palmer. *Dreaming of What Might Be: The Knights of Labor in Ontario, 1880–1900*. New York: Cambridge University Press, 1983.

Kelly, Gary. *The English Jacobin Novel; 1780–1805*. Oxford: Clarendon Press, 1976.

———. "Fiction and the Working Classes." In *The Cambridge Companion to Fiction in the Romantic Period*, edited by Richard Maxwell and Katie Trumpener, 207–34. Cambridge: Cambridge University Press, 2008.

———. Introduction to *Lydia Sigourney: Selected Poetry and Prose*, edited by Gary Kelly, 11–56. Peterborough, ON: Broadview Press, 2008.

Kelly, William P. *Plotting America's Past: Fenimore Cooper and the Leatherstocking Tales*. Carbondale: Southern Illinois University Press, 1983.

Kennedy, J. Gerald. "National Narrative and the Problem of American Nationhood." In Samuels, *American Fiction*, 8–19.

Kennedy, John Pendleton. *Horse Shoe Robinson: A Tale of the Tory Ascendency*. 3rd ed. Philadelphia: Carey, Lea and Blanchard, 1835.

Kerr, James. "Fiction Against History: Scott's *Redgauntlet* and the Power of Romance." *Texas Studies in Literature and Language* 29, no. 3 (Fall 1987): 237–60.

Kilcup, Karen L. "The Conversation of 'The Whole Family': Gender, Politics, and Aesthetics in Literary Tradition." In *Soft Canons: American Women Writers and Masculine Tradition*, edited by Karen L. Kilcup, 1–24. Iowa City: University of Iowa Press, 1999.

King-collect. "Classics Illustrated Comics: Identifying Reprints." *Ebay*. December 2, 2005. www.ebay.com/gds/CLASSICS-ILLUSTRATED-comic-books-IDENTIFYING-REPRINTS-/10000000000084872/g.html.

Kirby, William. *The Golden Dog: (Le chien d'or): A Romance of the Days of Louis Quinze in Quebec*. New York: Lovell, Coryell, 1877.

Knox, Vicesimus. "On the Efficacy of Moral Instruction." In Nixon, *Novel Definitions*, 234–35. First published in Vicesimus Knox, *Essays Moral and Literary . . . A New Edition*, 2 vols. London: Charles Dilly, 1782.

Kröller, Eva-Marie. "Walter Scott in America, English Canada, and Québec: A Comparison." *Canadian Revue of Comparative Literature* 7, no. 1 (Winter 1980): 32–46.

Lacombe, Patrice. *La terre paternelle*. Montréal: Fides, 1981.

Lacy, Thomas Hailes. *The Heart of Mid-Lothian; or, The Sisters of St. Leonard's. A Drama . . . in Three Acts. Adapted from Sir Walter Scott's . . . Novel, with Introductions from T. Dibdin's Play, W. Murray's Alteration of the Same, Eugene Scribe's Opera, and Dion Boucicault's Amalgamation of the Above, Colin Hazlewood's Adjustment and Re-Adjustment, J. B. Johnstone's Appropriation, and Other Equally Original Versions, Together with a Very Small Amount of New Matter, by T. H. Lacy*. London: Lacy, 1863.

Lamonde, Yvan, Patricia Lockhart Fleming, and Fiona A. Black, eds. *1840–1918*. Vol. 2 of *History of the Book in Canada*, edited by Patricia Fleming and Yvan Lamonde. Toronto: University of Toronto Press, 2004.

Bibliography 217

Lanoux, Armand, and Henri Mitterand. "Notes et variantes: Le ventre de Paris." In vol. 1 of Émile Zola, *Les Rougon-Macquart: histoire naturelle et sociale d'une famille sous le Second Empire*, edited by Armand Lanoux and Henri Mitterand, 1607–38. Paris: Bibliothèque de la Pléiade, 1960.

Laut, Agnes. *Lords of the North: A Romance of the North-West*. Toronto: Ryerson Press, 1920.

Leavis, Queenie D. *Fiction and the Reading Public*. London: Chatto and Windus, 1932.

Lee, Sophia. *The Recess, or, A Tale of Other Times*. London: Cadell, 1785.

Lemire, Maurice. "Introduction to Philippe-Joséph Aubert de Gaspé." In *Les anciens Canadiens*, edited by Aurélien Boivin, 7–76. Montréal: Les Presses de L'Université de Montréal, 2007.

Leprohon, Rosanna Mullins. *The Manor House of De Villerai: A Tale of Canada Under the French Dominion*. Edited by Andrea Cabajsky. Peterborough, ON: Broadview Press, 2015.

"Les 'Anciens Canadiens.' " *Bulletin des recherches historiques* 9, no. 8 (August 1903): 249–53. https://archive.org/details/lebulletindesrec09archuoft.

Lesperance, John. *The Bastonnais: Tale of the American Invasion of Canada in 1775–76*. Toronto: Belford, 1877. https://archive.org/details/cihm_08977.

———. "The Literary Standing of the Dominion." In *The Manor House of De Villerai: A Tale of Canada Under the French Dominion*, edited by Andrea Cabajsky, 216–31. Peterborough, ON: Broadview Press, 2015. First published in *Canadian Illustrated News*, February 24, 1877.

Levinas, Emmanuel. "Ethics as First Philosophy." In *The Levinas Reader*, edited by Seán Hand, 75–87. Malden, MA: Blackwell, 2005.

Levine, Robert S. "Race and Ethnicity." In Samuels, *American Fiction*, 52–63.

Lewis, Matthew G. *The Monk: A Romance*. London: J. Bell, 1796.

Lincoln, Andrew. *Walter Scott and Modernity*. Edinburgh: Edinburgh University Press, 2007.

Long, Robert Emmet. *James Fenimore Cooper*. New York: Continuum, 1990.

Lough, John, and Muriel Lough. *An Introduction to Nineteenth Century France*. London: Longman, 1978.

Loughran, Trish. *The Republic in Print: Print Culture in the Age of U. S. Nation Building 1770–1870*. New York: Columbia University Press, 2007.

Lubbock, Percy. *The Craft of Fiction*. London: J. Cape, 1926.

Lukács, Georg. *The Historical Novel*. Translated by Hannah and Stanley Mitchell. Lincoln: University of Nebraska Press, 1983. First published 1937 as *Történelmi regény*; first translation 1962 Merlin Press; this translation first published 1963 Beacon Press.

Lyons, Martyn. *A History of Reading and Writing: In the Western World*. Houndmills: Palgrave Macmillan, 2010.

———. *Reading Culture and Writing Practices in Nineteenth-Century France*. Toronto: University of Toronto Press, 2008.

Machar, Agnes Maule. *Roland Graeme: Knight: A Novel of Our Time*. Nepean, ON: Tecumseh Press, 1996. First published Montreal: William Drysdale, 1892; New York: Fords, Howard and Hulbert, 1892.

Mack, Douglas S. *Scottish Fiction and the British Empire*. Edinburgh: Edinburgh University Press, 2006.

218 Bibliography

Mackenzie, Henry. [from *The Lounger*, no. 20, June 18, 1975.] In Nixon, *Novel Definitions*, 235–38. First published in Henry Mackenzie, *The Lounger*, no. 20, June 18, 1785.

Manzoni, Alessandro. *On the Historical Novel*. Translated with an introduction by Sandra Bermann. Lincoln: University of Nebraska Press, 1984.

Marschner, Heinrich. *Der Templar und die Jüdin*. Libretto by W. A. Wohlbrück. Adapted by John P. Jackson. 1829.

Martineau, Harriet. *A Manchester Strike*. In *Illustrations of Political Economy: Selected Tales*, edited by Deborah Anna Logan, 137–216. Peterborough, ON: Broadview Press, 2004.

Matthews, Brander. *The Historical Novel, and Other Essays*. New York: Charles Scribner's Sons, 1901. https://archive.org/details/cu31924013355916.

Mauris, Joseph Claude. *The Heart of Mid-Lothian, A Romantic Tale, Founded on Facts*. London: J. Duncombe, 1820.

Maurois, André. *Prometheus: The Life of Balzac*. Translated by Norman Denny. London: Bodley Head, 1965.

Maxwell, Richard. *The Historical Novel in Europe, 1650–1950*. Cambridge: Cambridge University Press, 2009.

Mayer, Marianne, and John Rush. *Sir Walter Scott's Ivanhoe*. San Francisco, CA: Chronicle Books, 2004.

McCormack, A. Ross. *Reformers, Rebels, and Revolutionaries: The Western Canadian Radical Movement, 1899–1919*. Toronto: University of Toronto Press, 1977.

McCormick, John. *Theatre in Focus: Melodrama Theatres of the French Boulevard*. Cambridge: Chadwyck-Healey, 1982.

McCracken-Flesher, Caroline. *Possible Scotlands: Walter Scott and the Story of Tomorrow*. Oxford: Oxford University Press, 2005.

McElwee, Johanna. "The Nation Conceived: Learning, Education, and Nationhood in American Historical Novels of the 1820s." PhD diss., Uppsala University, 2005. www.diva-portal.org/smash/get/diva2:167469/FULLTEXT01.pdf.

McGill, Meredith L. "Copyright." In Gross and Kelley, *An Extensive Republic*, 198–211.

McGregor, Alan Leander. "The Historical Function of Historical Fiction: Walter Scott and James Fenimore Cooper." PhD diss., University of California, Berkeley, 1984.

McHoul, Alec. *Semiotic Investigations: Towards an Effective Semiotics*. Lincoln: University of Nebraska Press, 1996.

McKay, Ian. *Reasoning Otherwise: Leftists and the People's Enlightenment in Canada, 1890–1920*. Toronto: Between the Lines, 2008.

McKenzie, D. F. "The Book as an Expressive Form." In *The Book History Reader*, 2nd ed., edited by David Finkelstein and Alistair McCleery, 35–46. London: Routledge, 2002.

McNeil, Kenneth. *Scotland, Britain, Empire: Writing the Highlands, 1760–1860*. Columbus: Ohio State University Press, 2007.

McWilliams, John P. *Political Justice in a Republic: James Fenimore Cooper's America*. Berkeley: University of California Press, 1972.

———. "Revolution and the Historical Novel: Cooper's Transforming of European Tradition." In *James Fenimore Cooper Society Website*, edited by Hugh C. Macdougall (webmaster), n. pag. Oneonta: State University of New York College, 1999. http://external.oneonta.edu/cooper/articles/suny/1991suny-mcwilliams.html.

First published in *James Fenimore Cooper: His Country and His Art (No. 8)*, Papers from the 1991 Conference, edited by George A. Test, Oneonta and Cooperstown: State University of New York College, 1991, 25–36.

Millgate, Jane. *Scott's Last Edition: A Study in Publishing History*. Edinburgh: Edinburgh University Press, 1987.

Mitchell, Domhnall. "Acts of Intercourse: 'Miscegenation' in Three 19th Century American Novels." *American Studies in Scandinavia* 27, no. 2 (1995): 126–41. http://rauli.cbs.dk/index.php/assc/article/view/1462/1474.

———. "Authority in Fenimore Cooper's 'The Pathfinder.'" *American Studies in Scandinavia* 24, no. 2 (1992): 97–109. https://ej.lib.cbs.dk/index.php/assc/article/view/2610.

Mitchell, Jerome. *More Walter Scott Operas: Further Analyses of Operas Based on the Works of Sir Walter Scott*. Lanham, MD: University Press of America, 1996.

———. *The Walter Scott Operas: An Analysis of Operas Based on the Works of Sir Walter Scott*. University: University of Alabama Press, 1977.

———. "L'assommoir: Notice." In vol. 2 of Émile Zola, *Les Rougon-Macquart: histoire naturelle et sociale d'une famille sous le Second Empire*, edited by Armand Lanoux, 1532–1601. Paris: Bibliothèque de la Pléiade, 1961.

Mitterand, Henri. "Germinal: Étude." In vol. 3 of Émile Zola, *Les Rougon-Macquart: histoire naturelle et sociale d'une famille sous le Second Empire*, edited by Armand Lanoux, 1802–1938. Paris: Bibliothèque de la Pléiade, 1964.

———. "La terre: Étude." In vol. 4 of Émile Zola, *Les Rougon-Macquart: histoire naturelle et sociale d'une famille sous le Second Empire*, edited by Armand Lanoux, 1487–1608. Paris: Bibliothèque de la Pléiade, 1966.

Monarque, Georges. *Blanche d'Haberville; drame en cinq actes en vers*. Montréal: Librairie d'Action canadienne-française, 1931.

Monnickendam, Andrew. Introduction to *Clan Albin: A National Tale*, by Christian Isobel Johnstone, v–xxi. Edited by Andrew Monnickendam. Glasgow: Association for Scottish Literary Studies, 2003.

Moodie, Susanna. *Roughing It in the Bush, or, Life in Canada*. London: R. Bentley, 1852.

Moody, Jane. *Illegitimate Theatre in London, 1770–1840*. Cambridge: Cambridge University Press, 2000.

Moore, John. "A View of the Commencement and Progress of Romance." In Nixon, *Novel Definitions*, 358–61. First published in John Moore, ed., *The Works of Tobias Smollett, M.D. With Memoirs of His Life; To Which Is Prefixed a View of the Commencement and Progress of Romance*, 8 vols. London: B. Law, J. Johnson, C. Dilley, G. G. and J. Robinson, R. Baldwin, T. Becket, F. and C. Rivington, A. Strahan, F. Faulder, W. Richardson, W. Lance, W. Lowdnes, S. Hayes, G. and T. Wilkie, Ogilvy and Son, T. N. Longman, and Cadell jun. and Davies, 1797.

Moore, J. Quitman. "William Gilmore Simms." *DeBow's Review* 29, no. 6 (December 1860): 702–12.

Moretti, Franco. *Atlas of the European Novel, 1800–1900*. London: Verso, 1998.

Morgan, Lady (Sydney Owenson). *The Wild Irish Girl: A National Tale*. London: R. Phillips, 1806.

Morgan, Peter F. "Ruskin and Scott's Ethical Greatness." In *Scott and His Influence: The Papers of the Aberdeen Scott Conference, 1982*, edited by John H. Alexander and David Hewitt, 403–13. Aberdeen: Association for Scottish Literary Studies, 1983.

220   Bibliography

Muir, Edwin. *The Structure of the Novel*. London: Hogarth, 1928.

Murray, Padmini Ray. "Religion." In Bell, Finkelstein, and McCleery, *Ambition and Industry 1800–80*, 287–95.

Nakamura, Masahiro. *Visions of Order in William Gilmore Simms: Southern Conservatism and the Other American Romance*. Columbia: University of South Carolina Press, 2009.

Nelson, Dana D. "Cooper's Leatherstocking Conversations: Identity, Friendship, and Democracy in the New Nation." In *A Historical Guide to James Fenimore Cooper*, edited by Leland S. Person, 123–54. Oxford: Oxford University Press, 2007.

Neuburg, Victor E. *The Penny Histories: A Study of Chapbooks for Young Readers Over Two Centuries*. London: Oxford University Press, 1968.

Nixon, Cheryl L., ed. *Novel Definitions: An Anthology of Commentary on the Novel, 1688–1815*. Peterborough, ON: Broadview Press, 2009.

Odell, George Clinton Densmore, ed. *Annals of the New York Stage*. 15 vols. New York: Columbia University Press, 1927–49.

Olivero, Isabelle. "The Paperback Revolution in France, 1850–1950." In *Authors, Publishers and the Shaping of Taste*, edited by John Spiers, 72–87. Vol. 1 of *The Culture of the Publisher's Series*, edited by John Spiers, 2 vols. New York: Palgrave Macmillan, 2011.

Opfermann, Susanne. "Lydia Maria Child, James Fenimore Cooper, and Catharine Maria Sedgwick: A Dialogue on Race, Culture, and Gender." In *Soft Canons: American Women Writers and Masculine Tradition*, edited by Karen L. Kilcup, 27–47. Iowa City: University of Iowa Press, 1999.

Orwell, George. *Nineteen Eighty-Four: A Novel*. London: Secker and Warburg, 1949.

Owen, William. "In War as in Love: The Significance of Analogous Plots in Cooper's *The Pathfinder*." *English Studies in Canada* 10, no. 3 (1984): 289–98.

Pacini, Giovanni. *Ivanhoe*. Libretto by Gaetano Rossi. 1832.

Page, Eugene R. Introduction to "The Spy, A Tale of the Neutral Ground." In *Metamora and Other Plays*, edited by Eugene R. Page, 59–60. Princeton, NJ: Princeton University Press, 1941.

Pagel, Carol Anne Ryan. "A History and Analysis of Representative American Dramatizations from American Novels 1800–1860." PhD diss., University of Denver, 1970.

Paine, Thomas. *Rights of Man*. Edited by Claire Grogan. Peterborough, ON: Broadview Press, 2011.

Palmer, Bryan D. *Culture in Conflict: Skilled Workers and Industrial Capitalism in Hamilton, Ontario, 1860–1914*. Montreal: McGill-Queen's University Press, 1979.

Parent-Lardeur, Françoise. *Les cabinets de lecture: la lecture publique à Paris sous la restauration*. Paris: Payot, 1982.

Parker, Elizabeth, Eleanor Smith, Eliza Sinclaire, and Jane Lewis. [Students' Prizewinning Essays on "The Love of Novels."] In Nixon, *Novel Definitions*, 251–57. First published in *The Juvenile Library, Including a Complete Course of Instruction on Every Useful Subject*, vol. 1. London: T. Gillet, 1800.

Parker, Gilbert. *The Seats of the Mighty; Being the Memoirs of Captain Robert Moray, Sometime an Officer in the Virginia Regiment, and Afterwards of Amherst's Regiment*. Toronto: McClelland and Stewart, 1971.

Bibliography 221

Parsons, Coleman O. "Chapbook Versions of the Waverley Novels." *Studies in Scottish Literature* 3, no. 4 (April 1966): 189–220.

Partridge, Eric. "Fenimore Cooper's Influence on the French Romantics." *Modern Language Review* 20, no. 2 (April 1925): 174–78. doi: 10.2307/3714204.

Pederson, Susan. "Hannah More Meets Simple Simon: Tracts, Chapbooks, and Popular Culture in Late Eighteenth-Century England." *The Journal of British Studies* 25, no. 1 (January 1986): 84–113. www.jstor.org/stable/175612.

Pegge, Samuel (the Elder). [from *Gentlemen's Magazine*, no. 37, December 1767.] In Nixon, *Novel Definitions*, 239–40. First published in "T. Row," *Gentlemen's Magazine*, no. 37, December 1767.

Perron, Paul. *Narratology and Text: Subjectivity and Identity in New France and Québécois Literature.* Toronto: University of Toronto Press, 2003.

Phillips, Mark Salber. *Society and Sentiment: Genres of Historical Writing in Britain, 1740–1820.* Princeton, NJ: Princeton University Press, 2000.

Pierrot, Roger. *Honoré de Balzac.* Paris: Fayard, 1994.

Piketty, Thomas. *Capital in the Twenty-First Century.* Translated by Arthur Goldhammer. Cambridge, MA: The Belknap Press of Harvard University Press, 2014.

Pilbeam, Pamela M. *Republicanism in Nineteenth-Century France, 1814–1871.* New York: St. Martin's Press, 1995.

Pittock, Murray, ed. *The Reception of Sir Walter Scott in Europe.* London: Continuum, 2006.

Plant, Richard. "Drama in English." In *The Oxford Companion to Canadian Theatre*, edited by Eugene Benson and Leonard W. Connolly, 148–69. Toronto: Oxford University Press, 1989.

Popkin, Jeremy D. *A History of Modern France.* 3rd ed. Upper Saddle River, NJ: Pearson/Prentice Hall, 2006.

Porter, Jane. *The Scottish Chiefs: A Romance.* London: Longman's, 1810.

Price, Fiona. *Reinventing Liberty: Nation, Commerce and the Historical Novel from Walpole to Scott.* Edinburgh: Edinburgh University Press, 2016.

Pynchon, Thomas. *Gravity's Rainbow.* New York: Viking Press, 1973.

Ramsey, Colin T., and Kathryn Zabelle Derounian-Stodola. "Dime Novels." In Samuels, *American Fiction*, 262–73.

Rance, Nicholas. *The Historical Novel and Popular Politics in Nineteenth-Century England.* London: Vision Press, 1975.

Rans, Geoffrey. *Cooper's Leather-Stocking Novels: A Secular Reading.* Chapel Hill: University of North Carolina Press, 1991.

Raser, George Bernard. *The Heart of Balzac's Paris.* Choisy-le-Roi: Imp. de France, 1970.

Raudsepp, Enn. "Patriotism and Class Interest in *Les Anciens Canadiens*." *Journal of Canadian Fiction* 30 (1980): 106–13.

Reeve, Clara. Preface to *The School for Widows.* In Nixon, *Novel Definitions*, 132–33. First published in Clara Reeve, *The School for Widows. A Novel*, 3 vols. London: T. Hookham, Harrison and Co., and W. Miller, 1791.

———. *The Progress of Romance Through Times, Countries, and Manners: With Remarks on the Good and Bad Effects of It, on Them Respectively in a Course of Evening Conversations.* 2 vols. Colchester: W. Keymer, 1785.

Reid, Mayne. *The Free Lances: A Romance of the Mexican Valley.* London: Routledge and Sons, 1905.

222   Bibliography

―――. *The Rifle-Rangers, or, Adventures in Southern Mexico*. London: W. Shoberl, 1850.

―――. *The Scalp Hunters: A Romance of the Plains*. New York: Beadle and Adams, 1875.

Rémond, René. *The Right Wing in France: From 1815 to de Gaulle*. Translated by James M. Laux. 2nd American ed. Philadelphia: University of Pennsylvania Press, 1969.

Review of *Waverley, or 'Tis Sixty Years Since*, by Walter Scott. In Howard, *Waverley*, 493–95. First published in *Monthly Review*, 2nd ser., 75 (November 1814): 275–89.

Review of *Waverley, or 'Tis Sixty Years Since*, by Walter Scott. In Howard, *Waverley*, 495. First published in *Critical Review*, 5th ser., 1 (March 1815): 288–97.

Richards, Ivor A. *Principles of Literary Criticism*. 4th ed. New York: Harcourt, Brace, 1930.

Richards, Jeffrey H. *Drama, Theatre, and Identity in the American New Republic*. Cambridge: Cambridge University Press, 2005.

―――. *Theatre Enough: American Culture and the Metaphor of the World Stage, 1607–1789*. Durham, NC: Duke University Press, 1991.

Richardson, John. *Wacousta; or, The Prophecy: A Tale of the Canadas*. Toronto: McClelland and Stewart, 2008.

Richardson, Samuel. Preface to *Pamela*. In Nixon, *Novel Definitions*, 67–70. First published in Samuel Richardson, *Pamela; or, Virtue Rewarded. In a Series of Familiar Letters from a Beautiful Young Damsel, to Her Parents*. London: S. Richardson, 1740.

Rigney, Ann. *The Afterlives of Walter Scott: Memory on the Move*. Oxford: Oxford University Press, 2012.

Ringe, Donald A., and Lucy B. Ringe. "Historical Introduction." In James Fenimore Cooper, *Lionel Lincoln; or, The Leaguer of Boston*, edited by Donald A. Ringe and Lucy B. Ringe, xv–xl. Albany: State University of New York Press, 1984.

Robins, Madeleine, ed., and Norman Nodel, illustr. *Classics Illustrated: Sir Walter Scott: Ivanhoe*. New York: Acclaim Books, 1997.

Rogers, Pat. *Literature and Popular Culture in Eighteenth Century England*. Sussex: Harvester Press; New Jersey, NJ: Barnes and Noble Books, 1985.

Rossini, Gioacchino. *Ivanhoé*. Libretto by Émile Deschamps and Gustave de Wailly. 1826.

Rousseau, Jean-Jacques. *Julie ou la nouvelle Héloïse: lettres de deux amants habitants d'une petite ville au pied des Alpes*. Edited by Jean Marie Goulemot. Paris: Livre de Poche, 2002.

Rowson, Susanna. *Charlotte Temple: A Tale of Truth*. Edited by Clara Marburg Kirk and Rudolf Kirk. New York: Twayne, 1964.

Roy, Camille. *Nouveaux essais sur la littérature Canadienne*. Québec: Imp. de L'Action sociale limitée, 1914.

―――. "Philippe Aubert de Gaspé d'âpres les Anciens Canadiens." *La Nouvelle-France* 8, no. 4 (April 1909): 158–68.

"R.R.E." [from *Gentlemen's Magazine*, no. 57, December 1787.] In Nixon, *Novel Definitions*, 220. First published in *Gentlemen's Magazine*, no. 57, December 1787.

Russell, James. *Matilda; or, The Indian's Captive: A Canadian Tale Founded on Fact*. Three-Rivers, QC: G. Stobbs, 1833.

Bibliography 223

Rust, Richard Dilworth. "The Art of *The Pathfinder*." In *James Fenimore Cooper: New Historical and Literary Contexts*, edited by Wil M. Verhoeven, 177–84. Amsterdam: Rodopi, 1993.

———. "Historical Introduction." In James Fenimore Cooper, *The Pathfinder, or, The Inland Sea*, approved ed., edited by Richard D. Rust, xiii–xxvi. Albany: State University of New York Press, 1981.

———. "Textual Commentary." In James Fenimore Cooper, *The Pathfinder, or, The Inland Sea*, approved ed., edited by Richard D. Rust, 473–83. Albany: State University of New York Press, 1981.

Samuels, Shirley, ed. *A Companion to American Fiction 1780–1865*. Malden, MA: Blackwell Publishing, 2004.

Sand, George. "George Sand on Cooper." In *Fenimore Cooper: The Critical Heritage*, edited by George Dekker and John P. McWilliams, 271–76. London: Taylor and Francis e-Library, 2003. First published as "Fenimore Cooper," in *Autour de la Table*. Paris, 1856, 261–72, 281–82.

———. *Indiana*. Paris: Roret and Dupuy, 1832. Translated by Sylvia Raphael. Oxford: Oxford University Press, 2000.

———. *Mauprat*. Paris: Bonnaire, 1837. Edited and translated by Sylvia Raphael. Oxford: Oxford University Press, 1997.

———. *Le Meunier d'Angibault*. Paris: Desessart, 1845. Translated by Donna Dickenson as *The Miller of Angibault*. Oxford: Oxford University Press, 1995.

———. *La ville noire*. Paris: Paetz, 1860. Translated by Tina A. Kover as *The Black City*, 1st Carroll and Graf ed. New York: Carroll and Graf, 2004.

Sanders, Andrew. *The Victorian Historical Novel, 1840–1880*. London: Palgrave Macmillan, 1978.

Scott, Walter. *An Apology for Tales of Terror*. Kelso: James Ballantyne, 1799. www.walterscott.lib.ed.ac.uk/works/poetry/apology/home.html.

———. [*The Betrothed*] *Tales of the Crusaders*. Edinburgh: Constable; London: Hurst, Robinson, 1825.

———. *Le coeur de Mid-Lothian ou la prison d'Edimbourg*. Translated by Louis Vivien. Paris: P. M. Pourrtat, 1837.

———. [*Count Robert of Paris*] *Tales of My Landlord, Fourth and Last Series. Collected and Arranged by Jedediah Cleishbotham, Schoolmaster and Parish-Clerk of Gandercleuch. In Four Volumes*. Edinburgh: Robert Cadell; London: Whittaker, 1832.

———. *The Heart of Mid-Lothian*. Edited by David Hewitt and Alison Lumsden. Edinburgh: Edinburgh University Press, 2009.

———. *Ivanhoe*. Edited by Ian Duncan. Oxford: Oxford University Press, 1996.

———. *The Journal of Sir Walter Scott*. Edinburgh: David Douglas, 1890.

———. *The Lady of the Lake; A Poem*. Edinburgh: John Ballantyne; London: Longman, Hurst, Rees and Orme/William Miller, 1810.

———. *The Lay of the Last Minstrel: A Poem*. London: Longman, Hurst, Rees, and Orme; Edinburgh: Archibald Constable, 1805.

———. *Marmion; A Tale of Flodden Field*. Edinburgh: Archibald Constable; London: William Miller/John Murray, 1808.

———. *Minstrelsy of the Scottish Border: Consisting of Historical and Romantic Ballads, Collected in the Southern Counties of Scotland; With a Few of Modern Date, Founded upon Local Tradition*. 2 vols. London: T. Cadell Jun. and W. Davies, 1802.

224 *Bibliography*

———. *Oeuvres Completes.* Translated by Auguste-Jean-Baptiste Defauconpret. Paris: C. Grosselin and A. Sautelet, 1826–33.

———. *Oeuvres de Walter Scott.* Translated by Albert Montémont. Paris: Firmin-Didot frères, 1840.

———. *La prison du comté d'Edimbourg.* Vol. 4 of *Oeuvres complètes de Walter Scott.* Translated by Louis Barré. Paris: Librairie centrale des publications illustrées à 20 centimes, 1857.

———. *La prison du comté d'Edimbourg.* Vol. 7, pt. 1 of *Les veillées littéraires illustrées.* Translated by Louis Barré. Paris: J. Bry aîné, 1852.

———. *La prison d'Édimbourg.* Translated by Auguste-Jean-Baptiste Defauconpret. Paris: G. Barba, 1844.

———. *La prison d'Édimbourg, conte de mon hôte, par Sir Walter Scott, traduction nouvelle.* Translated by A. and P. Chaillot. Paris: F. Denn, 1829.

———. *La prison d'Edimbourg: nouveaux contes de mon hôte; recueillis et mis au jour par Jedediah Cleishbotham.* Paris: H. Nicolle, 1819.

———. *La prison d'Édimbourg: nouveaux contes de mon hôte, recueillis et mis au jour par Jedediah Cleishbotham, maitre d'école et sacristain de la paroisse de Gandercleugh.* Paris: Henri Nicolle, Ladvocat, 1821.

———. *La prison du Mid-Lothian ou la jeune Caméronienne.* Translated by Albert Montémont. Paris: Didot, 1835.

———. *Saint Ronan's Well: By the Author of "Waverley," "Quentin Durward," &c. In Three Volumes.* Edinburgh: Archibald Constable; London: Hurst, Robinson, 1824.

———. *Sir Walter Scott's Minstrelsy of the Scottish Border.* London: W. Blackwood, 1902. First published as Walter Scott, *Minstrelsy of the Scottish Border: Consisting of Historical and Romantic Ballads, Collected in the Southern Counties of Scotland; With a Few of Modern Date, Founded upon Local Tradition,* 2 vols. London: T. Cadell Jun. and W. Davies, 1802.

———. *Tales of My Landlord, Second Series. Collected and Arranged by Jedediah Cleishbotham, Schoolmaster and Parish-Clerk of Gandercleugh. In Four Volumes.* Edinburgh: Archibald Constable and Company, 1818.

———. *[The Talisman] Tales of the Crusaders.* Edinburgh: Constable; London: Hurst, Robinson, 1825.

———. *Waverley, or 'Tis Sixty Years Since.* Edited by Susan Kubica Howard. Peterborough, ON: Broadview Press, 2010. First published anonymously as *Waverley; or 'Tis Sixty Years Since,* 3 vols. Edinburgh: Archibald Constable; London: Longman, Hurst, Rees, Orme, and Brown, 1814.

Sedgwick, Catharine Maria. *Hope Leslie, or, Early Times in the Massachusetts.* New York: White, Gallaher and White, 1827.

———. *The Linwoods, or, "Sixty Years Since" in America.* Vol. 1. New York: Harper and Sons, 1835. https://archive.org/details/linwoodsorsixtyy01sedgrich.

———. *The Linwoods, or, "Sixty Years Since" in America.* Vol. 2. New York: Harper and Sons, 1835. https://archive.org/details/linwoodsorsixty02sedgrich.

———. *Married or Single?* Edited by Deborah Gussman. Lincoln: University of Nebraska Press, 2015.

———. *A New-England Tale; or, Sketches of New-England Character and Manners.* New York: E. Bliss and E. White, 1822.

Sellar, Robert. *Hemlock: A Tale of the War of 1812.* Montreal: F. E. Grafton and Sons, 1890.

Shaffer, Jason. *Performing Patriotism: National Identity in the Colonial and Revolutionary American Theater*. Philadelphia: University of Pennsylvania Press, 2007.

Shaw, Harry E. *The Forms of Historical Fiction: Sir Walter Scott and His Successors*. Ithaca, NY: Cornell University Press, 1983.

Sheppard, Alfred Tressider. *The Art and Practice of Historical Fiction*. London: H. Toulmin, 1930.

Shwartz, Susan. "Ivanhoe: Sir Walter Scott." In *Classics Illustrated: Sir Walter Scott: Ivanhoe*, edited by Madeleine Robins, n. pag. New York: Acclaim Books, 1997.

Sigourney, L. H. [Lydia Huntley]. *Sketch of Connecticut, Forty Years Since*. Hartford: Oliver D. Cooke and Sons, 1824.

Simmons, James C. *The Novelist as Historian: Essays on the Victorian Historical Novel*. The Hague: Mouton, 1973.

Simms, William Gilmore. *Eutaw: A Sequel*. New York: Redfield, 1856.

———. *The Forayers, or, The Raid of the Dog Days*. New York: Redfield, 1855.

———. *Katherine Walton; or, The Rebel of Dorchester*. New and revised ed. Chicago: Belford, Clarke, 1888.

———. "Modern Prose Fiction." *Southern Quarterly Review* 15 (April 1849): 41–83.

———. *The Partisan: A Tale of the Revolution*. New York: Harper and Bros, 1835.

———. *The Sword and the Distaff; or, "Fair, Fat and Forty," A Story of the South, at the Close of Revolution*. Philadelphia: Lippincott, Grambo, 1853.

———. *The Yemassee: A Romance of Carolina*. New York: Harper and Bros, 1835.

Simons, John. "Introduction: Why Read Chapbooks?" In *Guy of Warwick and Other Chapbook Romances: Six Tales from the Popular Literature of Pre-Industrial England*, edited by John Simons, 1–38. Exeter: University of Exeter Press, 1998.

Smith, Adam. *An Inquiry into the Nature and Causes of the Wealth of Nations*. London: W. Strahan and T. Cadell, 1776.

———. *The Theory of Moral Sentiments*. Edited by Knud Haakonssen. Cambridge: Cambridge University Press, 2002.

Smith, Charlotte. *Desmond: A Novel*. London: G. G. J. and J. Robinson, 1792.

Smith, Goldwin. "Walter Scott." In *The English Poets: Selections with Critical Introductions and a General Introduction by Mathew Arnold: Volume IV: Wordsworth to Rosetti*, 2nd ed. revised, edited by Thomas Humphry Ward, 186–93. London: Macmillan, 1892. https://archive.org/details/englishpoetssele04warduoft.

Spencer, Benjamin T. *The Quest for Nationality: An American Literary Campaign*. Syracuse, NY: Syracuse University Press, 1957.

Spiller, Robert E., and Philip C. Blackburn. *A Descriptive Bibliography of the Writings of James Fenimore Cooper*. New York: R. R. Bowker, 1934.

Stacey, Robert David. "Romance, Pastoral Romance, and the Nation in History: William Kirby's *The Golden Dog* and Philippe-Joséph Aubert de Gaspé's *Les Anciens Canadiens*." In Blair, Coleman, Higginson, York, and Gerson, *ReCalling Early Canada*, 91–116.

St Clair, William. *The Reading Nation in the Romantic Period*. Cambridge: Cambridge University Press, 2004.

Stephen, Leslie. "Leslie Stephen: Hours in a Library with Scott, *Cornhill Magazine*." In *Walter Scott: The Critical Heritage*, edited by John O. Hayden, 439–58. London: Routledge, 1995. First published in *Cornhill Magazine*, September 1871, 278–93.

226 *Bibliography*

Stephens, Ann S. "Malaeska, the Indian Wife of the White Hunter." In *Beadle's Dime Novels*, no. 1, June 9, 1860. www.ulib.niu.edu/badndp/dn01.html.

———. *Malaeska: The Indian Wife of the White Hunter*. New York: B. Blom, 1971.

———. *Malaeska; or The Indian Wife of the White Hunter*. In *Ladies' Companion*, February, March, and April 1839.

Stevens, Anne H. *British Historical Fiction Before Scott*. Basingstoke: Palgrave Macmillan, 2010.

Stevenson, Louise. "Homes, Books, and Reading." In Casper et al., *The Industrial Book, 1840–1880*, 319–31.

Stewart, D. *The Heart of Mid-Lothian, or The Affecting History of Jeanie and Effie Deans. Abridged from the Original [of Sir Walter Scott]*. Newcastle upon Tyne: Mackenzie and Dent, 1819.

Stowe, Harriet Beecher. *Uncle Tom's Cabin; or, Life Among the Lowly*. Boston: J. P. Jewett, 1852.

Strutt, Joseph. *Queenhoo-Hall, a Romance: And Ancient Times, a Drama*. 4 vols. London: John Murray; Edinburgh: Archibald Constable, 1808.

Sue, Eugène. *Les mystères de Paris*. Paris: Charles Gosselin, 1842. http://catalogue.bnf.fr/ark:/12148/cb314189929. Translated by Carolyn Betensky and Jonathan Loesberg as *The Mysteries of Paris*. New York: Penguin Books, 2015.

———. *Les mystères du peuple: ou, histoire d'une famille de prolétaires à travers les âges*. Paris: R. Deforges, 1977.

———. *Oeuvres illustrées d'Eugène Sue*. Paris: Maresq, 1850–55.

Taylor, Alan. *William Cooper's Town: Power and Persuasion on the Frontier of the Early American Republic*. New York: Knopf, 1995.

Teeling, Ed, and Paula Teeling. *Ivanhoe*. Long Island, NY: EDCON, 1993.

Terry, Daniel. *The Heart of Midlothian, a Musical Drama, in Three Acts; First Produced at the Theatre Royal, Covent Garden, Saturday, 17th April, 1819*. London: William Stockdale, 1819.

———. *L'auberge du grand Frédéric, comédie-vaudeville en 1 acte, de MM. Lafontaine et Léon* . . . Paris: Huet, 1821.

Théaulon, Emmanuel. *Faust: drame lyrique en 3 actes, par E. Théaulon*. Paris: Duvernois, 1827.

Théaulon, Emmanuel, Alexis Decomberousse, and Ernest Jaime. *Le père Goriot: drame-vaudeville en 3 actes/par MM. Théaulon, Al. Decomberousse et [E.] Jaime*. . . . Paris: Marchant; Brussels: Jouhaud, 1835. http://gallica.bnf.fr/ark:/12148/bpt6k104328x.

Thomas, Clara. Introduction to *Canadians of Old*, by Philippe-Joséph Aubert de Gaspé, vii–xii. Translated by Charles G. D. Roberts. Toronto: McClelland and Stewart, 1974.

Thorp, Willard. "Cooper Beyond America." *New York History* 35, no. 4 (1954): 522–39. www.jstor.org/stable/24470853.

Todd, William B., and Ann Bowden. *Sir Walter Scott: A Bibliographical History, 1796–1832*. New Castle, DE: Oak Knoll Press, 1998.

Tombs, Robert. *France 1814–1914*. London: Longman, 1996.

Traill, Catharine Parr. *Canadian Crusoes: A Tale of the Rice Lake Plains*. London: Arthur Hall, Virtue, 1852.

Trumpener, Katie. *Bardic Nationalism: The Romantic Novel and the British Empire*. Princeton, NJ: Princeton University Press, 1997.

Bibliography 227

Tulloch, Graham. "Essay on the Text." In Walter Scott, *Ivanhoe*, edited by Graham Tulloch, 403–62. Edinburgh: Edinburgh University Press, 1997.

Turner, Joseph. "The Kinds of Historical Fiction: An Essay in Definition and Methodology." *Genre* 12, no. 3 (Fall 1979): 333–57.

Vachon, Stéphane. *Les travaux et les tours d'Honoré de Balzac: chronologie de la création balzacienne.* Paris: Presses Universitaires de Vincennes, Université de Paris VIII; Montréal: Les Presses de l'Université de Montréal, 1992.

Vogel, Malvina G., and Pablo Marcos Studios. *Ivanhoe.* New York: Baronet Books, 1994.

Voltaire. *Candide.* Edited by Eric Palmer. Peterborough, ON: Broadview Press, 2009.

Wallace, Diana. *The Woman's Historical Novel: British Women Writers, 1900–2000.* Houndmills: Palgrave Macmillan, 2005.

Wallace, James D. *Early Cooper and His Audience.* New York: Columbia University Press, 1986.

Walpole, Horace. *The Castle of Otranto.* London: Tho. Lownds, 1764.

Watson, Charles S. *From Nationalism to Secessionism: The Changing Fiction of William Gilmore Simms.* Westport, CT: Greenwood Press, 1993.

Watt, Frank W. "The Growth of Proletarian Literature in Canada, 1872–1920." *Dalhousie Review* 40, no. 2 (Summer 1960): 157–73.

———. "Literature of Protest." In *Literary History of Canada: Canadian Literature in English*, edited by Carl F. Klinck, 457–73. Toronto: University of Toronto Press, 1965.

Watt, Ian. *The Rise of the Novel: Studies in Defoe, Fielding, and Richardson.* Berkeley: University of California Press, 1957.

Wertham, Frederic. *Seduction of the Innocent: The Influence of Comic Books on Today's Youth.* New York: Rinehard, 1954.

Wesseling, Elisabeth. *Writing History as a Prophet: Postmodernist Innovations of the Historical Novel.* Amsterdam: John Benjamins Publishing Company, 1991.

West, Jane. *The Loyalists: An Historical Novel.* London: Longman, Hurst, Rees, Orme, and Brown, 1812.

West, Michael. *Ivanhoe.* New ed. London: Longman, 1967.

Wheeler, Edward. *Deadwood Dick in Leadville: or, A Strange Stroke for Liberty.* Beadle's half dime library, no. 100. New York: Beadle and Adams, 1879.

White, R. S. *Natural Rights and the Birth of Romanticism in the 1790s.* Basingstoke: Palgrave Macmillan, 2005.

Williams, Raymond. *Culture and Society, 1780–1850.* New York: Columbia University Press, 1958.

Wilson, Thomas. *From The Use of Circulating Libraries Considered.* In Nixon, *Novel Definitions*, 221–23. First published in Thomas Wilson, *The Use of Circulating Libraries Considered; With Instructions for Opening and Conducting a Library, Either upon a Large or Small Plan.* London: J. Hamilton and T. Wilson, 1797.

Wimsatt, Mary Ann. *The Major Fiction of William Gilmore Simms: Cultural Traditions and Literary Form.* Baton Rouge: Louisiana State University Press, 1989.

Winship, Michael. "Distribution and the Trade." In Casper et al., *The Industrial Book, 1840–1880*, 117–30.

———. "The International Trade in Books." In Casper et al., *The Industrial Book, 1840–1880*, 148–57.

228 Bibliography

Witkowski, Claude. *Les editions populaires 1848–1870*. Paris: Les Amours des Livres, GIPPE, 1977.

Wollstonecraft, Mary. *Mary, A Fiction: And, the Wrongs of Woman, or, Maria*. Edited by Michelle Faubert. Peterborough, ON: Broadview Press, 2012.

Wood, Gillen D'Arcy. "Visual Pleasures, Visionary States: Art, Entertainment, and the Nation." In *A Concise Companion to the Romantic Age*, edited by Jon Klancher, 232–56. Chichester: Wiley-Blackwell, 2009.

Woodruff, Juliette. "A Spate of Words, Full of Sound and Fury, Signifying Nothing: Or, How to Read in Harlequin." *Journal of Popular Culture* 19, no. 2 (Fall 1985): 25–32.

Woolf, Virginia. *To the Lighthouse*. London: Dent, 1943.

Worrall, David. *Theatric Revolution: Drama, Censorship and Romantic Period Subcultures 1773–1832*. Oxford: Oxford University Press, 2006.

Wright, Gordon. *France in Modern Times: From the Enlightenment to the Present*. 4th ed. New York: Norton, 1987.

Zboray, Ronald J. *A Fictive People: Antebellum Economic Development and the American Reading Public*. New York: Oxford University Press, 1993.

Zola, Émile. *L'assommoir*. Paris: Charpentier, 1877. Translated by Leonard Tancock as *L'Assommoir*. New York: Penguin Books, 1982.

———. *Germinal*. Paris: Charpentier, 1885. Translated by Leonard W. Tancock as *Germinal*. New York: Penguin Books, 1963.

———. *Les Rougon-Macquart: histoire naturelle et sociale d'une famille sous le Second Empire*. Edited by Armand Lanoux and Henri Mitterand. 5 vols. Paris: Bibliothèque de la Pléiade, 1960.

———. *La Terre*. Paris: Charpentier, 1887. Translated by Douglas Parmée as *The Earth*. Harmondsworth: Penguin Books, 1980.

———. *Le ventre de Paris*. Paris: Charpentier, 1873. Translated by Brian Nelson as *The Belly of Paris = Le Ventre de Paris*. Oxford: Oxford University Press, 2007.

Index

Acclaim Books version of *Ivanhoe* 195–6
actualization of rights 30–1
adaptations: film adaptation of *Ivanhoe* 196–8; of *The Heart of Mid-Lothian* 55–9; operatic performances of *Ivanhoe* 192; *see also* stage adaptations; theatre
advertisements, in chapbooks 55–6
age of revolution, historical novel in 14
agency, and community 38
Aimard, Gustave 4, 88, 99–101, 102, 103
Allen, James Smith 110–11
Alves, Robert 1
The American Democrat, or, Hints on the Social and Civic Relations of the United States of America (Cooper, 1838) 73
American historical novels 67–75; authorship in early nineteenth-century America 89; circulation, impediments to 89; Indian captivity stories 92
Anderson, Benedict 52
The Antiquary (Scott, 1816) 36
Appleton 95
Arch, Stephen 68
Aubin, Penelope 9
authorship: 1790 Copyright Act 90; in early-nineteenth-century America 89
availability: of Balzac's novels in post-Revolutionary France 129–30; of chapbooks 53

Bakhtin, Mikhail 20, 39
Baldick, Chris 18
Balzac, Honoré de 4, 73, 80–1, 109–16; appeal of 133; capitalism in 134; early print history 126–8; novels, availability of 129–30; review of *The Pathfinder* 80–1; writing for stage 176
Barbauld, Ann Letitia 10
The Bastonnais: Tale of the American Invasion of Canada in 1775–76 (Lesperance, 1877) 159
Battle of Culloden 29
Baym, Nina 68
Beadle and Adams 102
Beattie, James 9
A Beautiful Rebel: A Romance of Upper-Canada in Eighteen Hundred and Twelve (Campbell, 1909) 159
Bellamy, Edward 162
Benjamin, Walter 19
Bentley, Richard 73, 93, 97
Bentley's Standard Novels 94
Berbéris, Pierre 119
Bibaud, Michel 173
bibliothèques 132
bildungsroman 155
Bird, Montgomery 74
Blackburn, Philip 94
Blair, Hugh 9
Blanche d'Haberville; drame en cinq actes en vers (Monarque, 1931) 174
Bolton, H. Philip 53
The Bravo: A Tale (Cooper, 1831) 74
British rule of Canada 148
Bulwer-Lytton, Edward 17
Burke, Edmund 14, 15
Burney, Frances 8, 29–30
Butler, Ronnie 117
Butterfield, Herbert 19

Cabajsky, Andrea 148–9
Cambron, Micheline 171

230 Index

Campbell, William Wilfred 159
Canada: 1774 Québec Act 148;
1840 Act of Union 148; *Club des Anciens* 150; development of the theatre 172; under French dominion 149; *Jean Rivard* (Gérin-Lajoie, 1862–1864) 157–8; *La terre paternelle* (Lacombe, 1846) 157–8; *Les anciens Canadiens* (de Gaspé, 1863) 150–7; *The Manor House of De Villerai: A Tale of Canada Under the French Dominion* (Leprohon, 1859–60) 148–9; modernization of 147–8; national progress 148; *In the New Capital: A Nineteenth-Century View of Ottawa in the Twenty-First Century* (Galbraith, 1897) 162–3; *The Preparation of Ryerson Embury: A Purpose* (Carman, 1900) 163–6; Rebellions of 1837–38 148; seigneurial system 148; Seven Years' War (1756–63) 148; Upper and Lower Canada, creation of 148; working-class fiction 160–2
Canadian Crusoes: A Tale of the Rice Lake Plains (Traill, 1852) 149
Candide (Voltaire, 1759) 47
capitalism 108–9; in Balzac 133, 134; criticism of in *Clan Albin* 29; ethics of self-interest 45–6; in *La comédie humaine* 118–19; labor relations in *Tales of My Landlord* 42–3; landed capital 119; modernization, impact on capital flows 119; in *The Pathfinder* 75–6; role in social relations 41; speculation 118–19
Capitalism in the Twenty-First Century (Piketty, 2014) 115
Carey, Matthew 92–3
Carey and Lea 64
Carlyle, Thomas, criticism of Scott 16
Carman, Albert 163–6
Carpenter, Kenneth 89
Caw, George 54
chapbooks 52; adaptation for stage 53; adaptations of new novels 53; advertisements 55–6; American production of 92; availability of 53; cheap tracts 53; content of 55; *The Heart of Mid-Lothian, or The Affecting History of Jeanie and Effie Deans* (Stewart, 1819) 55; *The Heart of Mid-Lothian* 59; *The Heart of Mid-Lothian, A Romantic Tale,*

Founded on Facts (Mauris, 1820) 56–7; *Jeanie Deans, and the Lily of St Leonard's* 60–1; popularity of 53; readership 54–6; styles used in 55; subjectivity in 55; *Waverley* versions 54
characteristics of modern life 44–5
Charlotte Temple: A Tale of Truth (Rowson, 1791) 67
Charpentier 130
Charvat, William 64, 99
Cheap Repository of Moral and Religious Tracts (More, 1795) 57–8
cheap tracts 53
children's books 54; *Cooper's Leather-stocking Tales for Boys and Girls: With Illustrations* (1892) 97; *Ivanhoe* (Scott, 1820) for school reading 195–6; *Jeanie Deans, and the Lily of St Leonard's* 60
Chronique du règne de Charles IX (Mérimée, 1829) 110
chronologies: and romance 11; transition to historical fiction 10
Cinq-Mars (de Vigny, 1826) 110
circulation 52; 1790 Copyright Act, impact on 90; expansion of, government's role in 90–1; impediments to 89; libraries 89; of periodicals in post-Revolutionary France 131–2
Clan Albin: A National Tale (Johnstone, 1815) 4, 27; capitalism, criticism of 29; editions 33; modernity in 47; rights 32–3; social justice in 30; as social philosophy 30
Cleland, John 9
Club des Anciens 150
Cobbet, William 16
Collins, Wilkie 16
comic book adaptation of *Ivanhoe* 193–4
communication: "effective communication" 2; reading as 11–12
community: *bildungsroman* 155; in *The Heart of Mid-Lothian* 31–2, 40–1, 43; historical community practices and modernity 38; in *Jean Rivard* 157–8
consequences of modernity 44–5
Constable, Archibald 51
content of chapbooks 55
Cooper, James Fenimore 64–5, 67–8, 72–3, 78–81; European trilogy

Index 231

73–4; influence on Aimard 99–102; Leatherstocking novels 65, 75, 94–5; popularity of, impact on theatre 177–9; print history of Cooper's novels 94–9; quality of reproduction in Cooper's novels 96; readership of Cooper's novels 95–7; satirical novels 73; travel narratives 74
copyright 126; 1790 Copyright Act 90; as tool of nation building 89–90
Cottin, Sophie 54, 109
Coward, David 103, 113, 175
crime novel 109
Critical Review, review of *Waverley* 13
Croker, John Wilson 14–15
Cromwell (Balzac, 1819) 109
Croxall, Samuel 8
Cullen, William 95
The Curé of St Philippe: A Story of French-Canadian Politics (Grey, 1899) 159

Dacre, Charlotte 8
Darley, Felix Octavius Carr 95
Darwin, Erasmus 9
Davison, William 59
de Cervantes, Miguel 10
de Gaspé, Philippe Aubert 149–57
de Kock, Paul 109
Deadwood Dick novels (Wheeler, 1877–97) 98
The Deerslayer, or, The First War-Path: A Tale (Cooper, 1841) 78, 99–101
Defauconpret, A. J. B. 98
Defoe, Daniel 8
Dekker, George 78, 81
Deserted Village (Goldsmith, 1770) 30
Desmond: A Novel (Smith, 1792) 8
Devey, Joseph 16–17
Devine, T. M. 36
Dibdin, Thomas 54, 58, 179–82
Dickenson, Donna 133
disembedding 35–6, 198n1
distribution, forms of 129
Doucette, Leonard 173
downmarket availability of chapbooks 53
dramatization: of *The Heart of Mid-Lothian* 179–86; and the novel 183
Ducray-Duminil, François Guillaume 109
Duffy, Dennis 156

Duncan, Ian 12, 34–5, 52
Duncombe, John 56–7

early reviews of *Waverley* 12–13
economic liberalism 108–11, 131
Edgeworth, Maria 10
The Edinburgh Juvenile Library 54
editions: of *Les anciens Canadiens* 171–2; of *Clan Albin* 33; of *The Heart of Mid-Lothian* 4, 28–47; of *The Pathfinder* 4, 73–82; of *Le père Goriot* 132–3; people's editions 94
"effective communication" 2
Elder, Henry 54
Elizabeth; or, The Exiles of Siberia (Cottin, 1806) 54–5
Ellis, Edward 98
empowerment, and reform 15
English Canada 158–9; development of the theatre 172
ethics 32–3; of self-interest 45–6; self-knowledge 46
Études de mœurs au XIXe siècle (Balzac, 1834–37) 130
Eutaw: A Sequel (Simms, 1856) 72

"Familiar Novel" 9
The Farther Adventures of Robinson Crusoe (Defoe, 1719) 8
Ferris, Ina 52–3
Ferry, Gabriel 101
Feuchtwanger, Lion 21, 65, 134
fictional representation of modernization in post-Confederation English Canada; Ginx's Baby (Jenkins, 1871) 160–2; *In the New Capital: A Nineteenth-Century View of Ottawa in the Twenty-First Century* (Galbraith, 1897) 162–3; *My Own Story: A Canadian Christmas Tale* (1869) 160–2; *The Preparation of Ryerson Embury: A Purpose* (Carman, 1900) 163–6; *Roland Graeme: Knight: A Novel of Our Time* (Machar, 1892) 162
fictional representation of the working class in post-Revolutionary France 135–6; *L'assommoir* (Zola, 1877) 135–7; *Germinal* (Zola) 140–1; *Le meunier d'Angibault* (Sand, 1845); *Les mystéres de Paris* (Sue, 1842–43) 99; *Les mystéres du peuple* (Sue, 1849–56); *La terre* (Zola, 1887) 141–2; *Le ventre de Paris* (Zola,

232 Index

1873) 135–7; *La ville noire* (Sand, 1859) 135
Fielding, Henry 9
film adaptation: of *Ivanhoe* 198n1; Robin Hood films 199n52
Flaubert, Gustave 18
Fleishman, Avrom 37
Fluck, Winfried 65
The Forayers, or, the Raid of the Dog Days (Simms, 1855) 72
formalism 19
Fortassier, Rose 127
Fourier, Charles 121n3
Frankfurt school philosophers 25n68
Franklin, Wayne 65, 73, 81
Frappier-Mazur, Lucienne 118
The Free Lances: A Romance of the Mexican Valley (Reid, 1888) 98
French Canada: *Club des Anciens* 150; development of the theatre 172; impact of historical novel 171–2; localization 172–3
French Revolution 15, 111
French translations of Cooper's novels 97–8
frontier politics 99–101
frontier romance 101–2
The Frontiersmen (Aimard, 1854) 99–101, 103
Fugitive Slave Act of 1850 72, 85n43

Gaines, William 194
Galbraith, John 162
Garneau, François-Xavier 149, 153
Garside, Peter 54–5
Gay, Sophie 109
genre: drama 54; in *The Heart of Mid-Lothian* 39; historical novel 1, 2–3, 7; "national genre of modernity" 26n100; romance 8; romance novels 9; social philosophy 30; travel genre 91; *Waverley* as emerging genre 8; the Western 98–9; *see also* historical novel
Gentlemen's Magazine 8
Germinal (Zola) 140–1
Gerson, Carole 149, 171
Giddens, Anthony 2, 35–6, 118, 190; on capitalism 41
Ginx's Baby (Jenkins, 1871) 160–2
Godey's Lady's Book 93
Godwin, William 10
GoGwilt, Christopher 20–1
The Golden Dog (Kirby, 1877) 159

Goldsmith, Oliver 30
Gosselin 98
Gravity's Rainbow (Pynchon, 1973) 3
Green, Sarah 8
Gregory, James 95
Grimes, E. Margaret 150
Gross, Robert 89
Guy Mannering (Scott, 1815) 36

Hamnett, Brian 21–2
Harris, Edward 177
Harris, Roy 2
Harvie, Christopher 51
Haynes, Christine 126
Haywood, Eliza 9
The Headsman, or, The Abbaye des Vignerons: A Tale (Cooper, 1833) 74
The Heart of Mid-Lothian, A Romantic Tale, Founded on Facts (Mauris, 1820) 56–7
The Heart of Mid-Lothian, or The Affecting History of Jeanie and Effie Deans (Stewart, 1819) 55
The Heart of Mid-lothian; or, The Lily of St. Leonard, a Caledonian Tale of Great Interest (1822) 58
The Heart of Mid-Lothian; or, The Lily of St. Leonard's (ca. 1819) 54
The Heart of Mid-Lothian (Scott, 1818) 4; actualization of rights 30–1; adaptations 55–8; community 31–2, 40–3; consequences of modernity 44–5; dramatization of 54, 179–86; Porteous Riots, history of 54; positive law 32; resolution of 43–4; universal representation of national society 35; varied use of genre in 39; word play in 28–9
The Heidenmauer: A Legend of the Rhine (Cooper, 1832) 74
Hemlock: A Tale of the War of 1812 (Sellar, 1890) 159
Henderson, Andrea 43
Highland Clearances 28
Histoire du Canada sous la domination française (Bibaud, 1837) 173
historical novel 1, 7; as act of modernity 2; in the age of revolution 14; American historical novels 67–8; combination with romance 11–16; comparison to melodrama 18; contemporary scholarship on 20–2; fiction, qualifying as historical 5n3; impact on French Canada

Index 233

171–2; as means of reform 14; mistrust of 19–20; modernity in 2; and the nation-state 2; prioritization over romance novels 9; reading, importance of 15; republican education, contribution to 67–70; transition from chronology 10
The Historical Novel (Butterfield, 1924) 19–20
The Historical Novel (Lukács, 1963) 21, 70
"historification" 2, 37
History of the Navy of the United States of America (Cooper, 1839) 73
The History of Tom Jones, a Foundling (Fielding, 1749) 9
Hobomok: A Tale of Early Times (Child, 1824) 67; Native Americans, characterization of 68
Home as Found (Cooper, 1838) 74
Homeward Bound, or, The Chase: A Tale of the Sea (Cooper, 1838) 74
Hope Leslie, or, Early Times in the Massachusetts (Sedgwick, 1827) 67–8; Native Americans, characterization of 68
Horse Shoe Robinson: A Tale of the Tory Ascendency (Kennedy, 1835) 68
Houghton & Mifflin 95

identity formation, impact on print circulation, 52
In the New Capital: A Nineteenth-Century View of Ottawa in the Twenty-First Century (Galbraith, 1897) 162–3
Indian captivity stories 74, 92
industrial capitalism 2, 135; actualization of rights 30–1; criticism of in *Clan Albin* 29; ethics of self-interest 45–6; labor relations in *Tales of My Landlord* 42–3; in *The Pathfinder* 75–6; social justice in *Clan Albin* 30; social philosophy 30
Industrial Revolution: capitalism, criticism of in *Clan Albin* 29; in Scotland 28, 36
inheritance as means of wealth 117–18
innovation, in publishing 128–9
inside/outside dynamic in *Tales of My Landlord* 42
interwar period, criticism of *Waverley* during 19

Ivanhoe: A Romance (Scott, 1820) 19, 110, 190–1; Acclaim Books version of 195; comic book adaptation of 193–4; film adaptation of 196–8; operatic performances of 192

James, G. P. R. 16
James, Henry 18
Jean Rivard (Gérin-Lajoie, 1862–64) 4, 157–8
Jeanie Deans, and the Lily of St Leonard's 60–1
Jeffrey, Francis 12
Jenkins, John Edward 160–2
John, Richard 90
Johnstone, Christian Isobel 4, 27
Jones, William 9, 196
journaux-romans 132

Kanes, Martin 127
Karcher, Caroline 67–8
Kaser, David 64
Katherine Walton; or, The Rebel of Dorchester (Simms, 1851) 71–2
Kelley, William 76–7
Kelly, Gary 53, 66
Kennedy, John Pendleton 68
Kerr, James 34
Kirby, William 159, 172
The Knickerbocker 93
Knights of Labor 162
Knox, Vicesimus 9
König press 173n18

La comédie humaine (Balzac, 1842–48) 109, 111; capitalism 118–19
La maison Nucingen (Balzac, 1838) 119–20
La peau de chagrin (Balzac, 1831) 127
La princesse de Clèves (La Fayette, 1678) 110
La terre paternelle (Lacombe, 1846) 157–8
La terre (Zola, 1887) 141–2
La ville noire (Sand, 1859) 135
labor relations: *Roland Graeme: Knight: A Novel of Our Time* (Machar, 1892) 162; in *Tales of My Landlord* 42–3
Lacombe, Patrice 157–8
Lacy, Thomas Hailes 184
L'Amour, Louis 98–9

234   *Index*

landed capital 119

large publishing houses, emergence of 93

L'assommoir (Zola, 1877) 137–40

The Last of the Mohicans: A Narrative of 1757 (Cooper, 1826) 67–8

Laut, Agnes 159

The Lay of the Last Minstrel (Scott, 1805) 10

Le coureur des bois, ou, les chercheurs d'or (Ferry, 1850) 101

Le meunier d'Angibault (Sand, 1845): and *Le père Goriot* 134

Le père Goriot (Balzac, 1835) 4, 98, 109–11, 115–20, 126; accessibility of 130–1; editions 132–3; literary impact of 132–3; localization 111–14; preface to 127; reproduction of 128; and Sand's *Le meunier d'Angibault* 134; stage adaptations 174–7

Le Petit journal 132

Le philosophe Anglois ou histoire de Monsieur Cleveland (Prévost, 1731–1739) 110

Le ventre de Paris (Zola, 1873) 135–7

Leatherstocking novels 65, 75, 94–6; influence on Western genre 98–9

Leather-Stocking Tales 94–5

Lee, Sophia 7–8

legislation: 1774 Québec Act 148; 1790 Copyright Act 90; 1791 Constitutional Act 148; 1819 Serre Laws 128; 1840 Act of Union 148; Post Office Acts of 1792 and 1794 90

Lemire, Maurice 154

Leprohon, Rosanna 148

Les anciens Canadiens (de Gaspé, 1863) 149–57; stage performance 173–4

Les aventures de Télémaque (Fénelon, 1699) 113

Les bandits de l'Arizona (Aimard, 1882) 103

Les chouans (Balzac, 1829) 99, 110

Les Mohicans de Paris (Dumas, 1854) 99

Les mystères de Paris (Sue, 1842–43) 99

Les mystéres du peuple (Sue, 1849–56) 134

Les pirates des prairies (Aimard, 1858) 101

A Letter to His Countrymen (Cooper, 1834) 73

Lewis, Matthew 14

libraries 89

Life of Scott (Lockhart, 1837) 18

Lincoln, Andrew 33–4, 35–6

The Linwoods, or, "Sixty Years Since" in America (Sedgwick, 1835) 68–9

Lionel Lincoln; or, The Leaguer of Boston (Cooper, 1825) 65–6

literary criticism: of the novel 8–10; nineteenth-century criticism of *Waverley* 12–18; twentieth-century criticism of *Waverley* 18

Lockhart, John Gibson 18

Lord Byron 13

Lords of the North: A Romance of the North West (Laut, 1900) 159

Loughran, Trish 89

Lower Canada, 1840 Act of Union 148

The Loyalists: An Historical Novel (West, 1812) 8

Lukács, Georg 1, 20–1

Lyons, Martyn 126, 129

Machar, Agnes Maule 162

Mackenzie, Henry 9

The Making of the English Working Class (Thompson, 1963) 21

Malaeska; or The Indian Wife of the White Hunter (Stephens, 1839) 74

The Manor House of De Villerai: A Tale of Canada Under the French Dominion (Leprohon, 1859–60) 148

Manzoni, Alessandro 18

Martineau, Harriet 17

Matthews, Brander 18

Mauris, Joseph Claude 56–7

Maurois, Andre 111

Maxwell, Richard 21, 110

McCormick, John 175

McElwee, Johanna 68

McHoul, Alec 43

McNeil, Kenneth 43

McWilliams, John 65, 72–3, 76

"meaning-as-use" 25n71

meaning-making: and circulation 52; historical process of 3; "historification" 2

melodrama, comparison to historical novel 18

Mérimée, Prosper 110

mistrust of the historical novel 19–20

modern publishing practices, emergence of 128

modernity 2; characteristics of modern life 44–5; consequences of 44–5;

Index 235

in *The Heart of Mid-Lothian* 31;
and historical community practices
38; and locale 43–4; and national
identity 35; in *The Pathfinder* 76;
place as "phantasmagoric" 37;
self-reflexivity of 33–4; time-space
relations of 27; trust, necessity of
40–1
modernization: in Canada 147–8;
impact on capital flows 119;
narratives of 99–101; taking control
of 47
Monarque, Georges 174
The Monikins (Cooper, 1835) 74
The Monk: A Romance (Lewis,
1796) 14
Monnickendam, Andrew 47
Monthly Review, review of *Waverley*
12–13
Moore, John 10
Moretti, Franco 2, 33–4
Murray, Padmini Ray 58
Musson of Toronto 172
*My Own Story: A Canadian Christmas
Tale* (1869) 160–2

Nakamura, Masahiro 70
narratives, of modernization 99–101
nation building: copyright as tool of
89–90; Scott's role in 51
National Anti-Slavery Standard 72
"national genre of modernity" 26n100
national identity 35;
"historification" 37
nation-state: early development of in
Le père Goriot 111–12; and the
novel 2
Native Americans: frontier politics
99–101; portrayal in Sigourney's
*Sketch of Connecticut, Forty Years
Since* 66–7
Nelson, Dana 78–9
Neuburg, Victor 92
"New Romance" novels 9
*New Travels to the Westward, or
Unknown Parts of America* 91
*A New-England Tale; or, Sketches
of New-England Character and
Manners* (Sedgwick, 1822) 67
the newspaper: and information
circulation 91
*Nick of the Woods, or, The
Jibbenainosay: A Tale of Kentucky*
(Bird, 1837) 74
Nineteen Eighty-Four (Orwell, 1949) 9

*Notions of the Americans: Picked Up
By a Travelling Bachelor* (Cooper,
1828) 73
*The Novels and Romances of J.
Fenimore Cooper* (1864) 97
*Novels and Tales of the Author of
Waverley* (Constable, 1819) 51
the novel: authorship in early
nineteenth-century America 89;
availability of 14; circulation 52;
Cooper's "new literary mode" 65;
crime novels 109; and dramatization
183; editions of 51; "Familiar Novel"
9; first-edition print runs
51; *journaux-romans* 132;
production of 92; republican
education, contribution to 67–9;
roman gai 109; *roman noir* 109;
romans- feuilletons 132; satirical
novels 73; war novels 12; *see also*
chapbooks; genre; historical novel

*Oeuvres complètes de M. James
Fenimore Cooper, Américain*
(1840) 98
Olivero, Isabelle 132
operatic performances of *Ivanhoe*
192
Opfermann, Susanne 68
Orwell, George 9
Owen, William 81
Owenson, Sydney 11

Paine, Thomas 14, 15
Pamela; or, Virtue Rewarded
(Richardson, 1740) 8–9
pamphlets 54
Parent-Lardeur, Françoise 109–10
Paris, in *Le père Goriot* 112–14
Parker, Gilbert 159
Parsons, Coleman 54
The Partisan: A Tale of the Revolution
(Simms, 1835) 70–1
The Pathfinder; or, The Inland Sea
(Cooper, 1840) 4, 73–5, 78–81;
reviews 93
Peat, Alexander 54
Pegge, Samuel 9
people's editions 94
periodicals: circulation in
post-Revolutionary France 131–2
Perron, Paul 149–50
petite bourgeoisie 133–4
Physiologie du mariage (Balzac,
1829) 109

236   Index

Pigault-Lebrun, Charles-Antoine-Guillaume 109
Piketty, Thomas 115, 117
Pilbeam, Pamela 109–10
Pitt, George Dibdin 184–5
politics: frontier politics 99–101; historical novel as means of reform 14; *see also* labor relations
popularity: of chapbooks 53; of *Waverley* 17
Porteous Riots, history of 54
Porter, Jane 11
Post Office Acts of 1792 and 1794 90
post-Revolutionary France: 1819 Serre Laws 128; availability of Balzac's novels in 129–30; circulation of periodicals 131–2; distribution, forms of 129; fictional representation of the working class 135–6; publishing in 126–8
The Prairie: A Tale (Cooper, 1827) 73
Precaution; A Novel (Cooper, 1820) 65
preface to *Le père Goriot* 127
The Preparation of Ryerson Embury: A Purpose (Carman, 1900) 163–6
the press: 1819 Serre Laws 128; information circulation 91
Prévost, Abbé 110
Price, Fiona 8
Priest, Josiah 92
print market: chapbooks, American production of 92; expansion of in early-nineteenth-century America 90; the newspaper 91; prose fiction, market for 109; *see also* circulation; publishers
print technologies: chapbooks 52–3; distribution, forms of 129; impact on reading 52; König press 173n18; *Le Petit journal* 132; in post-Revolutionary France 126–9; print history of Cooper's novels 94–9; reprinting of Cooper's novels in Europe 97–8; reproduction quality of Cooper's novels 96; *Romans à 4 sous* 132
publishers: of Aimard's novels 102; Appleton 95; Beadle and Adams 102; Bentley, Richard 73; *bibliothèques* 132; Carey and Lea 64, 92–3; Caw, George 54; Charpentier 130; Constable 51; Davison, William 59; distribution, forms of 129; Duncombe, John 56–7; Elder,

Henry 54; Furne 131; Gosselin 98; Houghton and Mifflin 95; Hurd and Houghton 95; large publishing houses 93; liberalization of 131; Mackenzie & Dent 56; Musson of Toronto 172; in post-Revolutionary France 126–8; Putnam 94–5; reworking of Cooper 95; Routledge 97; Ward and Lock 102; Werdet and Spachmann 127
Putnam, George 94

Quarterly Review, review of *Waverley* 14
Quentin Durward (Scott, 1823) 110

Racine, Jean 109
Rans, Geoffrey 79–80
Raudsepp, Enn 154
readership: of chapbooks 54–6; of Cooper's novels 95–7; expansion of in early-nineteenth-century America 89
reading: as communication 11–12; importance of 15; print technologies, impact on 52; in Victorian period 15–16
The Rebels, or, Boston Before the Revolution (Child, 1826) 68
The Recess, or, A Tale of Other Times (Lee, 1783) 7–8
Reeve, Clara 8
reform: cheap tracts 53; and empowerment 15; historical novel as means of 14
Reid, Mayne 98, 101
Religious Tract Society 58
remediation 4, 190; *see also* adaptations
Report of the Affairs of British North America 148
reprinting of Cooper's novels in Europe 97–8
reproduction: of Cooper's novels 94–5; of *Le père Goriot* 128
republican education, the novel's contribution to 67–9
responsibilities, and rights 31
The Restoration 108; speculation 118–19
reviews: Balzac's review of *The Pathfinder* 80–1; of *The Pathfinder* 93; purpose of 13–14; of *Waverley* 12–13; *see also* literary criticism

Revolutionary War novels: *The Linwoods, or, "Sixty Years Since" in America* (Sedgwick, 1835) 68–9; *Lionel Lincoln; or, The Leaguer of Boston* (Cooper, 1825) 65–6; *The Partisan: A Tale of the Revolution* (Simms, 1835) 70–1; *The Rebels, or Boston Before the Revolution* (Child, 1826) 68; *The Spy* (Cooper, 1821) 65, 67, 75, 149, 171, 177–9
Richards, I. A. 18
Richardson, Samuel 8–9
The Rifle-Rangers, or, Adventures in Southern Mexico (Reid, 1850) 101
rights, and responsibilities 31, 32–3
Rights of Man (Paine, 1791) 14
Rigney, Ann 95–6
The Rise of the Novel (Watts, 1957) 21
Robin Hood films 200n52
Roland Graeme: Knight: A Novel of Our Time (Machar, 1892) 162
roman gai 109
roman noir 109
romance novels 8, 9; and chronologies 11; combination with history 11–16; frontier romance 101–2; literary criticism 8–9; "New Romance" 9; subjectivity 11
A Romance of the Republic (Child, 1867) 72
Romans à 4 sous 132
Romans- feuilletons 132
Roseneath-Knocktarlitie 38–9, 42
Ross's Juvenile Library 54
Rousseau, Jean-Jacques 30
Routledge 97
Rowson, Susanna 67
Roy, Camille 150
Ruskin, John 15–16
Rust, Richard Dilworth 79, 94

Saint Simon, Henri de 121n3
sales of *Waverley Novels* 51
Sand, George 96, 133
satirical novels of Cooper 73
The Scalp Hunters: A Romance of the Plains (Reid, 1851) 98
scenery, Scott's descriptions of 37
Schwarz, Susan 195–6
Scotland: capitalism, criticism of in *Clan Albin* 29; Highland Clearances 28; *Waverley* as Scottish history 13

Scott, Walter 1, 4, 7, 27; classification of society 41–2; descriptions of scenery 37; dramatization of *The Heart of Mid-Lothian* 179–86; nation-building, role in 51
The Scottish Chiefs: A Romance (Porter, 1810) 11, 14
The Seats of the Mighty (Parker, 1896) 159
Sedgwick, Catharine Maria 67
Seduction of the Innocent: The Influence of Comic Books on Today's Youth (Wertham, 1954) 194
seigneurial system 148
self-interest, ethics of 45–6
self-knowledge 46
self-reflexivity of modernity 33–4
Sellar, Robert 159
Seven Years' War (1756–63) 148
Sigourney, Lydia 65–6
Simmons, James 16
Simms, William Gilmore 69–72; Border romances of 1838–42 71
Simons, John 92
Sketch of Connecticut, Forty Years Since (Sigourney, 1824) 65–6
Sketches of a History of Literature (Alves, 1797) 1
slavery: Fugitive Slave Act of 1850 72, 85n43; *National Anti-Slavery Standard* 72; *The Sword and the Distaff; or, "Fair, Fat and Forty,"* A *Story of the South, at the Close of Revolution* (Simms, 1853) 71–2; *Uncle Tom's Cabin; or, Life Among the Lowly* (Stowe, 1852) 72; in the United States 119
Smith, Adam 30
Smith, Charlotte 8
Smith, Goldwyn 17
social Justice, in *Clan Albin* 30
social management, as goal of *Waverley* criticism 15
social philosophy, *Clan Albin* as 30
speculation, in post-Revolutionary France 118–19
Spencer, Benjamin 102
Spiller, Robert 94
The Spy: A Tale of the Neutral Ground (Cooper, 1821) 65
St Clair, William 110
St. John, Percy Bolingbroke 102
stage adaptations: of chapbooks 53; dramatization of *The Heart of*

238   *Index*

Mid-Lothian 179–86; impact of Cooper's popularity on 177–9; of *Le père Goriot* 174–7; of *Les anciens Canadiens* 173–4
Stevens, Anne 7–8
Stevenson, Louise 94
Stewart, D. 55
Stowe, Harriet Beecher 71–2
styles, chapbooks' use of 55
subjectivity: in chapbooks 55; in romance novels 11
Sue, Eugène 99, 131
The Sword and the Distaff; or, "Fair, Fat and Forty," A Story of the South, at the Close of Revolution (Simms, 1853) 71–2
sympathy: in *Clan Albin* 32; and social progress 33
Symposium (Plato, ca. 385–70 BC) 120

Tales of My Landlord, Second Series (Scott, 1818) 4; inside/outside dynamic 42; puns used in 28–9; time-space relations of modernity 27; *see also The Heart of Mid-Lothian* (Scott, 1818)
Templeton, Laurence 190–1
Terry, Daniel 59–60, 182
theatre: development of, in English Canada 172; in French Canada 172, 174
Theory of Moral Sentiments (Smith, 1759) 30
Thomas, Clara 150
Thompson, E. P. 21
Thorp, Willard 97
time-space relations of modernity 27
To the Lighthouse (Woolf, 1913) 19
Tolkien, J.R.R. 196
tracts, religious tracts 58
Traill, Catharine Parr 149
translations: of Cooper's novels 97–8; of *Les anciens Canadiens* 171–2
travel genre 91
travel narratives of Cooper 74
Trumpener, Katie 7–8
trust, necessity of in modernity 40–1
twentieth-century criticism of *Waverley* 18

Uncle Tom's Cabin; or, Life Among the Lowly (Stowe, 1852) 71–2
universal representation of national society 35
Upper and Lower Canada, creation of 148

Vachon, Stéphane 111
Voltaire 47

Wallace, Diana 7–8
Wallace, James 97
Wallace, William, "historification" 37
Walter Scott and Modernity (Lincoln, 2007) 35–6
The Wanderer: or, Female Difficulties (Burney, 1814) 29–30
Ward & Lock 102
Warne, Frederick 97
Warne's Crown Library (1886–94) 97
Watson, Charles 71
Watts, Ian 21
Watts, Isaac 55
Waverley, or 'Tis Sixty Years Since (Scott, 1814) 1, 7, 11–12; adoption by canonical authors 52; chapbook versions 54; early reviews of 12–13; as emerging genre 8, 13; formalism in 19; impact on French literature 110; literary criticism 34; popularity of 17; production in Europe 110; sales of 51; twentieth-century criticism of 18; universal representation of national society 35
wealth: inheritance as means of 117–18; marriage as means of 108–9, 117–18; *petite bourgeoisie* 133–4
Wells, H. G. 16, 19
Welsh, Alexander 34
Werdet & Spachmann 127
Wertham, Fredric 194
West, Jane 8
the Western 98–9
Wheeler, Edward 98
White, R. S. 30
The Wild Irish Girl: A National Tale (Owenson, 1806) 11, 14
Williams, Helena Maria 30
Wilson, Thomas 8
Wimsatt, Mary Ann 70
Winship, Michael 96
Witkowski, Claude 129
Wollstonecraft, Mary 10
Wood, Gillen D'arcy 185
The Works of J. Fenimore Cooper (1849–53) 94–5

The Yemassee: A Romance of Carolina (Simms, 1835) 70

Zboray, Ronald 88, 96
Zola, Émile 17, 135–42